Ned Walworth

ROAD TO WAR
America : 1914–1917

PRESIDENT WILSON LEADING THE PREPAREDNESS PARADE IN
WASHINGTON, JUNE 15, 1916

ROAD TO WAR
America 1914-1917

BY WALTER MILLIS

BOSTON AND NEW YORK
HOUGHTON MIFFLIN COMPANY
The Riverside Press Cambridge

The Riverside Press
CAMBRIDGE · MASSACHUSETTS
PRINTED IN THE U.S.A.

TO

NORAH THOMPSON MILLIS

PREFACE

THE primary concern of this book is solely with the United States. The merits of the European struggle are beyond its scope, and it is no part of my purpose either to defend the German cause or to attack that of the Allies. Since it deals with an episode profoundly influenced by a passionate acceptance of the Entente case, much of it is necessarily devoted to a criticism of that case; the German contention had little influence and therefore is not for the most part relevant to the discussion. If this gives the book an appearance of relative hostility toward the Entente, that is simply an unavoidable consequence of the subject itself and implies no verdict whatever as between the European belligerents.

The book was designedly undertaken as an effort in interpretation rather than research. The purpose was less to unearth new facts than to assemble, from the many already available, a single and connected study that would include all of what seemed to be the significant elements contributing to a complex and much misunderstood passage in our history. It is surprising how few have attempted to do this. Since John Bach McMaster's 'The United States in the World War,' written in the high tide of war emotion, the only book I know of specifically devoted to the reasons for the American entry into the European conflict is C. Hartley Grattan's 'Why We Fought,' published in 1929. I have availed myself of Mr. Grattan's work, though my own approach has been a rather different one.

In pursuing it, I have not tried to read everything in the already immense literature bearing in one way or another upon the subject, though even so I find that my debts are extensive. The central diplomatic narrative rests, of course, upon the War Supplements to 'Foreign Relations,' for the official history, and upon 'The

Intimate Papers of Colonel House,' for the unofficial. These sources have been enriched from the memoirs, letters or biographies of Page, Gerard, Whitlock, Van Dyke and Herrick among the diplomats; of Bryan, McAdoo, Houston, Lane, Redfield and Baker among the Cabinet members; of Gompers, F. I. Cobb, Eliot, Schiff, Wanamaker and a number of others who were prominent during the period. For Roosevelt I have used, in addition to the published Lodge-Roosevelt correspondence, Henry F. Pringle's recent biography. Ray Stannard Baker's official biography of Wilson had not been carried into the war period; but I have used a number of recent studies of Wilson, and have taken several points from 'The Strangest Friendship in History' by George Sylvester Viereck, who has examined the Yale papers. Professor Seymour's recent 'American Diplomacy in the World War' supplies one or two details not included in the 'Intimate Papers.' I have used Mr. Tumulty's 'Woodrow Wilson as I Know Him' with reserve.

The German side of the story is based primarily upon Count Bernstorff's 'My Three Years in America,' together with the memoirs of Bethmann, Tirpitz, Falkenhayn, Hindenburg, Ludendorff and various other military and diplomatic leaders. For the Entente side I have drawn most heavily on the very useful 'The Letters and Friendships of Sir Cecil Spring Rice' by Stephen Gwynn, on Lord Grey's 'Twenty-Five Years' and on the recent 'War Memoirs' of Lloyd George, which prints a number of interesting documents.

Interwoven with the main theme are several more specialized subjects, each one of which might alone repay a considerable effort of research. In respect to each I have been obliged to lean pretty heavily upon one or two available guides. For the detailed operations of the war at sea, including statistics on the U-boats, sinkings, and so on, I have used 'The German Submarine War' by R. H. Gibson and Maurice Prendergast. The account of the Lusitania rests on 'The Lusitania's Last Voyage' by Charles E. Lauriat, Jr., the records of the British inquiry and the American court proceedings and (for Schwieger) an article by Lowell Thomas in the New York *American*, June 24, 1928.

For the preparedness agitation I have relied largely on Hermann Hagedorn's life of General Wood — an extremely interesting and suggestive book — and on Frederick Palmer's 'Newton D. Baker.' The correspondence of Theodore Marburg, edited by John H. Latané, was a principal source for the peace league movement; for what I have called the 'evangelistic' peace movement I have made much use of Jane Addams's 'Peace and Bread,' of 'The Political Philosophy of Robert M. La Follette,' edited by Ellen Tourelle and (for the peace ship episode) Jonathan Norton Leonard's biography of Henry Ford.

Thomas Lamont's life of his partner, H. P. Davison, is the most important source for the history of the private war financing. Alexander Dana Noyes's 'The War Period in American Finance' and 'Financial Chapters of the War' were most useful for the economic, as distinct from the banking, aspects of the situation. For the war propagandas I have drawn on H. D. Lasswell's 'Propaganda Technique of the World War' as well as other sources; the account of the German activities in the United States rests largely upon the report of the Senate investigation (Senate Document 62, Sixty-Fifth Congress, Second Session, 1919). Ray H. Abrams's 'Preachers Present Arms' supplied many of my quotations from the pulpits. For contemporary press comment I have made free use of the files of *The Literary Digest*.

These represent only the principal sources consulted. I have of course gathered details from many other volumes, while throughout I have drawn largely upon *The Congressional Record* and the contemporary newspapers. To the authors, editors and newspapermen concerned I must acknowledge my indebtedness, while relieving them of any responsibility whatever for the use which I have made of their work.

W. M.

March, 1935

CONTENTS

ILLUSTRATIONS

ROAD TO WAR
America : 1914–1917

'No man is wise enough, no nation is important enough, no human interest is precious enough, to justify the wholesale destruction and murder which constitute war.' ... These words, spoken in this place more than two years ago, I must reaffirm today. ... If you tell me that this war is fought for the integrity of international law, I must ask you why it is directed only against Germany and not also against England. ... If you say that it is fought in vindication of our national honor, I must ask you why no harm has come to the honor of ... Holland and Scandinavia. ... If you say that this war is a life and death struggle for the preservation of civilization against barbarism, I must ask you why we remained neutral when Belgium was raped, and were at last aroused to action, not by the cries of the stricken abroad, but by our own losses in men and money.

From a sermon by John Haynes Holmes, April 1, 1917.

The juxtaposition in the American people's character of Pacifism and an impulsive lust of war should have been known to us, if more sedulous attention had been paid in Germany to American conditions and characteristics.

Count von Bernstorff.

I. SUMMER 1914

i

THE Fourth of July, 1914, fell upon a Saturday. This meant a double holiday; and the nation gave itself to the pleasures of patriotic observance — to the speeches and the firecrackers, the parades, the ball games and the amusement parks — with nothing more arduous before it than the Sunday papers. From them it was to learn that the Republic's one hundred and thirty-eighth anniversary had passed without special incident in a placid summer world. At Newport the new America's cup sloops, the Resolute and the Vanitie, were tuning up for their first trials; while the challenger, Sir Thomas Lipton's latest Shamrock, would soon be on her way from England for the races to be held in September. Long Island was supplying, as it so often does, another mysterious murder for the fascination of the metropolitan area; while at Hammondsport Glenn Curtiss was still trying to get the great flying boat America — built for Rodman Wanamaker in the first serious attempt to fly the Atlantic — off the surface of Lake Keuka.

The country was suffering under something of a business recession, and only the week before the startling failure of the H. B. Claflin Company, an important drygoods firm, had introduced an ominous note. But leading merchants had hastened to announce that 'conditions in the drygoods trade generally are fundamentally sound,' and the President of the United States himself had formally declared that the nation was 'on the eve of the greatest business boom in its history' — 'signs of revival,' indeed, were already discernible upon the horizon. In the political field the great Theodore Roosevelt, an aging lion now but still showing the old fire, had stepped back upon the scene, leaving columns of speculation in his wake. Abroad, the celebrated Joseph Chamberlain had just died in England; the Ulster question was taking a most extraordinary turn; the French were having another army scandal. In the Old World, as also, perhaps, in the New, there did seem to be a certain sense of restlessness upon the air. However, that shocking business about the assassination of the Austrian heir apparent had already faded from the front pages, and it was necessary to hunt through the week-end correspondence in the feature sections to find any trace of it. There the diplomatic writers were still talking in their usual cryptic fashion about 'the gravest possibilities' — but they had been doing that ever since the first Balkan War, and it never meant anything.

Yet foreign affairs on that Sunday morning were a matter of the most active interest. The papers were full of special articles on the urgent and difficult problems of Mexico and the Caribbean, and it was to our foreign policy that the chief speech of the day before had been devoted. Standing in the open, before a great crowd in Independence Square in Philadelphia, President Wilson had chosen to explain and to defend his singular attempt to introduce idealism into international relations. For over a year, now, the country had watched its development with surprise, and with less than complete enthusiasm. It had given us already the Panama Canal tolls repealer and the attack on 'dollar diplomacy,' the Bryan peace treaties and 'watchful waiting.' It had produced as well such contradictory and exhilarating manifestations as the taking of Vera Cruz and the despatch of the first Army expeditionary force to land on foreign soil since the Spanish-American War. It offered a confusing challenge to many established conventions of patriotism and national interest, and the politically discerning had already found in it the most vulnerable aspect of the Administration's course. But as he stood in the July sunshine the President, with his tall figure and determined face, sounded again the lofty note, evoked the high vision in which he had almost taught the populace to believe:

The world is getting more complicated every day. Therefore, no man ought to be foolish enough to think he understands it, and that is the reason why I am glad to know there are some simple things in the world. One of those simple things is principle....

If I did not believe that the moral judgment would be the last judgment, the final judgment, in the minds of men as well as at the tribunal of God, I could not believe in popular government. But I do believe these things.... My dream is that as the years go on and the world knows more and more of America it ... will turn to America for those moral inspirations which lie at the basis of all freedom; that the world will never fear America unless it feels that it is engaged in some enterprise which is inconsistent with the rights of humanity; and that America will come into the full light of the day when all shall know that she puts human rights above all other rights and that her flag is the flag not only of America but of humanity....

I don't know that there ever will be another Declaration of Independence, a statement of grievances of mankind, but I believe if any such document is ever drawn, it will be drawn in the spirit of the American Declaration of Independence and that America has lifted the light that will shine unto all generations and guide the feet of mankind to the goal of justice, liberty and peace.

As these words were being read in the American newspapers next day, the German Emperor at Potsdam was giving that rather casual assurance to the Austrian Ambassador which now seems the most important single link in the long chain of causation that was about to drag a world into catastrophe. But no one, of course, knew anything about that.

ii

President Wilson's Fourth-of-July address was but a natural reflection of the peculiar backgrounds against which it was delivered. Sixteen months before an age had died. The Democratic party had returned spectacularly to power, and even British newspapers had proclaimed the beginning of 'what should be a new era.' The bright sun of Republican greatness, which had arisen in 1896 in the amiable image of Mr. William McKinley, had set at last in the fogs and confusions of 1912, leaving all the great protagonists of those golden years to discover, a little irritably, that their day was over.]

'Armageddon,' in the popular vocabulary, still referred to that curious battling for the Lord in which they had all gone down together. A new sense of age had come over them; a definite twilight had begun to deepen around those gods. Theodore Roosevelt had disappeared into the Amazonian jungles. Henry Adams, who had ruled so long as the esoteric pope of Lafayette Square, found it 'all very flat' and could discern 'not a trace of mental vigor' in the desert scene around him. The elder J. P. Morgan, the financial colossus of the period and the architect of so much in its economy, had died symbolically four weeks after the inauguration. E. H. Harriman was dead; John D. Rockefeller had taken up golf; the other giants of the times were passing into retirement. Mr. Taft had faded abruptly into a portly shadow; the gentle Archie Butt had gone down in the Titanic, together with John Jacob Astor, with Frank D. Millet, the painter, and so many other famous names. Mr. Bryce, that scholarly ornament of the imperial years and so established a fixture upon the national scene that one had almost forgotten he was the ambassador of a foreign power, had turned in his letters of recall and gone home in a quiet blaze of Anglo-American friendship; while Mr. Winthrop Chanler was writing to his successor, Sir Cecil Spring Rice, in a tone of philosophical melancholy:

> Enough of politics. Theodore and Cabot are both my friends. Older and war-worn and battered as they both are, they are still essentially as you knew them.... [Senator Lodge] is much aged but hearty and strong as ever. He shows his age by the whiteness of his hair and the intolerance of his political point of view as expressed

privately. In public I should say he is better than ever as a speaker....
At home he is quite different, does not argue, gets more excited and
vehement over trifles.... Theodore is the same old darling.... His
egotism has grown on him, but so has his fat.

Thus the twilight had darkened over Rooseveltian America
— its shadows serving to throw into only more brilliant contrast
the dazzling dawn of the Wilsonian era. 'No man,' the New York
World had happily exclaimed, 'has ever been elevated to the Presidency who was more fully the people's President than this college
professor who scorned alike the support of the bosses and the
support of Plutocracy.... If he succeeds... this nation will indeed
have a new birth of freedom'; and it was with the 'New Freedom'
inscribed upon their banners that the Democrats had come back
to office for the first time since Cleveland's day.

Washington had never seen so vast, or so happy, a throng as
that which filled its streets upon the day of the inauguration.
The huge inaugural parade wound on all afternoon and far into
the evening — until the fireworks began to go up from the White
House lawn — as a tangible manifestation of the great wave of
reform, of regeneration, of idealism which had been sweeping
the nation since two years before, and upon whose crest Mr.
Wilson and his party had ridden skillfully into power. It had been
generated by forces hidden, even more deeply than the reformers
themselves could understand, in the very structure of the new
industrial society which we were creating; it carried within it
profound contradictions. But in the spring of 1913 these were not
apparent. The long and hopeless battle of the muckrakers, the
good government leagues, the radical and reform leaders had
ended, incredibly, in victory. The past, with all its narrowness,
its stupidity and its fettering convention, was dead; the key to
the castle of the future had been discovered. It was a matter
simply of unlocking the door — of restoring government to 'the
people,' of overthrowing 'the bosses,' of curbing the 'predatory
interests,' of lowering (but not too drastically lowering) the tariff
and raising, in the industrial field, the standards of 'social jus-

tice.' A new, mystical vision of nationality had been evoked to override all questionings. The state took on a transcendental quality. No longer simply a dull, constitutional umpire between warring special interests, it now represented a sovereign unity which was to adjust all interests to 'common principles of right and fair dealing,' which was to protect the weak against the strong and the strong against the weak in accordance with a high idealism and a perfectly impartial justice.

Theodore Roosevelt himself had proclaimed that vision three years before in his speech at Osawotamie, giving it what today seems a strangely suggestive name. 'I do not ask for over-centralization; but I do ask that we work in a spirit of broad and far-reaching nationalism when we work for what concerns our people as a whole.... The New Nationalism puts the national need before sectional or personal advantage.... The New Nationalism regards the executive power as the steward of the public welfare.' It was a stirring concept; the New Freedom (to Mr. Roosevelt's subsequent and intense disgust) was largely to appropriate it, for it supplied a social sanction under which all things became easy. The aging Adams might confide his disdain to his correspondence, but to the spokesmen of the new era it seemed a time no less of intellectual than of social and moral regeneration. Looking back upon it from a sadder pinnacle of experience, Frederic C. Howe, that veteran of reformers, was to confess that in the years from 1911 to 1914 it seemed to him 'that a new dispensation was about to be ushered in.' He summed it up:

It was good form to be a liberal.... Conservative lawyers, bankers and men of affairs stepped out from their offices and lent their names to radical movements.... The younger generation was to achieve the things that had been denied my own.... It would not stop with economic reform; it would bring in a rebirth of literature, art, music and spirit.... The spirit of this young America was generous, hospitable, brilliant; it was carefree and full of variety. The young people in whom it leaped to expression hated injustice. They had no questions about the soundness of American democracy.... They believed ... that the truth would make us free.

One great field of governmental activity, however, the New Freedom had largely omitted to consider. The cultivated, esoteric mysteries of international affairs had held but the slightest interest for Mr. Wilson; throughout a long career devoted to the study of government he 'had given surprisingly little attention to foreign relationships and diplomacy.' The martial splendors and imperial ambitions in which the Rooseveltian age had risen and flourished meant little to the liberal idealism of 1912, of which Mr. Wilson had made himself the mouthpiece. 'In this country,' as Mr. Elihu Root was later to observe, 'international law was regarded as a rather antiquated branch of useless learning, diplomacy as a foolish mystery and the foreign service as a superfluous expense.' War, if not an impossibility, was at least a barbarous anachronism; and in 1910 Mr. Andrew Carnegie had set up his $10,000,000 endowment for its abolition.

Yet it was not entirely by accident that a progressive social movement which based its theology upon a new concept of national power and union should have found one of its leaders in the martial Colonel Roosevelt, who had always been so fascinated by foreign policy. It was only natural that the New Freedom, which appealed to nationalism to enforce peace, justice and liberty in the domestic sphere, should have thought of the American nation as an active force for peace and justice in the international world as well. It simply accorded with tradition when a mood of evangelical reform at home expressed itself, from time to time, in superior admonition to foreign powers whose governments oppressed their benighted peoples under the chains of militarism and reaction. Unfortunately, no one saw that the same forces which had produced the colossal armaments and imperialist foreign policies of the European industrial powers were already beginning to work beneath the surface of our own economy as it grew more closely to resemble theirs; while no one appeared to realize to what profound contradictions this tendency toward righteous intervention upon the world stage might lead.

The New Freedom believed in a vague, uncritical way in

international peace, arbitration and disarmament. Mr. William Jennings Bryan, its Secretary of State, had been preaching arbitration in *The Commoner* for years, and even Mr. Wilson had joined the American Peace Society in 1908. He had readily assented when Mr. Bryan, on being offered the State Department, had outlined his project for 'cooling-off' treaties with the nations of the world. Upon the eve of the inauguration Mr. Bryan had publicly declared it to be the 'imperative duty of the United States... to set a shining example of disarmament.' This proposal had naturally shocked all the militarists and conservatives. Yet even in his own party no one took Mr. Bryan very seriously as a statesman, and few could have really intended to sink the Navy. The New Freedom preferred merely to assume that the United States would always be found upon the side of righteousness in world affairs. It was more inspiring, when one thought of the matter at all, simply to think of the nation as a moral 'arbiter,' happily leading more barbarous and less pacific peoples toward the light. Mr. Walter Hines Page, that cultured though perhaps rather conservative voice of the New Freedom, had been chosen as its Ambassador to the Court of St. James's. A month or two after he reached his new post he was cheerily writing home: 'Nothing else would give such a friendly turn to the whole world as the President's coming here. The old Earth would sit up and rub its eyes and take notice to whom it belongs.' A more experienced age may detect a certain flaw in this method of promoting friendliness; but Mr. Page was convinced (in those days) of 'the complete divorce of European politics from fundamental morals,' so a program of peace based upon American world 'mastery' — in a purely moral plane, of course — may well have seemed logical to him.

Foreign policy had played no part in the electoral campaign. Yet a curiously premonitory thought had passed through Mr. Wilson's mind a few days before his inauguration. 'It would be the irony of Fate,' he had mused, 'if my Administration had to deal chiefly with foreign affairs'; and almost immediately the great ironist had begun to spin her web. Within a few days after taking office the Administration discovered itself with the Chinese consortium, the Japanese land question in California, and a Mexican revolution upon its hands. By May 15, less than two and a half months after the inauguration, the President was facing war with Japan as a serious possibility. That crisis passed; but at the Cabinet meeting on the 23d 'Mexico loomed up... as an ugly problem,' and this crisis, unfortunately did not pass.

The issue was over the recognition of the latest revolutionary President, General Victoriano Huerta. 'The President and Bryan,' as Mr. Houston, the Secretary of Agriculture, noted in his diary, 'were opposed to recognition. I emphatically opposed it as immoral.' It was the characteristic note. Secretary Houston's reasoning was simple. The Huerta government, he thought, was 'bad in origin and purpose'; besides, recognition would merely enable it to get a loan from American bankers which would in turn permit it to fasten its despotism upon the Mexican people. What more was necessary? Despotisms abroad and bankers at home were equally the enemies of a movement dedicated to popular government and the control of 'predatory interests.' General Huerta was not recognized.

The result was that disorders in Mexico continued to endanger American life and property. Yet if idealism and democracy, 'good' government and social justice were principles adequate to the solution of domestic problems, they should be enough for foreign policy as well. The disorders would have to be accepted. It was absurd to risk the lives and welfare of one hundred million Americans in a protective intervention which would chiefly benefit those 'vested interests,' those great corporations, bankers and oil magnates against whom the people's struggle was to be waged at home. It was equally absurd to impose their candidate upon the helpless Mexicans. 'We shall yet prove to the Mexican people,' President Wilson informed a restive Congress in August, 'that we know how to serve them without first thinking how we shall serve ourselves.' If individual Americans in Mexico were endangered, 'we should earnestly urge all Americans to leave Mexico at once.' And then a really fine ethical concept was introduced which was to find its echo in a far greater crisis:

> We can afford to exercise the self-restraint of a really great nation which realizes its own strength and scorns to misuse it.... The steady pressure of moral force will before many days break the barriers of pride and prejudice down, and we shall triumph as Mexico's friends sooner than as her enemies.

Unhappily, however, the steady pressure of moral force did not triumph. All through that tremendous summer and fall, as the Administration's great program of domestic reform was being pushed to enactment, the Mexican problem remained as an irritant and a distraction. The Mexican people seemed somehow not to appreciate our imperious desire to serve them by compelling them to be a democracy. Even at home it appeared that moral force, however attractive in the domestic sphere, was less popular when applied in foreign affairs. An ethical foreign policy seemed to lack the glamour of the old-fashioned and more martial variety. The American citizens refused to leave Mexico; the oil companies were supplied with powerful emotional weapons with which to combat the Wilsonian statesmanship. Wider international complications also began to develop; there were British as well as American citizens in Mexico, and the Monroe Doctrine itself might be placed in jeopardy. Joyfully Mr. Wilson's political opponents began to detect an Achilles heel in the otherwise impregnable popularity of the New Freedom. It only hardened the Presidential determination; and in October Mr. Wilson was generalizing his Mexican policy into a broad philosophy of foreign relations:

> I want to take this occasion to say that the United States will never seek one additional foot of territory by conquest.... We dare not turn from the principle that morality and not expediency is the thing that must guide us, and that we will never condone iniquity because it is most convenient to do so.

To the New Freedom the New Diplomacy had now been added.
It had been hammered out suddenly, under a great press of
other and seemingly more important affairs, to meet unexpected
exigencies of foreign relations and practical politics. The thoughtful might have perceived that its effect need not always be pacific
nor its practical application always easy.   Yet by the end of the
year there was reason to believe that it would ultimately solve
the immediate problem in Mexico. It had not restored order
there; but it was undermining General Huerta's position, and the
President in his annual message in December was able to strike
a confident note. Huerta's power, he announced, was crumbling
'and the collapse is not far away. We shall not, I believe, be
obliged to alter our policy of watchful waiting.'

iii

So 1913 passed into history, and the year 1914 was ushered in.
It was welcomed by a nation still in a mood of stirring, of evangelical, optimism. If the business world still appeared to be suffering under a strangely lingering anaemia, it was a condition which
surely could not last. 'The new year,' in the distinguished opinion
of the New York *Times*, 'opens in hope, with opportunity, with
the certainty of good things, good business and carefree minds,
if only the opportunity be availed of.' The economic slackness,
such as it was, derived after all from world rather than domestic
phenomena; the Balkan War at the end of 1912 and the military
alarms which had spread from it through Europe had evidently
had a good deal to do with the business recession, and now that
cloud had happily passed. The *Times* observed:

> One of the greatest wars of modern times, and altogether the great-
> est expenditures upon armaments in history, are the natural basis of
> hope for avoidance of the speedy repetition of what would be a
> calamity too great for the world to endure. Out of war peace ensues.

And the *Review of Reviews* declared in its issue for January,
1914:

Regarding mankind as a whole, the thing most to be deplored is war, and the thing most to be desired and definitely worked for is peace.... There can be no doubt concerning the high motives of our foreign policy, and its benevolent attitude toward other countries.... There is no danger of our becoming an aggressive military power. The world is moving away from military ideals; and a period of peace, industry and world-wide friendship is dawning.

The new President stood, it seemed, upon a higher pinnacle of popularity than any other President of recent times had ever attained. Yet already the first, fresh bloom upon the New Freedom was beginning to wear away. The natural recalcitrances and inertias of humanity were beginning to reassert themselves; and even Democrats were showing that they were human. 'Marse Henry' Watterson, that mighty pillar through so many years of Jeffersonian Democracy, was manifesting a certain restlessness. The editor of the Louisville *Courier-Journal* still declared himself a follower of the President:

But I shall not follow him blindly, because he appears to me a most self-centered, ambitious man, and I dread the ascendancy of such men; because he is an undoubted experimentalist, and experimentation is a dangerous thing in government.... Before him now appears the danger line.

It was a note which was to be heard with increasing emphasis in the months that followed. For as the year advanced, the difficulties only accumulated; the bright promise of those New Year forecasts only dimmed. The economic recovery did not come. A speculative liveliness in the opening weeks of 1914 seemed to have nothing behind it and presently died away. Mr. McAdoo, the facile Secretary of the Treasury, found the country full of 'a propaganda of pessimism which apparently had its source nowhere and in nothing,' and he suspected conspiracy among 'the interests.' The interests — and the Republicans — did not wait upon suspicion; there was undoubtedly a sense of creeping paralysis upon the air, and they had no hesitation in tracing it to the lowered tariff, to the Administration's anti-trust activities

and to 'governmental interference.' It was with satisfaction that
Senator Lodge in April discovered that 'the business condition
here is very bad,' and he despatched a pleasantly gloomy bulletin
to meet his old friend, Colonel Roosevelt, now on his way home
from Brazil. 'I feel greatly alarmed about the outlook, for I fear
we are on the edge of a condition which will cause great suffering
in all directions. It is not the fault of business' — and so patently
had to be the fault of the Democrats.

The President set a jaw of now recognized obstinacy and dismissed the 'temporary depression in certain quarters' as not only
'psychological' but 'artificially created.' Nevertheless, at the
end of April the protagonist of the New Freedom was sending
United States troops into Colorado to suppress striking coal miners
in a bitter industrial war. Possibly there were deeper forces at
work than either the President or the bankers understood. Indeed,
in retrospect one now seems to feel through all the first six months
of 1914 a curious feverishness, a sense of strain and excitement
beneath the confident surfaces of the times. At home and abroad
events seem to take on a suddenly violent, ominous or erratic
quality, as if in evidence of a change impending. Today one sees
those months illumined, not by the long, level rays of a placid
sunset, but by the last strange and sultry twilight before the bursting of a hurricane. In Europe the war danger was officially over;
yet the Germans and the French were perfecting their huge new
army increases. Berlin, in the Christmas season, had been agitated
by the 'Zabern incident' in which an irascible subaltern had
sabered an Alsatian peasant, and there had been much international editorializing about Prussian militarism. And now our
own Mexican problem was suddenly to take a most extraordinary
— and strangely militaristic — turn.

In December the President had confidently consigned it to
'watchful waiting'; by mid-January it had abruptly revived again.
The Republicans in the House were declaring our foreign policy
to be 'the laughing-stock of the world,' and a wave of damaging
criticism was running through the press. In February the bandit

general Villa managed to kill a British subject, and Mexico became even more an international issue. Mr. Wilson was unmoved. But with his public it served only to stimulate the new passion for the glamours of a 'strong' policy; the anti-Administration elements were now happily at work compiling lists of atrocities committed against American citizens, while Mr. Wilson's own special representative in Mexico was by this time appealing for the use of force to aid the Carranzista opposition against General Huerta.

Suddenly and unaccountably — for was it not the people who suffered in war and was not a democracy like the United States therefore peace-loving by definition? — there had developed a powerful popular pressure for military action in Mexico. Action of some sort, if only to forestall a full-dress intervention, had already begun to seem politic even to some of the leaders of the New Freedom when, in the early days of April, there came the fantastic 'Tampico incident.' A party going ashore from one of our naval vessels off that port was arrested by the Huerta forces; the men were released immediately, but when Admiral Fletcher demanded a salute to repair the insult to our flag, it was refused. Here was a pretext for action which certainly could not be set down as instigated by oil barons. In a quick decision, the President authorized a peremptory despatch to the recalcitrant Huerta; the fleet was ordered to hold itself in readiness, and Mexico became a front-page sensation of the first rank.

Was it too much of a sensation? In a moment either of policy or of pique the President had snatched up the tremendous engines of brute power lying always ready to the hand of those who control the modern state. But once raised? The letters and telegrams poured in, enthusiastic in their congratulations; Washington was at an intense pitch of excitement; the deep thrill of war was running through the nation, but General Huerta, unfortunately, was not yielding. That unexpectedly dangerous situation would have to be brought to an end. On April 19 an ultimatum was despatched. There was no reply. The President found himself trapped in his own rash intransigence. To avoid humiliating retreat he must now go forward. Early on the morning of April 21, Mr. Wilson, apparently never supposing that the Mexicans would resist an actual show of force, authorized the seizure of the customs house at Vera Cruz by the squadron lying off that harbor; and a few hours later the strings of boats were going in, packed with armed and excited men despatched for the first time since 1898 upon the conquest of foreign soil.

The landing took place before noon. The same evening the despatches were at the White House — four Americans killed, up to that time, and twenty wounded, with the fighting still in progress. The Mexicans had resisted. So swift, and so irretrievable, were the consequences of the word which Mr. Wilson himself had given less than twelve hours before. It was a first bitter and uncalculated fruit of the New Diplomacy.

With the public, however, there seemed to be no hesitations. The great headlines sprang from the front pages; there were columns of war despatches, war preparations, war fever. For a moment it seemed doubtful whether the bloody process, once released, could be checked. At a press conference a day or two later the President looked 'preternaturally pale, almost parchmenty.' But for a man of the President's temperament there was but one solution for an emotional issue of that character. It was to insist that the policy, whatever its consequences, had been right; besides, if more trouble was now to come it would not be Mr. Wilson's fault, but General Huerta's. In the end, further bloodshed was avoided; but all that summer an American army of occupation remained in possession of Vera Cruz.

iv

Thus, as the spring days lengthened pleasantly into the summer of 1914, foreign policy — in Mexico and the Caribbean — was already appearing as a possibly major issue. Yet Americans were not wholly unaware of a far greater and more tragic drama slowly

developing upon a greater stage.   Financial writers had used it to
explain the singular persistence of economic depression; political
observers, though badly informed, at least knew that there were
dark forces at work in the world beyond the Western Hemisphere.
The first shadows had begun to fall long years before; and the
Balkan War, the blackest of all, had come in October, 1912, at
the very moment that the New Freedom was marching to its
victory.   At the height of Mr. Wilson's Presidential campaign the
war headlines had burst through the political speeches in a
strangely prophetic counterpoint; and barely a week before the
election an editorial-writer of the New York *Tribune* had paused
to note their significance:

> It is scarcely conceivable that one of the [great] powers could
> become engaged in the present war without being followed into it by
> others.... It is indeed something like a genuine European war that
> this country would... have to fear.

All through the final winter of Mr. Taft's Presidency the alarm-
ing headlines continued to recur: 'Great European War Looms
on Horizon,' 'Europe Drifting Toward General Conflagration,'
'Fear Again Rises of Great European War.'   In December, 1912,
Mr. Henry Adams was reading a letter from his friend, Sir Cecil
Spring Rice, then British Minister at Stockholm:

> Isn't it curious that we are all supposing ourselves to be standing
> on the edge of the most terrific disaster (for Europe) which has ever
> taken place?   Even the hardened dip. looks a little solemn when the
> subject is alluded to at dinner.   The appearance of the *Red Man* in
> a particularly realistic manner, in the middle of the cocked hats
> and laced coats, has had rather a calming effect....But this isn't, yet,
> the real thing.   Austria may at this moment have given the order
> which may lead Europe to a several years' war.

It was even more curious, perhaps, that they were all passively
accepting the possibility of that frightful calamity being unleashed
'at any moment by one slight act, based on what look to you the
meanest of motives.'   But the diplomatist went on to point out that
in reality it would be 'a peoples' question — the struggle for exist-

ence between races,' and therefore unavoidable. It was an analysis
which Spring Rice himself was to forget when the order did come,
nineteen months later; at the time, however, the 'Red Man'
slowly withdrew and the cocked hats were left to resume the
decorative tenor of their way. Yet in March, as Mr. Wilson was
arriving in Washington for that splendid dawn of the new era,
there came the news of the great armament increases in Germany,
France and England. 'Europe,' said a Paris despatch to the New
York *Tribune* on March 23, 1913, 'is thus trembling on the verge
of one of those periodic crises at which the outbreak of a general
war is apparently merely a matter of chance. Both France and
Germany are swept by waves of chauvinism; each is accusing the
other of wilful provocation.... Belgium, frightened at the warlike
preparations of its neighbors, is about to reorganize its army.'

No war did come; yet the war atmospheres lingered (as a later
age might put it) like the acrid stench of poison gas after a barrage.
Two years before Mr. Norman Angell had proved in 'The Great
Illusion' that modern war could not pay. The immense sensation
produced by that rather simple thesis is sufficiently suggestive as
to the attitude of the times. The peace movement took on a new
determination, and in 1913 Dr. David Starr Jordan, director of
the World Peace Foundation, was asking in his 'War and Waste':

> What shall we say of the Great War of Europe, ever threatening,
> ever impending, and which never comes? We shall say that it will
> never come. Humanly speaking, it is impossible.

Perhaps so; and on January 1, 1914, the New York *Times* gave
front-page display to an interview in which Mr. David Lloyd
George, the radical British Chancellor of the Exchequer, argued
that the peoples were sick of armaments and that the time had
come for reducing British naval expenditure. Yet at a dinner
party a few days before, Ambassador Page had learned from
Admiral Jellicoe that the latter never, day or night, was beyond
telephone reach of the Admiralty for more than half an hour.
'The Admiralty,' the Sea Lord had told him, 'never sleeps.' Mr.

Page did not think that they really expected a German naval attack on a half-hour's notice; but 'they talk all the time of the danger and probability of war;... and they are all the time prepared.'

Unfortunately, Mr. Page, like the other representatives whom Mr. Wilson had scattered through Europe — like most American diplomats, indeed, in the opening years of the twentieth century — knew almost nothing about European diplomacy. The Ambassadors and Ministers of the New Freedom were for the most part men of cultivation and intellectual rather than political distinction. The eminent Myron T. Herrick at Paris was a hold-over from the Taft Administration; he had gone out, however, partly for the 'holiday' and partly to help Mr. Taft out of a patronage predicament, and his longer time upon the scene appears not to have given him a much deeper grasp of European politics than the new men enjoyed. Mr. Page at London had long been celebrated as an editor and publisher of liberal views and brilliant mind. Mr. Thomas Nelson Page at Rome was a writer. The distinguished Dr. Henry van Dyke, churchman, educator and poet, filled the post at The Hague. The somewhat pompous Penfield at Vienna had been a consular and diplomatic agent in Cleveland's time; in the intervening years he had travelled and written on diplomatic subjects and so was an at least distant approach to a 'career diplomat.' Mr. Brand Whitlock at Brussels had been a reform Mayor of Toledo; from this blight of practical politics he was saved, however, by the fact that he was also a novelist. Only one of the major appointments had a slight suggestion of the unworthy about it; and a faint note of superiority can be detected in the references which the other members of this constellation of the talents made to Judge 'Jimmy' Gerard — who had been sent to Berlin as a gesture to Tammany.

The great men of the Republican party — Roosevelt and Root and Lodge and Taft — had had their contacts, during the imperial years, with the fashionable world of European affairs; they had even been played at times (whether or not they realized it) as

AMERICAN AMBASSADORS ABROAD

Above: Ambassador Walter Hines Page at a garden party in London just before the outbreak of war. In the group from left to right are: Sir William Mather, Lady Mather, Mrs. Page, Ambassador Page, and the Honorable Miss Mather.

Below: Ambassador James W. Gerard (marked with X), at an American sports meet in Berlin, July 4, 1914.

pawns in the ceaseless, intricate and insane game of European diplomacy. It was all new to the Democratic Ambassadors. Like most of their more cultivated countrymen, they approached those brilliant societies with an odd mixture of patriotic superiority and private awe. Irresistibly flattered by their new intimacy with the great and the socially overpowering, they never, in that last brief twilight of a dying age, succeeded in penetrating very far into its shadows. Their attitude was that of the ordinary literate American — the whole continent was sunk in a morass of monarchic foolishness and immoral 'militarism' with which the United States had little concern.

All Europe was drunk with 'militarism' — but of course the Germans were more militaristic than the French or British. Was it not the autocratic Kaiser who was always rattling the saber against his peaceful and democratic neighbors? And who could doubt the liberalism, the enlightened purposes and the high public ethics of British constitutional monarchy? Ambassador Gerard, enjoying himself hugely amid the heavy brilliance of the court at Potsdam, began to realize that the problem of Europe was a somewhat more complex matter than these easy generalizations would suggest. But Mr. Page, according to his biographer, had throughout his life entertained a 'reverent respect' for 'English history, English literature and English public men'; and as he fell under the sad, gracious charm of Sir Edward Grey the reverence passed almost into adoration. It was not the best state of mind in which to make an accurate appraisal of the satanic forces at work beneath the surface of European politics.

Yet even Mr. Page perceived, as the Balkan War receded without clearing the unhealthy atmosphere around him, that some forces were at work, that 'a great European war' was bound to come if the continent could not find some way of escape from the tragic armed truce in which it had involved itself. Mr. Page's own idea of the way was a singular one. In August, 1913, he drew up a memorandum on the subject for private circulation among friends in the United States. Europe, he felt, would never disarm; the only other solution was 'to find some common and useful work for these great armies to do.' In the prosecution of such a 'great, unselfish task' the United States might even lead the way. Indeed —

> May there not come such a chance in Mexico — to clean out bandits, yellow fever, malaria, hook-worm — all to make the country healthful, safe for life and investment, and for orderly self-government at last? What we did in Cuba might then be made the beginning of a new epoch in history — conquest for the sole benefit of the conquered, worked out by a sanitary reformation. ... And the tropics cry out for sanitation, which is at first an essentially military task.

This striking vision of the backward peoples crying out to be sanitated in order to save Western military imperialism from itself was never to be realized. In advancing it, however, Mr. Page was apparently only embroidering upon a hint which he had received from another statesman, who, already engaged upon these great subjects, was to exercise a profound influence over events.

As early as January, 1913, while the Balkan crisis was at its height and while Mr. Taft was still in the Presidency, 'Colonel' E. M. House of Texas, lunching quietly with a friend, had confessed to a great ambition. Colonel House had spent the better part of his life as a skillful amateur of American party politics. Already the guide and confidant of the President-elect and one of the chief architects of Mr. Wilson's victory, he was now looking for broader fields in which to exercise his peculiar talents. Like so many other educated minds before him, he was succumbing to the dignified, glamorous and dangerous lure of foreign policy. He confided to his friend that he proposed 'to get Governor Wilson to let me bring about an understanding between Great Britain, this country and Germany in regard to the Monroe Doctrine'; but beyond that, and as a necessary condition to the attempt, it would also 'be my endeavor to bring about a better understanding between England and Germany.' It was, if any date at all can be set for so vague an event, the beginning of the American intervention in Europe.

Colonel House was as complete a stranger to the diplomatic world as the new Ambassadors, and seems to have known little more about European politics. It did not deter him from his quiet pursuit of this enticing and stupendous object. His first thought had been that 'we could encourage Germany to exploit South America in a legitimate way' and thus cure the deep-seated ills of Western imperialism. But when in May he was lunching with Count Johann von Bernstorff, the German Ambassador at Washington, the vision had already begun to enlarge. 'I suggested that it would be a great thing if there was a sympathetic understanding between England, Germany, Japan and the United States.... They could ensure peace and the proper development of the waste places.' Count Bernstorff was unexpectedly encouraging; he even suggested 'that perhaps China was the most promising field at present for concerted action.' House was pleased; and that summer he was in London with Page, meeting still greater statesmen and repeating to Sir Edward Grey what Bernstorff had said. 'My purpose,' he artfully explained to his diary, 'was to plant the seeds of peace.'

House was greatly taken with the English. When Sir William Tyrrell, Grey's secretary, arrived in Washington in November, 1913, as an informal emissary to smooth out Anglo-American relations over Mexico, House was delighted with his attitude. By this time the Colonel was dreaming 'of a sympathetic alliance between the two countries.' Is it surprising that Sir William, steeped in the tense air of armed Europe, should have 'expressed a willingness to co-operate'? Sir William, in fact, was perfect. To House and to the President he spoke of 'the necessity of curbing armaments,' and discussed the maleficent power of international bankers and the indications that 'an armament trust... was creating war scares' in a manner nicely calculated to win the heart of the New Freedom. Under this expert fertilization, House's ideas rapidly expanded. On December 2 he was confiding to Tyrrell that 'the next thing I wished to do was to bring about an understanding between France, Germany, England and the United States, regarding a reduction of armaments, both military and naval.' France, significantly, had appeared in the happy picture; Japan, Latin America and the waste places seem to have dropped out.

Sir William was most flattering in his kindly encouragement; he even consented to advise House as to the best 'procedure.' Oddly enough, the Englishman thought he should go to Germany first— though carefully warning him that 'the Minister of Marine, von Tirpitz, was a reactionary.'

> He thought I should proceed quietly and secretly, but should secure an audience with the Kaiser and say to him, among other things, that England and America 'had buried the hatchet' and there was a strong feeling that Germany should come into this good feeling and evidence their good intention by agreeing to stop building an extravagant navy, and to curtail militarism generally.

Sir William assured him that in such a program the British would 'co-operate'; he even went farther, and actually promised 'to give me all the memoranda passed between Great Britain and Germany upon this question of disarmament, in order that I might see how entirely right Great Britain had been in her position.' Dutifully, House noted it all down in his diary, and ten days later he was laying this curious project for international peace before the President. Neither of them, apparently, even noticed with what skill Sir William had managed to convert House's altruistic project about the waste places into a projected Anglo-American alliance against Germany — to crush the naval threat which Great Britain alone had been unable to overcome in the negotiations of 1912. Mr. Wilson seemed almost 'enthusiastic'; and it was decided that House should make the visit to Berlin, just as Sir William had instructed him to do.

The decision was apparently a rather offhand one. Perhaps nobody really thought of Colonel House's ambitious scheme as a practical matter; the President, at all events, seems to have given only the most casual attention to a proceeding which would certainly have been of the first importance if it had been intended as a serious move in national policy. But the Colonel eagerly matured his project; moreover, the unhealthy state of Europe was sufficiently

apparent in the early months of 1914, and when at the end of
April House again asked his chief whether he really wished him to
undertake the journey, the President answered: 'The object you
have in mind is too important to neglect.' House sailed for Germany on May 16, 1914.

Today there hangs about the slight figure of Colonel House, as
it passed in the weeks that followed through the capitals of Europe,
a strong suggestion of innocence in a den of suspicious gangsters.
With Berlin came the first shock of reality, and it appalled him.
'The situation,' he wrote to the President, 'is extraordinary. It is
militarism run stark mad. Unless some one acting for you can
bring about a different understanding, there is some day to be an
awful cataclysm.' The Germans, laboring under the disastrously
mistaken impression that because he was called 'Colonel' he was
a military man, entertained him at all sorts of military shows. They
took him to an airfield where 'a man named Fokker' was performing
the 'most dangerous and curious maneuvers'; and as a special
compliment to his supposed status, his audience with the Kaiser
was arranged for the great *Schrippenfest* — a military ritual festival
— on June 1. It all served most unhappily to reinforce the tuition
which Sir William Tyrrell had been kind enough to supply.

Nevertheless, the Colonel was able to grasp the fact that the
problem was more intricate than he had thought. He met Tirpitz,
who turned out to be slightly less an ogre than represented; he met
everyone else — except Bethmann-Hollweg, the German Chancellor — and he had a long, private conversation with the Kaiser.
The Kaiser, too, was encouraging, just as the English had been.
The monarch's personal peculiarities were something of a strain,
but House 'found him much less prejudiced and much less belligerent than Tirpitz. He declared he wanted peace because it
seemed to Germany's interest. Germany had been poor; she was
now growing rich, and a few more years of peace would make her
so.' He heard another side to the naval controversy; he heard
about 'encirclement' and about the German fears of being crushed
between France and Russia whenever England should consent.

House, enjoying all the optimism of ignorance, summed it up as on the whole 'satisfactory,' and departed to sow the seeds of peace with the Triple Entente.

He was in Paris in the first week of June, but discovered that he could do nothing — the mercurial French were too full of the Caillaux trial for serious statesmanship. He merely passed a 'quiet week' there before going on to London. In the British capital the 'season' was at its height, and he was plunged into a whirl of notables. He met all the best people, in or out of politics; he talked with Haldane and Lloyd George as well as with the Foreign Secretary and the Prime Minister. Page told him that his work in Germany was 'the most important done in this generation'; Sir Edward Grey was 'visibly impressed.' Earnestly House repeated what the Germans had told him, advised the British how to conduct their foreign policy, warned them about 'the German aerial strength' and actually proposed that he, Sir Edward and the Kaiser should meet ' in some way' at the Kiel Regatta, which was about to take place. But oddly enough 'this was not gone into further.' Though the conversations were many and long, there was always a certain vagueness as House approached this point. Sir Edward listened with the gravest courtesy as this singular American ran on; the Foreign Minister was even 'very fair' concerning the necessity 'for Germany to maintain a navy commensurate with her commerce and sufficient to protect herself from Russia and France.' Yet whenever it came to some positive action, some specific message that House might take back to Berlin, there was always a mysterious difficulty. The French and Russians would not understand. In France, Colonel House had not found 'the war spirit dominant'; he felt sure, he told them, that France would 'welcome our efforts for peace.' But nothing happened.

It was in the midst of these dinners, luncheons and exciting conversations that the Austrian heir apparent was assassinated at Sarajevo. The event left no impress upon the published papers of Colonel House, who was proposing to solve the problem of European peace. On July 3 there was another luncheon. Tyrrell told him that Sir Edward would like him to convey to the Kaiser the 'impressions' he had obtained, but would not send 'anything official or in writing, for fear of offending French and Russian sensibilities.' Though House stayed on for another week or two in the July weather, this was about the best that he could get. Evidently it was not enough to warrant that triumphant return to Berlin, bearing the dove of world peace upon his shoulder, of which the Colonel had dreamed. Instead, he sat down and wrote a long personal letter to the Kaiser, expressing his 'high hopes' and pointing out how 'much has been accomplished.' He had a congratulatory letter from Mr. Wilson and felt 'happy,' according to Page; but on July 21 he sailed for the United States.

On his last day in London, Tyrrell brought him another message from Sir Edward, 'which was to the effect that he wished me to know before I sailed that the Austro-Serbian situation was giving him grave concern.'

V

The American people, of course, were wholly ignorant of this essay in amateur diplomacy, undertaken in their name. Europe itself, with its rumors of wars and its spectacular armaments, might make glamorous reading in the Sunday feature sections but it was all remote enough to the ordinary citizen. On the morning of Monday, June 29, it is true, the assassinations at Sarajevo were announced by all the New York newspapers with staring headlines and long and accurate despatches upon the shocking details of the murder. Vienna, London, Paris, Berlin, alike spoke of the most serious 'possibilities,' and one or two of the local editorial comments were ominous in tone. Yet the war scares had come so often, and the whole thing was so far away. In Washington, Mr. Houston, though a Cabinet member, gave the whole matter only the most 'passing interest.' Count Bernstorff, the German Ambassador, had been dining with his Spanish colleague at the Metropolitan Club when the news came. Both realized at once its menacing character, but they 'found little interest in the matter among the Americans in the club.'

The news suggested nothing to House and Page in London. At Paris, Mr. Herrick, whose successor had at last been named, understood that the situation 'was not considered alarming' and so continued with his plans for relinquishing his post. The despatches interrupted Mr. Whitlock as he was at work, in his summer home outside of Brussels, upon a new novel of rural life in Ohio. The Archduke meant little to him; while as for Sarajevo (which was only the capital city of Bosnia) he had never even heard of it. 'I had not the least idea where it was in this world, if it was in this world.' Mr. Gerard, enjoying fashionable society and nautical romance at Kiel, saw the sudden flutter of excitement. But 'that night we dined on board the yacht of the Prince of Monaco. All the diplomats and notables whom I met during the afternoon and evening seemed to think that there was no chance that the tragedy ... would lead to war.'

On Tuesday, June 30, a Vienna despatch to the New York *Times* spoke of sentiment for 'a punitive war upon Serbia,' while an interview with a Hungarian Count who was visiting in New York supplied some further hints. The assassination, he said, was really the fault of Russia — it was due to Russian 'propaganda.' The reporter accepted the word, unaware of how soon and how dramatically it was to enter the language. Already, however, more immediate events were crowding the affair into the background. That morning there was announced the sensational indictment of Mr. Charles S. Mellen of the New Haven Railroad; it was recognized as the first frontal attack of the Administration's war upon the 'interests,' and that was a more exciting war than anything in Europe.

By Wednesday morning the assassination had vanished altogether from the front pages. The *Times* had a London despatch reporting that Signor Marconi's attempt to speak across the Atlantic by wireless telephone might actually be made within the next three months. There was a prominent local headline on the front page: 'City Bank Bids For World Trade.' With the new era in American finance foreshadowed by the passage of the Federal Reserve act, the news account said, the National City Bank had decided 'to engage in a world-wide plan to assist in building up the foreign trade of the United States through the establishment of branches abroad.' More arresting than either of these matters, however, was the formal re-entry of Theodore Roosevelt into American politics. At Pittsburgh on the evening before he had made his first political address since the campaign of 1912. It proved to be an unsparing attack upon the policies of President Wilson.

The New Freedom nevertheless held to its course. Far away in London Colonel House and Mr. Page were still busily sowing the seeds of peace around expensive dinner tables; while at Kiel Ambassador Gerard was lunching with Grand Admiral von Tirpitz aboard his flagship, and was finding that celebrated monster 'an amiable sea dog, combining much political and worldly wisdom with his knowledge of the sea.' The 'A. B. C.' conference at Niagara Falls — at which the Argentine, Brazil and Chile had been invited, by another original stroke of the New Diplomacy, to help us out of the Mexican muddle — had at last reached an agreement which appeared to bring that crisis to an end. So the Fourth of July arrived, and President Wilson at Philadelphia was restating, as has been said, his faith in 'principle' as the true guide to the use of the influence and power of the United States in international affairs, and was kindling anew the high, if dangerous, belief that the flag was 'the flag not only of America but of humanity.'

Another golden week slipped away. On Sunday, July 12, Mr. Page was composing for the President another of those long, chatty letters which so much delighted Mr. Wilson. It was chiefly about Mexico and the quaint habits of the British aristocracy, but in the midst of it the Ambassador paused to note, almost parenthetically:

But Grey is greatly disturbed over the danger that comes of the Servian unrest against Austria. Both Russia and Germany are mobilizing on the South. The infernal near-Eastern country is worse than Mexico.

That was all. The Ambassador was misinformed about the mobilization, but one is struck by the cheery carelessness with which he accepted such a report. That same Sunday readers of New York newspapers searched in vain for any reference to the Balkan danger in the week end cable sections, where the sidelights and backgrounds of the European news were customarily reported. The *Tribune's* Berlin despatch was devoted to the lively problem of mixed bathing in the Wannsee. The *Times* had an editorial, 'Prepared for War,' but that referred to the exciting events in Ulster. In the same paper's feature section, however, there was a fullpage article by Yves Guyot, former French Minister of Public Works, upon the menacing absurdity of the colossal European armaments. It stressed the complete absence of any valid cause for war; the talk of war, it suggested, was largely manufactured by the military men and diplomatists themselves. 'Everybody remembers,' M. Guyot wrote, 'the optimism of Benedetti on the eve of 1870. All diplomats fear to endorse the role of dupes, and, fearful of being accused of having disregarded perils, they invent them.' Can one say even now that M. Guyot was wrong? His article ended upon a question:

> One supposes that, in the ordinary relations of life, people will act in a rational manner. Is it too much to ask that the men who control the various great nations act in a similar manner? I would put this simple question to them: 'How is it that the expenditures for armaments are increasing when the causes of war are diminishing?'

How indeed? Barring some of the customary wild talk in such distant places as St. Petersburg or Vienna (very badly reported in the American press), peace appeared to reign profoundly. It certainly reigned in the embassies and legations of the New Freedom's diplomats. Mr. Whitlock returned to his novel of rural life in Ohio. On July 13 Ambassador Penfield at Vienna was preparing a long-winded, full-dress despatch for the State Department upon the consequences of the Sarajevo tragedy; in Mr. Penfield's mind they seemed to concern only the succession to the Austro-Hungarian throne. But farther down the Danube, and also on July 13, Mr. F. E. Mallett, the American Vice-Consul at Budapest, was likewise writing out a report: 'The impression prevails at present in Budapest that a war between Austria-Hungary and Servia is unavoidable, and that hostilities will begin soon after the crops are harvested....' It was the only warning despatched to the State Department by any of its representatives until after the crisis had reached every front page in the world. But cable tolls were high; and Mr. Mallett unfortunately confided it to the mails.

Mr. Mallett's despatch began its leisurely journey across Europe and the Atlantic; at home, the daily current of news flowed on. Count Bernstorff, who had received no word from Berlin to encourage his own forebodings, sailed for his usual summer vacation in Germany. Sir Cecil Spring Rice, the British Ambassador, was in England; M. Jusserand, the French Ambassador, was in France. The new rotogravure section of the New York *Times* was printing photographs on Sundays of Carson's volunteers drilling in their cloth caps and bandoliers; even the Ulster war, however, was now being submerged beneath the gorgeous Parisian scandal of the Caillaux trial. So the July days went by. General Huerta at last resigned the Mexican Presidency and fled the country. Colonel House sailed for home. President Wilson flung a bombshell into the fortresses of reaction by entering suit to dissolve the New Haven railroad merger and calling for the indictment of its directors. At Newport the America's Cup yachts were getting on famously.

That week, too, a heat wave of unusual intensity swept the country, setting new records for the year in many cities. On Thursday, July 23, a temperature of 100 was recorded at Chicago, and a publicity-seeking physician got into the papers by asserting that a 'wave of insanity' was also appearing as a direct result of the excessive temperature. In New York on the same day there was intense heat and great suffering; but suddenly in the evening the dead air broke under a wild thunderstorm of 'hurricane velocity.' The lightning flashes leapt, reverberated and died away; and the relieved millions had no inkling of the other storm which had burst that day in Europe across the last sultry summer of the world as they knew it.

No one, outside of a few diplomatists, politicians and financiers in Europe, had any real inkling; no one in America seems to have had any understanding of even the possible danger. The surface of the European news during all the second and third week of July had been cheerfulness itself. Business men, anxiously scanning the horizon for signs of the much-heralded revival, were no doubt puzzled by the unaccountable slackness on the New York Stock Exchange, but it was set down to 'foreign selling' and allowed to go at that. Only today, as one turns the fragile newsprint pages which record the last days of that vanished world, is one struck by the foreign market stories, which from July 15 onward reported the growing heaviness of the European bourses. Never more than a paragraph or two, and buried under small headlines in the cavernous recesses of the financial sections, they day by day announced the sagging prices and steady pressure of selling coming from Vienna — and St. Petersburg. They were of small consequence except to a few expert speculators then. Reading them today one seems to catch the faint, dripping sound of the lifeblood of nineteenth century Western civilization, ebbing secretly away in the darkness.

II. THE HURRICANE

i

IN the United States even more, perhaps, than in Europe the appalling suddenness of the paroxysm in which that civilization perished was itself a factor of far-reaching consequences. The New York *Times* on Friday, July 24, announced the Austrian ultimatum to Serbia as a matter of serious but not of sensational importance. A brief editorial recognized in only a cautious and theoretical way a threat of that 'general war' which had so often been discussed and in which no one, really, believed. Just one week later the exhausted diplomats of Europe were finally throwing in their cards; the impossible had occurred and, barring miracles, the general war had come. There was no time to think, no opportunity for assessing causes, examining backgrounds and establishing reasoned attitudes. In seven days the framework of an age was shattered; the mind rebelled under the fearful abruptness of the blow and the emotions too readily took command.

The alarm came overnight. On Friday most of the newspapers were unconcerned; on Saturday morning the headlines were leaping from all the front pages: 'Europe At Point of War,' 'European War in the Balance.' The cables pouring in from London, from Berlin, from Vienna and Belgrade were of the gravest character. The general war, said the London correspondent of the *Times*, could 'only be averted by a complete backdown of one of the two great triplices into which the European powers are divided,' and that alone should have been enough to show that the general war was inevitable. Yet most of the New York editors naturally hesitated to proclaim it. One, Mr. Frank H. Simonds of the *Evening Sun*, who happened to have some first-hand knowledge of recent European history, did see clearly not only what was happening but the essentially impersonal character of the enormous disaster which had been precipitated. In a long editorial that Saturday afternoon he gave a comprehensive analysis of the whole background of the crisis, and one which was notably impartial. Alone he understood that the Austrian attack on Serbia was not a merely wanton aggression, but Austria's 'declaration of a determination to fight for her own existence' against the 'attrition of intrigue.' Neither side could now back down without accepting destruction; and the great war had come at last, not because anyone had willed it, but because it was the only issue from the tragic fears and rivalries of the past half-dozen years. The article now remains to show that such a detached and scientific view was not beyond the leaders of American opinion had they striven to achieve it. Unfortunately, it is chiefly interesting today for the fact that its implications were so soon forgotten by everybody — including, perhaps, Mr. Simonds himself. It created a brief sensation, which was immediately swept away in the furious rush of events.

Already the New York *Tribune* had advanced a far simpler and emotionally more satisfying interpretation; Austria, it decided, must be forcing war on Serbia through greed for the territorial booty which had fallen to the latter in the Balkan wars. Everywhere this idea, requiring no prior knowledge of the problem, was quickly seized on. With Sunday morning there came bigger and blacker headlines. In the New York *Times* they stretched across four full columns — something very rare with the conservative newspapers of that day:

> AUSTRIA BREAKS WITH SERVIA;
> KING PETER MOVES HIS CAPITAL;
> RUSSIA IS MOBILIZING HER ARMY;
> BERLIN AND PARIS MOBS FOR WAR

The news stories followed in a rushing torrent:

Berlin, July 25 — The capital is afire tonight with the war fever....
The crowds which had been waiting since 6 o'clock greeted the
announcement with frenzied cheers. Hats were thrown into the air
and shouts of 'War! War!' reverberated up and down the street.

Paris was no less frenzied, and if anything even more aggressive:

Paris, July 25 — Tonight's crowds on the boulevards are shouting
'To Berlin!'... Belief is that Austria's break with Servia means the
beginning of the big war so long prepared for by the powers. The
popular idea is that Germany planned it as a 'coup de theatre' while
all her rivals of the Triple Entente are occupied at home.

Did our hurried editorial-writers, snatching at the cables as they
came in and trying under pressure to assess a situation in its very
nature almost inconceivable, pause to recognize that first deft
propagandist touch? By Monday, they all knew that Europe was
on the verge of the abyss; most of them, however, were following
the lead, not of Mr. Simonds, but of the *Tribune*. The sedate and
ordinarily careful *Evening Post* loftily waved aside its competitor's
erudition; talk of 'long-smoldering backgrounds,' it implied, was
all very well but of no present moment — obviously the whole
crisis was the fault of the Austrian militarists. Our traditional
sympathy for small peoples (where our own interests were not
involved) was quick to awake, and the liberal, Democratic New
York *World* had a flaming cartoon of the Austrian wolf about to de-
vour the innocent lamb of 'little Servia.' The *Times*, probably the
most influential American newspaper in matters of foreign affairs,
arrived at the solemn verdict that Austria was the guilty party:

Austria has made the recent assassinations a pretext for renewing
on a large scale her efforts to increase her power in the Near East....
The war news from Vienna is read here with loathing and a sense of
shame.

The assassinations at Sarajevo were dismissed as a mere pretext,
obviously for the simple reason that they were already a month old.
At the time it had been freely prophesied in the American press

that they might mean the dissolution of the Austro-Hungarian Empire, but what that might imply was now forgotten. The *Times* expressed no loathing for the war news from St. Petersburg — no doubt because there was so little significant news of any sort available from that capital. And Paris was insistent. Again on Monday American readers learned that a 'Paris despatch to the London *Times* sees a German plot. The present crisis is "the result of a deliberately planned scheme"...'

It is impossible to blame the editorial writers for guessing; that was their unhappy duty. Their failure was in not realizing that their efforts were only guesses, based upon ignorance and inadequate information and already confused by the fogs of special pleading. As the crisis rapidly deepened, they jumped only the more rashly to unsound conclusions — which, by the fatal tradition of editorial 'consistency,' were bound to influence the whole future course of their papers' policies. Daily the strain increased, the fearful excitement grew. On Wednesday the *Times* headlines had widened to five columns. For many today the most vivid recollection of that fatal week is the steadily lengthening parade of headline type across the face of the morning news. With Wednesday morning there came the announcement of the Austrian declaration of war on Serbia. The peace of Europe, the headlines shrieked, was 'Now in Kaiser's Hands,' and Americans could not understand that the Kaiser, no less than all those other statesmen, was a prisoner of that tragic game of European diplomacy at which all the powers had so long been playing.

The Berlin cables, unlike those from Paris, neglected to allege an enemy conspiracy. Rather, they were content to point, in a methodical way, to the obvious fact that if Russia mobilized, German mobilization must follow automatically, and that thereafter no halting would be possible. But the overwhelming importance of Russia escaped American commentators, and there were no appeals in the American press to Russian militarists to stay their hand.

By the middle of the week the reality was at last sinking in —

and something of its possible significance for the United States was just beginning to be realized. Wheat prices were soaring at Chicago, while the stock market in New York was breaking to panic lows as the main tide of European selling came pouring over the cables. Currents of private opinion were already beginning to set strongly in the direction indicated by the editors. Prominent men were hastening to demonstrate the profundity of their intellects by leaping for the popular side; and Mr. Samuel Gompers, that rather pompous voice of the people, was formally announcing that war was being 'inaugurated by Austrian royalty to divert the people's attention from their own ills.' For 'the aggrandizement of an effete royalty, men are to be arrayed against each other to kill men, to create countless widows and orphans.'

Reporters hastily digging out our few military experts found most of them, strangely enough, more realistic, more inclined to suspend judgment, and more sober. The aging General Nelson A. Miles — hero of our own comic-opera war of sixteen years before — did not seek to assess the blame, but he knew that what was coming was to be no comedy. The general war, he said, would 'demonstrate the wisdom of a parliament of reason and of justice for the settlement of international controversies.' The civilians now rushing into print were far more impassioned — for most of them, naturally enough, were those whose prejudices were already violently engaged. The distinguished physicist, Michael Pupin, gave a fiercely propagandist interview in support of Serbia. Dr. Pupin was a Serb by birth; and this interview was one of the first in which innumerable influential citizens were to appeal to their countrymen not as Americans but as bitter partisans in the European struggle. Those who did this in the German interest were later to be excoriated as 'hyphenated Americans.' The much greater number who, like Dr. Pupin, performed the same service for the Allies were only applauded as patriots. Indeed, at the White House a reporter was already putting a direct question to Mr. Wilson as to whether the United States should not intervene in the defence of Serbia.

'Unless a miracle is wrought,' the morning *Sun* announced on Friday, the last day of July, 'there is going to be a general war in Europe.' That day, too, the *Times* printed the first war map — with its short black line, representing the Austrian positions around Belgrade, which was so soon to stretch across the whole face of a continent. No miracle was wrought. 'All quarters,' said a London cable, 'believed that the beginning of Armageddon was only a matter of hours.' That Friday morning the London Stock Exchange suspended trading, and an hour later the New York Stock Exchange, receiving a convergent torrent of selling from every European capital, likewise closed its doors. It brought home the tremendous magnitude of the disaster with a smashing vividness. The world was collapsing, and Americans suddenly found themselves engulfed in the host of immediate and pressing personal problems which it involved for them. Thousands of American citizens, it was now suddenly remembered, were being left stranded in a Europe at war. At home the cotton exchanges followed the security markets into suspension; the clearing house banks in New York did not know whether they could remain open; there was no money, no possibility of doing business, no knowledge as to the outcome.

Everything was happening at once, at home and abroad, and everything was inconceivably disastrous. On Saturday morning there was a ray of hope — 'Czar, Kaiser and King May Yet Arrange Peace' — but during the day the hope died. That afternoon in Paris and Berlin the mobilization decrees were signed; and on the morning of Sunday, August 2, the New York *Times* spread its great streamer headline across the full eight columns of the front page:

GERMANY DECLARES WAR ON RUSSIA, FIRST SHOTS ARE FIRED;
FRANCE IS MOBILIZING AND MAY BE DRAWN IN TOMORROW;
PLANS TO RESCUE THE 100,000 AMERICANS NOW IN EUROPE

'The bloodiest war ever fought on earth,' cried the *Times* from the head of its editorial columns, 'and the least justified of all wars since man emerged from barbarism has apparently begun.' Its rotogravure section published with the same issue was still carrying romantic photographs of the Irish Nationalist and Ulster volunteers, drilling for that little war in Ireland which had already been forgotten. So quickly had Armageddon come.

Like other newspapers, the *Times* in a long editorial was already arraying itself irrevocably on the side of the Entente powers. The thought process was as natural as it was unsound. Ignorant of the backgrounds, forgetting the Sarajevo assassinations and neglecting the importance of Russia from the outset, American opinion had first grasped the crisis in the conveniently simple terms of a wanton Austrian attack upon 'little Servia.' When the attack was pressed home, the harried editorial writers snatched at the hope that Germany would restrain her ally; when Germany did not — for reasons which were inexplicable because the commentators had no real understanding of the actual situation in Europe — they were led automatically to the conclusion that Germany, animated by some secret and satanic purpose, must be deliberately forcing on the war. That, obviously, explained everything. It was ready, it was simple and it was psychologically satisfying.

Indeed, it was psychologically essential. When the crisis came, as Spring Rice had told his friend Mr. Adams months before, it would really be 'a peoples' question — the struggle for existence between races,' though it would be precipitated by some 'slight act, based on what seem to you the meanest of motives.' In the presence of overwhelming disaster, the human mind must find mean or criminal motives to 'explain' it. Somebody must be responsible. There must be some personal criminal upon whom to discharge all that sudden sick horror and dismay. The *Evening Post*, striving gallantly through the storm to gain the judicial attitude, thought it a 'melancholy futility' to attempt to fix the blame, but in the next breath emphasized the 'terrible miscalculation of which Germany was guilty' in consenting to the Austrian ultimatum. Long before the great war propagandas began to develop from abroad, the leading organs of American opinion, through the interplay of haste, ignorance and their own psychological necessities, had begun to distinguish in the German Empire a vast, malignant power which alone and for its own atrocious ends had plunged the world into this stupendous catastrophe.

The improbability of that analysis implied only that it must be buttressed at once with every straw of 'proof' that could be discovered or invented.

> The war speech of the German Emperor from the window of his palace [the *Times* editorial page exclaimed] was a piece of pompous humbug. 'The sword has been forced into our hands,' forsooth, and he demands of Russia and of France an explanation of the mobiliza- tion of their troops, when from many sources it has been disclosed that German mobilization has for days been under way.

The *Times* may have owed this fictitious disclosure to the astute stream of insinuation which had been flowing out of Paris from the first days of the crisis; but if such 'proofs' had not been sup- plied others would have been invented. In fact, they were. 'Militarism' was instantly seized upon as a basic cause of the disaster — and since in the minds of most Americans this had come to mean German militarism primarily, it fortified the im- perious necessity for belief. An equally superficial theory of the fundamental causes operated from the very beginning in the same way. It was all due to the undemocratic machinations of the Central European 'autocracies.' As early as August 2 the *Times* was proclaiming the crusade for 'the crushing out of the imperial idea, the end, once for all time, in those three empires of the absolute rule and the substitution for all powerful sovereigns and their titled advisers of an executive with power to carry out only the will of the people.' Thus was posed that curious enigma which was to puzzle the more skeptical down to the spring of 1917. How was a victory which must include victory for Romanoff absolutism to assist in crushing out the imperial idea? It did not matter; the war of 'democracy against autocracy' was already joined in our newspapers, and in still another way it supplied a 'reason' that would satisfy the overpowering need for a moral verdict.

That Sunday night Mr. McAdoo, the Secretary of the Treasury, was sitting up until the small hours with the great financial magnates in New York, hastily devising means for keeping the nation going. The crowds were in the streets; the anxious were besieging the cable offices for news of relatives abroad; editors were mobilizing all available forces to cover the greatest news story which had ever broken; innumerable personal and national problems were springing with a burning urgency out of the white heat of that terrific excitement. And then on Monday there came the slow, the majestically self-righteous swing of Great Britain into her place upon the Allied line. It changed the whole character of the crisis — and of its impact upon American opinion.

ii

Secretary Houston, one of the more influential members of the Wilson Cabinet, was to confess that he watched the developing crisis almost with indifference — until there came the British ultimatum to Germany. Then, as he put it, 'I had a feeling that the end of things had come.... I stopped in my tracks, dazed and horror-stricken.' He was but one among many. In spite of the long popular tradition of Anglo-American hostility, the influence of the British viewpoint upon the United States was in fact enormous. Politicians might placate an Irish constituency or stir our bumptious nationalism with a little tail-twisting now and then; but those more cultivated elements which dominated our intellectual, political and financial life still found in London their unacknowledged capital.

The educated leaders of the New Freedom were steeped in British literature more deeply than the old-fashioned politicians. As a student of domestic government, President Wilson throughout his life had been profoundly influenced by English ideas and political institutions; while our rare experts in the elegant fields of foreign policy had modelled themselves for a generation upon the giants of British liberal imperialism. Our own imperialist adventure at the turn of the century had been largely in imitation of those romantic splendors; Mr. Kipling himself had sung us forward to 'take up the white man's burden,' and the statesmen of those years — Roosevelt and Lodge, Root, John Hay, Taft, Leonard Wood — had rejoiced to create an empire almost as glorious and perhaps even more righteous than that of Great Britain.

At the time of the Spanish-American War, Great Britain alone had supported us against what we believed to be a European cabal chiefly instigated by Germany; and as the Anglo-German rivalry developed in the years that followed, our high priests of foreign policy repaid the service by orienting the American attitude in accordance with the British interest. Twenty years before the League of Nations, John Hay, as Secretary of State, had dreamed of bringing the United States onto the international stage to guarantee a world peace based on the existing British predominance. Mr. William Randolph Hearst had raised the rabble against him and President McKinley had cautiously refrained from the adventure, but that view of world politics lingered on in high places. So did a certain tradition of hostility toward Germany which, running back to the Samoan incident of the late 'eighties, had been greatly strengthened by the peculiar conduct of Admiral von Diedrichs at Manila. As the Kaiser continued to make foolish speeches he continued to be held up as the chief incendiary of Europe. Many of our serious thinkers had come to believe with Page and House in an Anglo-American 'understanding' as the best basis of universal peace, and Great Britain's action in 1914 could not in any event have failed to sway profoundly all the more elegant and distinguished leaders of American opinion. But one circumstance gave to Great Britain a tremendous hold upon American opinion itself. London was not only the cultural and social capital of our wealthier and more influential classes; so far as European events were concerned it was our newspaper capital as well.

For years the American public had received its day-by-day

picture of Europe through a distinctly British perspective. Few American newspapers at that time maintained European staffs of their own; while those which did found few trained American foreign correspondents to man them. There were one or two capable American newspaper men in Berlin, but there were probably none at all in St. Petersburg, while even the Paris correspondents concentrated mainly upon social and artistic news rather than political reporting. Both our newspapers and our press associations tended to cover European politics from London. Their London bureaus had general supervision over the correspondents on the Continent; the news was largely assembled in the London bureaus and forwarded by them. It was often heavily filled out with information or 'background' material derived from the British newspapers and magazines — simply because they had so much better sources than the American staffs — while the common language and the lack of competent American writers often made it convenient to employ Englishmen in the American organizations. The New York *Times*, which perhaps gave more serious attention to European events than any other American newspaper, had an Englishman, Mr. Ernest Marshall, as the head of its London bureau, and his subordinates were largely Britishers. Its Berlin correspondent, Mr. Frederick William Wile, was an American, but the *Times* shared him with Northcliffe's *Daily Mail*, a leader in the anti-German propaganda in England. The New York *World's* London correspondent was an Irishman who had never worked in the United States; his staff, like Mr. Marshall's, was largely composed of British newspaper men. So was that of the *Sun*. Those correspondents who were American citizens, moreover, had often lived so long abroad as to absorb the British viewpoint. The dean of the American correspondents in London, Mr. Edward Price Bell of the Chicago *Daily News*, had arrived fresh from college to remain there for the rest of his active life, and it was naturally impossible for the others not to reflect the atmosphere by which they were daily surrounded. The whole arrangement was simply a matter of convenience, economy and the absence of any very lively American interest in European affairs; the result was, however, that the American view of Europe was normally and unavoidably colored very deeply by the British attitude. Ordinarily, perhaps, it made little difference. In the midst of a world crisis in which the British interest was to be wholly engaged upon one side, the effect was bound to be unfortunate.

Up until the last days of the crisis, of course, the British themselves were unaware of how deeply their interests were to be engaged; while their Liberal newspapers and journalists, at least, were doing their utmost to hold a fair balance. Through all the earlier stages this lent a considerable impartiality both to the London cables and the American front pages. But by Monday, August 3, it was apparent that Great Britain was herself upon the verge, if not already in, and London was impartial no longer. Our papers displayed the British press comment. The London *Times* spoke with its mighty voice: the die was cast — Germany was largely to blame. The *Daily Mail*: 'Germany is plainly revealed as the aggressor.' The *Morning Post*: 'We must stand by France.' If the British, cried the New York *Times* in its agony, should enter the war, then Americans could know that they had no alternative. 'We must feel that they have acted with clear minds and under a deep sense of their accountability.' Great Britain could do no wrong. It is noticeable that the *Times* had failed to 'feel' as much concerning any of the other great powers involved; but once more it was a type of reasoning which escaped the laborious exercise of thought and so met the pressing need of the hour.

In Washington, that Monday, Congress was rushing through Mr. McAdoo's emergency fiscal legislation, and had little time to think of the larger aspects of the crisis. The Senate did pause to adopt a resolution 'deprecating' the war (as one correspondent put it); while the moralist in the White House summoned the newspaper men and urged them to eschew all unverified rumor and excitement. The United States, Mr. Wilson told them, 'owes it to mankind to remain in such a state of mind that she can help the world.' Nobody, of course, paid the slightest attention. That very afternoon in London, as the King and Queen drove through the cheering crowds to Parliament, a group of Americans at the Carlton Hotel cheered and yelled with the rest, and one mighty Yankee voice sang out above the tumult: 'New York is with you!' The King 'bowed and smiled to the greeting.'

New York was. On the morning of August 4, its great newspapers were all but unanimous. Only the Hearst press — cold, as always, to the British — and the New York *Herald* had managed to retain some intelligent neutrality, and neither carried much weight among those more cultured souls who took an interest in 'affairs.' The *Times*, finally seduced by Sir Edward Grey's address to Parliament, had joined the Allies lock, stock and barrel. Germany's invasion of France was 'aggression, pure and simple.' The *Tribune* and the intellectually distinguished *Evening Post* had yet to find anything particularly shocking in the invasion of Belgium or to perceive those great moral issues in which (as they were so soon to discover) the war had been joined. They still ignorantly assumed that Great Britain was fighting for her own national interests, but they supported her no less cordially on that account. It was not, in those early days, the conservatives, for whom the *Tribune* spoke, who saw in the Allied cause a holy crusade for the rights of humanity. It was the liberals, the progressives, the leaders of reform and the standard-bearers of the New Freedom. 'Autocracy or Democracy' was the heading above the long and flaming editorial in the New York *World*. As early as August 4, and with only the slightest of prompting from the propagandas and publicists of the Entente, the liberal, the enlightened and the Democratic *World* had itself adopted what now seems the shallowest of all the war rationalizations:

All the machinery of progress [the *World* concluded] is stopped by the hand of autocracy. The Kaiser plunges Europe into the most devastating conflict known to human history.... And about what? Ostensibly... in order to protect her own interests. In reality because the reactionary party of Germany was determined to invite a general

European conflict in order to stay the advancement of political reforms....

It was a logical analysis; it was complete and consistent and, because it was utterly damning, it satisfied the intense emotional demands of the moment. Yet at no point did it correspond even remotely to the actual history which it sought to explain — as is readily granted today even by those who still feel that the Austrian and German governments must bear a major share of the responsibility for the disaster. Mr. Simonds's informed interpretation of ten days before had long since gone swirling down the torrent of events; in its place American editors had evoked out of their own brains, emotions and partial information a largely legendary concept of the crisis — which no one had time either to consider or to criticize.

By the evening of August 4 the immense catastrophe had become complete and irretrievable; and on Wednesday morning, August 5, the great banner heads went marching like fate across every American breakfast table:

ENGLAND DECLARES WAR ON GERMANY; BRITISH SHIP SUNK;
FRENCH SHIPS DEFEAT GERMAN, BELGIUM ATTACKED;
17,000,000 MEN ENGAGED IN GREAT WAR OF EIGHT NATIONS;
GREAT ENGLISH AND GERMAN NAVIES ABOUT TO GRAPPLE;
RIVAL WARSHIPS OFF THIS PORT AS LUSITANIA SAILS.

The thing had happened.

The United States had issued her formal proclamation of neutrality, but in the huge crowds which gathered about the newspaper bulletin boards to cheer each fresh declaration of war it was noticed that the cheers for the Entente powers drowned out those for Germany and Austria. New York City was already overrun with reservists, many of them penniless, pouring in to catch the steamers that would bear them into greater horrors than any dreamed of. They marched through the streets with bands and their national flags, one side often falling afoul the other until presently Mayor Mitchel had to forbid foreign flags of any sort. Others besides reservists were straining to be off. The celebrated General Leonard Wood was in Washington demanding that he be despatched as 'observer' to the scene of action. Mr. Richard Harding Davis, the greatest, the most elegant and most Kiplingesque of our 'war correspondents,' caught the Lusitania and was borne out to sea — and to the slow discovery that in war on this stupendous scale war correspondents, like the rest of military glamour, were but quaint anachronisms.

The Bank of France was reported (erroneously) to be opening a big war credit — all of $5,000,000 — with J. P. Morgan & Co. The U.S.S. Tennessee was being hurriedly loaded with gold dollars and rushed abroad to the rescue of the tourists now jamming every American consulate and embassy in Europe — in the panic-stricken discovery that they were stranded in a world where civilization had broken down, where letters-of-credit had no meaning and whence security had fled. In Paris and London other Americans were rushing into government offices with their offers of assistance, or into the newspapers with their sympathy and support. In every belligerent country the intellectuals, the publicists, the journalistic and official spokesmen, were desperately rationalizing the national cause — forgetting facts and remembering 'reasons' — and the first results of the process were already pouring over the cables. On August 5 the New York *Times* published a column and a half justification of the British entry into the war under the signature, oddly enough, of no less a liberal and a pacifist than Mr. H. G. Wells:

That trampling, drilling foolery in the heart of Europe that has arrested civilization and darkened the hopes of mankind for forty years — German imperialism and German militarism — has struck its inevitable blow.... Never was a war so righteous as is the war against Germany now.... [The military outcome] will be more or less definitely decided within the next two or three months. By that time, I believe, German imperialism will be shattered, and it may be possible to anticipate the end of the armaments phase of European history. France, Italy, England and all the smaller Powers of Europe are now pacific countries. Russia... will be too exhausted for further adventure. Shattered Germany will be revolutionary.... The way will be open at last for all these Western powers to organize peace. That is why I, with my declared horror of war, did not sign any of these 'stop the war' appeals.... Now is the sword drawn for peace.

Mr. Wells, like the rest of us who were to adopt his argument, is now aware of the baseless character of that reasoning. Yet one can hardly accuse him of seeking, on August 5, 1914, deliberately to mislead American opinion; rather, it was himself whom he was misleading, in a passionate effort to re-establish his own intellectual integrity. The effect, however, was the same; and the 'war to end war,' like the war to end 'autocracy,' had entered the American ideology long before President Wilson had even thought of endowing it with the great power of his rhetoric. Mr. Wells's contribution, moreover, was but the first wavelet of the flood which was to roll in without interruption for two and a half years thereafter — from the Allied side. But not from the German. On August 5 the British Navy dredged up and cut the German cables, and on August 6 there was not a single Berlin or Vienna date-line in the American press.

It was also on August 4 and 5 that President Wilson despatched to all the belligerent governments his telegraphic proffer of good offices 'in the interest of European peace, either now or at any other time.'

iii

Our somnolent State Department, where Mr. William Jennings Bryan ruled placidly and idealistically over his deserving Democrats, had not really awakened into activity until the crisis was in full career. It was not until July 28, five days after the Austrian ultimatum, that the first thoroughly alarming cables began to come in from the ambassadors; while as late as July 31 Mr. Bryan was just remembering to wire all representatives in Europe for daily telegraphic reports on the situation. The war broke upon our government even more suddenly than upon our newspapers, and gave it even less time in which to assess its problem and formulate its policy. The idea of an American mediation, however, was as spontaneous as the shock and horror springing from the disaster itself. There was a resolution in the Senate on August 4 urging the President to undertake a settlement 'by mediation or arbitration'; the Chicago *Examiner* was in the same days telegraphically inviting all the prominent men it could think of to form a 'world-wide committee' to stop the war, and countless others must have seized at the same thought — which accorded so well with that mood of superior virtue in which we were accustomed to regard the benighted governments of Europe.

The earliest official suggestion arrived at the State Department with those first cables of July 28, in the despatch from Ambassador Herrick at Paris. German mobilization, he reported, would mean war, and he believed that 'a strong plea for delay and moderation from the President of the United States would meet with the respect and approval of Europe.' Even in those first days, mediation, in Mr. Herrick's excited mind, was being colored into a proposal for what would have amounted to an American intervention on behalf of the Entente powers to halt the Germans. The despatch went immediately to the White House. Did the President grasp the unneutral implications of the suggestion? He rejected it, at any rate; and instead of issuing at once the 'plea for moderation' he cabled late that night to Ambassador Page at London, asking his advice as to a sounder course of action. 'Is there in your opinion any likelihood that the good offices of the United States... would be acceptable or serve any high purpose?'

Mr. Page was asked for his own opinion; unfortunately, he responded by giving Sir Edward Grey's. Already Mr. Page was far gone beneath the spell of that austere nobility. 'I think I shall never forget yesterday,' the infatuated Ambassador reported to Mr. Wilson. 'There sat this always solitary man — he and I, of course, in the room alone, each, I am sure, giving the other his full confidence.' It was a dangerous illusion for a diplomatist at a moment like that one. On his own responsibility Page begged Sir Edward to inform him 'if the good offices of the United States could at any time or in any possible way be used,' and received the Foreign Minister's polite and cautious thanks. When the President's telegram arrived a few hours later, Mr. Page replied to it merely by reporting this offer of his own and saying that he would renew it. Meanwhile, however, the life of European civilization was ebbing fast. The State Department had to insist again; and it was not until six days later that the Ambassador at last found time to give his opinion that there was 'not the slightest chance' of any result from a proffer of good offices. By that time, of course, there was none. It was the first of many instances in which Mr. Page was to prove an unsatisfactory representative.

In the meanwhile, all the foreign offices had been busily pouring in their official versions of the calamity. As early as August 4 the French Foreign Office was forehandedly protesting to Mr. Herrick (and 'all civilized nations') against Germany's 'violation of its international obligations,' and on that basis was reserving its own right 'to use such reprisals as may be found necessary.' Sir Cecil Spring Rice was inventing a subtly ingenious explanation for Colonel House's benefit: 'You came so near making a general war impossible that the war party in Berlin and Vienna became alarmed... and... took advantage of the Archduke's murder... to precipitate matters, believing that... it was now or never.' It is very difficult indeed not to see the diplomat behind that striking theory of the war's origin. On August 2 Mr. Page was under the impression that the true cause of the war was simply race-hatred between 'the Slav and the Teuton' and that the conflict was being forced because the time seemed 'favorable to Russia.' Twenty-four hours later he knew better than that. 'The Foreign Office informs me,' he reported, 'that the Czar gave his personal assurance... that not a Russian soldier should pass the frontier unless Russia were attacked.... All opinions here therefore point to Germany as the determined aggressor.' And all Mr. Page's doubts were set at rest next day when Sir Edward himself kindly 'explained at length the designs of Germany.'

The President finally issued his tender of good offices anyway, in a somewhat softened form; but our own editorial pages cried that mediation was useless now, and the State Department early resigned itself to the hope that at some future date we might be 'in better position to exert our influence for peace.' Yet the episode served to fix the idea of an American intervention in mind; and it now shows how early there appeared the confusion between a neutral intervention to secure a mediated or 'negotiated' peace and an intervention, in effect belligerent, to secure peace (as Mr. Herrick had suggested) through supporting the Entente against the Central Powers. Few American statesmen in those hurried hours seem to have noticed the difference. It was not only in the United States, however, that the President's offer awoke the idea of an American intervention. Sir Edward Grey both noted the difference and very shrewdly analyzed the possibilities. He was later to record his method of reasoning:

If there were stalemate on both Western and Eastern fronts there would be a pause, in which the voice of reason might be heard. Germany would then have lost the hope of victory.... On the other hand, the Allies might reflect that, to resist a German attack was one thing, to advance and to conquer Germany another and very different thing. It might seem preferable to make peace on terms that, though short of victory for the Allies, would be anything but victorious terms for Germany. In such a situation the influence of the United States would be invaluable.

Invaluable, that is to say, to the Entente. Sir Edward, it must be remembered, was fresh from the original but suggestive diplomatics of Colonel House; and he explains that an 'early opportunity' was taken of putting his views before Mr. Page. On August 7 the American Ambassador was summoned to the Foreign Office; it was to be a week before the British Expeditionary Force had landed upon the Continent, but British diplomacy had already initiated its first skillful offensive.

I explained to the United States Ambassador today... [that] of course, if the Germans won easily against the French they would listen to nothing. If, on the other hand, the French and Russians won easily, they would insist that Germany should receive a lesson. What terms of peace would be fair would depend upon how things went.... I knew that President Wilson wished to mediate, and, whenever there appeared a fair opportunity of stopping the war by mediation, we should, I felt sure, throw our influence on the side of it.

[American 'mediation,' in other words, would be prepared as a last-line reserve which the Entente might call up, in case both sides were beaten to a standstill. Unless such a case arose, mediation from the United States — which must necessarily impose limits upon possible Allied victory — would not be welcome. To penetrate that fairly simple situation would not seem to have called for any very profound diplomatic skill, but it all went over the head of the devoted Mr. Page. Sir Edward was not of so crass a nature as to maintain that might made right. He felt only that 'what would be fair would depend upon how things went'; and since the matter was put so genteelly as that, Mr. Page was content to wait until the United States should receive the summons from the Foreign Office. That an American response to such a summons would not be, exactly, 'mediation' seems not to have occurred to him.]

iv

Long before the politely non-committal replies to Mr. Wilson's proffer of good offices began to come in from the belligerents, however, the State Department had found itself engulfed in a tremendous press of more immediately practical issues. On the morning of August 4 the passengers in the crack German liner Kronprinzessin Cecilie, a day or two out on their way to Europe, awoke to discover the ship at anchor surrounded by the familiar but unexpected scenery of Bar Harbor. It was as near as any of them were to get to Europe on that voyage. Practically the whole of our great trans-Atlantic commerce had vanished overnight. The ships did not sail; the elaborate and delicate financial machinery which moved the tides of ocean traffic simply disintegrated on the spot. The first shocks of the collapse, moreover, were already being transmitted throughout our whole domestic economy. Cotton, which had been selling at 13 cents in the latter half of July, slumped to 11 cents by the second week of August and continued dropping fast. Wheat, on the other hand, was floating off to new highs, even as the freight jams began to accumulate upon the export wharves. And on August 6 the first British contraband list arrived at the State Department — a mild enough affair compared to what was soon to come, but enough to suggest the immediacy with which war in Europe must affect many intricate complexes of American interest. Already there loomed upon the horizon the forest of problems concerning contraband and blockade, 'neutral rights' and 'neutral duties,' through which the United States and her citizens would have to find their path.

In this matter the State Department acted boldly and promptly. A few hours after the receipt of Mr. Page's cable announcing the contraband list, a circular telegram went out asking all belligerents if they would accept the Declaration of London — that codification of sea law in war time which had been signed by all the principal powers at the conference in 1909, but which had not, unfortunately, been ratified. This seemed the simplest and most obvious way of regularizing a situation which was bound to be difficult; and it represented our first move in support of our strictly national interests, as distinct from our more idealistic aims of peace and humanitarianism. From that time onward these two aspects of American policy were to develop concurrently, and were often to get rather badly mixed in the process.

The protection of our trade, however, was but one problem among many. Abroad, our embassies and legations suddenly found themselves overwhelmed with the responsibility for the diplomatic interests of all Europe, besides being charged with the immediate care of the distressed nationals of half a dozen belligerent powers. Problems of neutrality accumulated. Our representatives were correctness itself as far as the etiquette and the ritual went; but Page, Herrick and Whitlock never troubled to conceal

their complete sympathy with the governments to which they were
accredited, and too rarely stopped to consider the falsity of the
situation into which this might lead them. As the German battle
line came rolling down the central plain of Belgium in the first
fortnight of August, Mr. Whitlock at Brussels was suddenly confronted with a decision. The Belgian court was about to evacuate;
should he go with it or stay by his legation? The State Department incautiously left it to Mr. Whitlock's judgment. He stayed,
of course — with the result that for the next two and a half years
we were to have a Minister accredited to the Belgian Government
and wholly in sympathy with it upon German occupied territory.
Mr. Whitlock himself understood that this was a 'wholly anoma-
lous' situation, though the anomaly never seemed to trouble him.
Theoretically representing the interests of the United States in
Belgium, it was inevitable that he should become in fact a representative of Belgian and Allied interests behind the German
lines. It was impossible to prevent the Allied propagandas from
exploiting his dramatic position, or to prevent the Germans from
being thoroughly irritated by an unwarranted interference which
they had no means of ending. On the whole, the Germans were
to bear it with a surprisingly good grace, but it was of no help in
keeping the people of the United States uncompromised.

The eminent and influential Americans with connections or
interests in Europe were of even less help. The wealthy colony
in Paris found its emotions violently engaged. Mr. James Stillman,
the head of the great National City Bank, who had passed into
semi-retirement in his Paris mansion some years before, at once
'made it very plain that he was no neutral' and went the rounds
of the leading French statesmen, offering relief and suggesting
'projects toward financing.' Mr. E. H. Gary, the powerful chairman of the United States Steel Corporation, had been in Paris on
a holiday when the disaster came; he was duly convinced that
'Germany *wants* war.' Mrs. W. K. Vanderbilt, James Gordon
Bennett, Mrs. Harry Payne Whitney, James Hazen Hyde, Whitney
Warren were some of the other prominent Americans who had

lived in and loved France and who became passionate Franco-
philes. Mr. Andrew Carnegie sat in his mansion at Skibo with
'all my air castles' of world peace, as he said, 'fallen about me like
a house of cards'; but he supported the British declaration of war.
There were Americans in Berlin rallying similarly to the German
cause, of course, but there were far fewer of them — and they were
much less influential.

Was a mere proclamation of our neutrality enough to maintain
it? On August 10 the French chargé d'affaires was formally
addressing himself to Secretary Bryan: 'I was surprised to read in
the press the declarations which the representatives of Germany
and Austria thought fit to make to your Excellency as to the way
hostilities were started.' He was pained at such propagandist
impropriety; he would not imitate it, therefore, but instead he
would simply 'rectify' these 'incorrect statements.' He did so, at
length. On the 14th the Kaiser gave an extensive interview to
Ambassador Gerard formally blaming the war on Russia and
England. 'As early as August 18 and repeatedly thereafter,' said
a later note from President Poincaré to President Wilson, 'we
have had occasion to denounce outrages [by Germany] to Your
Excellency.' Already our State Department was the harried battle
ground of official criminations and self-exculpations. Then on
August 15 the Japanese suddenly startled the world (and American
diplomacy) with the discovery that the obligations of peace,
humanity and the Anglo-Japanese alliance compelled them immediately to relieve the Germans of the 'entire leased territory of
Kiaochow, with a view to eventual restoration of the same to
China.' So Japan was in the war. All in all, neutrality was
clearly presenting a complex problem.

The press was of no assistance. The thought processes by which
the New York newspapers had achieved their analysis of the war
quickly spread through the press in every section of the country.
A few scattered journals did pause to ask whether the nation
might not be making up its mind too hastily, but save for the German language press and one or two English language papers

published in heavily German communities, the verdict for the Allies was very nearly unanimous. The Milwaukee *Free Press* sadly announced that it had 'gone through our exchanges since the beginning of this war in an endeavor to find a just and reasonably correct representation of Germany's position,' but had 'not found one.' As early as the first week of the war the great London *Times* had made the peculiar but satisfactory discovery that 'Americans are now beginning to appreciate that the rise of Germany to the power and influence hitherto enjoyed by Great Britain would be a development inimical to American interests and a menace to the freedom of the United States as a world power.' Mr. Theodore Roosevelt himself, that mighty nationalist, was already declaring himself impressed by the 'very friendly feeling of this country toward England' as against a 'genuine apprehension of German designs.' Sir Cecil Spring Rice (who, as a close personal friend of Mr. Roosevelt, had been laboring for years to implant such apprehensions in the statesman's own mind) hastened to report this to his superior, Sir Edward Grey. 'This seems,' he noted, 'the feeling of the native American; but there are other elements, and the influence of the Germans and especially the German Jews is very great.' He went on:

> Your name here is one to conjure with.... A Wesleyan Bishop told me that it was seldom in this world that anyone was so clearly in the right, and he will say so to his people. All the State Department are on our side except Bryan, who is incapable of forming a settled judgment on anything outside party politics. The President will be with us by birth and upbringing, but he is very much in the hands of some of our worst enemies.

On Saturday, August 15, Secretary Bryan despatched a note to J. P. Morgan & Co. 'In the judgment of this Government,' it pointed out, 'loans by American bankers to any foreign nation which is at war are inconsistent with the true spirit of neutrality.' It was a first, and very wise, step toward a positive neutrality policy, and it served to forestall such loans — for the time being. But perhaps even more than that was needed. By a coincidence as unfortunate as it was tragic, the one most commanding leader of the nation had been snatched from public problems at precisely the most critical moment. On August 6 Mrs. Woodrow Wilson, undoubtedly one of her husband's chief sources of strength and judgment, died suddenly at the White House. Just as the whole outer world was breaking up before him, the President's inner world went to pieces in his hands. It is difficult to assess the full influence of this violent personal shock upon the history which followed. Some believe that it operated throughout the whole of the next year or two to withdraw the President from contacts he would otherwise have maintained and from problems he might otherwise have met more promptly; for the ensuing week, at any rate, it distracted him from all save the most urgent of immediate business. The funeral took place at the White House on Monday, August 10; the President and his family at once left for Rome, Georgia, where Mrs. Wilson was buried. Whether he would in any event have sought to recall the nation to a safer perspective, one cannot say; but when on August 19 he at last issued his 'appeal by the President of the United States to the citizens of the Republic, requesting their assistance in maintaining a state of neutrality during the present European war,' it was already far too late.

The effect of the European War upon the United States, Mr. Wilson rightly and prophetically pointed out, would depend 'upon what American citizens may say and do.' The American people were drawn from every one of the warring nations; it meant that to excite partisan passions would be easy, to allay them would be difficult. Very seriously the President urged his fellow-citizens to remember that they were 'Americans all,' to think first of the United States and her interests and to avoid divisions which would not only be 'fatal to our peace of mind' but which would render 'impartial mediation' by the United States an impossibility.

I venture, therefore, my fellow countrymen, to speak a solemn word of warning to you against that deepest, most subtle, most essential breach of neutrality which may spring out of partisanship, out of passionately taking sides. The United States must be neutral in fact as well as in name during these days that are to try men's souls. We must be impartial in thought as well as in action, must put a curb upon our sentiments as well as upon every transaction that might be construed as a preference of one party to the struggle before another.

It was the voice of high statesmanship; it was also the simplest of common sense. And its point was to be missed completely — even, perhaps, by the President. Colonel House dashed off a letter to his chief congratulating him upon 'one of the finest things you have ever done,' and then continuing to discuss the war in terms which suggest how passionately (and how hastily) the Colonel had himself already taken sides. An Allied victory might, he granted, have the slight drawback of making Czarist Russia supreme upon the Continent, but a German victory would mean 'the unspeakable tyranny of militarism for generations to come,' the abandonment of all hope of 'permanent peace' and ultimately 'trouble for us.' The truth was that the nation was already so overwhelmingly partisan toward the Allies that only the German sympathizers seemed to be partisan. By a curious paradox, it was the very weakness of the German sentiment (now trying to overcome its unpopularity by noise) which exaggerated its importance. The President's appeal was generally taken as a reproof only to the vociferous pro-Germans, and so was everywhere applauded. Only much later, when it appeared that this wise injunction might operate in both directions, was the idea of being 'impartial in thought' raised as a reproach to the President. It survives today as an enduring reproach to those shallow critics who never remotely grasped the profound importance of its implications.

The appeal served, if anything, merely to confirm the great majority in a sentimental partisanship it had adopted from the first days of the crisis. But history, in the meanwhile, had been moving. Already those crowds of young men who had surged through the European capitals cheering and yelling for war were being sucked into the great engines of mobilization which they had themselves helped to set in motion. The vast machinery of slaughter, so long prepared, so carefully oiled and tested by every European great power, had begun to grind at last in earnest. Across the whole face of a continent the troop-trains packed and jammed with exultant youth were rolling inexorably to collision; the civilian mass armies, sown with the dragon's teeth of many years, had sprung into existence overnight and were flowing out of every concentration area to their own destruction. In the capitals the first joyous excitement of war still reigned; but on the border lines of Europe there was already war itself. In Upper Alsace, before Belgrade and in the streets of Liege there had appeared the first thin wedges of primeval savagery and death which were to widen, deepen and coalesce into the great chasm that was to engulf a generation of mankind.

In Brussels our Minister, Mr. Whitlock, had been passing the most exciting fortnight of his life. Liege, they knew, had fallen on August 7, but the communiqués said it didn't matter. The streets were full of glamorous, anachronistic uniforms; the flags fluttered bravely in the unusually perfect weather and Brussels was 'lovelier than ever.' Everybody was in a fever of enthusiasm and patriotism and activity; everybody, suddenly, was in the army. To the east, of course, men must be fighting; but even when a whole squad of American war correspondents — Richard Harding Davis, Frederick Palmer, John T. McCutcheon, Irvin Cobb — miraculously appeared out of the blue, it was still more like Kipling than like war. They dashed cheerfully about in big automobiles, innocent of passes or credentials, reporting skirmishes, reporting Uhlans, trying to guess where the 'big battle' that everyone anticipated would be most likely to take place. But then there were rumors. The Liege gateway had fallen; what might in fact be coming through it? What was really happening? All at once the government was gone from Brussels, and in the street Mr. Whitlock ran into a troop of Belgian cavalry that was not gay. They were 'weary, haggard men, unkempt, with grimy faces, their uniforms grey with dust.' Then suddenly all the flags began to flutter down; the Germans were at the gates of Brussels.

Next morning — it was the day of President Wilson's appeal to his countrymen — Mr. Whitlock was hurrying out to see their entry. A little before noon his party encountered the first grey-clad pickets in their spiked helmets coming through; after them marched the infantry, and finally a long column of the famous lancers. So that, they supposed, was that. Having seen the spectacle, they started for home:

> And as we turned into the Boulevard Bischoffsheim there was the German Army.... There, up and down the boulevard under the spreading branches of the trees as far as we could see, were undulating, glistening fields of bayonets and a mighty, grey, grim horde, a thing of steel, that came thundering on with shrill fifes and throbbing drums and clanging cymbals, nervous horses and lumbering guns and wild songs. And this was Germany! ... We sat there in the motor and stared at it. No one spoke for a long time.

For hours the tide flowed by, until Mr. Whitlock's eyes were weary, his emotions exhausted. He went away, coming back later on to see the end. There was no end. Rank after rank they poured on into the dusk, artillery and trains, cavalry and the singing infantry — 'Heil Dir Im Siegenkranz,' 'Lohengrin,' and, amazingly enough, a song to the tune of 'Every Little Movement Has a Meaning All Its Own.' Mr. Whitlock gave it up. So did Mr. Richard Harding Davis — or tried to. But 'all through the night, like the tumult of a river when it races through a canyon, in my sleep I could hear the steady roar of the passing army.' In the morning he was at his window, but that unbelievable river of men and steel poured onward as before. For three days and nights on end it flowed through Brussels without a break or pause — the mightiest torrent of armed power that any of them were ever likely to see — and disappeared into the silences of the south. With what result? The flood had passed; it was swallowed up in space and time, and nothing penetrated the thick veils of censorship to show the outcome. Battering her way with the great 42-

centimetre howitzers — engines of the new warfare more irresistible than anyone had dreamed of — Germany had overrun nearly the whole of Belgium and deployed one million of the finest fighting men on earth along the northern frontiers of France. The rest was mystery. There was no 'big battle.' This was war.

III. WAR IN EUROPE

i

OUR public had received from its own newspapers in the very
first days of the crisis the basic elements of what was to be perfected as the Allied thesis of the war. Americans were now to
be surprised, shocked (and naturally pleased) to discover how
everything that they read as the war progressed simply confirmed their first judgment. What they overlooked was the source
of nearly everything that they read. No one paid much attention
to the disappearance of the German side of the story with the
cutting of the cables; no one stressed the possible influence of the
Allied censorships upon the color of the news, all of which now
had to pass through these controls. Few, indeed, even realized
that the Allies, because of the ownership and routing of the cables,
could edit the news coming from Germany by way of the European
neutrals almost as readily as they could edit that originating in
their own territory. According to an Associated Press representative on the Continent, it was possible to get neutral despatches to
the American papers for only a week or two after the outbreak of
the war; 'after that it was entirely a matter of hazard, or one of
writing from the British point of view.' By early autumn an
editor of the Chicago *Tribune* was even beginning to suspect that
the British censors were not only eliminating what they did not
like from the continental despatches but interpolating their own
material. Our public, however, for a long time thereafter still

naïvely assumed that it was the suppression of only military secrets in which the war censorships were interested.

There were many things that the American people never understood about the reporting of the war. At the outset the leading American newspapers ran into the difficulty that no American correspondents were allowed upon the Allied front. Their recourse was to utilize the services of the British newspapers. From September the New York *Times*, *Tribune* and *World* regularly bought the advance proofs of the London *Chronicle*, *Morning Post* and *Daily Telegraph*, using this material in their own news columns and syndicating it throughout the United States. The British for their part early assigned their ablest and most effective popular writers to the reporting of the war, and American editors were eager to print the work of such men as Philip Gibbs, H. M. Tomlinson or H. W. Nevinson. Nor was the 'informing' of American opinion left to any such casual arrangements as these. 'Practically since the day war broke out,' as Sir Gilbert Parker cheerfully admitted afterward, 'I was responsible for American publicity.'

Sir Gilbert soon had a large propaganda office at work near Victoria Station — under the aegis, it was vaguely supposed, of the Foreign Office. Here American correspondents were delighted to receive articles gratis from such priceless but patriotic pens as those of Kipling, Wells, Galsworthy, Arnold Bennett and (until presently he fell into disgrace) George Bernard Shaw. The articles were only a beginning. Sir Gilbert arranged propagandist interviews with the leading British statesmen — men formerly as inaccessible as Everest to anyone so base as a reporter — thus flattering the American press as he 'educated' it. He distributed propaganda material broadcast to American libraries, educational institutions and periodicals; he was particularly careful to arrange for lectures, letters and articles by pro-Ally Americans rather than by Englishmen; while he himself established relations 'by personal correspondence with influential and eminent people of every profession in the United States, beginning with the university and college presidents and scientific men and running through all the

ranges of the population.' It was the complete and skillful technique later to be developed by many other propagandists, lobby-
ists and public relations counsel; but Sir Gilbert, unlike a number
of his successors, was never to run afoul of a Congressional investigation into his activities.

As the war went on and the agony deepened every possible
means of influence was to be exploited by the intelligent directors
of Allied publicity. They were, of course, to spread their share of
actual mendacities — such things as the celebrated corpse-factory
legend, for example — but one may doubt whether all of the
deliberate inventions and distortions put together were of much
consequence. The overwhelming effectiveness of the Allied
propagandas in the United States is not to be explained by any
particular superiority in technique or subtlety in misrepresenta-
tion. Rather is it to be found in the predisposition of the American
public to receive the propaganda, in the nearly absolute Allied
command over all channels of communication and opinion and
in the passionate and sincere conviction of the Allied propagandists.
One of the greatest of the qualities which have made the English
a great people is their eminently sane, reasonable, fair-minded
inability to conceive that any viewpoint save their own can possibly
have the slightest merit.

From the very first the best propagandists of all were the Americans who gave their passionate and vocal sympathies to the Allied
cause. Second only to them were the great men of British letters
who had been read and revered throughout the United States
and whose sincerity was never, of course, in question. Sir Edward
Grey, in his first letter to Mr. Roosevelt after the outbreak of the
war, introduced 'J. M. Barrie and A. E. W. Mason, some of whose
books you have no doubt read' and who were already on their way
to the United States. 'Their object is, as I understand, not to make
speeches or give lectures'; it was merely 'to meet people, particularly those connected with Universities, and explain the British
case as regards this war.' Lord Bryce, that distinguished liberal,
that great authority on American politics, that friendly pillar,

through so many years, in the American scene, threw himself into a patriotic correspondence with Americans from the outset. He 'lent his pen readily to the development of the British case,' as his biographer observes, and sought by every kind of high-minded suggestion to embroil the American people in its defence.

But the British overlooked nothing. At the annual convention of the American Federation of Labor that fall the regularly accredited delegates from the British Trades Union Congress, who usually came, were missing; in their stead, however, there turned up 'two British labor men,' Mr. James Seddon and Mr. Albert Bellamy, who were eagerly received and questioned about the war by the American labor chieftains. Mr. Gompers himself was 'glad to get the benefit of their observations'; and he listened with interest as Mr. Seddon gave him 'a line on the nature and methods of German propaganda in England' and thus forewarned him against the wiles of the Germans in the United States. Unfortunately, Mr. Gompers did not know that Mr. Seddon had been recommended by the British Foreign Office to Sir Cecil Spring Rice with the note that he was going out 'to do spadework in the American trade unions.' But then, as Mr. Gompers himself observed in a different connection: 'Americans were unaccustomed to the subtleties of international propaganda and secret service work, and we had to learn much before we could protect ourselves from the penalties of ignorance.'

It is hardly remarkable that the picture of the actual hostilities, as it now began to come in filtered through these agencies of transmission and annotated in these many ways, should have turned out to be one vast and (quite literally) incredible indictment of Germany. One of the first of the atrocity stories was in the New York *Herald*, under a Brussels dateline, as early as August 6: 'The Germans fired on stretchers containing wounded being cared for by the Red Cross service at Vise, a small town near the Dutch frontier.' On the very next day, curiously enough, the New York *Times* carried on its front page a short, propagandist despatch from Antwerp of a different sort. Glowingly it described the heroism with which Belgian civilians were resisting the advancing German armies:

> The inhabitants of Bernot received them with a heavy fire from the roofs and windows. Even the women fought, and a girl of eighteen shot an officer dead with a pistol. She was captured and executed.

In the excitement of the moment someone in Antwerp had blundered badly; he had forgotten that in war it is an atrocity for civilians to shoot soldiers and legitimate ground for reprisals. By the time the Germans were making their first protest, on August 18, against the Belgian *francs tireurs*, such corroboratory evidence from the Belgian side had vanished from our press. Naturally, no one for a moment believed the Germans.

As the terrible grey tide came rolling across the Belgian plain a vast fog of atrocity stories rolled and spread before it, drifting rapidly through the Allied countries and over the Allied cables into every quarter of the world. From the first moments of the war our Legation at Brussels had been hearing the most dreadful rumors — stories of old men, women and children brutally shot, of nuns violated, of the most frightful savageries perpetrated. Mr. Whitlock, of course, had no way of verifying the stories; but he clung to his skepticism for only a day or two, and then yielded wholly to conviction. It was on August 26 and 27, after Brussels had fallen and Mr. Whitlock and his Legation were within the German lines, that the report came of some horrible tragedy at Louvain. The Germans were wantonly burning the city and murdering its inhabitants by the hundred. Young Mr. Hugh Gibson, Mr. Whitlock's first secretary, hurried out with some other diplomats on August 28 to see what was really going on. The place was in ruins — there was no doubt of that — and the dead bodies both of civilians and of German soldiers were lying in the streets. The Germans, however, all told them that the *francs tireurs* had precipitated the disaster. Mr. Gibson was with a friendly group of German officers and men near the railway station when 'suddenly several shots rang out... and the whole place was instantly in an uproar.... Apparently a number of civilians... had deter-

mined to sell their lives as dearly as they could. They had gathered
in the ruins of the houses fronting on the station and had opened
up on us.' Mr. Gibson's whole account is hostile in tone to the
Germans, but the only shooting which he reports having seen himself was this affair, which was begun by the Belgians.

Much later, when the destruction of Louvain had been raised
by the Allied propagandas into one of the great crimes of 'German
savagery,' the Germans tried to get Mr. Gibson to testify before
their official inquiry into the tragedy. Mr. Whitlock refused to
permit anything so 'unneutral' as that; besides, as the Minister
later sapiently observed, Mr. Gibson had no way of knowing that
the people who fired into the German troops were really civilians,
or even Belgians. It is unfortunate that the simple rules of evidence were never applied with equal rigidity to the testimony
from the Allied side. Had this been done it would never have
disproved the fact that the invasion of Belgium was a savage,
bloody and terrible business — for war is in its essence savage,
bloody and terrible — but it might have suggested not only that
the great mass of alleged atrocities were pure fictions but that the
savagery itself could not be ascribed to any peculiar inhumanity
in Germans.

The American press, however, which like everyone else had
lightly talked and thought of war so long, was stunned by the
dread visage of war itself. It could not be war which was responsible for these horrors; it must be the Germans. Before the
end of August 'indignant protest' was appearing on many American editorial pages, and on September 3 the aging 'Marse Henry'
Watterson spoke suddenly from his Louisville *Courier-Journal*:

> May Heaven protect the Vaterland from contamination and give
> the German people a chance! To hell with the Hohenzollerns and
> the Hapsburgs!

From this day forward Marse Henry 'in the face of attack,
abuse and deprecation... stuck to his task of educating the whole
world' to the belief that 'the military ideals and the conception of
Kultur as personified in the Hohenzollern and Hapsburg dynasties

could not exist on the same planet with the American conception of liberty.' Yet it was to be a long time before the notion was to penetrate even his mind that if such were actually the case the United States might reasonably be expected to do its share in eliminating the Hohenzollerns from the planet.

August yielded to September; the idea of a world actually at war began slowly to sink in, but about the progress of the war itself there was singularly little news. As the Allied armies fell back, the correspondents were naturally debarred from reporting what was really going on. The atrocity story filled the void. One group of the American newspapermen in Belgium had been overtaken by the German advance and had continued thereafter with the German armies. Early in September a bundle of Allied and neutral newspapers fell into their hands; they were astounded and shocked by what they read concerning the operations they had just been witnessing. Harry Hansen, Irvin Cobb, John T. McCutcheon, Roger Lewis and O'Donnell Bennett despatched a joint cable to the Associated Press:

> In spirit fairness we unite in declaring German atrocities ground-less as far as we were able to observe. After spending two weeks with German army accompanying troops upward hundred miles we un-able report single instance unprovoked reprisal. Also unable confirm rumors mistreatment prisoners or non-combatants.... Numerous investigated rumors proved groundless.... Discipline German soldiers excellent as observed. No drunkenness. To truth these statements we pledge professional personal word.

But it was of no use, either then or later. Mr. Eric Fisher Wood, an attaché of our Paris Embassy, who was on the Marne battle-field immediately after the German retreat, uncovered 'no in-stance' of wanton brutality although he cross-examined the people of the recently evacuated towns. By that time, however, Ambas-sador Page was reporting from London the long catalogues of atrocities of which he had been told. 'It is impossible longer to doubt the wholly barbarous conduct of the Prussians,' he wrote; and, since he doubted no longer, he made the remarkable official proposal that the Carnegie Foundation be asked to appoint a commission to investigate and proclaim this barbarity to the world. So tremendous had the furore become that the German Emperor on September 7 despatched a personal message to President Wilson, calling upon him to witness the atrocious conduct of the Belgian civilians, which had necessitated the repressive measures adopted at Louvain. 'My heart bleeds,' the Kaiser unwisely added, 'when I see that such measures have become unavoidable and when I think of the numerous innocent people who lose their home and property.' Even Bethmann-Hollweg's blundering honesty about the scrap of paper did not open so magnificent an opportunity to the Allies as this attempt at the artistic touch. M. Poincaré, the President of France, instantly seized upon it. 'Germany,' he informed Mr. Wilson, 'aware of our protests, is now trying to confuse the issue and to lay up mendacious pretexts for indulging in fresh atrocities. In the name of flouted right and outraged civilization, I send to Your Excellency an indignant protest.'

President Wilson very wisely gave it up. By that time a commission of eminent Belgians had arrived in the United States to lay before him the results of the official Belgian inquiry into the atrocities. To the Kaiser, to M. Poincaré and to the commission alike he replied, with a prudent correctness, that the verdict would have to be left to 'the opinion of mankind'; while the State Department, a little belatedly, began to impress upon its representatives abroad the importance of a genuine neutrality and of minding their own business. The mass of American opinion, however, poured out a storm of withering sarcasm upon the Kaiser's 'bleeding heart,' and the Belgians toured the nation to all but universal acclaim.

There was one great voice, it is true, which struck a discordant note; it was none other, strangely enough, than that of Theodore Roosevelt. 'I am sure,' he wrote in *The Outlook* on September 23, 'the sympathy of this country for Belgium... is very real.' Yet it would be 'folly to jump into the gulf ourselves to no good purpose, and very probably nothing that we could have done would have helped Belgium' since Germany had been compelled to violate her territory by the iron law of self-preservation. For the Germans, Mr. Roosevelt felt at that time, there could be 'nothing but... praise and admiration due a stern, virile and masterful people' and 'hearty respect for their patriotism and far-seeing self-devotion.' The truth was — and how could the American people have so completely overlooked it? — that the militarists were by no means confined to the German army command. But Mr. Roosevelt was soon drastically to revise his opinions; and in the meanwhile the visit of the Belgian commission was to stand as one of the first brilliant propagandist strokes of the war.

The statesmen of the Central Powers, on their side, were utterly unprepared to meet these tremendous engines of publicity so suddenly mobilized against them. Considering the fierce vituperation which was to be poured out upon 'German propaganda' it is remarkable that throughout 'it was the Germans who had a minimum of co-ordinated propaganda effort.' The idea that publicity might have anything to do with war was slow to penetrate the rigid military classicism of the Great General Staff. Only gradually did there dawn upon them the ominous importance of what Count Burián (soon to succeed to the Austrian Foreign Office) called 'the American riddle.' There is a queer glimpse of von Jagow, the German Secretary of State for Foreign Affairs, hurriedly demanding books, novels and information on the United States in the first days of the war, and desperately learning about America in those tremendous hours from Mr. Booth Tarkington's 'Turmoil.' Count Bernstorff, who had been on leave in Germany when the crisis broke, was rushed back to Washington with hardly more instruction than that he was to 'enlighten the government and the people on the German standpoint.' He was told to take along Dr. Bernhard Dernburg, a former Colonial Secretary, and Geheimrat Heinrich Albert of the Ministry of the Interior; their function was originally, however, only to raise money and purchase supplies. As far as organized propagandas went, the Germans had scarcely realized at that time that there could be such things.

Yet by the time Count Bernstorff landed at New York on August 23, it was already clear that the task of presenting 'the German standpoint' to a strongly hostile opinion would be a large one. The sole means of untrammelled communication with Germany was through the two German-owned wireless stations at Sayville, Long Island, and Tuckerton, New Jersey; and these the United States Government seized, with a punctilious sense of its neutral duty to the Allies, to prevent their being used to direct the German commerce raiders still at sea. The Ambassador was not even permitted to receive code messages through these stations until the code book had been deposited with the American authorities, while the amount of news which they could transmit was limited. On September 5 the New York *Times* printed a Berlin despatch received direct through Sayville; it was the first report from the Central Powers not filtered through the Allied censorships which that mighty journal had published since the cutting of the cables a month before. In time it was possible to develop a fair-sized trickle of direct news by wireless, helped out by the mail and telegraphic matter which could be got past the Allied censors from the neutral countries. The whole never approached in volume the vast flood which was continually poured out from every Allied source.

The German censors themselves were less than clever. They would eliminate everything not rosily favorable to their own side, thus giving the Allies an excuse for suppressing the remainder as obviously inadmissible 'enemy propaganda.' When this German news did get through, moreover, American readers were quick to dismiss it themselves on the same grounds. The Allies had only to play upon an opinion overwhelmingly disposed in their favor; the Germans faced the far more difficult technical problem of winning an opinion powerfully prejudiced against them. It was a problem they never solved. For the most part they merely imitated, in a rather plodding fashion, the Allied methods, and they could

never understand (they seem not to understand even now) why
the results were so lamentably different.

When prominent Germans, like Kuno Francke or Professor
Münsterberg of Harvard, leapt to perform for the German case
the service which Lord Bryce and so many other prominent
Britons were performing for the Allies, they were shocked and hurt
by the difference with which their activities were regarded. When
eminent Americans of German ancestry, like the Ridders in New
York, defended the Central Powers with the same passion which
innumerable other Americans were bringing to the support of the
Entente, they were dismayed to find that in their case such
efforts were held to be akin to treason. Their response — as human as it was unwise — was to speak with only greater anger and
violence. Since they had no news to work with, however, they
were compelled to invent argument; not unnaturally, the argument was frequently mistaken or exaggerated and so easily
discredited. The first German propaganda was as native and
spontaneous as the first Allied propaganda. But where the Allied
case was now absorbed unconsciously through every morning
newspaper, the German case was noisily presented by an angry
and plainly ill-informed minority and so clearly stamped as mere
partisanship. It did the German case little good.

Ambassador Bernstorff could face his problem with more
detachment than the German-American, and he had a far more
skillful touch. He had barely landed in the United States before
he had begun his long and astute campaign through the American
press. Reporters were delighted to find cigars, refreshments and
unfailing helpfulness and courtesy perpetually on tap at the German Embassy in Washington and at a special news bureau set
up in the Ritz Carlton Hotel in New York. The Ambassador,
at a time when Ambassadors were still clothed in sanctity, was
the most accessible of men. Uncomfortably factual interviews
with him, even articles over his signature, began to flower in the
American press, and the Allies (whose own Ambassadors were
under no necessity of adopting such tactics) were furious at so

gross a violation of diplomatic etiquette. It was uphill work; but Count Bernstorff persevered, and presently Mr. Page was sending eloquent testimony from London as to its effectiveness. He forwarded a collection of British press clippings with the comment: 'Great denunciation is expressed in all papers of what is called "Count Bernstorff's publicity campaign."' Before long Dr. Dernburg, who found the purchase of supplies impossible, had been converted into an official spokesman in the United States for the German case, while Dr. Albert was at the head of the propaganda organization with which the Germans sought feebly to combat the paralyzing superiority of the Allies in a branch of warfare to which Clausewitz had paid too little attention.

Their difficulties were from the first appalling. The invasion of Belgium was soon exploited to a point at which it was useless even to attempt a defence. When the appeals for aid for the starving Belgians began to come in, offering a sudden practical outlet for the overwrought American emotions, the response was immediate — and the Allies found themselves in possession of still another incomparable propaganda weapon. That the relief of suffering could in any way compromise our neutrality hardly occurred to the Americans who poured out their contributions; but the Allied leaders understood very well that every request for funds in that cause was a concealed demonstration of German brutality and every answering dollar a vicarious blow for the Entente. Appeal after appeal was made in the United States; and among those who appealed was Sir Gilbert Parker himself, who, as Americans had not been told, was 'responsible for American publicity.' He rushed to Holland, whence he poured out his letters:

> I am here, on the borders of Belgium, watching the refugees flee-ing... from their devastated country. Many towns and cities are absolutely destroyed. Countless homes are in ashes. Unless America renders immediate aid, starvation will destroy more Belgians than have been killed in the war.

Americans did not ask whether this might be exaggerated;

they did not know that the threat of starvation came, at the moment, not from the Germans — but from the British Navy! In mid-October Mr. Whitlock was working earnestly, in co-operation with the German authorities and a Belgian committee, to rescue starving Belgium from the British blockade. The Admiralty was at first cold to the idea, but it ultimately saw the light. In London a certain Mr. Herbert Hoover — an American engineer and promoter long intimately connected with British and Belgian mining interests — was enlisted to organize the charity, and the celebrated C. R. B. — the Commission for the Relief of Belgium — was launched upon its career. The Germans thus freed themselves from the costs and troubles of rationing Belgium, but at an extortionate price. Month in and month out thereafter American millions were to flow into the Belgian Relief, every penny doing its part to cement the emotional alliance with the Entente Powers.

The prompt organization of the American Ambulance in Paris and of the even more spectacular Lafayette Escadrille worked powerfully to the same end. Ambassador Herrick had been showing his sympathy with the French in many grossly indiscreet ways. When the French Government retreated to Bordeaux he was reckless enough to remain in Paris as Mr. Whitlock had remained in Brussels, and he had become a hero for it, not only in France but in the United States as well. Again our neutrality was unfortunately impaired; but though his successor, Mr. Sharp, was already on the ground, President Wilson hesitated to replace him. When a very solemn and earnest group of young Americans filed into Mr. Herrick's office to ask if they might enlist in the French army, the foolish old man read and explained to them the laws of neutrality, then closed the book and burst out: 'That is the law, boys, but if I was young and stood in your shoes, by God I know what I would do.' They cheered, shook hands with the Ambassador, and went out to enlist — and to be killed, most of them. Their names are now famous — Lufberry, Prince, Kiffin Rockwell — and their 'influence upon sentiment at home,' as Mr. Herrick later boasted, 'was tremendous.'

So was that of the American Ambulance, a direct creation of
Mr. Herrick's. Secretary Bryan almost alone seems to have been
worried as to the correctness of Mr. Herrick's neutrality, and on
one occasion sent a query as to whether this American hospital
service was taking care to succor German wounded as well as
French. By a remarkable coincidence it was discovered that
there was not a German in the hospital; but the Ambassador
rushed out one of his military attachés with a searching party,
and by good luck they found three mangled but still living Germans. One died on the way in and was dumped unceremoniously
upon the roadside; the other two survived, and Mr. Herrick was
able to telegraph Washington that they were caring for Germans.

Mr. Herrick was at last pried out of the Paris Embassy at the
end of November, though the French did their best to retain so
useful an ally and many in the United States likewise urged that he
be allowed to remain. As it was he sailed loaded with honors and
compliments from the Entente governments; he was enthusias-
tically received at home; Mr. Roosevelt (whose opinions were
progressing very rapidly) lamented that he was not President of
the United States and a movement to make him so was instantly
set on foot. Americans of German sympathies could only watch
such developments in a growing anger and despair. At every
point they were upon the defensive. Before August was out there
had arrived the British 'White Paper' in which the documentary
history of the war's origins was skillfully edited for the education
of the world. It was the first of the famous rainbow-tinted book-
shelf contributed by all the belligerent and ultimately some, even,
of the neutral powers. The Germans were prompt with their
'White Book,' but once more they were stupid, and by trying to
claim too much seemed to convict themselves of mendacity in
everything. The pundits compared the documents and were
convinced. Some of our pro-Ally statesmen even tried to have
them spread upon the records of the Senate for the damnation
of Germany; fortunately, this idea was squelched, but the New
York *Times* conceived an even better one.

It sought to have several eminent American lawyers argue the responsibility for the war from the evidence as presented by the two publications. They were to act as though they were attorneys for the respective governments and the books were their briefs. Those approached to sustain the German case not unnaturally refused, unless they were permitted to go beyond the narrow and obviously fragmentary ground covered by these published documents. The *Times* thereupon enlisted the eminent legal talents of the Honorable James M. Beck, a former Assistant Attorney General of the United States, to analyze both volumes and give his opinion. Mr. Beck seems not to have doubted his ability to arrive, upon these partial and patently unsatisfactory disclosures, at a sound judgment; and the *Times* solemnly printed his flaming defence of the Allies and castigation of the Central Powers under the headline 'The Evidence in the Case.' It was so instantly popular that it was reprinted in pamphlet form; it was translated into many languages; it sold '400,000 copies in England alone.' Mr. Beck expanded it into a book, dedicated to King Albert, which — all the more effective because it had the appearance of being a dispassionate judicial analysis — was to run into many editions as another triumph of pro-Ally propaganda.

General von Bernhardi was discovered almost at once. As early as August 9 the New York *Times* had given the whole front page of its Sunday magazine section to an article on the 'remarkably prophetic book' which had 'foretold Germany's war plans.' Here the emphasis was simply on Bernhardi's technical strategic ideas, not upon the immorality of his philosophy of war; it did not take long, however, for the propaganda possibilities to be realized, and within a week or two Bernhardi's 'Germany and the Next War' was launched upon its curious career. Its sales were enormous; it was reprinted by the million to flood the United States as well as the Allied and other neutral countries. Mr. Owen Wister was reading it before the end of August — with lamentable results. It is hardly necessary to add that no one took the trouble to unearth and reprint the similar works of similar obscure military philosophers and chauvinists in the Entente countries or the United States.[1] Bernhardi, moreover, served but to point the way to a whole vast field lying ready for exploitation. Nietzsche, Treitschke and the invaluable literature of the Pan-German League were instantly laid under contribution, and the stupefied Germans discovered themselves convicted before world opinion on the evidence of a few writers whom the vast majority of Germans had never read or never even heard of.

By September 24, Ambassador Spring Rice, writing home from Washington, had almost brought himself to believe the marvellous truth:

> Here popular opinion is almost unanimous in our favor, except among the Germans who raise a continual shriek and poison the wells, as usual.

'Instinctively,' Sir Cecil believed, Americans felt that 'our struggle is the same as their old ones for personal freedom.' Perhaps they had been assisted to this view by something more than pure 'instinct,' but as to the result there could be no doubt.

ii

It was scarcely a state of mind to qualify the United States as an impartial mediator. Yet the bright vision of a neutral intervention by a humane and pacific America to rescue the Old World from itself would not down. On September 5, while the exhausted armies were still locked in their vast struggle along the Marne, Ambassador Bernstorff was dining in New York with a group of our

[1] That these existed has often been pointed out. Kirby Page has gathered whole chapters of examples, including a pre-war endorsement of Bernhardi by Lord Roberts, a pre-war advocacy of atrocities by Captain Charles Ross, later a British major general, and our own General Sheridan's conclusion that 'the proper strategy' requires that 'the people must be left nothing but their eyes to weep with.' Becker notes that the year 1912, when Bernhardi's book was first published, also saw a volume in which our Admiral Mahan argued that 'European civilization might not survive' should arbitration ever replace armaments and so destroy 'its fighting energy.' And the great Theodore Roosevelt once urged the United States to 'perform those deeds of blood, of valor, which above everything else bring national renown.'

great German-Jewish bankers and merchants. Mr. Oscar Straus
was generously full of the idea of mediation; he was astounded
when the Ambassador assured him that Germany 'had not desired
the war and would certainly be ready at the first suitable opportunity for a peace by understanding.' This discovery that the Central
Powers were not wholly bent upon rapine and slaughter seemed
so sensational to Mr. Straus that he rushed at once from the dinner
table to the Washington train. He was at the State Department
next morning with his news; Secretary Bryan immediately summoned the German Ambassador, and the upshot was the despatch
of our second mediation 'feeler' through the Ambassadors abroad.

At once the Allies were in a panic. 'Nothing,' Spring Rice
accurately perceived, 'would tend to win over the public here so
much as the belief that we had refused a fair offer of peace.'
Yet Sir Edward Grey had himself observed that what was fair
'would depend upon how things went'; and with the Germans in
possession of all Belgium and Northern France it was plain that
any fair offer (if it was to be one of genuine mediation) must
represent a very considerable degree of success for Germany.
Thus early were the Allied statesmen confronted by the difficult
logical problem of proving that by continuing to fight until they
had won they would not be opposing peace. In haste Spring
Rice consulted 'some of our friends here' and received the shrewd,
if perhaps treasonable, advice 'that we should at once declare that
the Allies are anxious for peace with guarantees of permanency.'
Thus early was the solution, which the Allies were to employ
regularly thereafter, suggested to them — by their friends in
America. Vigorously the Allied statesmen played to this lead.
It was because of their devotion to 'real' and 'permanent' peace
that they must go on with the slaughter until Germany was
completely crushed and they were completely victorious. American opinion readily acquiesced in this view, and the 'Straus move'
was easily turned.

Only the much despised Mr. Bryan seems to have had the
common sense to understand that 'the responsibility for continu-

ing the war is just as grave as the responsibility for beginning it' and that if the United States was to play the mediator at all it could only do so by bringing both sides to negotiation before a crushing victory had been won by either. Even President Wilson in those days was accepting House's conclusion that 'if Germany won it would change the course of our civilization and make the United States a military nation,' and showing himself, to the eyes of his adviser, 'as unsympathetic with the German attitude as is the balance of America.' But he still seemed not fully to realize that a 'mediation' in this spirit must inevitably become an intervention on behalf of the Entente. No one realized it except the shrewd spokesmen of the Entente itself; and they continued earnestly to implant the idea of this sort of 'mediation' in Mr. Wilson's mind.

Ambassador Page was tireless in his suggestions. 'Be ready,' he wrote the President as early as August 9, 'for you will be called on to compose this huge quarrel'; and he never ceased to harp upon the thought, except when some practical proposal to this end was in the air. Spring Rice explained to Sir Edward that 'the line' he was taking was to say that Great Britain 'had no objection whatever to the President keeping in touch with the warring powers, because the time will almost surely come when the one Great Power which is neutral will have to use its good offices, and also because we have a perfect confidence in the rectitude of the President, his perfect fairness and his understanding of our point of view.' It poured in from every side. Ambassador Herrick reported the universal Allied opinion that 'the United States should in the end play a great role and exert a restraining influence'; while Lord Bryce, whom Mr. Wilson had always revered as a teacher, contributed his hope that 'a time may arrive... when an offer of mediation from you as the greatest and most respected neutral may be helpful' — if only 'My dear Mr. President' wouldn't make it now.

It is hardly strange if Mr. Wilson, as the long months dragged by, did begin to suspect that he might be almost as great a man as the Allies told him that he was. The pressure was strong; yet at the moment the President seems to have been fairly resistant to it, for House was pained to find him (on September 28) 'singularly lacking in appreciation of the importance of this European crisis.' But Colonel House himself, already the great expert on Europe, could not leave so enticing a subject alone. The 'Straus move' had barely collapsed before the Colonel was trying his own hand, free from any bucolic meddling by Mr. Bryan's official State Department. There was a curious passage in which House sought to bring Bernstorff and Spring Rice together to start private peace negotiations in the secrecy of House's New York apartment. The German was willing enough; the Englishman indignantly refused to speak with anyone so 'thoroughly unreliable' as Bernstorff. It ended finally with the Colonel artfully prompting Spring Rice to despatch a cable to Sir Edward:

> G[ermany] is doing her best to put E[ngland] in the wrong by causing a belief that E is rejecting G's friendly overtures. It would be dangerous for E to persist in *non possumus* attitude.... It would be of advantage to all three [Allies] that G should be forced to show her hand.

Hopefully House waited for Sir Edward to rise to this bait. Nothing happened. A fortnight passed while House kept putting off the German and Austrian Ambassadors. At last, when House pushed Spring Rice about the cable, the latter admitted that it would probably be a long time before there was any answer. 'Germany should be badly punished before peace was made.' It is just possible that the bait had been upon the other hook, and that it was the Colonel who had risen.

At any rate, making peace was clearly not going to be so easy as it looked. With October, the Battle of the Marne had been fought and won; the 'race to the sea' had ended, and as the exhausted armies settled down to their four years of stalemate some first idea had begun to dawn on all these statesmen of the enormous, the appalling, horror with which they were attempting to deal. Realization came slowly. The newspapers, few if any of whose correspondents had been permitted the sight of an actual battle, gave scarcely a hint of the truth. But some of the better informed were beginning to get an inkling of it. Mr. Wood, of our Paris Embassy, was on the corpse-strewn fields of the Marne immediately after the battle lines had passed, and his diary was full of strange and dreadful things. He was struck by one curious phenomenon. In a hospital train he found seventy-five men who proved to be quite unwounded, but who were in such 'a state of nervous collapse' that they had been sent back. Mr. Wood guessed that there must be many more such cases, as otherwise these wrecks would simply have been shot as cowards, but he found the French authorities 'reluctant to discuss the matter.'

The word 'shell-shock' had not yet entered the language, but the emotional shocks were already pounding upon the mind. There was a passionate letter from Mr. Page to the President:

> The ferocity of it, which visibly becomes greater every week, passes anything felt by any men in modern times. It's a death grapple. All preceding mere 'wars' are not in the same class of events. It means the extermination, not of the people of either nation, but the utter extermination of the system of either one or the other — English free institutions or German military autocracy. But in fact the men of both nations will be more nearly exterminated than anybody yet realizes.

Even the British public had not grasped the true 'horrors of it.' He spoke of the 'shells and acres of bloated human bodies, careless of sun or rain, giving only a stench.' It was no longer 'the same world it was last July.' How was it possible in that incomprehensible nightmare to think rationally, to remember the humdrum interests one was supposed to represent, to retain a cold sense of proportion? For the sensitive and impressionable Page it was not possible; and perhaps this was not wholly to his discredit. But Colonel House, in the private little State Department he was now developing in his home on East Fifty-Third Street, was undismayed by this titanic passion and agony. 'It is my purpose,' he informed his diary at the end of September, 'to make a drive

at the President and try to get him absorbed in the greatest
problem of world-wide interest that has ever come, or may ever
come, before an American President.' On October 3 he summarized the results of his first attempt: 'Bernstorff and Dumba
say their countries are ready for peace talks but the difficulty is
with England. Sir Cecil says their statements are made merely
to place England in a false position.' Yet the Colonel was not
dashed by this *impasse*. He had himself begun to have some
suspicions of the British insistence upon the total destruction of
Germany; he was even remembering that the Kaiser had not
wanted the war and was not directly responsible for it, and he
now proposed to write Sir Edward that there was 'a growing
impatience' in the United States because of the prolongation of
the conflict. With Mr. Wilson's sanction he would continue his
altruistic efforts — behind the back of Mr. Bryan, whom all these
thinkers regarded as beneath consideration.

iii

This growing impatience which the Colonel had detected in his
countrymen was not wholly disinterested. American business
had been slack enough in July; by October it was prostrate.
'Bank checks drawn in the whole United States during August
decreased 19 per cent from the year before; in September and
October the decrease was 25 per cent.' The Stock Exchange was
still closed. With the first thunderclap of war our maritime trade
had disappeared; it was a 'shattering blow' to the whole of our
economy. Presently the sea lanes were reopened, but the first
efforts to rebuild our economic machinery only brought the
dawning realization that nearly the whole of our lucrative trade
with Germany and Austria-Hungary had somehow gone, and
gone for good, in the disaster. The indirect effects upon our
domestic commerce and industry were widespread and paralyzing.

It took time to grasp the fact that this had occurred; it took even
longer to understand how it had been brought about. Everybody

knew, of course, that under international law the Allies were free to blockade Germany if they could. Unfortunately for the Allies, however, geography and the German Navy combined to render this impossible, and no 'blockade' in the precise legal sense of the word was ever declared against the Central Powers. It was also understood that the Allies had the right to seize 'contraband' destined for the enemy wherever they might find it upon the high seas. 'Contraband,' however, was supposed to mean actual munitions of war — guns, shells, artillery carriages, infantry equipment and so on. The ordinary articles of commerce, even food, might also be seized as 'conditional contraband' in cases where it could be proved that they were directly destined for the use of the enemy's armed forces; but otherwise they could only be interfered with through the institution of a blockade of the enemy's ports, not only regularly declared but also effective in fact.

Such, at any rate, were the broad principles. That there was a distressing vagueness about their detailed application, and a lamentable confusion in the precedents, had long been recognized; and this had led to the attempted codification of the rules in the Declaration of London of 1909. It was true that the Declaration had failed of ratification. Its authors, however, had designed it simply as a statement of what existing law and precedent required, and that seemed to make it clear that in the absence of a formal blockade American exporters and importers would be free enough to carry on their normal trade with the civil populations of Germany and Austria-Hungary.

Yet if the Allies found themselves unable to establish a legal blockade of the Central Powers, they also found themselves in full command of all the sea routes leading to them and to the contiguous neutrals — Scandinavia, Holland, Italy, Switzerland and the Balkans — through which they might be supplied. With the Royal Navy standing unchallenged over every avenue by which goods might enter Germany and Austria-Hungary, the Allies naturally had no intention of permitting them to do so, whatever the dubious niceties of international law might seem to require.

From the very first the project of starving the Central Powers into submission — and that meant starving their civil populations as well as their armed forces — was cheerfully announced by the Allied press and public men. In the way of this project there stood but one difficulty. That was the United States.

The Central Powers could not be isolated from the world without the destruction of some of our best markets and the excision from our economy of about 13 per cent of our foreign trade. It was a point which our own statesmen were slow to appreciate. As early as September Ambassador Dumba was complaining to Colonel House against the British 'starvation campaign' and urging that the United States assert its rights against British navalism. 'He forgets to add,' was the Colonel's profound and scornful comment, 'that England is not exercising her power in an objectionable way, for it is controlled by a democracy.' The British statesmen, however, had a shrewder grasp of the realities. They never lost sight of the inconvenient fact that the United States not only had a direct material interest in keeping open the trade routes to Germany but also possessed the power to do so if she ever chose to exercise it. The Allies, moreover, had already announced themselves in every propagandist utterance as the defenders of international law, and it would be distinctly embarrassing if the taint of illegality should ever be attached to their suppression of our commerce. With a skill and foresight which one can only admire, the British Foreign Office (very materially assisted, it must be said, by Ambassador Page) now advanced over the thin ice presented by this delicate problem. Gradually, cautiously and with every sort of ingenious expedient, the rules were to be shaped to the desired end. Nowhere did international law appear to be clearly violated; nowhere was there any abrupt departure from the precedents we cited nor any rude rejection of the arguments which the State Department soon found itself elaborating. The only plain fact was that American commerce with the Central Powers had ceased. It was to have all the mystery of a conjuring trick.

The State Department had begun with the attempt to settle the whole question by securing acceptance of the Declaration of London. This would have solved the problem at the outset; unfortunately, it would also have made the throttling of Germany quite impossible. Sir Edward countered skillfully on August 22 by accepting the Declaration in its entirety — save for one or two slight 'modifications.' They were such, it is hardly necessary to say, as to render the instrument valueless for the protection of American commerce. At the same time the British began rapidly expanding their lists of 'absolute' and of 'conditional' contraband. A large share of our foreign commerce normally moved in British bottoms; these were suddenly unavailable for trade with Germany or the contiguous neutrals. Neutral shipping could not get insurance with the near-monopoly of Lloyds, or was restrained by the vague threats of possible seizure which the British were in no haste to clarify. The cable censorship through which the Allies controlled the news was equally useful for preventing the transaction of business with the Central Powers.

Practically nothing was moving between the United States and Germany. For a special reason the State Department was goaded to fresh efforts. The war had caught us just as the great Southern cotton crop was coming upon the market, and Germany was normally the second largest taker of American cotton. To the South the blow was prostrating; and the Solid South was a chief pillar of the Administration's political power. Before the end of August influential Southern Senators were imploring Mr. Bryan to arrange in some way for the shipment of raw cotton to the Central Powers, for it was already evident that 'we will probably lose one-third the value of our cotton crop... or in the neighborhood of $250,000,000.' The industrial Northeast, already passionately pro-Ally and always slow to understand its dependence upon the hinterlands, dismissed such cries as only the perennial wailing of the agrarian; to the South, however, it was a matter of desperate earnestness. Yet cotton was not even on the contraband lists. The State Department found itself simply fighting the air.

Nor was Mr. Page of much assistance. On September 15 he reported cheerily to House that 'everything is going well here, I think. The British Government is most considerate of us in all large ways. The *smaller questions* of ships and prizes, etc., are really in the hands of the Admiralty... and they are conducted on a war basis.' The italics are not Mr. Page's. A few days earlier he had been running on in his fluent way to Mr. Wilson:

> I have dealt so candidly and frankly with Sir Edward Grey and so completely given him my confidence that his candour and confidence in me are now my shield and buckler.... I think he has told me every fact at every stage in this troublesome journey so far.

What Mr. Page could never understand was that the foreign secretaries of fighting powers cannot afford to give anyone their confidence. It was only very much later that Sir Edward was to reveal what he was actually thinking in those days:

> After Paris had been saved by the Battle of the Marne the Allies could do no more than hold their own.... The Allies soon became dependent for an adequate supply [of their own war needs] on the United States. If we quarreled with the United States we could not get that supply. It was better, therefore, to carry on the war without blockade, if need be, than to incur a break with the United States about contraband.... The object of diplomacy, therefore, was to secure the maximum of blockade that could be enforced without a rupture with the United States....
>
> It was evident that the first step was to put on the list of absolute contraband all the articles that were essential for armies under modern conditions; and the second and more important step was to get the United States to accept that list.... There were articles that in old days had been of little or no use to armies but were now essential to them. Would the United States dispute our right to put some of these on the list? They might do so on the ground that they were articles of general use for general commercial as well as for military purposes.... It would be politic for us not to make the list too large at first.

It was for this reason that Sir Edward vetoed the early proposal to declare cotton absolute contraband — a decision which he afterward maintained 'was right.' It was; especially as little or no cotton moved anyway.

Such practical calculations as these, however, were foreign to our own more altruistic diplomatists, like House and Page; and they scarcely guessed at the power which they might hold over British blockade policy until long after it was too late to exercise it. But there was one American official who was more alert. Mr. Robert Lansing, the Counselor for the State Department, was a lawyer with a highly developed sense of the importance of legalities, and he remained unimpressed by Great Britain's 'consideration.' After the British reply on the Declaration of London, Ambassador Spring Rice had sensed that 'something was up among the lawyers of the State Department' and had detected a distinct chill in the atmosphere. His intuition was soon verified. In the absence of Secretary Bryan, Mr. Lansing had devised a Note in protest against the British 'modifications' of the Declaration.

Colonel House happened to be visiting at the White House when Mr. Lansing submitted it, on September 27, to the President. Its terms made the Colonel's hair rise; instead, however, of merely recommending that it be toned down, he conceived the more remarkable idea of submitting it first to the British Ambassador. The next day he was in secret session with Spring Rice over the formidable document; the Ambassador (who confessed to Sir Edward that he was 'really astonished at the tone in one or two of the paragraphs') was naturally loud in his alarms. If the Note went as drafted there would be a 'big catastrophe'; it would be 'almost a declaration of war'; it would produce another Venezuela incident. Such a crisis, Spring Rice skillfully suggested, 'would never have arisen if the State Department had talked the matter over with him frankly in the beginning.' House — perhaps forgetting in his excitement that the Venezuela incident had resulted, as a matter of fact, in a complete back down by Great Britain — hastened to submit the Note to the British representative for revision; together they devised the cable which should actually be sent, and agreed, as House innocently noted, 'to be absolutely frank with one another' in the future. Thus was the first important American diplomatic effort of the World War secretly watered down by the intended recipients. It finally went off to Mr. Page in the revised version; Mr. Lansing thereafter did his best to stir his own Ambassador into putting the matter as strongly as possible, but Mr. Page (who did not hesitate to water down the State Department's protests on his own responsibility when he thought best) had no sympathy with anything which might hamper the British war effort. It is to be doubted whether Lansing's adjurations were of much effect.

Sir Edward gracefully temporized, and went on expanding the contraband lists. Mr. Lansing responded with fresh protests and further insistence upon the Declaration of London; but Mr. Page could not see what difference the Declaration of London made anyway, and in a personal appeal to the President announced that in the shipping controversy he feared 'we are getting into deep water needlessly.' This singular communication at last aroused Mr. Wilson, and he replied at once:

> Beg that you will not regard the position of this Government as merely academic. Contact with opinion on this side the water would materially alter your view.... I must urge you... to use your utmost persuasive efforts.

There ensued some frantic cabling, but Mr. Page's utmost was evidently not enough to persuade Sir Edward that he was on dangerous ground, and Great Britain flatly declined to accept the Declaration even in slightly compromised form. On October 22 Mr. Lansing gave it up; our request was formally withdrawn, and the United States retreated to the previously existing rules and precedents of international law, without reference to the London codification. It was a complete surrender; the British were overjoyed and Sir William Tyrrell himself came to the American Embassy to express his immense pleasure and relief. Page's own comment to the President was that the outcome had had a 'most admirable effect all around' — which was no doubt true enough, if one neglected our cotton farmers, our industrial unemployed

PRESIDENT WILSON AND COLONEL HOUSE, NEW YORK, 1915

and our export merchants. And also, it should be added, our political relations with the Central Powers.

Great Britain had won easily in the first, and therefore the decisive, skirmish. After that, with the exercise of only a little care and skill, the foreign trade of the United States might be made to wait upon the military necessities of the Entente Powers; and it is a fact that from that time on every issue which arose between the United States and Great Britain was settled in accordance with the British view. The completeness of this reverse was due partly to Mr. Page, partly to Washington's inability to understand how great was its own power over the Entente, but chiefly to the emotional sympathy for the Allied cause entertained at that time, not only by the American press and vocal public but by House, the State Department and the President himself. They could not bring themselves to contemplate a German victory; and the strongest argument of the British was not their fictitious threat of war but their plea that the measures they took were 'essential,' as Spring Rice put it, 'to our existence.' As long as that plea carried weight with our statesmen and the corresponding plea from Germany did not, the United States was unavoidably a silent partner of the Entente.

iv

To this result, moreover, somewhat less elegant factors were already beginning to contribute. There was, unfortunately, about to be an election; and the thoughtful might early have perceived that American foreign policy would not remain uncomplicated by American domestic politics. At the Congressional elections of November, 1914, the Wilson Administration, which had ridden so triumphantly into power upon the great wave of regeneration and reform, would have to meet its first test. It was an event for which the sleepless professionals of politics had long been preparing; and if the sudden coming of the greatest disaster in human history had tended to upset their calculations, it had in no way diverted them, of course, from their major preoccupation. The greying and irascible Senator Lodge had been caught by the war in London. One of the shrewdest of the Republican professionals, he was also his party's ranking member upon the powerful Foreign Relations Committee of the Senate. It was his firmest conviction that politics should stop at the water's edge — and that beyond it the Republicans should have undisputed control. Already preparing to confound the Democrats by an assault upon their foreign policy in the Caribbean, he did not hesitate to give out an interview in London on August 23 making political capital out of Mr. Wilson's neutrality policy as unduly favorable to the Germans.

Like other eminent Republicans who had dabbled, through their years in power, upon the fringes of the European question, Senator Lodge had great difficulty in conceiving that mere Democrats could possibly be equal to piloting the nation through the vast issues which had now opened. Yet when the Senator got home to take part in the Congressional campaign, it was to make the distressing discovery that the populace was almost as ignorant of foreign affairs as the Democrats. He had intended to make a great play with Mr. Wilson's cravenly pacific attitude toward Mexico; with a real war raging terribly in Europe, however, it seemed that peace had actually become popular. 'I was told,' as he later wrote to his friend, Mr. Roosevelt, 'that it would not do to attack the Administration on Mexico because people felt generally that Wilson had kept us out of war. That statement had upon me the same irritating effect that it evidently had on you.' The evidence was correct; nothing, Mr. Roosevelt replied, had irritated him more than the caution of his own Progressives toward the 'noble and humanitarian peace policy' which they were so misguided as to discern in Mr. Wilson.

The Colonel's unhappiness was deepening. Those fires of social reform which he had incautiously set alight in 1912 were already burning very low in his own breast. In their place there raged an ever more consuming personal hatred of Woodrow Wilson, the man who had so deftly profited by them, and T. R. yearned to maneuver himself back upon the firm platform of orthodox Republicanism, from which alone it would be possible to deliver an effective attack upon the 'schoolmaster.' The ties which still bound him to the bright host he had led forth two years before were now gall and weariness; yet they could not be broken too abruptly. Mr. Roosevelt barnstormed through half a dozen states that fall, campaigning for Progressive candidates. But as he went, chafing under his inability to assail Mr. Wilson's pacifism, the roars of a far greater battle were constantly in the ears of that life-long militarist.

From the beginning Mr. Roosevelt's deepest sympathies were probably with the English; in the September *Outlook*, however, he had shown himself capable of understanding the German side, he had upheld with Mr. Wilson the traditional American policy of neutrality and he had recorded his opinion that 'probably nothing we could have done would have helped Belgium.' But as his campaign train rolled across the countryside scarcely a month later, his ideas were undergoing alteration. Throughout the imperial years the foreign department had been Mr. Roosevelt's especial pride, the scene of his most resounding triumphs. It was a final bitterness now that to Mr. Wilson, of all men, there should have come the greatest opportunity in foreign affairs ever likely to present itself to an American Administration. 'For the first time since he had left Washington,' according to Mr. Oscar King Davis, who travelled with him, 'he felt an eagerness to be again at the White House.' It was an eagerness which made it simple for the Colonel to convince himself that if he had been he would have acted differently — and far more effectively — than the bungler who sat on the Colonel's throne.

Already Mr. Davis perceived the truth; already the Colonel had made himself believe that if only he had been President he could have prevented the outbreak of the European War. Mr. Davis asked how. Mr. Roosevelt had developed the full theory — by urging the American interest, under the Hague Conventions, in 'preventing the violation of Belgium' he would have compelled

Germany to yield and so saved the world. 'But what,' he went on, 'could be expected from an Administration that has at its head a college professor who has never had anything but an academic interest in foreign affairs?' What, indeed? Mr. Roosevelt had convinced himself; and it was a conviction in which he was never afterward to be shaken. For the moment he could not reveal it to the world. The American people might be profoundly sympathetic toward the Allies, but their first emotion, in those early days of the carnage, was an even more profound satisfaction in the thought that they were out of it. Fervently the simple creatures rejoiced in the Atlantic Ocean and in the Washingtonian policy of neutrality, which Mr. Wilson had basely pre-empted. It seemed that 'the bulk of our people,' as Mr. Roosevelt sadly confided to Sir Edward Grey on October 3, 'do not understand foreign policy,' and it was terribly discouraging. But as the campaign train rolled back at last to New York, the Colonel told Davis that now he had paid all his debts — he was a free man at last. With a glow of martyrdom he proposed to throw himself into the task of arousing the people 'to an active sense of their duty in Europe,' a duty (as he did not add) which must clearly begin with the throwing out of Woodrow Wilson.

The Democrats suffered at the polls, but not so heavily as to lose either House. It left the regular Republicans almost as unhappy as Mr. Roosevelt. In the early summer they had been cheerfully certain, observing the deepening economic stagnation, that their opponents were 'on the rocks.' Now the truth was apparent: Mr. Wilson had become almost by accident the Peace President; the outbreak of world war, though it had greatly intensified the depression, had actually saved the Democrats instead of destroying them. More than ever was it clear that if the Republicans were to win back the Presidency in 1916 they must do so upon the difficult terrain of foreign policy. But how? Here fate was kind. At the very outset she thrust into their hands an instrument ideally suited to their rather special requirements — the great weapon of Preparedness.

War is terrible; it is also glamorous, and because of its appalling terror it exercises a compelling fascination. Americans might thank God for the Atlantic Ocean; they might tremble at the sight of Europe — and yet experience a strange temptation to imitate her. It was something akin to that faint impulse which has half prompted the most normal of men to hurl themselves from the top of a tall building or under the wheels of an oncoming express train. It was the unparalleled political virtue of Preparedness — 'against war' — that it offered a means of imitating Europe, yet on the understanding that this was merely to preserve us from her horrors. It provided the thrill, at the moment that it promised to prevent the damage. There could scarcely be a more perfect combination with which to approach, at such a moment, so emotional a public as our own.

One of the American people's profoundest illusions about itself, of course, was its belief in its own 'non-militaristic' character. This was a great source of our detestation for the Germans. The American people would have been shocked to learn that precisely the same forces which had built the great armaments of Germany (and of France, Russia and Great Britain as well) were already at work in the United States, as we reached a similar stage of industrial, political and social development. Yet it was a fact. We overlooked the obvious and striking parallel between President Roosevelt and the German Emperor; we did not realize that the terrible von Tirpitz had sat at the feet of Admiral Mahan and that the German Navy was founded squarely upon the philosophy of the American navalist. Even less was it realized that (consciously or unconsciously) our own General Leonard Wood had in turn sat at the feet of von Tirpitz, and had devoted himself, long before the outbreak of the European War, to the upbuilding of an American militarism by the same modern and realistic methods wherewith the German had so brilliantly and disastrously succeeded.

Leonard Wood was our most distinguished professional soldier; he had shone for years in the Rooseveltian radiance, and in April, 1914, he was just concluding his tour of duty as Chief of Staff, the highest office in the Army. Like Admiral Tirpitz, General Wood never questioned his own patriotism, nor is it necessary for others to do so. It is sufficient to say that his patriotism, like that of the Grand Admiral, was at the service of an intense personal ambition, a fondness for political maneuver and an intuitive sense of the new importance of publicity. When the fresh glories of the Spanish War and colonial pro-consulship began to fade, Wood found himself (as the German had done) stagnating in a small, old-fashioned service of no popular importance. He chafed at so narrow a field for talents which he rightly felt to be beyond the average; and he would have been more than human if he had not convinced himself that the national interest imperatively demanded that this field be enlarged. Like Tirpitz, he set himself to enlarge it.

In one respect the Grand Admiral had enjoyed the advantage; he had his Kaiser until the end while Wood lost his Roosevelt at the beginning. It required only a greater energy and skill. The basis of the effort, of course, was the new demand of American industrialism for armament orders at home, for the opportunities of foreign markets and foreign adventure, for the disciplines of military patriotism to preserve the social structure against its developing internal strains and stiffen it to support the world competitive struggle. Here were the General's inexhaustible supplies, alike of emotional and of more material resources; all that was required for their utilization was pressure and propaganda. As long as he was Chief of Staff Wood could operate directly upon the Congressional committees, but he understood that Congress was really the last, not the first, fortress to be taken. He became indefatigable in lectures, dinner gatherings, personal contacts with appropriately powerful people. He lent encouragement and material to the new school of military propagandists who were appearing with magazine articles and books on 'military policy' and 'national defence.' And as early as 1913 he had evolved the most subtle of all the engines with which he was finally to convert the United States to militarism.

These were the voluntary citizens' training camps, the origin of what was later known as the 'Plattsburg idea.' It was in the summer of 1913 that Wood opened the first two of these camps with 222 students in all — for the most part college undergraduates. Ostensibly, the camps offered to patriotic young men a chance to equip themselves at their own expense with the military training which Congress had basely failed to provide; actually, General Wood was never under any illusions as to the military value of the experiment. 'We do not expect,' he wrote at the very beginning, '... to accomplish much in the way of detailed military instruction,... but we do believe a great deal can be done in the implanting of a sound military policy.' The camps, to state it more bluntly, were designed from the start to be (as their successors still are today) not practical schools of war but seminaries whence propagandists for preparedness might be distributed through the civil population. General Wood was not really trying to provide an officer reserve; 'he was seeking,' as his own wholly loyal biographer puts it, 'to develop missionaries in the cause of patriotic service.' Four camps, with three times as many novitiates, were organized for the summer of 1914. General Wood was inspecting one of these camps at the moment that the great hurricane broke — to fertilize, beyond all hope or expectation, the ground which he had been so diligently sowing.

Thus, even before the outbreak, preparedness already had the beginnings of an effective pressure organization behind it. The Allies were now to lend it powerful assistance. From the beginning every Allied spokesman assiduously spread the conviction that a German triumph in Europe would mean an immediate German attack upon the Monroe Doctrine, if not upon the United States itself. So instant, so universal, was this move that as early as September 3 Ambassador Bernstorff was directed to enter official denial at the State Department that his Government intended 'to seek expansion in South America.' No one, however, believed the Germans any longer, and General Wood only the more diligently fanned these new flames of propaganda. He was sta-

tioned now on Governor's Island, in the heart of the powerful
and pro-Ally Northeast, a five-minute ferry ride from all the more
important diners out in the United States and from the incomparable sounding board of the New York press. He 'talked preparedness day and night to whomever would listen,' wrote letters,
made speeches, buttonholed everyone. And soon the results began
to show. With November, influential editors were calling him
into conference; letters began to flow in demanding data or giving
encouragement; presently a civilian friend and collaborator,
Frederic L. Huidekoper, came back from a tour of the battle
fronts to found the National Security League — which was to
become one of the chief organs of nationalistic patriotism and
preparedness.

Yet Washington remained strangely hostile to all this patriotic
ardor. In November no less an emissary than Colonel House was
lunching at Governor's Island, and asking for 'memoranda and
data to hand the President.' But nothing came of it. Actually,
House found the President balky. Mr. Wilson had no interest, it
seemed, in military glamour; he suspected the soldiers, he was
afraid of labor union opposition, while his Democratic majority
in Congress reflected the old-fashioned but well founded distrust
of great military castes in a democratic state. Worse than that,
he told House — what it seems that even a military expert might
have guessed by that time — that 'no matter how the great war
ended there would be complete exhaustion, and, even if Germany
won, she would not be in a condition seriously to menace our
country for years to come.' 'I combatted this idea,' House complacently noted, but it was of no use. He found Mr. Bryan in
positively 'violent' opposition. The Secretary of State saw even
more clearly than the President that there was not 'the slightest
danger' of a Teutonic invasion; but this very obvious piece of
common sense served only to convince House that Mr. Bryan was
as 'innocent' as 'my little grandchild, Jane Tucker.'

The agitation was taking hold with the public, but the President, in his annual message to Congress in December, suddenly

threw cold water over the whole preparedness idea. Mr. Roosevelt ground his celebrated teeth in fury; and two weeks later General Wood ostentatiously appeared before the Merchants Association in New York, with 1500 people acclaiming him. It was an act of insubordination sufficiently flagrant to make the whole position clear — and to delight the Republicans. From the moment that the war broke in Europe, any political tyro would instinctively have sought to exploit the tremendous emotional energies which it generated. Preparedness, glamorously martial and yet by definition wholly pacific, was the ready and the incomparable instrument. Mr. Roosevelt and the Republicans alike now turned to make use of it in earnest.

V

Already, however, there were stealthily arising problems more serious and more immediate than anything foreseen by the romantics of preparedness. It was all very well to draw fearful pictures of a German invasion in the next war, but it served only to conceal the situation into which we were rapidly drifting in respect to the current one. By October it began to appear that the sudden plunge into the economic abyss had been, in some miraculous fashion, arrested. Southern cotton farmers might still be destitute; great numbers of unemployed might still be on the streets. In New York, however, an 'outlaw' securities market had developed upon the sidewalk before the closed doors of the Stock Exchange, and its prices 'caused surprise.' Presently some faint hint, even, of a recovery was discernible in these 'outlaw' quotations, while foreign exchange began to turn in our favor as the Allied governments came heavily into our markets for food, raw materials, commodities of all sorts. Was it possible that a European war could be profitable?

As the autumn days shortened toward that first winter of the war, Mr. H. P. Davison, a leading partner in the great House of Morgan and whole-hearted in his sympathy for the Allied cause, was distressed to observe the 'helter skelter and at times almost frantic' fashion in which different Allied purchasing agencies were bidding against each other in the American markets. The recklessness with which they were forcing up prices and wasting their money upon American pockets offended Mr. Davison's 'idea of orderliness in purchasing'; besides (in the words of Mr. Thomas Lamont, Mr. Davison's partner and biographer) it was 'developing uneven spots in the American markets, not conducive to stable industry here.' At once Mr. Davison perceived it to be the Morgan company's patriotic duty to undertake the purchasing job for itself, thus rescuing American industry from the 'demoralization' of too sudden wealth. On November 26 he sailed to lay this inspiration before the British Government; a similar idea, he found, had already occurred to them, and he was welcomed 'cordially.'

There were many other American bankers, manufacturers and promoters who discerned, even sooner than the Allies themselves, the opportunities for high (and highly profitable) service to humanity and the Entente held out by the immense scale of the new warfare. Nor was it solely a matter of food and raw material, even in those early days. In September Ambassador Bernstorff had heard of a French military mission at the Bethlehem Steel Works (happy name!), and by early November its head, Mr. Charles M. Schwab, was climbing stairs in 'evilly-lighted' London offices, arranging fat contracts for war munitions. He also arranged for direct cable communication with the Admiralty, the messages to be coded and decoded by the Chief Naval Censor himself — a convenience which was 'followed throughout the war.' Count Bernstorff charged that he had taken no less than $100,000,000 worth of munitions orders. This was denied; but it was noticeable that when Mr. Schwab debarked again at New York it was with the cheery announcement that the era of a 'big business revival' was imminent. In November the dollar rose again to par with the British pound, and on November 13 Spring Rice was happily reporting that 'everyone is talking of booming trade and increasing exports. This all depends on our keeping the sea open and consequently it is the rule of England on the sea that is preventing a financial catastrophe here.' But the cotton farmers and the unemployed did not think so; the boom was still all in the future, and there were others to whom the Royal Navy did not appear in quite so beneficent a light. However profitable it might be to sell to the Allies, it would have been even more profitable to sell to the Germans also — more profitable and, from the political viewpoint, far less embarrassing.

As early as August 28 Representative Towner of Iowa, speaking on the floor of Congress, had clearly foreseen the danger. To ship 'food and clothing' to the Allies, he had warned his countrymen, was 'to aid them in their great struggle with Germany and Austria.' At best we would be fortunate if we could avoid being drawn into the war; but to encourage even commercial exports to one side, when the other was debarred from our markets, would be 'to invite our own entanglement.' His fate was that of other Cassandras; few saw the relationship between these lucrative new markets and our own neutrality, and the Allies' commercial purchases mounted rapidly. The sale of munitions, however, was another matter. Activities like those of Mr. Schwab were quick to arouse our old-fashioned, evangelistic pacifism, of which Mr. Bryan was so representative a voice. It was a sentiment deeply rooted in the South and West — great areas remote from Europe, without the industrial Northeast's material interest in munitions contracts, and so ignorant as to feel that the sale of armaments to Europe was indistinguishable from the sale of small-arms to a gang of homicidal maniacs. When Congress convened in December, it was to meet a flood of bills calling for an embargo upon the export of munitions.

The leading bill was introduced by Senator Hitchcock of Nebraska, a pillar of the Democratic majority. Unfortunately, the movement was presented as one of humanitarian idealism, rather than as a severely practical way of preserving the United States from involvement in the war. Even more unfortunately, it at once enlisted the enthusiastic support of the pro-German minority. They plunged into a propaganda campaign which made it only too easy to discredit the whole idea as mere Teutonic treachery; besides, the sale of munitions was lucrative. Even so Spring Rice, always nervous, took instant alarm. He hurried off adroit warnings to Grey. Should the Administration threaten to support the embargo, he suggested, 'it will become necessary to point out that such unneutral action will disqualify the government from the office of impartial mediator. And this impartial mediation is the most cherished ambition of the President.' On December 11 Sir Edward 'unofficially' suggested that the Hitchcock bill 'would be special legislation passed while war is in progress making a radical departure from a long-established custom' and so a definitely 'unneutral act.' Loudly the Allies and their American sympathizers re-echoed this view, and Mr. Bryan soon reassured Spring Rice that the Hitchcock bill was without Administration endorsement. Curiously enough, no one appeared to notice that Sir Edward, at the very moment that he protested the 'unneutral act,' was forcing the European neutrals to adopt precisely the same sort of munitions embargo. But in their case, it worked in favor of the Allies.

Thus Mr. Wilson missed a valuable opportunity. There was really nothing whatever in international law to forbid a munitions embargo applying equally to all belligerents. To have supported the measure would of course have opened the President to a furious attack from the pro-Ally Americans and from the gentlemen who were getting the munitions contracts; at the time, however, few if any munitions had actually been exported, and the embargo would not have been the body blow either to American prosperity or to the Allied war effort which it would have been later on. The export of raw materials and commercial supplies would have supported all the prosperity we needed; the Allies would have been driven sooner to organize their own munitions manufacture, as the Germans did, and the net result might well have been far more satisfactory to them as well as to the United States. Doubtless the Germans would still have resented the commercial exports, but without the deep sting of bitterness which came with the thought that one's son had been eviscerated by a shrapnel shell made in America. Afterward, when a great munitions industry had been organized in the United States and the Allies were dependent upon it in earnest, it was too late; at the time, we might have preserved a much greater share of practical neutrality at relatively small cost.

Unfortunately, few were alive in those days to the importance of practical, as distinguished from formal, neutrality. The Morgans were allowed to set up their purchasing agency and our earnest seekers after contracts to continue unchecked. The Allies could buy from us; the Germans could not, and could not prevent the Allies from doing so, and that seemed all there was to it. But suppose the Germans should react against this situation? That they might invent a way occurred to no one. Mr. Gerard at Berlin was reporting that 'my job is made harder by these sales of munitions'; a growing bitterness toward the United States was not difficult to detect in the Central Powers. It seemed nothing which the American Government need worry about. Yet far back in the first week of September Mr. Whitlock at Brussels had encountered our naval attaché from the Berlin Embassy, passing through on his way to see the fighting. 'They have an invention at sea,' this officer told him, 'that will create the same staggering sensation in the world that the [42-centimetre howitzers] have.' And on November 7, just as Mr. Schwab was happily invading important offices in London, the Chief of the German Naval Staff was laying before Grand Admiral von Tirpitz 'a draft of a declaration of the submarine blockade of the whole coast of Great Britain and Ireland.'

Von Tirpitz, according to his memoirs, was doubtful; as yet they had too few submarines for such a job, and international law (which meant the United States) looked like an obstacle. But the Grand Admiral, a master as always of the publicity, began putting out his feelers. In November an American correspondent was invited down to Kiel and shown all over the submarine base with its magnificent new boats — capable of keeping the sea, they told him, as long as the crews could stand it. 'New Submarines at Kiel Awaiting the Chance to Strike' was the headline over his column story in the *World* on November 30. He had failed, however, to catch the hint that they might strike at something other than the Allied naval vessels. But a little later von Tirpitz himself was receiving Mr. Karl Wiegand, Berlin correspondent of the United Press, and two days before Christmas there was another story in the American papers, reporting the Grand Admiral's remarks:

> America has not raised her voice in protest and has taken little or no action against England's closing the North Sea to neutral shipping. What will America say if Germany declares submarine war on all enemy merchant ships?

But nobody seemed to pay much attention.

vi

At any rate, Colonel House's private little branch of the State Department seemed not to notice it. Colonel House was too occupied with higher things. In September the Colonel's first efforts as a peacemaker had not turned out too well, but that only led him, from October onward, to enlarge his ideas. In his long letter to Page on October 3 he had endeavored to review his immense problem, to consider actual peace terms, to project some idea of the future which he should aim to create. The Allies, he thought, 'could readily stand on the general proposition that only enduring peace will satisfy them,' and to the establishment of this happy condition the Colonel saw 'no insuperable obstacle.' Indeed, it was simplicity itself. Once the war was ended 'and the necessary territorial alignments made,' Colonel House had decided, the 'best guarantee of peace' would lie in every European nation 'guaranteeing the territorial integrity of every other nation.' In addition it would be well to suppress the private manufacture of armaments and to make sure that 'all sources of national irritation' were removed so that 'no sore spot can grow into a malignant disease.' Thus did Colonel House, seeking to establish the bases for American mediation in October, 1914, outline the central ideas upon which the Versailles Treaty and the League of Nations were in fact to be erected five years later. Where had he got them?

They were in the air — and in the Allied propagandas. Almost from the first days of the conflict, the peace sentiment in the United States had tended to divide itself into two distinct movements, more or less confused at first but developing into an ever sharper opposition as the war progressed. On the one side there was the more vulgar, the more simple-minded and evangelical form of pacifism which clung to the quaint notion that the way to establish peace was to put an end to war. William Jennings Bryan, if not exactly its leader, was one of its more distinguished heads; Jane Addams was already, that fall, touring the colleges in its behalf; the elder La Follette was to lend it the grim voice of his determined probity; Lillian Wald, David Starr Jordan and others were devoted workers, and it was to gain a powerful though disastrous recruit in Mr. Henry Ford. This was the movement which supported the arms embargo, opposed preparedness, insisted that the merits of the European quarrel were no concern of the United States and demanded that American influence should be exerted not toward deciding the war but toward bringing it to a stop on whatever terms might be practicable. It was promptly, though unjustly, convicted of German inspiration; the ostentatious support it received from the pro-German and Irish elements seemed to prove the charge, and it was never to count for much in the seats of power.

It was from the other current of peace sentiment that Colonel House had preferred to draw his inspiration. This movement was of a far more elegant, more cultivated and more intellectual character; it fitted much more easily into the established scheme of things, and carried no such threats to the social and economic order as lurked obscurely within the program of the evangelists. Ex-President Taft was to become one of its chief leaders; Mr. Elihu

Root was to give it aid and comfort; Dr. Eliot of Harvard and Dr. Nicholas Murray Butler of Columbia, Mr. Hamilton Holt and Mr. Theodore Marburg were among its distinguished liberal supporters, and it was even to find room, strangely enough, for pacifists of a more martial character. For this was the movement which crystallized about the rather different and more militant idea (already current before the outbreak of the war) of establishing peace by setting up a world league which would be prepared to fight for it.

It was the misfortune of the Bryanite pacifists that their program unavoidably tended to favor the Germans; for the same reason, it was the great strength of the peace league movement that it worked with an equal partiality to support the Allies and to promote our intervention on their behalf. For was not the Entente, after all, just such a peace league as these altruists envisioned, fighting desperately to preserve the world against the menace of a Prussian 'aggression'? Were not the Allies fighting for 'permanent' peace? In general the peace league movement confined itself to suggesting that the United States should enter such a league after the war was over; yet unavoidably it prepared the ground for the idea of an American intervention to end the war, in a way that would make the 'permanent' peace system possible. If the Entente was fighting for a 'permanent' peace which the United States would help to guarantee, how could the United States reasonably refuse to aid them? The Bryanites abhorred war, rather than the Germans. Insensibly, the peace league men could be brought to abhor the Germans, rather than war.

One can only admire the skill with which the Entente statesmen worked to channel the humanitarian American impulses toward peace and mediation into unconditional support for the practical war aims of the Entente. The ablest of them saw from the beginning that the United States was their greatest hope, and one of their greatest dangers. She might bring them military victory; but she must not be permitted to do so at the price of exacting political defeat. Toward the end of October Ambassador Page received, indirectly, a message from Sir John French, the British Commander-in-Chief. It was evidently intended for President Wilson, and Mr. Page hastened to transmit it to him. Already, it seemed, the British soldier realized that a stalemate had been reached; the 'probability was that the war would end in a drawn war.' Another year of it, at any rate, would leave the armies still only trampling back and forth over the bloody ground of Northern France; and moreover 'by that time somebody will know approximately the number of men that are killed.... Then a great revulsion will come. Not only will the neutral world rise up and say that this slaughter must cease, but the combatants themselves will say so and will at least be receptive to a suggestion.' Reading Mr. Page's letter today, one can understand how cautiously the British Commander-in-Chief was working to insure a 'suggestion' of the desired sort. The letter went on:

> The President of the United States will be called upon to mediate — to lay down a broad principle or two by which the struggle may be ended.... And the broad principles would be such as these: Every country must maintain its nationality — Belgium must be Belgian, of course; Alsace-Lorraine must be French, if they are French and so wish to be; Schleswig-Holstein Danish if they are Danish and wish to be; Poland, the same principle; the South German States to go with Austria if they so wish, etc., etc.; the Slav states now Austrian become Russian. The German colonies are left as pawns to trade with in working out the details of the bargain. As for the discouragement of big armies and navies — that's more difficult.... Let great armies and navies be discouraged by treaties. (Here the thought was not very clear; it had not been thought out by the soldier.)

Yet these principles of 'mediation' were suggested as appropriate to a situation in which it was assumed that undefeated German armies would still be fighting everywhere on foreign soil! One is often compelled to wonder, in reviewing those years, how Mr. Wilson ever came to be regarded as the author of what is now loosely summarized as 'Wilsonism.' To find the celebrated principle of 'self-determination' thus advanced by a British army commander, long before Mr. Wilson ever adopted it, as a device for inducing the Americans to convert a drawn war into total Allied victory may seem surprising. The surprise grows less, however, as one discovers again and again that nearly every one of the great principles upon which President Wilson insisted at Versailles actually originated in the strategic or diplomatic necessities of the Allies. It may have been naïve of the President to demand the fulfillment of these principles after the practical purposes for which they were invented had been attained, but at least it is hardly fair to fasten their paternity upon him.

It is difficult to suppose that Sir John French was really much more interested in the self-determination of peoples in October, 1914, than he was in the manner whereby big armies and navies were to be 'discouraged.' There were some Americans who could appreciate the true implications of this kind of pacifism. One was Mr. Jacob Schiff, the Jewish banker, who saw and said, in a letter to the New York *Times*, that if the war was to go on 'until one country is beaten into a condition where it must accept the terms the victor chooses to impose ... the peace thus obtained will only be a harbinger of another war.' Twenty years later we know the truth of that statement; at the time, the peace league propaganda helped to conceal it, while Mr. Schiff could be disregarded as a patent pro-German. It was less easy to disregard Mr. William Jennings Bryan, who, if a bucolic idealist, was also Secretary of State of the United States. On November 13 Spring Rice was recording, in a letter to Sir Arthur Nicolson, his amused contempt for a diplomatist who imagined that if the United States was to 'mediate' at all it could only be on a basis of genuine mediation in a drawn war.

> Bryan spoke to me about peace as he always does. He sighs for the Nobel Prize, and besides that he is a really convinced peaceman. He has just given me a sword beaten into a plowshare six inches long to serve as a paperweight.... No one doubts his sincerity, but that is rather embarrassing for us at the present moment, because he is always at us with peace propositions. This time, he said he could not

understand why we could not say what we were fighting for. The nation which continued war had as much responsibility as the country which began it....

I felt rather cross and said that the United States were signatories to the Hague Convention, which had been grossly violated again and again without one word from the principal neutral nation. They were now out of court. They had done nothing to prevent the crime, and now they must not prevent the punishment.

Mr. Bryan's very sensible reply was that the war had reached a stalemate, there was no longer any chance 'of an issue satisfactory to any Power.' Why, therefore, should not both sides say what they were fighting for and invite the United States to assist them in making peace then and there? The Ambassador was pained at such simple-minded common sense.

I asked him if he thought that under present circumstances Germany would give up Belgium and compensate her for her suffering. If not, how could the United States Government go on record as condoning a peace which would put the seal on the most disgraceful act of tyranny and oppression committed in modern times? I didn't believe there was a man in the country not a German or a Jew who could advocate such a cause. — He got rather angry and said that if that was what we wanted why did we not say so?

They could not, because this was not a fraction (as Mr. Page already knew) of what they really wanted; and Sir Cecil deftly shifted the conversation. It is not surprising that the Allies found Mr. Bryan's peace proposals 'embarrassing' — for they were genuine peace proposals. Unfortunately, those emanating from Colonel House were of a much less inconvenient character.

By the beginning of December Colonel House was again becoming urgent. The country was really suffering under the effects of the war; and Congress, in which those Southern and Western sections which suffered most were heavily represented, was about to convene. With military stalemate in Europe apparently offering the opportunity, the domestic pressure upon Mr. Wilson to offer his services once more as a peacemaker was growing severe. 'The President,' House wrote to Page on December 4, 'desires to start peace parleys at the very earliest moment, but he does not wish to offend the sensibilities of either side.' It was to prove a fatal reservation. Mr. Page replied at once, laying down Sir John's Carthaginian terms as the only ones it was useful even to talk about with the British. Sir Edward, on the other hand, was more shrewd. Suddenly on December 20 there appeared Sir Edward's answer to the artful cable which House and Spring Rice had concocted far back in September.[1] The British Foreign Minister now agreed that 'it would not be a good thing for the Allies to stand out against a proposal which embraced indemnity to Belgium and a satisfactory plan for disarmament.' House was delighted with such evidence of progress; he laid the cable before Mr. Wilson, who was 'elated' and 'wanted to know whether I could go to Europe as early as the coming Saturday.'

The future was suddenly more roseate than could have been hoped. House had already seen Bernstorff, who had at once agreed to the beginning of negotiations, for Count Bernstorff was no less subtle than Sir Edward in his cautious play for American support. But two days before Christmas, just as House was preparing to take ship upon his new mission of peace, Spring Rice brought word of another cable from Sir Edward. In agreeing to consider peace on the basis of a Belgian indemnity and disarmament, it now appeared, the Foreign Minister had been expressing only a personal opinion. He had not taken it up even with his Cabinet, much less with his allies. More than that, there were, after all, certain territorial questions to be considered — Alsace-Lorraine, Constantinople to Russia, perhaps...? Colonel House was an amateur in the hands of masters. The Colonel and the President, to whom he took this news, decided to drop it until they heard more from the Allies. So the war went on; Christmas — the first bitter Christmas in wartime — came, and the Colonel's third peace venture (counting the one he had undertaken in the spring,

[1] Page 80.

before the outbreak) ended in failure on the eve of the festival of
the Prince of Peace.

For the Colonel and the President had resolved not to 'offend
the sensibilities of either side.' Actually, they had far less fear of
offending German sensibilities than those of the Allies; but it was
only by offending both sides, and pretty sharply, that they could
have hoped for any success along the pathway of mediation.
Seven months later this truth was to dawn upon Colonel House,
and he was to glimpse the opportunity which he had squandered.
On August 4, 1915, the first anniversary of the war, he wrote:

> The President's judgment... was that last autumn was the time to
> discuss peace parleys.... I believe if one could have started peace
> parleys in November, we could have forced the evacuation of both
> France and Belgium and finally forced a peace which would have
> eliminated militarism on land *and sea*. The wishes of the Allies were
> heeded with the result that the war has now fastened itself on the
> vitals of Europe and what the end may be is beyond the knowledge
> of man.

The italics are not House's. In 1914 he had not thought enough
about militarism 'at sea.' He had not clearly apprehended the
basic elements in the outbreak of the war nor sufficiently analyzed
the sources and significance of his own ideas about the organization of peace. He did not even know whether he was mediating or
intervening. In August, 1915, House may have overrated (as
statesmen so frequently do) the chances of success had he followed
a different course; but it is now clear that the course which he did
follow was a futile one. The opportunity did not recur. In
diplomacy, as the ten million dead of the World War were to
attest, one cannot afford to be seven months late.

vii

This altruistic effort at mediation sprang, at bottom, out of the
material distress which the war had imposed upon the country.
Perhaps the trouble was that the two aspects of American policy

were not better correlated. The arrangement under which Colonel House privately presided over the altruism while it was left to Mr. Lansing at the official State Department to wrestle with the defence of our material trade interests was not a happy one.

Had the two departments been combined, for example, the Colonel might earlier have realized the importance of militarism 'at sea.' In November Governor Colquitt of Texas was declaring that the South had been ruined by the destruction of its cotton export trade, that thousands of its people were 'starving' and that 'American ironclads' should be sent 'to England's door' to enforce our rights. Throughout that fall the 'Buy-a-Bale-of-Cotton' movement was spreading through the country, in a feeble attempt at relief. The charitable were called upon to purchase cotton at 10¢ a pound (it was selling commercially down to 6¢), and the homes of prominent politicians and wealthy business men were blossoming with shaggy cotton bales on their front porches. In November, too, Mr. Elbert Gary, chairman of the United States Steel Corporation, came back from Europe to find the nation 'in the grip of the worst depression that he or any one of his generation had seen. Tens of thousands of people in New York City alone were out of employment.' According to Mr. Tumulty, the President's private secretary, from the latter part of October onward 'the pressure upon us at the White House for satisfaction at the hands of England grew more intense each day.' But across the street, where the 'lawyers at the State Department,' as Spring Rice scornfully called them, were struggling with the problem, the chances of ever getting any satisfaction at all seemed only to fade more and more mysteriously away behind the mountain ranges of correspondence that were now daily accumulating.

On October 22 the United States had formally withdrawn her insistence upon the Declaration of London and had entrusted her maritime rights to 'the existing rules of international law.' Only gradually was the painful truth to sink in that, for most practical purposes, there were none. Today it is impossible to follow in detail the steps whereby the Foreign Office was — with delicacy, but with persistence, determination and great thoroughness — to inculcate that lesson. One can distinguish only the higher peaks in those documentary *massifs* which the process left behind it. In general, the position was that in the absence of a formal and close blockade the United States was entitled to carry on her commerce with the civil populations of Germany and Austria unhindered. This position it was essential for the Allies to overcome if they were to apply their 'economic pressure,' and through a series of ingenious devices they now proceeded to overcome it.

The first requisite was to transfer to their lists of 'absolute contraband' (specific war munitions) every article of peace-time commerce which they thought could be included without too much risk of protest from the United States. Practically everything else became 'conditional contraband.' [1] Conditional contraband could be confiscated only upon proof of its destination to the armed forces of the enemy; it was the British prize courts, however, which passed upon the 'proof.' They found little difficulty in inventing rules of evidence adequate to almost any occasion, while the inordinate costs and delays which they were able to impose upon the 'suspected' shipper merely in bringing his case to trial were a sufficient weapon in themselves. The contraband rules, as interpreted and enforced by the overwhelming Allied command of the sea lanes, were alone enough to end practically all the direct trade into German and Austrian ports.

There remained the indirect trade by way of the European neutrals. On this matter the 'law' was more dubious, but the doctrine of 'continuous voyage,' which had been stoutly upheld by the United States in the Civil War, could be cited to authorize the enforcement of the contraband rules against this trade as well. Here there was the added difficulty that it was necessary, even in the case of absolute contraband, to prove enemy destination; but once more the British prize courts were to rise to every emergency. So catholic were the standards of proof which they ultimately established, that the mere fact that a 'suspicious' cargo was

[1] See p. 83.

headed in the general direction of Scandinavia or Holland was enough to convict it of enemy destination.

The contraband rules and the prize courts between them thus provided the 'legal' basis for what amounted to an offshore block-ade — in itself illegal — of the Central Powers. This foundation was not laid, however, without strenuous challenge from the United States at almost every step. From the beginning the State Department found itself overwhelmed with demands for action from American shippers, from cotton farmers, from oil, copper and packing interests as well as from the pro-Germans; and as it took up the innumerable specific cases of seizure or interference which they presented, it was soon vigorously denying the legality of the Allied contraband lists, of their prize court methods, of nearly every other device by which they asserted a right to prohibit American commerce with Germany and Austria.

This constrained the Allies to proceed with caution, and left many possible loopholes in their blockade. But if the legal founda-tion was shaky, it was still quite adequate to support the remarkable extra-legal superstructure which they were now to raise upon it, and which became in fact their chief means of channelling the foreign trade of the United States to the service of their own ends. If the law was doubtful, the threats made in its name were not. While the State Department was defending the legality of this or that cargo, the shipper was confronted by the fact that it was being held up — at enormous cost to himself. The State Department could give him no guarantee against losses of that kind; the British consular agents, on the other hand, could. The American shipper very soon began to seek out the consular agents rather than the State Department; and very soon these foreign consuls were passing upon the export trade of the United States, approving whatever was intended for or desired by the Allies, and condemning any-thing which could be remotely suspected of the crime of 'enemy destination' to every sort of interference and annoyance which an inventive officialdom could devise.

Rapidly this system was expanded. To the threats of confiscation at sea other pressures were soon added. Beginning in October, the British embargoed the export from their own territories of such essential raw materials as wool, meat, rubber and manganese, upon which American manufactures were largely dependent. Protest only brought the rather contemptuous reply from Mr. Page that since the United States would give no guarantee against the re-export of these materials to the Central Powers, Great Britain obviously had to lay the embargo itself. To this unquestionably reasonable contention the State Department could find no good reply; yet our industry had to have the raw materials. The result was that the American manufacturers entered directly into agreements with the British Government under which they imposed the embargo themselves — and the British secured another powerful lever for the control of the American manufacturers. The Allies, moreover, could soon hold out bribes as well as threats. As their war demands began to develop the American industrialist and exporter saw that they held the promise of markets far too lucrative to be risked by laying oneself open to suspicion of trading with the 'enemy.' The celebrated 'black lists,' which found their genesis in this state of affairs, did not come until very much later, but before the end of 1914 the British were already asserting a very direct authority over large areas of the American economy.

Similar controls were established, in essentially the same way, on the other side of the Atlantic. By threatening to cut off the entire foreign trade of the European neutrals — vital, of course, to their existence — the Allies forced them to participate in the blockade. In some cases their governments embargoed munitions exports (an 'unneutral act,' as Sir Edward had called it, when the United States proposed to do the same) thus rendering impossible the transit trade into Germany. For the most part the neutrality question was evaded, however, by the establishment of ostensibly private trading corporations which accomplished the same purpose. By November one of the first of these, the Netherlands Overseas Trust, had been set up in Holland. This concern gave its own assurances to the British Government that goods consigned to it would not be re-exported to Germany; the Royal Navy thereupon consented to grant free passage to everything consigned to the trust — and it naturally followed that goods shipped to any other Dutch consignee would be subjected to every costly impediment which could be applied. Thus were the European neutrals in effect compelled to violate their neutrality and forego the rich transit trade which would otherwise have been theirs, yet by arrangements which in law at any rate were purely 'voluntary' and private.[1]

Thus at both ends of the Atlantic passage, American trade with the Central Powers was subject before the end of 1914 to a 'voluntary' system of British supervision as astonishing in its extent as it was probably abhorrent both to domestic and international law. One hesitates to think of the storm of popular outrage which would have resulted had the Germans been in a position to exert one tenth of the interference which was scarcely noticed (except by those not inconsiderable interests which suffered) when practiced by the Allies. It was of course to take much time before the full system was perfected. But already cotton cargoes en route to Europe were being solemnly unloaded at New York and X-rayed, bale by bale, at the American shipper's expense and under the eyes of British officials, lest they might carry concealed contraband. American manufacturers and exporters were being formed into the first of the trade associations which, acting in effect as the agents of a foreign power in American industry, were rigidly to enforce every order from Downing Street, and to act — despite anti-trust laws — in complete restraint of American trade with the Central Powers.

The State Department, curiously enough, actually connived in the whole process. Throughout all that fall and winter it did

---

[1] For many reasons — not all of them creditable to the Allies — the control of the trade by way of the European neutrals was never made complete until after the American entry into the war. This does not alter the principles involved, and if anything served only to increase the irritation of the American interests which suffered under the very great measure of control which was enforced.

carry on (as well as it could through the resistant medium of Mr. Page) a running fire of correspondence and protest upon all the more important individual cases. Yet their very number and complexity offered to the British every resource of evasion, confusion and delay. In extreme cases the British would even buy the contested cargoes at prevailing prices. What more could the shipper ask? It was a difficult argument to rebut; yet the effect was still to close the lucrative German market and, while giving the shipper his profit on one cargo, to deny him the profits he might have made on countless others. Deeper and deeper the State Department sank into a morass of words without substance — a nightmare battle with phantoms in which no blow ever seemed to strike home and every victory turned out to be a triple defeat. To make progress in that fashion was impossible, and the Department soon developed a tendency to leave individual cases for 'unofficial' settlement between the shippers and the British authorities, while it concentrated its own efforts upon the broad principles of contraband and prize court law. The State Department, in other words, turned to attack the foundations upon which the elaborate superstructure of 'voluntary' control was being erected; yet by encouraging the 'unofficial' settlement of the individual cases it was facilitating the very methods whereby that superstructure was being set in place.

'Sir Edward,' Page cheerfully wrote to House on November 9, 'values American friendship more than anything else of that kind.... To this day he hasn't confiscated a single American cargo.' He did not have to; there were so many other ways of achieving the same end. The American public, moreover, paid relatively little attention to the controversy — at best a dull and unexciting affair compared to the bloody despatches from the fighting fronts. As the year ran out, however, and as the blockade continued to close in upon our trade like a choking fog, at once impalpable and yet ever more impenetrable, the tempers in the State Department began to run short. A note of sharpness began to enter our formerly polite representations; patience with the emotional Spring

Rice began to wear thin; Mr. Page was rather abruptly warned to pay more attention to the interests of the nation he was supposed to represent and less to those of Great Britain. Spring Rice, always wavering between truculence and abject pessimism, began to see specters of the most extraordinary kind:

> The German-Jewish bankers are toiling in a solid phalanx to compass our destruction. One by one they are getting hold of the principal New York papers, and I was told today that the New York *Times*, which had a courageous Jew at its head who manfully stood up for the Allies, has been practically acquired by Kuhn, Loeb & Co. and Schiff, the arch-Jew and special protégé of the Emperor. Warburg... is a member of the Federal Reserve Board.... He practically controls the financial policy of the Administration and Paish and Blackett had mainly to negotiate with him. Of course it was exactly like negotiating with Germany.... Since Morgan's death the Jewish banks are supreme and they have captured the Treasury Department.

If it sounds like madness that is but another testimonial to the deepening shadows of war insanity into which everyone was sinking.

In November and December still another straw was to be laid upon the camel's back. On November 4 Secretary Bryan received official notice from the British Government that thereafter 'the whole of the North Sea must be considered a military area.' From the beginning of the war both Germans and British had sown mines off each other's ports; already the British had used this fact as a reason for 'advising' all neutral shipping to call at British ports on their way into the North Sea. Thus they would learn what routes were clear of mines — and greatly facilitate the task of searching their cargoes for contraband. In October, however, a German auxiliary cruiser ran the supposedly airtight British naval cordon and sowed mines off the west coast of Ireland, on the trade route from America. The Admiralty was quick to see another opportunity. On the theory that no German could have conceivably eluded their vigilance they now announced that

Chief of the Naval Staff laid before Grand Admiral von Tirpitz 'the draft of a letter to the Foreign Office, in which he requested their approval of the opening of a submarine campaign at the end of January, the English Channel and all the waters surrounding the United Kingdom to be declared as a war zone.' If the United States permitted the English to do it she surely could not raise difficulties when the Germans followed their example? Von Tirpitz was not convinced even so; 'our experiences,' he truthfully observed, 'have unfortunately made it clear that Germany must pay more respect to the commercial interests of the neutrals than England.' But the Foreign Office (according to Tirpitz) was bolder; it believed it could justify such a declaration, and the plan went forward.

Of all this the American statesmen were naturally ignorant. But even without the new complications which it threatened, the blockade question was sufficiently serious. On November 5 Spring Rice was anxiously inquiring of House:

Do you gather that an attack will be made on the Administration by Congress for remissness about contraband matters? As a matter of fact [though it hardly was] all the protests of the Administration have been successful. But owing to changed conditions of modern war it is evident that the definition of contraband must be changed.... A *just* cause of complaint would be the seizure of goods really destined for neutrals and we are making arrangements by which such goods will be hall-marked by the sender here if he wishes it.

That, of course, was the point — we rejected the whole body of devices whereby Great Britain was making us an accessory to the blockade of Germany. That 'hall-mark' was the badge of our subjugation to the status of an ally of the Entente. On December 3 Ambassador Page was bluntly informed that there was 'sharp criticism in this country' of British high-handedness, and that something would have to be done. This new stiffness at last appears to have prodded Page into some realization of the true position, and he replied on December 7 with a proposed 'working arrangement' with Great Britain, in which he had attempted to

consolidate the whole intricate problem — markedly to the
British advantage.

Was this, one wonders, the celebrated occasion afterward recorded by Sir Edward Grey? 'Page came to see me at the Foreign
Office one day and produced a long despatch from Washington
contesting our claim to act as we were doing in stopping contraband going to neutral ports. "I am instructed," he said, "to read
this despatch to you." He read, and I listened. He then said:
"I have now read the despatch, but do not agree with it; let us
consider how it should be answered!"' Long after the war was
over a friend once remarked to Sir Edward that this was all very
well, but what would the Foreign Minister have said if one of his
own Ambassadors had offered to advise the government to which
he was accredited upon how to answer one of Grey's despatches?
'"Ah, well," he responded diplomatically, "Page and I stood in
very special relations to one another" — which was certainly true.'
It certainly was, and the point need be labored no longer. As Sir
Edward put it in his own memoirs: 'The comfort, support and
encouragement that [Page's] presence was to the Secretary for
Foreign Affairs in London may be imagined.'

The opposite effect which this presence had on Mr. Bryan and
Mr. Lansing may likewise be imagined; and indeed, Page's influence was already waning rapidly. Mr. Bryan replied to Page's
'working arrangement' with the hint that he had better try again;
but this only brought another proposal like the first — and after
that the State Department was to take matters into its own hands.
On the day after Christmas there was despatched over Mr.
Bryan's signature a long, a formal and a severe protest: 'Note to
Great Britain Protesting Against Seizures and Detentions Regarded as Unwarrantable.' We protested the strained and illegal
methods with which the contraband lists had been enforced; we
protested the diversion of ships; we protested the seizure of food
cargoes upon the flimsiest of suspicion that they might be destined
for the German armed forces rather than the civil population; we
protested the refusal to pass conditional contraband unless con-

signed to the Allied control organizations in the European neutrals; we protested the uncertainty as to what would and would not be interfered with which the British used as one of their great weapons for intimidating lawful commerce. The Note declared:

> The present policy of His Majesty's Government toward neutral ships and cargoes exceeds the manifest necessity of a belligerent and constitutes restrictions upon the rights of American citizens on the high seas which are not justified by the rules of international law or required under the principle of self-preservation.

This was strong language. It was also to prove totally ineffective.

IV. THE PRIZE COURT—AND THE TORPEDO

i

AT the beginning of 1915 few in the United States could have seriously anticipated an American participation in the war. In a weighty editorial the New York *Times* remonstrated with 'Our English Friends' for their impatience with our continued neutrality. We might reprobate the Germans as militaristic menaces to the peace and safety of civilization, but surely the Allies could not expect us to take any action in the matter. It was a common attitude; nor did it seem to be an inconsistent one. Yet in fact the coils were tightening; already all the chief causes of our entanglement had been firmly established and already war was the most likely outcome.

For the urgent problem thus posed it was Mr. Wilson's duty to find a satisfactory solution. At the beginning a variety of solutions were theoretically possible. Any one of several policies — strict and effective neutrality, impartial intervention to force a peace, intervention in alliance with the Entente, even intervention on the side of Germany, for that matter — might, if consistently pursued, have been made to yield relatively satisfactory results. Unfortunately, the course actually adopted represented only a confused attempt to follow them all, with the result that it became increasingly difficult to succeed with any. Fate, weaving her rhythmic pattern, was now gradually to narrow the field within which our diplomatists could act; each year the possible solutions open to us were fewer than the year preceding; each year American statesmanship was to attempt policies which could only have been practicable had they been adopted months before. 'Last autumn,' as House said of his peace effort, 'was the time' — and it was a note which was to run in solemn counterpoint throughout the history. It is not surprising that our statesmanship was finally to prove incompetent to arrest or to control the mighty forces with which it sought to deal, and that under its guidance the nation was in the end thrust helplessly down into the abyss of war, the victim rather than the master of its destiny.

On January 1, 1915, however, such futures were not foreseen. Even in New York, which was closer to the war than most of our cities, the conflict left curiously little impress upon the New Year celebrations. 'Record Revels Usher in 1915,' exclaimed a head-line, 'Broadway's Largest Crowd.' At the restaurants 'the fox-trot and the one-step' had 'raged everywhere.' Despite war and blockade 'there was more real champagne in evidence... than there had ever been before.' It is true that at all the watch-night services there had been prayers for peace; while just before mid-night someone in the crowd outside Trinity Church in lower Broadway had struck up 'It's a Long Way to Tipperary.' The crowd had joined in the singing of all the national airs and war songs, but as the clock began to strike they turned to 'The Star-Spangled Banner.'

At the hotels 'money poured out for the pure joy of celebrating not only the new year but the confident assurance that money will be more plentiful in 1915.' So everyone wished to believe; so the editorial writers predicted. Actually, 'at the beginning of 1915,' according to a later survey, 'there was no sign of recovery in our manufacturing industries.' Bank checks drawn during the whole first quarter of 1915 were to prove the smallest in years, less by 10 per cent than in the corresponding period of 1914, which had been a dull time. Wall Street still 'prayed for peace'; and only at the Produce Exchange, where wheat was at startling highs, did they 'pray for the war to go on.' Yet the nation was at peace in

a warring world, and the possibility that virtue might be its own
reward was quite apparent to the thoughtful. The *Times* was,
perhaps, just faintly pharisaical:

> We have oversupplied ourselves with forces of production and they
> are idle in unusual proportion.... The promise of the new year is that
> we shall accomplish a peaceful penetration of the world's markets to
> an extent we have never dreamed of. What others have shed blood
> to obtain through politics and force we shall attain while bestowing
> our benevolence.... It is a new translation of the old beatitude, re-
> vised: 'Blessed are the keepers of the peace for prosperity shall be
> within their homes and palaces.'

Such elevated sentiments were scarcely calculated to soften the
shock, the anger and the dismay with which the publication of
the strenuous American protest against British trade restrictions
was received in Great Britain. The Note appeared in full in the
morning papers of January 1. To the publics on both sides of the
water, who had but imperfectly followed the diplomatic history
behind it, it came as the first important official action taken by the
Government of the United States in regard to the European war.
Yet it was not against Germany that it was directed; it was against
the Allies!

Mr. Page in London was grieved by the 'shirt-sleeve tone' of the
State Department. Lord Bryce hastened to express to his American friends his distinguished disappointment over the fact that the
United States had never protested against 'such a flagrant breach
of public law as the invasion of Belgium.' The circumstance that
the invasion of Belgium had not affected our national interests
while the suppression of our trade affected them very directly
escaped Lord Bryce. It escaped the British press even more completely. Sir Edward warned House that British opinion was 'un-
favorably' impressed. Spring Rice gave way to enraged despair;
he was certain that all America would be pro-German within six
months and talked wildly about boycotting the State Department.
Instead, he ultimately called upon Mr. Bryan with representations
that today seem to verge almost upon the insulting. At the begin-

ning of the war, he suggested, the British people had observed 'a distinct and purely American sentiment which was stirred by the wrong done Belgium'; now his countrymen were convinced that under pressure of an organized 'independent force in the heart of the American people' the United States was adopting 'an attitude of partiality in the present war and of hostility to Great Britain.'

Oddly enough, large sections of American opinion only echoed these reproaches. Mr. Roosevelt, that bellicose nationalist, plunged into a faintly treasonable correspondence with his old friend and fellow bird lover, Sir Edward Grey, in which he advised the Foreign Minister how to deal with the American protests — 'even if you are right and we are wrong.' Prominent newspapers warned the President to proceed with caution lest he fall into the traps prepared for 'amiable statesmen' by German intrigue. Yet the press, perhaps, was no longer altogether representative. On January 8 Senator Stone of Missouri, chairman of the powerful Foreign Relations Committee of the Senate, addressed a long letter to Mr. Bryan enumerating point by point the many ways in which it was charged that the Administration had shown partiality for the Entente. The State Department soon replied, exculpating itself with technical appeals to shadowy legalities. But Congress, now actively debating the arms embargo resolution, showed signs of passing it.

At the same time, the Bryanite, or pacifist, peace movement was gaining strength and consciousness. It had received interesting reinforcements from abroad. During that winter Mrs. Pethwick Lawrence, an Englishwoman, and the brilliant Hungarian, Rosika Schwimmer, were preaching a crusade throughout the country against 'the common enemy of mankind.' Between them they inspired Jane Addams to found the Women's Peace Party, dedicated to urging the immediate discussion of reasonable peace terms. The organization was launched on January 10 at the New Willard Hotel in Washington, before a group of some 3000 women. Miss Addams, however, got next to no serious attention in the newspapers; while there was that other, more elegant and more militant peace movement in the field. Its liberal leaders were already deep in the work out of which the League to Enforce Peace was later to grow. In close correspondence with a similar group in England, including the Bryces, the Morleys and other distinguished exponents of British Liberalism, they were developing the theory — far more inspiring than Miss Addams's — that 'the shortest road to enduring peace is the crushing of the military class in Germany.' They did not regard it as necessary to include the military class of Russia, France, Great Britain or the United States in this project; but they might have guessed where it was leading them when they suddenly received the support of none other than Mr. Roosevelt — the nation's most influential militarist.

Throughout all this period it is difficult, it is impossible, to regard the ex-President — aging, jealous, envenomed with a personal fury against the Princeton schoolmaster — as an idealist. Yet Mr. Wilson had committed himself, it seemed, to the traditional policy of neutrality. Mr. Roosevelt now tossed Washington, Jefferson and Monroe into the discard to announce a policy of complete 'entanglement' in Europe quite as drastic as that to which the name of his great enemy was long afterward to become attached. 'Utopia or Hell' was the title of his flaming manifesto:

> The only alternative to war, that is to hell, is the adoption of some plan substantially like that which I have advocated. . . . What I propose is a working and realizable Utopia. My proposal is that the efficient civilized nations — those that are efficient in war as well as in peace — should join in a world league for the peace of righteousness. This means that they shall by solemn covenant agree as to their respective rights, which shall not be questioned; that they shall agree that all other questions arising between them shall be submitted to a court of arbitration. And that they shall also agree — and here comes the vital and essential part of the whole system — to act with the combined military strength of all of them against any recalcitrant nation.

When four years later President Wilson had brought this exact proposal, even to the word 'covenant,' to realization; when he was giving the last ounce of his strength to the insistence that the sanctions of Article X were 'the vital and essential part of the whole system,' Mr. Roosevelt was no longer living. At the moment, Mr. Roosevelt did not foresee his enemy in such a role. The 'dreadful wrong' done to Belgium, he thought, was 'really not quite so contemptible' as the 'short-sighted and timid inefficiency' of Mr. Wilson's acquiescence in this wrong, 'which we had solemnly undertaken to oppose.' The existence of any such solemn undertaking had escaped Mr. Roosevelt at the time, as it has escaped all later students, but consistency seldom trammelled the Rough Rider. Miss Addams's movement he could regard as 'silly and base,' an effort of 'foolish and noxious' women; but to this more enticing form of pacifism he now gave himself with abandon.

If Wilsonian neutrality made Mr. Roosevelt an internationalist, perhaps this Rooseveltian internationalism assisted to confirm Mr. Wilson in his neutrality. At any rate the President's Jackson Day address at Indianapolis on January 8 sounded like a direct reply to these noble excursions into the field of foreign entanglement.

I, for one, would prefer that our thoughts should not too often cross the ocean but should center themselves upon the policies and duties of the United States. If we think of the United States, when the time comes we shall know how this country can serve the world. I will borrow a very interesting phrase from a distinguished gentleman of my acquaintance and beg that you will keep your moral powder dry.

And with that one skillful shaft the President passed on to a long discussion of strictly domestic problems. Yet if the President kept his own moral powder dry, the indefatigable House did not. Whatever the newspapers might say, Colonel House knew that the military situation had reached a deadlock, and the ardor of the peacemaker burned as brightly within him as within Mr. Roosevelt. He had barely abandoned his third attempt in December before he was launching a fourth. He had now convinced himself that the Central Powers were ready for peace on terms at least favorable enough for the British to accept. There were, of course, the incorrigible French and Russians with their demands for territorial conquest; but perhaps, as he wrote to Page in January, Sir Edward could be induced to put pressure on them? Page might hint that if the Germans should make a peace offer which was not sympathetically received by the Entente 'neutral sentiment... would veer toward them.'

Colonel House, as always, underestimated the true depth and magnitude of his own suggestions. He was suffering from that fatal tendency of the negotiator to imagine that with a word here, a hint there and a few quiet little conversations over the coffee cups the destinies of peoples might be transformed and the mighty torrents of human history channelled to any desired end. He was in Washington on January 12, and in a twelve-minute talk with the President before dinner 'it was decided that I should go to Europe on January 30.... It was time to deal directly with the principals.' After dinner the President read aloud to the family gathering and Europe was not even mentioned again. It is another of the several instances which leave one wondering just how seriously the President took his unofficial ambassador.

Next day the irascible Spring Rice found himself again confronted by the House menace — which he supposed they had successfully laid the month before. But the new threat of peace proved easy to handle. Sir Cecil was 'sulky' and full of his grievances about our pro-German tendencies; and under this barrage the Colonel hastened to explain that he did not intend to discuss specific peace terms with the Germans. He was merely going to throw the 'great moral strength' of the United States behind 'a permanent settlement.' Sir Cecil not unnaturally cheered up at once. He insisted upon calling in Jusserand and Bakhmetieff (the Russian Ambassador); they in turn arrived in a 'violent' mood; in turn Colonel House brought them round by explaining the advantages of getting the United States to expose German treachery and unreliability — and the whole party was soon 'merry' and 'offering me every facility.' Thus simply had House's mission been transformed, even before it began, from an intervention for peace into an intervention on behalf of the Entente. And the President had so little understanding of, or so little interest in, the true problem that he could still let him go. The leave-taking was in fact of an affecting character, and Mr. Wilson showed his confidence in his friend by going down to the station himself to see him off. Colonel House duly sailed on January 30, in the Lusitania.

But Spring Rice was taking no chances. Far down below the Colonel's comfortable cabin there doubtless sailed with him the diplomatic pouch carrying the verbal torpedo which the Ambassador had paused to implant beneath the Colonel's happy enterprise. Jusserand, Bakhmetieff and the Belgian Minister, he advised Sir Edward, were all three convinced that whatever assurances House might have got from Bernstorff were 'simply part of the plan to get the Allies into assuming attitudes inconsistent with one another on the peace question.'

ii

While Colonel House, innocent of such suspicions, departed to work for peace, other forces continued no less busily to work in an opposite direction. Actual shipments of American munitions to the Allied battle lines were still negligible, but the contracts continued to roll in and the hopes to mount. On January 16 the Cunard liner Orduna sailed from New York carrying one hundred and fifty-five peaceable passengers and, lashed in full view upon her forward deck, two fourteen-inch guns consigned to Liverpool — some of the first fruits, it was believed, of the new activity in Mr. Schwab's little town of Bethlehem, Pennsylvania. In London only the day before Mr. Davison of J. P. Morgan & Co. had been receiving the Prime Minister's 'hearty thanks' for all that he had done to 'co-ordinate' British purchases in America. Mr. Lloyd George was no less appreciative; Lord Kitchener was in 'high spirits' and expressed to the American banker his 'great faith in the United States.' Mr. Davison, touched by such distinguished confidence, modestly declared that there were many more of his countrymen who would be glad to do as much for the Allies. The remark was snatched up for translation to a higher sphere; the King's Secretary asked permission to repeat it to the King himself.

If the munitions supply, moreover, was just beginning to develop, the more usual commodities were pouring into the Allied storehouses in ever greater volume. On the other hand, the control system which made sure that none got to Germany was taking rapid strides toward perfection. Officially the cotton trade to Germany was totally free of restriction — and indeed on January 9 a cargo of American cotton did actually arrive at Bremen. But the trade proceeded thereafter in the thinnest possible trickle; and cotton Senators continued to make strenuous and embarrassing protest. Inspired by the vivacious Secretary McAdoo, the Administration made one attempt to strike at what was really the heart of the whole difficulty — the utter dependence of American foreign commerce upon Allied shipping. A sweeping bill was introduced providing for the purchase and operation by the United States Government itself of a fleet of merchant vessels. The mere existence of such a fleet would have levelled almost the whole structure of the Allied trade controls. Instantly the Republican opposition (materially assisted, of course, by the loud threats and protests of the Allies) discerned here a proposal to buy, not ships but a war with the Entente. Worse than that, they likewise discerned a first entering wedge of government ownership, which was, naturally, a far more dreadful threat than war. Possibly it was this menace to the rights of property which concealed from them the absurdity of imagining that the Allies could ever go to war with their own supply base. But the fact that the interned German liners were almost the only ships available for purchase lent color to the war argument; the Republicans at last felt that they had a political issue which they could fight on, and (with no thought of partisan politics, as the great Elihu Root impressively explained) they set themselves to talk the Democratic ship bill to death.

Two final attempts were to be made by private citizens, under the concealed inspiration of the German Embassy, to break the blockade. To test this question of utilizing the interned German ships one of them, the Dacia, was bought by a bona fide American citizen, regularly transferred to American registry and despatched with a cotton cargo to Germany. The British at once announced that they would seize her as an enemy vessel. To test the Allied contention that food was not being denied illegally to the German civil population, the Wilhelmina, a ship of unquestionable American registry, was chartered by an American commission house, loaded with food and consigned to the firm's own representative, an American citizen, in Hamburg. Since there was even less ground in law for interfering with this steamer, the British press proclaimed the even more imperative necessity for stopping her. Had either test succeeded, as a matter of fact, it would have been next to impossible to reconstitute the blockade without admitted and flagrant violation of that 'international law' of which the Allies were the devoted defenders. But the American Government showed no real sign of making any determined fight in either case, strong though its position would have been had it done so. The Germans gave it up.[1]

If the United States thus permitted all her rights of trade with Germany to go by default, it remained only for the Germans to act themselves. Each fresh failure to defend our trade with the Central Powers, each fresh step toward placing our economic power at the service of the Entente, was simply another weight in the scales of calculation which all during the month of January were hanging balanced in the minds of the German authorities.

[1] Rightly, as the sequel showed. There was a lot of half-hearted correspondence; in the end the Wilhelmina's cargo was seized, though the British paid for it. The Dacia's fate was more curious. On Mr. Page's artful and singularly treasonable suggestion, the British allowed her to be captured not by themselves but by the French — who were still popular in the United States and with whom it would have been necessary to take up the whole question from the beginning. The State Department again sustained defeat.

Should they, or should they not, declare the great submarine war against 'English freight-space'?

Mr. Gerard was reporting that even the friendly Zimmermann Undersecretary of Foreign Affairs, seemed not to care whether there was trouble with the United States or not; the Yankees could hardly injure them more than they were doing already, and besides, if it came to a break, the German-Americans and the Irish would start a revolution. 'I thought he was joking, but he was actually serious.' At any rate, the Germans knew from the beginning that the submarine would mean trouble with America. Yet it was the British who had already declared the North Sea a 'war zone'; and having acquiesced in that, would not Mr. Wilson be compelled to acquiesce when the Germans made it one in earnest? On January 18 there was a conference at General Headquarters. Von Tirpitz by this time was eager; but the Foreign Office legalists — nervous now over Italy as well as the United States — were opposed. In the end the Kaiser dared not risk it — 'he must first get a clear political vision, etc.' Yet the sailors were too confident of their great weapon; there was too little in the American attitude and in the existing military position to outweigh them, if only half their hopes were justified. Two days after this indecisive conference Mr. Gerard, accurate and intelligent as always, was reporting that Germany would 'soon undoubtedly try to blockade England with submarines.'

In January, 1915, the economic life of Germany had been scarcely affected by the 'starvation war.' But the year-end statistics were coming in, and she knew, as a French naval writer has since dispassionately observed, 'that as the months went by the Allied action would become intensified.... She was still breathing normally, but was haunted by fears of suffocation; she beheld herself as it were a fortress already beset, a state of mind which was becoming an obsession.' Nor did the Allies, whatever humanitarian sentiments they might find it necessary to adopt in their legal argument with the United States, leave her in any doubt as to their purpose. In Paris Mr. Winston

Churchill, First Lord of the Admiralty, gave an exuberant interview:

> Germany is like a man throttled with a heavy gag. You know the effect of such a gag.... The effort wears out the heart, and Germany knows it. This pressure shall not be relaxed until she gives in unconditionally.

The sole question for the German statesmen was whether retaliation with their own kind of gag would prove effective enough to warrant the unavoidable risks of complication which it involved. How much could their little flotilla of submarines (numbering at that time only sixteen boats in active service) really accomplish? 'For the first time in history,' the British First Lord announced in this same interview, 'England can say, "The sea is free."'... Our most important victories never brought us security comparable with that which we enjoy today.' Unfortunately for the effect, two days before this statement appeared S.M.S. U–21, rising off the port of Liverpool, hundreds of miles behind the protecting screen of the British fleet, had sunk three British merchant steamers in swift succession. The next day, on the opposite side of England, another submarine sank three more merchantmen — all of them being torpedoed without warning, in flagrant violation of international law. Two more cargo ships had been destroyed, by more legal methods, off Havre and one off the Dutch coast a little earlier. It was in these days, it seems, that the Chancellor, Bethmann-Hollweg, became convinced.

With his assent the Chief of the Naval Staff, Admiral von Pohl, hastened to draw up the scheme. A proclamation was prepared declaring the waters around Great Britain to be a zone of war, in which belligerent merchantmen would be subject, after February 18, to being sunk on sight and neutrals must accept the risk of destruction through mistaken identity. Even for this latter and more dangerous clause Great Britain had offered some color of a precedent by warning neutral merchantmen against the risk from Allied patrols unless they 'strictly' obeyed Allied sailing directions. If this concept of a maritime war zone could be made to stand at all, moreover, it must surely require that neutrals would proceed, as they did in land war zones, only at their own risk. The Chancellor, ill-informed as to the technical possibilities of the submarine, agreed to the proclamation. There remained only the Kaiser; and Admiral von Pohl now 'took the Kaiser by storm.' The War Lord was to inspect the fleet at Wilhelmshaven on February 4; and on the boat journey through the harbor to the flagship the confident Admiral secured the fateful decision upon which so much history was to hang.

Barely twenty-four hours later the newspapers of the United States were blazing with the headline: 'Germany Proclaims a War Zone.' At the precise moment when American resentment against the British trade controls might conceivably have produced some tangible result (if it was ever to do so) the Germans had created a diversion in which all thought of the trade controversy was soon to be swallowed up and lost.

iii

It is true that the first reception was one of comparative calm. This was partly, no doubt, because it was still so difficult for anyone to conceive (after six month's study of the war through Allied eyes) that the Entente arms were other than invincible. There were some who were outraged. 'This is inconceivable,' Mr. Frederic R. Coudert, the distinguished international lawyer, exclaimed to the reporters. 'An absolutely unprecedented stroke of barbarism!... Such an atrocity as this is not in any way justified by law or morality.' Yet even Mr. Coudert supposed that it merely indicated the depths of 'desperation' to which the Central Powers had been reduced; while most adopted the view of the Allied spokesmen that the thing was technically too absurd for serious consideration. In New York, Baltimore and other seaports the representatives of the British shipping companies 'were inclined to treat the whole matter as a bluff. "They can't get away with it," "Business as usual," "No suspension of sailings" — these are some of the remarks made by officials of the trans-atlantic lines.' There was even a cable from Liverpool, where the Lusitania (bearing Colonel House) was expected. No alarm, it said, was felt for that great ship; the authorities were confident that the big, fast liners were in no danger from submarines. At the State Department a few days later reporters were told that the United States would probably make no protest. Comparison showed the German war zone decree to be very like the earlier British one, and 'it dawned upon the officials here today that the German Government had executed a rather neat and clever counter diplomatic stroke.'

In the meanwhile Colonel House's mind was upon higher things. Watching the cold, grey leagues of the North Atlantic rolling endlessly away from the Lusitania's decks, he was struck by a happy inspiration about that troublesome disarmament difficulty. It was simplicity itself! At the peace conference all major nations should merely agree to cease the manufacture of munitions for ten years; armies and navies would thus remain as they were, eliminating the obstinate problem of relative strengths, while with time everything would grow 'automatically obsolete' and there would be the end of the whole business. And the money saved would pay the war debts. Unhappily, as they came in under the Irish coast the Colonel's mind was recalled to less transcendental realms. The passengers were full of the new submarine war; approaching St. George's Channel they noticed, with mingled emotions, the boats being uncovered and swung out, and then the sudden appearance at the Lusitania's monkey gaff of the Stars and Stripes! Colonel House discreetly omitted to observe this latter phenomenon himself, but others did and there were big stories about the stratagem in the American newspapers. It was a sudden suggestion that there might, after all, be more complications in this submarine affair than had at first appeared; more than that, it lent color to the German contention that they could not guarantee the safety of neutral ships in the war zone because the Allies were misusing neutral flags.

Our pro-Ally press proved equal even to this situation. If the Lusitania had been compelled to misuse our flag, the Philadelphia *Ledger* severely observed, the 'one effect' should be 'to provoke an immediate declaration against the barbarous policy which Germany proposes to enter upon.' At the State Department they were less biassed and more logical; unfortunately, all they saw in the flag episode was an opening for a conventionally adroit move in the routine chess game of diplomacy. On February 10 a stiff note was despatched to Germany:

> If the commanders of German vessels of war should act upon the presumption that the flag of the United States was not being used in good faith and should destroy on the high seas an American vessel or the lives of American citizens, it would be difficult for the Government of the United States to view the act in any other light than as an indefensible violation of neutral rights.

Thus flatly — and far too hastily — was the war zone concept rejected. To the argument that the Germans had been authorized to adopt it by our acquiescence when it was invented by the British, we replied upon the technically correct, if practically irrelevant, ground that we hadn't acquiesced. Were we not, indeed, still protesting British illegalities? And to prove it another note was despatched on the same day to Great Britain, energetically protesting the misuse of our flag. This protest was of course to go the way of all our others; yet in the German note we had added — incautiously, even recklessly — that we would hold Germany 'to a strict accountability.' It was a phrase which President Wilson was later to have cause to regret.

The trouble was that nobody really appreciated the importance of what even Mr. Wilson called the Germans' 'extraordinary threat to destroy commerce.' Our diplomatic pieces were simply pushed about the board in accordance with the rules; it seemed a sound bit of play, and if it was also totally neglectful of the grave problem in statesmanship which the German note had raised before American policy, who had time to notice that? The New York *Times* thought it showed 'our diplomacy at its best.' Both notes, another commentator observed, were 'heartily approved by our people' for their 'fearlessly impartial' neutrality. Both sides had been slapped equally upon the wrist; and when presently the February 18 deadline came and went, nothing very much happened — except that the British authorities moved promptly and ably to exploit the situation to their own advantage.

Outwardly the British spokesmen bent all their energies to denouncing the barbarity of the submarine campaign. As a matter of fact, however, it had come as a godsend. The calculations of the British Admiralty convinced them that the Germans as yet had too few submarines to make any serious inroads upon their commerce if only the merchant ships would risk the inevitable sinkings. On the other hand, as Mr. Winston Churchill has put it, 'we were sure that [the submarine war] would offend and perhaps embroil the United States; and that in any case our position for enforcing the blockade would be greatly strengthened. We looked forward to a sensible abatement of the pressure which the American Government was putting upon us.' On this realistic appreciation of the situation they immediately extended their great project to starve the German civilians into submission. On February 12 there suddenly went forward the complete answer, which we had been awaiting since December 28, to our formal and vigorous protests against the British trade restrictions. It was a long and learned argument; naturally it conceded nothing — and was more or less overlooked in the excitement. And on March 1 Ambassadors Spring Rice and Jusserand presented at the State Department two Notes Verbales, flatly prohibiting all further neutral trade either to or from the German Empire.

The offshore blockade of Germany, which the Allies had for so long been prevented from announcing by the fact that an offshore blockade was illegal, had now been decreed. It frankly prohibited the importation of all goods — contraband, conditional contraband and free list alike — while it also prohibited exports from

Germany, something which the contraband rules in theory could not touch. That the new measure was a violation of international law and a denial of established neutral rights the Allies were forced to admit; they justified it only as legitimate reprisal against Germany's prior violation in the declaration of the submarine war. The American Government was once more, of course, vociferously to protest; equally of course the protests were to be unavailing, and from this time onward the United States was to lose all rights to direct trade of any kind with the Central Powers.

It is easy to see in retrospect that the situation had reached a point at which it could only be dealt with as a whole and on terms of the broadest statesmanship. Unfortunately, so multitudinous were the rank trees of controversy surrounding the State Department's lawyers that they were unable to see the jungle in which they were involved. Mr. Bryan seems to have striven for the detached view with more common sense than the others, but the ground was unfamiliar to him and besides, nobody had any respect for Mr. Bryan. And at the White House President Wilson's hand lay strangely lax upon the controls; for the President had largely confided his foreign policy to the management of Colonel House. The President did nothing. Colonel House did worse than nothing. It was not upon the pressing practical issues of the war that the Colonel's eyes were fastened but upon the remoter glories of peace. If the State Department failed to see the wood for the trees, the Colonel even more lamentably failed to see the trees for the wood — and the Colonel was to prove but an indifferent woodsman.

From Berlin Mr. Gerard had been doing his best. On February 11 he cabled:

> It is my conviction ... that if a reasonable peace proposition were offered Germany very many men of influence would be inclined to use their efforts to induce Germany to accept the proposition.... If peace does not come immediately a new and protracted phase of the war will commence.... It will be fatal to hesitate or wait a moment; success is dependent on immediate action.

Mr. Gerard saw clearly that with the military advantage lying everywhere with the German armies, any practicable peace proposal must at most represent a draw. If it was peace which Washington wanted, it could only get it by forcing both sides to cry quits; if our government did not wish to put pressure on the Allies, then it must keep its hands off altogether. Washington did neither. It was delighted with the magic 'possibilities' opened by Mr. Gerard's cable — and largely missed their implications. The Ambassador wanted action. What he got was Mr. Wilson's instructions to refer everything to Colonel House, who had been 'fully instructed and commissioned' to act 'in all these matters.'

Indeed, Mr. Gerard had already done so. 'Germany will make no peace proposals,' he had written the Colonel in London, 'but I am sure if a reasonable peace is proposed *now* (a matter of days, even hours) it would be accepted.' And to Washington he cabled urgently: 'Yours about Colonel House received. Favorable moment is passing'; but if House could bring a 'secret, reasonable' offer to Berlin he thought it would be accepted. The offer must represent realities, however; the Allies could get the evacuation of Belgium, Gerard thought, but no indemnity, and would have to pay in colonial territory and perhaps in cash for the evacuation of Northern France. Entrusted to Colonel House's hands, unfortunately, the whole matter simply came to a dead stop, in the soft yet resistant medium of Allied statesmanship, like an express train in a snowdrift.

For days the Colonel had been busily 'negotiating' in the highest circles in London. He had been lunching on terms of the happiest intimacy with Grey, or dropping in at the Foreign Minister's house in Eccleston Square to discuss 'nature, solitude, Wordsworth' before getting down to the business of diplomacy. He had been quietly seeing all the best people. He had been sympathetic; it was unnecessary, as Grey quickly sensed, 'to spend much time putting our case to him.' And he had managed 'from the first' to leave Sir Edward 'in no doubt... that he held German militarism responsible for the war.' Thus the Colonel gave away his hand.

The Allies could not rudely repel the successive 'peace offensives' from the United States. Their problem was to retain our sympathy, and develop us as potential military support, for their own nationalistic war aims, many of which they dared not even avow. They had to do so, moreover, while actively suppressing our commercial rights. Our interest in peace and humanity, however, was their one great means for solving this difficult problem, and when Colonel House began by convincing them that he held German militarism to be responsible for the war, everything was easy. Deftly they sought to draw him into committing the United States to such specific terms of peace as would represent a settlement not only 'just' but also satisfactory from the practical viewpoint of the Entente. Here the Colonel was shy; it did not matter, however, for there was a less direct approach. From the beginning 'there was one thing Grey was fairly insistent upon,... that we should come into some general guaranty for world-wide peace' on the conclusion of the war. This accorded with House's own train of thought, and though he was scarcely empowered to commit the American people to the radical departure from their traditional policy which it must involve, he seems to have given them encouragement.

Unhappily, it was in the midst of all these sympathetic felicities that Mr. Gerard's urgent suggestions arrived. There was also an invitation from Zimmermann for House to come to Berlin — and a hint of peace in it. Should House make the visit? The moment had come to strike, and strike hard — if it was peace that the Colonel was trying to negotiate. But the Colonel had been too skillfully swathed by this time in the British viewpoint. What he actually did was to show these communications to Sir Edward. They must, Sir Edward instantly declared, be taken up with the Prime Minister. Asquith solemnly combined with Grey in rejecting the very idea of any such terms as those hinted at by Berlin; both men strongly advised the Colonel against making a visit to Germany — until Germany had suffered a few severe military reverses! And House, dutifully bowing to this eminent opinion, informed his principal in the White House of his objections against going on to Berlin.

President Wilson rather abruptly awoke, and there came a sharp cable:

> If an impression were to be created in Berlin that you were to come only when the British Government thought it an opportune time to come, you might be regarded when you reach there as their spokesman rather than mine.

It was obvious; but the amateur diplomat failed to see the unwisdom of placing American policy at the command of Downing Street, and the only result was a long letter (on February 23) warning the President that the Germans were trying to use him. For the rest, nothing could be done at the moment. If Sir Edward knew of this letter, as he doubtless did, he must have permitted himself a quiet smile at the ease with which Colonel House had once again been rendered harmless.

In the meanwhile, moreover, the peace question had got badly entangled in the more immediate issue of the submarine war. In spite of the adroit correctness of our simultaneous notes on the submarine and on the misuse of our flag, this sharp practical matter would not down. In Washington Count Bernstorff was imploring Mr. Bryan to take some action toward warning American citizens and American ships that the war zone was really dangerous. The Secretary of State was 'incredulous' and thought the Germans were merely bluffing; but Ambassador Gerard in Berlin did not. While pressing for peace with one hand he was pressing with the other for some kind of workable compromise of the trade and submarine questions that would preserve the United States from the involvements now clearly threatening. For Mr. Gerard, as even House presently had to admit, was 'different from some of our representatives, inasmuch as his point of view is wholly American'; and indeed, one cannot fail to be struck by the extent to which every suggestion for some kind of resolute and practical action seemed to originate with this political appointee, whom our great brains of diplomacy were so much inclined to patronize. The Ambassador now cabled his own hopes that:

You can force England [by threatening an arms embargo] to permit foodstuffs and raw material to enter Germany, in which case proposed blockade will be withdrawn and in all probability I can arrange that no further reference will be made to the question of export of arms and ammunition. If you cannot arrange with England, then I can arrange convoy of American ships by American war vessels... under our guarantee to carry no contraband.

Thus stirred, the Department ordered Page (on February 16) to work for an agreement not to withhold food-stuffs, at least, from the German civil population. 'A policy,' he was instructed to suggest, 'which seeks to keep food from non-combatants, from the civil population of a whole nation, will create a very unfavorable impression.... It will certainly create... a strong revulsion of feeling in this country.' But all that this produced was Mr. Page's announcement, clearly more in sorrow for the Department's ignorance than in anger against it, that 'I do not see a ray of hope for any agreement between Germany and England whereby England will permit food to enter Germany under any condition.' This was received in Washington on the evening of February 20. An hour later the State Department despatched to Great Britain and to Germany its own official suggestion of a compromise. It was plainly useless to wait upon Mr. Page.

Briefly, we proposed that all foodstuffs imported from the United States be distributed in Germany to the civil population alone by an American agency similar to the Belgian Relief. Great Britain would agree not to interfere with such shipments. Germany would abandon the use of submarines against merchant vessels except by the normal process of visit and search. Both sides would refrain from the indiscriminate sowing of mines and the misuse of neutral flags.

Naturally, it came to nothing. Germany replied on the 1st of March; she would accept, but only on condition that raw materials were included under the same terms as foodstuffs. The reply of the British, on March 15, was an indignant rejection of the whole affair. With an abler representation at London the issue, despite the German reservation, might have been pressed to some sort of adjustment which would not only have tended to right the sinking balance of our neutrality but would have regularized a situation plainly loaded with peril to ourselves. But the chance, like so many others, was lost. March 1, moreover, the day of the German reply, was also the day chosen by the Allies to declare their own illegal blockade. The British, like the Germans, did not want to compromise the submarine war. It had proved far too useful to them.

Nothing was done. In London the liberal British journalist, Mr. F. W. Hirst, frankly told House that the President should take an active stand against the blockade. Mr. Hirst stressed the patent fact that by embargoing all exports to all belligerents, Mr. Wilson could force the British Government 'to do practically what he desired'; he urged that the President should 'lay down a new code of international law and insist upon every nation living up to it.' House contented himself with pointing out to Mr. Hirst, in a superior way, 'some of the difficulties' this would involve. In Washington Spring Rice was surprised and shocked to hear Mr. Bryan speak 'in severe language of British disregard for the law of nations.' The bucolic Secretary actually 'seemed to regard the torpedo and the prize-court with equal abhorrence,' and appeared almost hurt when the Ambassador spoke harshly of the 'deep and painful impression' which such heresy would produce upon London. But Spring Rice was to find comfort with his intimates among the Republican leaders, who knew so much more about foreign affairs than the ignorant Democrats. Mr. Elihu Root, the great patriot and statesman, soothed him in private by explaining that the Administration's foreign policy was in reality simply a play to the galleries of domestic politics.

The press was hardly more helpful than the Republican confidants of Spring Rice. In a column editorial upon the legalities, the *Times* managed completely to miss the real point involved and so solemnly to endorse the lawfulness of a measure which the British themselves had never claimed to be other than a departure from established law. But the *Times* had long been rather more pro-Ally than the Allies — so much so, in fact, as to lead to a Congressional investigation, which gave the opportunity indignantly and righteously to deny that it was taking British gold. This fact having been established, it occurred to no one, of course, to ask the more important question as to whether it was taking British ideas, and loftily it continued to do so. Many other papers, it is true, did begin to show a certain irritation as something of the meaning and extent of the Allied interdictions upon our commerce began to come home. Through March and April the *Literary Digest* was able to cull some pretty sharp comment from all parts of the country. Yet the editors generally appeared to feel that nothing much could be done about it; there came no clear lead from Washington, and the opportunity to take matters into our own hands and insist upon some regularization of the war at sea slipped fatally away.

In London, of course, Colonel House was as diligent as usual, and the new issue did give him an opportunity of reviving his project of a trip to Germany. It was in connection with the submarine threat that Sir Edward and his secretary, Sir William Tyrrell (House's old friend and tutor of the year before) had let drop the suggestion that a permanent guaranty of complete freedom of the seas to all merchant ships in war time might well be included in the peace settlement.[1] House had seized upon this idea; and presently a letter came from Zimmermann hinting that it might serve as a basis for the compromise of the sea war while hostilities were still in progress. The British now had their own blockade established, and had little reason to fear any rashness on the part of the Colonel. Sir Edward agreed that perhaps the time had come for House to visit Germany; and thus authorized the

---

[1] This was the seed from which there grew the Freedom of the Seas included by Mr. Wilson in the Fourteen Points. Again one observes an important element of 'Wilsonism' originating, not with Mr. Wilson, but in the necessities of Allied diplomacy.

peace emissary set forth again, in the second week of March, upon his altruistic travels.

He made little progress in Paris. The unreasonable French (whom House appears to have regarded rather in the light of engaging but difficult children) were insisting upon all sorts of grandiose territorial conquests far beyond the nobler peace terms which House and Grey had been discussing. He went on to Berlin, arriving on March 20 to confront an even more baffling situation. Zimmermann actually turned out to be almost as noble and as peace-loving as Sir Edward himself. He found Rathenau on that first evening 'almost pathetic' in his urgings that the United States should not cease her peace efforts. Everywhere he heard the same note. Yet some strange obstacle persisted. Could it be that 'the people in both Germany and England have been led to expect more than is possible of realization'?

On the day that Colonel House reached Berlin the White Star liner Adriatic sailed from New York with one hundred and fifty armored cars for the Allied battle lines and three hundred passengers. (W. E. Corey, a former president of the United States Steel Corporation, and his wife were among them, on their way 'to look after their château near Versailles.') The Orduna sailed the same day with one hundred and ninety-five passengers and two more fifteen-inch rifles from Bethlehem lashed on her main deck, to say nothing of quantities of lighter ordnance and shell-cases in the hold. In Berlin they were telling Colonel House that if peace was really what the United States wanted, the quickest way to get it would be to embargo munitions exports. The Colonel thought the idea the sheerest 'nonsense' and went on with his negotiation. He dropped the seed about the freedom of the seas on receptive ground; but as to peace, the scales were at last falling from his eyes. It was not peace for which the fighting peoples yearned; it was peace with victory — and that was a different matter. 'I am somewhat at a loss as to what to do next,' he wrote the President; and finally after a week of conversations, 'I leave sadly disappointed.'

'Some way has to be thought out,' he wrote the President on the eve of his departure, 'to let the Governments down easy with their people. That is almost, if not quite, our hardest problem.' In the Irish Sea on the day before the liner Arabic, carrying two hundred passengers, was chased into Liverpool by a submarine, which fired two torpedoes at her. Fortunately, both missed. But the day after, March 28, the liner Falaba, outward bound to West Africa with one hundred and forty-seven passengers and thirteen tons of ammunition, was torpedoed off the Scilly Isles. One hundred and four lives were lost — among them that of Mr. Leon Thrasher, an American citizen.

Was it only with the foreign peoples that the Colonel's problem lay? All the irritation over the British blockade was forgotten in the cry of outrage which burst from our astounded editors. 'Piracy,' 'barbarism run mad,' 'a triumph of horror,' 'assassination,' 'shocking bloodthirstiness,' 'massacre,' 'a crime against humanity' were some of the phrases with which the pro-Ally newspapers of the Northeast struggled to express their indignation over this relatively small addition to the toll of human life (a daily five thousand or so) which the war was taking week in and week out. Perhaps they were right to be shocked. There was less reason, however, for surprise that the Germans had thus reacted — as they had given full warning that they would — against a blockade which the Allies had declaredly adopted in order to starve Germany into surrender.

iv

Before Congress rose in March the Republican patriots in the Senate (reinforced by seven conservative Democrats) had talked Mr. McAdoo's ship purchase bill to death with prodigies of oratorical heroism. Senator Smoot offered himself up for eleven and one-half solid hours upon the altars of patriotism and party; Senator Burton talked 'without visible effort' for thirteen hours on end, and upon one occasion cots had to be brought into the

Senate cloak-room to receive the exhausted forms of these warriors as they sank down from their superhuman exploits. The nation was at length saved for private ownership and the bill successfully destroyed; but the arms embargo proposal, more or less by accident, was dragged down in the wreck. It is quite possible that the embargo might have passed had it ever been brought to a vote; as it was, the ship filibuster blocked the way and Spring Rice could breathe again, though uneasily.

For the Germans, on the other hand, the failure of the embargo — the failure, indeed, of every American action or representation which might have disadvantaged the Allies — was but added proof that whatever they were to get they must get by their own exertions. Their propaganda bureau redoubled its activities. Unweariedly the interviews and apologia and assaults upon the Allies flowed from Dr. Dernburg's pen, while Herr Albert raised the money wherewith to disseminate them or secretly prompted Americans of German sympathies to take up the cause. This was, after all, hardly more than Sir Gilbert Parker was doing for the Entente; while Dr. Dernburg — an official and acknowledged spokesman of his government — was simply giving the American public from the German side a fraction of the sort of thing which it was getting from the Allies with every newspaper cable. But his activities seemed very reprehensible to our impartial pro-Ally press. Our editors consistently overlooked the critical importance of the Allied censorship, which should have been their first concern. Schreiner of the Associated Press estimated that at this time 'nearly three-quarters of the despatches written by American correspondents in Central Europe' were perishing under the shears of the British censors. It was scarcely unreasonable of the Germans in the United States to try to make good something of the deficiency.

Unfortunately for their cause, however, they did not stop with propaganda. In order to check the growing stream of munitions, the German Embassy was beginning to buy up and hold such supplies. Count Bernstorff and his military attaché, Captain Franz von Papen — for whom Fate was to reserve so curious a destiny — were organizing the Bridgeport Projectile Company, ingeniously designed to take shell orders from the Allies which would never be filled, as well as to pre-empt available supplies of machinery, material and labor. There was nothing illegal in this; and Count Bernstorff declares that throughout he was careful to keep his own operations within the limits of American neutrality law. He did not, however, have full control over his more exuberant military and naval attachés; while he had none at all, of course, over the occasional exploits conceived by wandering German patriots in the United States. It was one of these, Werner Horn, who on February 2 tried unsuccessfully to blow up the international railway bridge at Vanceboro, Maine, over which he supposed that Canadian munitions were being shipped for export through American ports. The affair was fantastic enough; it created a sensation at the time, however, and was later to be remembered. More serious were the activities of a young German naval reserve officer, Franz von Rintelen, who arrived secretly on April 3 with some sort of official mission to do something about the munitions exports. Captain Rintelen was not discovered until afterward, but his presence soon began to be felt. Was there really a vast German conspiracy in the United States? As early as January the New York *Herald* had been working up a nice little scandal over the false passports allegedly being forged by von Papen and his naval colleague, Captain Boy-Ed, for the use of returning reservists, and it helped to implant the conspiracy idea. Such things, however, were but the first distant mutterings of the later storm.

But early lightnings in another quarter were now developing impressively. In December the President had been severe about preparedness; yet as Congress worked onward through the winter it was proving an enticing subject. New preparedness organizations were springing up beside the National Security League, under the delighted patronage and encouragement of General Wood. He 'supplied them with irrefutable data'; he lent them his offices; he even lent them his aide, Captain Gordon Johnston. One of them was the American Legion,[1] which proposed to enroll 250,000 young men to serve voluntarily as the Army reserve which Congress cravenly refused to provide for. Mr. Roosevelt and his four sons instantly joined. Indeed, as early as the preceding autumn Mr. Roosevelt had been plotting at the Harvard Club in New York (something of a center for these elegant, if subversive, movements) to raise a 'Roosevelt Division of mounted infantry' all his own, and lead it to battle in the event of war — whether with Mexico or Germany being a matter of indifference. The brief glories of San Juan Hill were flowering again in T. R.'s imagination, upon a grander scale. By the middle of February he was swearing the newspapermen to secrecy about it; he was deep in strategy and tactics with old Rough Riders and young military men; he was even riding forth from Sagamore Hill to do command problems over the peaceful scenery of the North Shore of Long Island. But there was one penetrating comment upon these martial exercises: 'Mrs. Roosevelt chuckled. "Both you men," she said, "are exactly like two small boys playing soldiers. It's a lovely game."'

It was; and the preparedness agitation rolled onward. Mr. Garrison, the conservative Secretary of War, was irritated by General Wood's gross insubordination, but he was infected all the same. One cannot avoid the thought that Mr. Daniels, the Secretary of the Navy, was more interested in preparedness against the Republicans than against Teutonic invasion; but at all events he began to lend encouragement to the idea of bigger and better naval appropriations. By March the American Legion was filling the headlines and becoming a subject of controversy. Mr. Garrison ordered General Wood to drop it (an order not exactly obeyed) but put the scholars of the War College to work upon 'a complete and exhaustive study of military policy.' Various books began to appear describing imaginary wars in which unprepared America suffered all manner of disastrous and humiliating defeats — usually

[1] Not to be confused with the present American Legion.

at the hands of Germany. They proved a popular and dramatic form of propaganda. 'America Fallen; A Sequel to the European War' came out in April. It recounted, with a wealth of fascinating and convincing technical detail, how Germany was at last forced to make peace in 1916, and how she immediately thereafter fell upon the United States, brushed our Navy and Army aside without difficulty and compelled us to pay the indemnity which had been assessed upon her by the Entente. A public without the benefit of later sad experience may be forgiven for not realizing the impossibility of collecting war costs even from allies, to say nothing of defeated enemies; but it does seem that some of our now numerous military experts might have noted the obvious military — as well as political and social — fallacies in this demonstration. None did; and by April Mr. Garrison was already thinking of resigning from an Administration which was 'too Bryanistic' and too pacifistically cold to preparedness. General Wood, on the other hand, was already thinking of making himself President on the 'defence' issue.

Mr. Roosevelt had long since confided to Senator Lodge his considered opinion that 'this Administration is the very worst and most disgraceful we have ever known.' Unhappily, his benighted countrymen still obstinately refused to agree with him; and Mr. Lane, the Secretary of the Interior, felt that the President, though weak in the conservative citadels of the Northeast, was 'strong west of the Alleghanies' and 'growing daily in the admiration of the people.' On the surface, indeed, matters were being handled adroitly enough; the dangers all lay hidden beneath. If Mr. Roosevelt despised the President for his virtues, the public too easily applauded him for his omissions. Yet their first consequences were proving unexpectedly satisfactory. Spring was coming on the Western Front, bringing new drives and new slaughter. Again the bloody mills were grinding; but the process was exerting a more powerful suction than before upon American farms and factories, drawing out their produce and pumping back a rejuvenating stream of dollars. As the serried ranks of Europe's youth went down again into their agony, a corresponding breath of life was felt in American business undertakings. In March American sub-contractors got the largest single munitions order which had yet been placed in the United States; on April 1 the New York Stock Exchange lifted the last of the restrictions which had survived from the closure. The last trace of the war panic had vanished; the dollar was above par and the future was suffused with a rosy glow — a far happier tint than that dark, clotted crimson of which it was the reflection.

Spring was coming. J. P. Morgan and Company were getting their Allied purchasing bureau in running order. Mr. Morgan himself had run across to England in March to discuss, it was thought, the big loans which would soon be necessary, with sterling dropping so fast, if the bureau was to continue to purchase and so continue to shower its blessings upon the American wage-earner and capitalist. Even Spring Rice was in a more philosophical mood. They must be patient with Mr. Wilson, he was reporting to Sir Edward, and remember that 'to be re-elected... is his principal preoccupation.' 'It is, I think, useless,' the Ambassador went on, 'to depend on these people for help or for practical sympathy'; but cotton and copper were fortunately going up, there seemed to be 'a very general prosperity' and one therefore had little to fear from the dollar-chasing Yankee.

Spring was coming. The military geniuses in their cloistered headquarters were once more filled with their illusions of smashing victory, and civilian hopes of peace were again being trampled beneath the feet of the marching columns. Italy was now seen to be upon the verge. Passing through Rome Colonel House had heard the rumors. In Paris in the April weather he found the whole place full of hate, hope and territorial ambitions, and was finally forced to admit that 'for the moment it is impossible to harmonize' the fiercely clashing war aims. He summed up the sad truth for Mr. Bryan: 'Everybody seems to want peace, but nobody is willing to concede enough to get it.' It was the insoluble dilemma (had he only known it) which had confronted him in

the happy spring of 1914, in that remote age before Sarajevo; now
twenty years later, after all the misery and wealth poured out
upon its solution, it is the insoluble dilemma still. Colonel House,
of course, saw it in no such gloomy terms as that; but 'for the
moment' he gave it up and went back to London to take consola-
tion with Sir Edward.

Here a fresh disappointment awaited him. Even the Freedom
of the Seas idea collapsed when the British took the inexplicable
notion that it was a German proposal. As a means of adjusting
the submarine and trade questions it was simply 'not a fair proposition'; though after the war was over it might be practicable —
provided Germany would enter 'some League of Nations where
she would give and accept the same security as other nations gave
and accepted.' Thus was the whole episode used to bring House
back again to the idea of American action to enforce peace on
Germany — as delicately as if Sir Edward had planned it all
when he first sent House to Berlin. Perhaps he had. It was in
these same days that he was lending every encouragement to the
new peace league enthusiasts in America, assuring them, through
intermediaries, that he was 'anxious to have the United States
come out strong for such a league' and was even 'perfectly willing
to stand for the use of force in connection with it.'

But this ended the Freedom of the Seas as far as the existing
struggle went; and the submarine war — that jagged rock in the
channel down which American policy was steering — remained
unseen and unprovided for. Yet the Germans were in bitter
earnest. On April 16 their official communiqué announced that
'a captured French officer asserted that French artillery had
unlimited quantities of American ammunition at its disposal.'
On April 3 von Tirpitz was at G.H.Q. 'The Kaiser,' he noted,
'has really given in now and has granted absolutely free action to
the submarines.' In Washington Count Bernstorff, more and more
convinced that the American Government 'still underestimated
the dangers of the situation,' considered taking action on his own
accord. About the middle of April he 'held a meeting in New

York with representatives of the other German administrative departments, and in view of the great responsibility incumbent upon us we resolved, on the motion of Dr. Dernburg, to issue a warning to the press in the form usually adopted for shipping notices.' An advertisement was drawn up. 'Travellers,' it began, 'intending to embark on the Atlantic voyage are reminded that a state of war exists....' It was intended to appear on Saturday, April 24, and succeeding Saturdays thereafter. But there was a hitch, and in the end it missed the April 24 insertion.

No doubt the motive was more to frighten away the traffic than to avert the danger of complications with the United States. Yet after the death of Mr. Thrasher in the Falaba anyone might have seen that this danger was imminent. At least one other man did see it. On April 23 Mr. Bryan, more and more troubled by the course which events were taking, sat down to write a long and serious letter for the President. He noted the contrast between the attitude we had taken with the Allies and that which we were increasingly adopting toward Germany. He continued:

> If we oppose the use of submarines against merchantmen we will lay down a law for ourselves as well as for Germany. If we admit the right of the submarine to attack merchantmen but condemn their peculiar act or class of acts as inhuman, we will be embarrassed by the fact that we have not protested against Great Britain's defence of the right to prevent foods reaching non-combatant enemies....
>
> I venture to suggest an alternative, an appeal to the nations at war to consider terms of peace. We cannot justify waiting until both sides, or even one side, asks for mediation. As a neutral we cannot have in mind the wishes of one side more than the wishes of the other side.

But President Wilson had declared that he would hold the Germans to 'strict accountability.' Mr. Bryan's alternative must have seemed fantastic to him. Yet it was actually the alternative to which Mr. Wilson was himself desperately to resort a year and a half later — when the time for it had long gone by.

Already April was running out; spring was well advanced and there were the first lovely hints of summer in the air. In the long scars that ran across the face of Europe the first bloody 'failures' of the new campaign had been recorded, and the diligent impresarios of the staffs were preparing more. In peaceful America Mr. Owen Wister was already 'hard at work preparing to write "The Pentecost of Calamity"' — that dreadful piece of dripping invective against the Germans which was to have an enormous sale when it came out, though it is forgotten now. In Washington Mr. Wilson was debating what to do over the Falaba matter. And in the cold, grey waters off the west of Britain two submarines were working southward, tossed upon the great Atlantic seas. On April 28 one of them sank an Admiralty collier off the Hebrides; next day she sank another off County Mayo; on the 30th her sister sank a third collier and a merchantman off the southwest corner of Ireland, just where the great steamer track from the United States led in on the way to Liverpool.

On the last day of April the pennants were flying at the submarine base at Wilhelmshaven as another U-boat slipped her moorings and passed down to sea, going to the relief of these two. Senior Lieutenant Schwieger conned her out through Borkum Roads and prepared to take up the long, perilous journey to the Western Ocean. He was one of the ablest officers in the service and is said to have been one of the most popular — a youngish man of good education, afterward remembered by his friends for his gaiety, his 'urbane courtesy' and his 'kindness toward the officers and men under him.' The land sank and was gone; the escorting destroyer left them and the U-20 wallowed on alone, under routine orders to raid whatever enemy shipping she might find. There is no evidence of more specific instructions; and apparently it was only by coincidence that at about the same hour compositors in the New York newspaper offices were setting up an advertisement for insertion next day. 'Notice!' it said, 'Travellers intending to embark on the Atlantic voyage are reminded that a state of war exists....' They set the signature: 'Imperial German Embassy, Washington, D.C., April 22, 1915.' Then they boxed it up in some heavy black rules and put it to bed beside the customary notice in which the Cunard Line announced the sailing of the Lusitania on the morrow.

Next day, Saturday, May 1, there was the usual cheerful crowd at the pier to see her off. It was an ordinary sailing, like those of peace time. The crowd waved to the passengers as she backed into the stream, and the passengers — there were 1257 on board — waved back. Many of them had seen Count Bernstorff's notice that morning, but few gave it any serious thought. They were warned, it had told them, that British vessels were 'liable to destruction' and that 'travellers sailing in the war zone on ships of Great Britain and her allies do so at their own risk.' It was just German bluff and swagger; it could not, anyway, apply to that great and swift ship, protected by her speed, her many bulkheads, her distinguished (and rather heavily American) passenger list and by the power of the Royal Navy. Indeed, some who had taken the trouble to ask about the submarine risk when they bought their tickets had been readily assured that there was none — the Lusitania would have naval convoy through the war zone.

The liner, with just under two thousand souls in all on board, and with forty-two hundred cases of rifle ammunition in her hold besides some empty shell-cases and other supplies for the Allied armies, passed down the bay and out by Ambrose. Off the Scilly Isles that same day three more ships were attacked by submarines; of this the passengers, of course, were ignorant. They were unaware of the four vessels destroyed in the preceding three days near the waters through which they were to pass, and they naturally knew nothing of the submarine which had left Wilhelmshaven the day before. Their lives, moreover, were in the keeping of the Cunard Line and the Royal Navy, and they had no worries. The voyage proved pleasant.

Captain Turner, the Lusitania's master, afterward testified that he had seen the warning notice, 'or something of the sort,' but had paid no attention to it. The New York offices of the line thought so little of the matter that they did not even trouble to report it when they cabled the usual notice of the sailing to the home office. The newspapers picked it up as something of a joke, however, and the London press had accounts of it. 'Berlin's Latest Bluff; Ridiculed in America' said a headline in the *Daily Telegraph*. The Lusitania held on her way, the passengers greatly enjoying the sunny weather and smooth seas. The U–20 also held on her way, dodging patrols and minefields or perhaps lying on the bottom as the racing screws of a destroyer went by over head. The consorts whom she was going to relieve continued their activities. On May 3 another steamer was destroyed; on May 4 — the Lusitania was in mid-Atlantic by that time — a submarine was seen off the Fastnet, the usual landfall on the road from America. Rapidly these several events shaped themselves to their appointed conjunction; swiftly these little groups of lives — unconscious chessmen in the hands of the vast, impersonal processes of war and policy, of duty, habit and accident — were borne onward to the collision which was their destiny. And beyond and behind their drama the enormous, the unrealizable agony and horror of the Great War itself went on — with its roaring artillery, its flaming destruction, its tortured hospitals, its breadlines and bereavements, its lies, its hatreds and its heroisms — in the face of a statesmanship as impotent, in all countries, to control the gigantic tragedy as it now was to avert the little one.

In Washington there was more trouble. Of the three vessels attacked on May 1 off the Scillies one was the American tanker Gulflight, the first American-flag ship to fall victim to the torpedo. She did not sink, but three lives were lost and it meant another 'incident.' Less and less adequate did the legal talents of the State Department appear amid these strangely inescapable mazes. On May 2 Mr. Page in London was writing letters — he was so often writing letters! — in a thoughtful mood. 'Peace?' his pen asked the white paper. 'Lord knows when! The blowing up of a liner with American passengers may be the prelude. I almost expect such a thing.' The idea seems suddenly to have fascinated him, and in another letter he recurred to it: 'If a British liner full of American passengers be blown up, what will Uncle Sam do?

That's what's going to happen.' It seems odd that the thought had occurred to so few in the three months which had elapsed since the German declaration.

But it now began to appear that a distressing lot of questions about this business had been left unanswered. From Washington the President cabled House in London to ask advice about the Gulflight. 'I believe,' the Colonel primly replied, 'that a sharp note indicating your determination to demand full reparation would be sufficient in this instance. I am afraid a more serious breach may at any time occur.' This answer was cabled on May 5. The Lusitania was getting in toward Ireland by that time. The same day a sailing vessel was torpedoed and sunk off the Old Head of Kinsale. The U–20 had arrived upon her cruising ground.

The steamer track to Liverpool skirts the whole southern coast of Ireland. Fastnet Light, on its rock beyond Cape Clear at the southwest corner of the island, is the landfall; the Old Head of Kinsale, some forty miles farther along, is the next prominent headland, whence the usual course continues under the coast for another hundred miles to Coningbeg Lightvessel and so through St. George's Channel into Liverpool. Nothing was simpler for the submarines than to lie off these marks and gather in whatever might be coming along; and it was in just this way that they had been collecting their bag during the whole time that the Lusitania had been approaching. With the land to cut off escape on one side, it was an ideal ground for the U-boat's purposes — so long as the traffic continued to follow the beaten path instead of swinging right out into the open water between Ireland and Cornwall.

On the 6th of May the Lusitania was beginning to smell the land. That day Mr. Page was writing again: 'We all have the feeling here that more and more frightful things are about to happen.' That day Captain Schwieger sank two more steamers on the Liverpool track. In the Lusitania the passengers were interested to note that the lifeboats had been uncovered and swung out. It had become a formality as one approached the celebrated war zone; and it gave them a pleasantly exciting thrill, no doubt, to experience that faint, distant brush of the dark wings of war. But it amounted to nothing.

About eight o'clock that evening there was a wireless message, from the naval command at Queenstown to the Lusitania:

Submarines active off the south coast of Ireland.

She had her first warning. At eight-thirty — the passengers were taking their after-dinner coffee by that time — the wireless was busy again. This was a general warning:

Avoid headlands. Pass harbors at full speed. Steer mid-channel course. Submarines off Fastnet.

In the quiet dusk on the Lusitania's bridge Captain Turner acknowledged it and paid no attention. To have left the Irish coast altogether would not have been difficult, but would have involved many extra miles and some uncertainty in navigation. Besides, it was a general warning — just common stuff for the tramp captains, the master may have thought. They held on, intending to make the Fastnet their landfall as usual, though giving it a fairly wide berth. In the first class lounge the passengers were enjoying the customary benefit performance in behalf of those in peril on the sea. Presently it was over and they were turning in. A couple of hundred miles ahead the U-20's people in their sweating little iron prison were enjoying as best they could the fresh air and the brief security of the night.

From time to time the Admiralty warning came again, but it appears to have meant little to the Lusitania. Indeed, Captain Turner, anxious not to beat the tide over the bar at Liverpool, actually reduced his speed from 21 to 18 knots, thus lessening by so much his ship's principal defence. He might better have consumed the time by zigzagging, in accordance with the standing Admiralty instructions for submarine-infested waters; but Captain Turner labored under the stupidly mistaken idea that zigzagging was necessary only after a hostile submarine had been sighted.

He had nearly two thousand lives in his keeping, but at sea one comes to do things by habit.

The morning, May 7, came in foggy; it prevented their picking up the land and so determining an exact position. They knew they were somewhere off the Fastnet, just where the Admiralty warnings placed the danger, but thought they were about twenty miles out. Captain Turner set his course parallel with the coast; because of the fog he again reduced speed — to fifteen knots, which was no more than the surface speed of the German submarines — and began to announce his presence with the fog-horn. Less than a hundred miles away by this time Captain Schwieger also found himself buried in fog. His fuel was running low; he had only two old torpedoes — 'not so good' — remaining, and he set his course for home around the west of Ireland. Ignorant of each other, the two vessels were brought nearer and nearer through the fog with every turn of their propellers.

As the morning wore on the fog lightened and burned away, to leave a beautifully sunny day with a smooth, almost glassy, sea. The Lusitania's speed was restored, but only to eighteen knots. At eleven-twenty-five there was another message from the Admiralty:

> Submarines active in southern part of Irish Channel. Last heard of twenty miles south of Coningbeg. Make certain Lusitania gets this.

If Captain Turner was less than alert, so was the Admiralty. It left the Lusitania in ignorance of the actual sinkings which had been taking place on and near her course; it now sent a message which, giving no indication as to *when* the submarine had been 'heard of,' was next to useless. Coningbeg was far ahead, and Captain Turner, left to assume that the submarine was still there, continued as before. Passengers coming on deck for a stroll before lunch saw the line of the Irish coast low on the horizon to the north. At twelve-forty there was still another Admiralty warning:

> Submarines five miles south of Cape Clear, proceeding west when last sighted at 10:00 A.M.

This danger was astern and could reasonably be dismissed. The general instructions had been to 'avoid headlands' and 'steer mid-channel.' Sighting Galley Head at this juncture, Captain Turner's decision was to run closer in to the coast in order to determine his exact position. At twelve-forty he altered course so as to close in with the headlands he had been advised to avoid.

In London that morning Colonel House found himself with a full and pleasant schedule. Sir Edward was to take him for a little tour of Kew Gardens, now lovely with spring; afterward they were to go on to Buckingham Palace, while there was to be a dinner to himself and Mrs. House at the Embassy that evening. The Colonel and his distinguished host reached Kew before the gates were opened, but the porter let them in and they rambled for a time in that place of peace and sweetness. 'I have never seen the gardens so beautiful,' the Colonel told his diary. 'It is to me one of the superlatively beautiful spots in England. Grey showed me the different trees and told me something of them. The black-birds were singing, and we talked of how different they were to those in far-away Texas.' It must have been a strangely idyllic moment amid all the tragedy and horror of the war; yet however sweetly a bird might sing, that subject could never be thrust far below the surface of the mind, and presently they were back upon it again.

> We spoke of the probability of an ocean liner being sunk, and I told him if this were done a flame of indignation would sweep across America which would in itself probably carry us into the war.

Was House getting farther away from Texas than he quite realized? The stroll came to its end; they left the gardens and an hour later were with the King. Again, 'We fell to talking, strangely enough, of the probability of Germany sinking a transatlantic liner.' It was the King who said: 'Suppose they should sink the Lusitania with American passengers on board?'

The Lusitania's passengers at just about that moment were going down to luncheon — their last on board, as they would be in Liverpool in the morning. Perhaps they were congratulating themselves upon the beauty of their final day. The ship drove steadily onward; it was warm, and there was only a touch of sharpness in the spring breeze that came in through the open portholes of the dining saloon — which were but twenty-five feet above the sparkling surface of that smooth, enticing sea.

V. THE LUSITANIA

i

AT twelve-forty Captain Turner had changed course to the northeast and stood in toward the coast. In spite of what ticket agents may have told prospective passengers, there had never been any thought of a convoy. There were no patrols upon the scene. As a precaution two lookouts had been stationed on the forecastle head, an extra man in the crow's nest and a man at either end of the bridge; they scanned the placid ocean, but saw nothing. They had not been twenty minutes on their new course, however, before something saw them. Ten or fifteen miles away, the little group of men on the low conning tower of the U–20 had suddenly made out the masts and four funnels of a 'large passenger steamer' just appearing over the western horizon ahead of them.

It was a chance encounter. The U–20 was already on her way home. The steamer was crossing her bows, and so far away that it would have been impossible for the submarine to have caught up had the liner remained on that heading. Here, however, Captain Turner's fatal proximity to the coast again betrayed his ship. Had the meeting occurred in the open sea the submarine would not have attempted to give chase; as it was, it was obvious to Captain Schwieger that the liner must soon turn toward him again in order to avoid the land. Five minutes later, the U–20 had slipped beneath the surface; Captain Schwieger put her on a northerly course to intercept, and from that moment the single, secret eye of the periscope never left the Lusitania.

For an hour the two vessels ran onward toward the coast. The Lusitania's passengers were now coming up from lunch, and forward on the promenade deck Mr. Elbert Hubbard and his wife were watching the low Irish hills approach. The Old Head of Kinsale was taking shape by this time — it was not more than ten or fifteen miles away. At one-forty Captain Turner, now near enough to get a good 'fix' upon it, ordered the course changed once more. The Lusitania swung back again to starboard, steadying upon her former heading parallel to the coast. In the control room of the U–20 Captain Schwieger saw that his guess was right. An attack was now possible. He ordered full speed upon the motors.

On the Lusitania's bridge a junior officer had begun methodically taking a 'four-point bearing' on the Old Head of Kinsale. This is a highly accurate method of determining a vessel's position — an unnecessarily accurate method under the circumstances, it would seem, for it requires that the ship be held upon one course for a considerable period — the one most dangerous proceeding in submarine-infested waters. Unfortunately, Captain Turner thought that zigzagging was useful only after a submarine had been sighted, and the six lookouts saw nothing. In the control room of the U–20 there was no sound except the steady drone of the motors and the rattle of the chain hoist as the periscope was adjusted up or down. Captain Schwieger watched; forward the torpedo crew waited, as they had so often done before. On the Lusitania's bridge the navigation work had been going on for nearly half an hour. Below upon the promenade deck Mr. Hubbard was cheerfully remarking to a shipboard acquaintance that he might not be precisely welcomed in Germany, because of the little essay he had just written called 'Who Lifted the Lid Off Hell.'

As the remark passed his lips, that bright, mechanical eye peering ceaselessly through the waves was barely seven hundred yards off the starboard bow of the Lusitania. Rapidly Captain Schwieger saw her swim across the hairlines of his eyepiece. 'Fire,' he said.

In the compartment forward a hand moved, and there was a hissing rush of air. The torpedo crew stood, counting off the seconds in their blind little pocket beneath the sea. The seconds ticked away — and ended in a deep, muffled roar that shook the submarine. It was a hit.

ii

A shout from the forecastle, 'Torpedo coming on the starboard side!' was the only warning. The people on the bridge had just time to see the track when they felt the shock and the crash of the explosion — like 'the slamming of a heavy door' — followed after a perceptible interval (according to the 'overwhelming' evidence of the survivors) by a second detonation. It seemed to have a quite different sound from that made by the torpedo; it 'may possibly,' as Captain Turner afterward testified, 'have been internal.' The ship only trembled, but the debris leapt up to the mastheads, and a lifeboat hanging forty or fifty feet above the waterline was shattered. Captain Schwieger at his periscope observed the unexpected violence of the effect and noted it in his log:

> Shot hits starboard side right behind bridge. An unusually heavy detonation follows with a very strong explosion cloud. (High in air over first smokestack.) Added to the explosion of the torpedo there must have been a second explosion. (Boiler or coal or powder.) The superstructure over the point struck and the high bridge are rent asunder, fire breaks out and smoke envelops the high bridge.

The hit had come at just ten minutes past two. In the first crisis everyone supposed that they at least had plenty of time. No one imagined that such a ship as the Lusitania could be sunk quickly by one torpedo, if indeed one hit could sink her at all. The Titanic, ripped open to the sea through something like one-third of her length, had floated for two and a half hours. Captain

Turner's first thought was to beach the vessel, and he ordered the helm put down. Some minutes were lost in this way; it was very soon apparent, however, that the damage was serious.

Already the Lusitania had taken up a heavy list to starboard and was settling by the head. From below the crew were tumbling out upon the boat deck and preparing to lower away the lifeboats. There was no panic, but the passengers were now streaming up the companionways, hunting lifebelts, milling about in an increasing confusion. Aside from swinging out his boats, Captain Turner had made no real preparation for abandoning ship. There had been no general drills; the passengers had not even been assigned to boat stations; lifebelts were not distributed about the decks. Most of the belts, on the contrary, were in the cabins, and many who gained the deck in the first rush had to go below again to find them. This added to the turmoil. On the port side the women and children were already taking their places in the boats. Peremptory orders were cried from the bridge, however, not to lower and for the crew and passengers to get out again. The officers shouted that there was no danger, that the ship would right herself; doubtless they still thought so, while Captain Turner afterward explained that he was afraid of the boats being lost through reaching the water while there was still way on the ship. The result was that many of the crew simply abandoned the port side boats and went elsewhere; while when an attempt was at last made to lower them the list had become so heavy that it was impossible to get them down over that side. Of the eleven port side boats only two ever reached the water; one was so badly damaged on the way down that it filled and sank, the other was lost in some other way.

Perhaps five minutes had gone by. The ship seemed to hang for a few moments, and then continued to heel over. One passenger, who knew something about ships, was convinced that the end was coming quickly. Going below to get some papers, he had to walk in the angle between the floor and the wall of the passage, while the water was so near the portholes that he judged she must be filling through dining-saloon ports on the deck below, which he had noticed to be standing open when he was at lunch. Another five minutes or so elapsed. It was now clear to everyone that the Lusitania was going with a fearful rapidity. On deck they were working at the starboard boats in earnest. The officers and many of the crew did their best; everything, however, was more or less hit-or-miss; there was discipline, but little order. According to a survivor:

> One boat, full of passengers, was being lowered. The man at the bow was not lowering fast enough and an officer shouted to him to hurry up. He threw off a bight, lost control of the rope, and the bow dropped, throwing the passengers into the water. A minute later a second boat, which seemed about to get safely away, also got out of control and fell upon the people struggling in the water. I can see that sight yet.

There was one invisible witness to the horror. In his log Captain Schwieger noted what he saw in the lens of his periscope. 'She has the appearance of being about to capsize. Great confusion on board, boats being cleared and part being lowered to the water. They must have lost their heads.' Schwieger had not supposed, any more than the rest, that a single hit would suffice to kill the ship, and he was apparently waiting until she had been abandoned in order to deliver the *coup de grâce* with his one remaining torpedo. But at two-twenty-five he noted: 'It seems that the vessel will be afloat only a short time.' It was too much for him; he dropped below periscope depth and stood away. 'I could not have fired a second torpedo into this thing of humanity attempting to save themselves.' The submarine could have rendered no assistance, and he supposed that the naval patrols would be at once upon the scene.

A scant fifteen minutes had passed since the torpedo had struck. The passengers were clinging in helpless masses along the starboard side of the deckhouse, the towering funnels leaning far out above them and the water creeping rapidly along the deck from the now almost submerged bow. The foremost of the eleven boats on the starboard side had been cleared; two more had been lost in lowering, a fourth had been smashed by the explosion. As the water lapped back along the rail it began to float the after boats level with the deck, but the upper works were leaning dangerously down over them. One, filled with women and children, was afloat in this way, but the bow falls jammed, and it was impossible to clear them in time. The head of the forward davit caught the boat as the ship settled, upended it and threw the occupants into the sea. The five aftermost boats were cleared, making six in all which were successfully launched, with a total capacity of about three hundred and sixty persons, though there were probably fewer in them. As for the twenty-six 'collapsibles' — crosses between lifeboats and life rafts, which were stowed beneath the regular boats — it was impossible to do more than cut their lashings in the hope that they would float free. Many of them did so, and helped to save a large number of lives.

In her last moments the Lusitania seemed to roll back to an even keel; her stern simply subsided into the water, as if the whole after part had filled. Captain Turner, a strong swimmer, was floated off his bridge as the water came over. Looking back he saw the tall funnels go under one by one; there was a great, groaning sigh, a last rush of steam and air above the funnel tops, the mastheads vanished and there was nothing but the placid and smiling sea, dotted over a great area with the immense mass of floating debris and the heads of swimming people, the few life-boats riding among them. In just eighteen minutes after the shot was fired, the Lusitania was on the bottom. 'The wreck,' Captain Schwieger noted, 'must lie off the Old Head of Kinsale, lighthouse bearing 358° true, fourteen sea miles off in 90 metres of water. The shore and lighthouse are clearly seen.'

There had been 1257 passengers and 702 members of the crew on board — 1959 souls in all — of whom 1195 were lost. Of the 159 American passengers, 124 perished. There were many harrowing details. There were 129 children on board; 94 of them were lost. Among these children there were 39 babies, of whom only four were saved. A heartrending photograph was widely published afterward; it was a family group showing Mrs. Paul Crompton of Philadelphia and her six children, all seven of whom were lost. Among the Americans, both Mr. Elbert Hubbard and his wife were lost. The wealthy young sportsman, Mr. Alfred Gwynne Vanderbilt, was last seen heroically trying to get the children into the boats. Charles Frohman, the theatrical manager, perished; so did Charles Klein, the author of 'The Music Master,' and Justus Miles Forman, a young writer whose war play, 'The Hyphen,' had recently appeared on Broadway.

For this appalling loss of life it does not seem possible, in spite of the official whitewashing,[1] to relieve either the Admiralty or the ship's officers of all blame. With the sanction of the British Government, the Cunard Line was selling people passages through a declared war zone, under due notice that its ships were subject to being sunk on sight by a power which had demonstrated its ability and determination to do so. Yet the Admiralty's warnings seem curiously sketchy. This great vessel was placed in the hands of a master who did not even know that zigzagging was necessary before a submarine had been sighted. Captain Turner took almost no real precautions, either to avoid attack or to deal with emergency should it come. Boat drills on the way over, for example, were confined to five-minute exercises with the two boats kept ready for such minor accidents as a man overboard. The impression left by the whole episode is that nobody really conceived the possibility of an attack upon the Lusitania, and that the ship was actually navigated more or less by routine. In the result, Captain Turner managed first to run her right on top of the enemy

[1] By the British Wreck Commissioner, who held an inquiry immediately afterward. The proceedings were hasty; there was little real cross-examination, and the commissioner's findings were too obviously swayed by war emotion to be of much value. Somewhat more thorough was the work of the American court which in October, 1918, adjudicated the damage claims against the Cunard Line arising from the disaster. This court, however, was also sitting in an atmosphere surcharged with wartime passion and propaganda, while the question was one of legal rather than moral responsibility. The line was held free of all liability.

The World.

"Circulation Books Open to All." "Circulation Books Open to All."

VOL. LV. NO. 19,638. NEW YORK, SATURDAY, MAY 8, 1915. PRICE [...]

DON'T FORGET!

The Sunday World To-Morrow

TWO TORPEDOES SINK LUSITANIA; MANY AMERICANS AMONG 1,446 LOST; PRESIDENT, STUNNED, IN SECLUSION.

LUSITANIA, HER CAPTAIN, AND PLACE WHERE SHE WAS HIT

Cunard Liner Attacked by Two German Submarines Off the Irish Coast, and Goes Down in Fifteen Minutes—Luncheon Being Served at the Time—Survivors Picked Up From Lifeboats and Taken to Queenstown, Forty Miles Distant—Regarding 1,254 Passengers and 850 of Crew Aboard, Cunard Line Says: "First Officer Jones Thinks 500 to 600 Are Saved"—Ship Left New York Last Saturday With Many Americans, Including Prominent New Yorkers, Who Disregarded German Warning Not to Sail.

(Special Cable Dispatch to The World.)

LONDON, May 8.—The Cunard liner Lusitania was torpedoed by German submarines shortly after 2 o'clock yesterday afternoon, ten miles off the Old Head of Kinsale, on the south coast of Munster, Ireland. At least two Submersibles attacked her.

She sank fifteen minutes later. The company states that no warning was given her.

A statement issued by the Admiralty says the total number of survivors of the Lusitania is 658, which would make the loss of lives 1,446, as the Lusitania carried 1,254 passengers and 850 crew when she sailed from New York, May 1.

It is believed only a few first class passengers were saved as they thought the ship would remain afloat and made little effort to escape.

The tug Stormcock has returned here, bringing about 150 survivors of the Lusitania, principally passengers, among whom were many women, several of the crew and one steward.

"Describing the experience of the Lusitania the steward said:

"The passengers were at lunch when a submarine came up and fired two torpedoes, which struck the Lusitania on the starboard side, one forward and the other in the engine-room. They caused terrific explosions.

"Capt. Turner immediately ordered the boats out. The ship began to list badly immediately.

"Ten boats were put into the water, and between 400 and 500 passengers entered them. The boat in which I was approached the land with three other boats, and we were picked up shortly after 4 o'clock by the Stormcock.

"I fear that few of the officers were saved. They acted bravely.

"There was only fifteen minutes from the time the ship was struck until she foundered, going down bow foremost. It was a dreadful sight.' "

An official statement issued by the Cunard Steamship Company said:

"First Officer Jones thinks from 500 to 600 were saved. This includes passengers and crew, and is only estimated."

A despatch to the Chronicle from Queenstown says that "seven torpedoes were discharged from the German attacking craft, one of them striking the Lusitania amidships."

This would indicate that at least two submarines were arrayed against the liner. Even the newest type of the undersea boats carries but six tubes, and most of them have only four.

A despatch coming from Kinsale at 7 o'clock says that at 3.30 two lifeboats were intercepted six miles off Old Head by the motorboat Elizabeth and convoyed by a Cork tug, which took from one 63 sengers and from the other 16, most of them women and children. They were taken to Queenstown.

These survivors said that the Lusitania got two torpedoes, the first of which struck her on one side. She canted toward the land, and received the second on the starboard side.

They said a heavy list so port followed, and the Lusitania remained afloat for only ten min only six lifeboats could be launched. These contained about 300 passengers.

Other reports say that the first of the torpedoes struck the liner near her bows, the second its way into her engine room. Terrific explosions followed, and great volumes of water po through the seams.

Captain W. T. Turner

WASHINGTON, SILENT, AWAITS ADVICES ON AMERICANS' FATE

[...] When, After Receiving Official News From Queenstown Says [...]

A. G. VANDERBILT DROWNED, IS REPORT AT QUEENSTOWN

LONDON, May 8 (4.42 A. M.).—The Times Queenstown correspondent says that some of the survivors who have arrived there report that 1104 Captain Vanderbilt was drowned.

Underwood & Underwood News Photos

THE S.S. LUSITANIA

The lower photograph shows the boat equipment as carried at the time she was sunk. The six boats which reached shore are the foremost and the last five, beginning with the one here shown swung out. The 'collapsibles' can be distinguished stowed just beneath the regular lifeboats. The double portholes seen in a row just forward of the small steamer are those of the dining-saloon, through which the ship may have filled.

and was then caught with the slightest of preparation to handle the consequences.

Yet with the best of preparation it would have been impossible to abandon such a ship within eighteen minutes. The real reason for the tremendous death roll was the fearful suddenness with which she sank — and there some sense of mystery still lingers. Assuming that the torpedo hit against a bulkhead, it could hardly have opened more than two main compartments, and the ship was designed to float with two compartments filled. The Germans and German sympathizers seized at once upon that second explosion, which 'may possibly have been internal,' and claimed that the ship must actually have been destroyed through the detonation of munitions in her cargo. But the rifle cartridges known to have been aboard could not have been touched off all at once, and there is not the slightest ground for supposing that she carried undeclared and illegal explosives. Schwieger himself (and it gives one greater confidence in the authenticity of his published log) thought of the boilers or an explosion of the coal dust in the bunkers before he thought of munitions. There have been many other hypotheses. Open portholes may have hastened the end. The automatic system for closing the watertight doors may have failed, or the torpedo may have interrupted the control mechanism. In the first minutes an order was given to trim the ship with the port side tanks; if it was obeyed, it must have helped to destroy her last reserve of buoyancy.

Yet a bunker explosion seems the most likely explanation; and in whatever degree omissions or mistakes may have contributed to the catastrophe, they could not alter the fact that the primary reason why the Lusitania went down was that a German submarine fired a torpedo point-blank into her side. Her passengers had been murdered — much as they would have been, for example, had the Chemin de Fer de l'Est taken a trainload of them within sight and range of the German artillery. The ninety-four lost children were murdered, as were the German babies upon whom there fell the brunt of Mr. Churchill's 'economic pressure'

— or even, one might add, as the German youths would have been murdered for whom the Lusitania's 4200 cases of rifle ammunition were destined. War is murder. The Lusitania's passengers might, of course, have stayed out of the war zone — an option which was not open to the conscripts who were daily slain by the thousand — while a reasoned understanding of the full details of the tragedy might have mitigated somewhat the emotional responses to it. But the passengers were dead; and within twenty-four hours after the Lusitania's mastheads had disappeared, the great mass of pro-Ally sympathizers in the United States, the overwhelming majority of the editors and immense numbers of their readers were alike beyond any reasoned judgment, sense of proportion or an ability, even, to analyze clearly what had taken place.[1]

iii

The first news was at the American Embassy in London by four o'clock that afternoon; it said nothing, however, about the loss of life, and the staff was busy with the preparations for the dinner that evening to Colonel and Mrs. House. 'At about seven o'clock the Ambassador came home; his manner showed that something extraordinary had taken place.' It was too late then to postpone the dinner; and the bulletins began to arrive with the guests. All through the evening Mr. Page read them out to his company as they were received. The affair was 'one of the most tragic in the social history of London.' The gowns, the jewelry, the white ties and shirt-fronts, gleamed elegantly through

---

[1] The same afternoon Captain Schwieger fired his last torpedo at a freighter, but missed; he then continued safely homeward. Legend, in the Allied countries, was to accord him agonies of remorse and was even to take him to a miserable and haunted death in Peru after the war. Actually, while commanding the larger U-88 in September, 1917, he perished with all his crew on a British mine barrage. He seems to have been shocked by the loss of life in the Lusitania, but to have regarded his own part in it as merely what had been required of him in the line of duty. Captain Turner held several smaller commands during the war. One, a transport, was torpedoed under him in the Mediterranean; again he swam off the bridge and was saved. The close of the war ended his sea service, though he lived on in retirement until 1933.

an atmosphere 'of dumb stupefaction.... If anyone spoke it was in a whisper,' and behind all the whispers there ran one word — War. All those handsome ladies and gentlemen were convinced that the United States would declare war immediately — 'on this latter point several of the guests expressed their ideas, and one of the most shocked and outspoken was Colonel House.' Had not the amateur diplomatist been saying the same thing to the King that very morning? That the President would act with the utmost energy Colonel House took for granted.... 'We shall be at war with Germany within a month,' he declared.

They stayed late, breaking up at last in a portentous silence. Four o'clock in London is only eleven o'clock in Washington and New York; and the banner headlines were marching all that afternoon across the faces of the evening papers. Secretary Lane cancelled an appointment with Secretary Redfield: 'I have two friends on the Lusitania.' Ambassador Bernstorff had taken the afternoon train to New York; so had Mr. Paul Warburg and another banker. The papers came on at Philadelphia, and at New York they found Mr. Jacob Schiff waiting on the platform to warn his brother-in-law that the news was true. The Ambassador had planned to attend a benefit performance of 'The Bat' being given that evening for the German Red Cross. The engagement was cancelled and he locked himself in his hotel against the besieging hosts of the reporters. When he left next day, he tried to run their blockade through a side door, but was detected. 'Several cars filled with reporters followed me to the station and pressed round me so persistently that I was unable to shake them off. I could only refuse to make any statement.... Finally, I succeeded in forcing my way through the infuriated and howling mob of pressmen and reaching the train.'

One hundred and twenty-four American citizens had been murdered off the Irish coast. On Saturday, May 8, the morning papers were shouting the news in bigger and blacker headlines than they had used since the early days of the war, and their editorial pages were blazing with horror and indignation. 'From our Department of State,' cried the New York *Times*, 'there must go to the Imperial Government at Berlin a demand that the Germans shall no longer make war like savages drunk with blood.' The *Tribune* closed its philippic with an appeal to a moving passage in our history: 'The nation which remembered the sailors of the Maine will not forget the civilians of the Lusitania!' Mr. Roosevelt leapt shrieking into print: 'This represents not merely piracy but piracy on a vaster scale of murder than old-time pirates ever practised.' From the violently pro-Ally Northeast the great wave of shock, outrage and denunciation spread through the newspapers, at least, of every part of the country. Only two English-language papers in the United States — one in St. Louis and the other in Milwaukee — could be found defending the sinking. The Memphis *Commercial Appeal* was ready 'to consider a declaration of war.' From Louisville the great voice of Marse Henry Watterson thundered in vivid imagery:

> Truly, the Nation of the black hand and bloody heart has got in its work.... The decree of Satan went forth from Berlin. The instruments of Satan were forged at Essen. There was but a single Satanic abatement. Satan's Ambassador at Washington — shameless in his infamy, under the sign manual of Satan's Embassy, insolent in its disregard of law or consequences — gave warning.... Shall any just man say that Count von Bernstorff is not guilty of murder?

That war is murder was something that our public had never quite been able to grasp. Marse Henry plunged onward to complete his figure:

> This holy Sabbath every pulpit in America should send a prayer to God in protest;...and more than all — the Christian President of the United States, a cool and brave man, sprung from a line of heroes and saints — ceasing longer to protest, should act, leaving no doubt...that he is...a leader of men and nations, and that he holds aloft the Sword of the Lord and Gideon!

It is useless to continue. 'Condemnation of the act,' as the surprised editors of the *Literary Digest* were forced to leave it, 'seems to be limited only by the restrictions of the English language';

while the language had hardly given out before the pencils of the cartoonists were reinforcing it with every kind of stirring and terrible visual appeal. The preachers sprang to take Marse Henry's advice. A few, like Bishop Greer, could urge the nation to think calmly; more typical was the cry of the Rev. John Henry Jowett that 'it is a colossal sin against God and it is premeditated murder.' Nor did the passion stop with ministers and editors who, like Marse Henry, were long past military age. Within a couple of days a group of young men of eminent (and for the most part Republican) families were fiercely telegraphing the President to demand that adequate measures, 'however serious,' be taken to 'secure full reparation and guarantees.' Among the names appended were those of Elihu Root, Jr., Theodore Roosevelt, Jr., young Mr. Hamilton Fish, young Mr. Bob Bacon, John G. Milburn, Jr., a Wickersham, a Devereaux, and others of no less lofty lineage.

This spontaneous blaze of passion was at once, of course, fanned vigorously by every agency of Allied propaganda. Mr. Page hastened to pour out for the President his 'interpretation' of 'opinion here':

> The United States must declare war or forfeit European respect. So far as I know, this opinion is universal. If the United States come in, the moral and physical effect will be to bring peace quickly and to give the United States a great influence in... so reorganizing the world as to prevent [a] recurrence [of war]. If the United States submit... [she] will have no voice or influence in settling the war or in what follows for a long time to come.

Again the Ambassador was playing upon what he supposed to be the weakness of his chief. Perhaps it was. Mr. Wilson burned the almost insolent despatch; but 'after all,' he too generously commented, 'this does not express Page's own opinion, but what he takes to be public opinion at the moment in Great Britain.' Such a reaction might, indeed, affect 'our influence for good.' It was a dangerous thought; however, Mr. Page was distressed to find that in this supreme crisis nobody in Washington appeared to be paying much attention to him. They did not even acknowledge his communications, and he was 'frequently obliged to get his information about the state of feeling in Washington from Sir Edward Grey'! It is possible that all of them were still overrating the Presidential egotism.

All day on Saturday, May 8, the 'largest crowds since the war began' were milling before the newspaper bulletin boards in New York, many of them calling for war. Dr. Eliot decided that 'our flag should be somewhere in the trenches' and went over to preparedness. Mr. John Wanamaker, the great Philadelphia merchant, had originally adopted an attitude of scrupulous neutrality. Among those lost in the Lusitania, however, was one of his shoe salesmen (he had been bound for Russia to arrange delivery on one of the biggest war contracts that had been given out) and the disaster put Mr. Wanamaker 'into the war.' Yet whether such prominent leaders of the Northeast were really representative of the rank and file for whom they were so lightly preparing the agonies of battle may be open to some question. General Wood, with opportunity of the most dazzling kind now trembling just beyond his grasp, dropped an angry note into his diary: 'Rotten spirit in Lusitania matter. Yellow spirit everywhere in spots.' Was it possible?

Perhaps it was. The Northeast, moreover, was not the nation. Secretary Houston happened to be in California when the disaster came. He was to meet a delegation of Los Angeles business men that morning; the Secretary was full of the news, but the business men merely 'talked for a few minutes about the tragedy without excitement' and did not mention the subject again through the rest of a long morning. 'Nor did any reporter of any local newspaper seek to interview me on the matter,' though Mr. Houston was one of the most influential members of the Cabinet. 'No citizen brought it up during the remainder of my stay in the West, which lasted several weeks.' The European conflict 'seemed out there to be very far away'; those extraordinary people, it appeared, were just not 'contemplating the possibility of our becoming involved.'

Yet, strangely enough, if one looked twice at all that flood of righteously outraged press comment, one might begin to have one's doubts about the East and center as well. When it came to what the editors wanted done about the crime there was an unfortunate vagueness. A hurried telegraphic analysis of some thousand newspaper editorials of the days immediately following the sinking showed that, however recklessly the editors might inflame the warlike passions of their readers, less than one per cent of them actually demanded war. Many cried, with Marse Henry, for the promptest 'action,' the sternest of demands upon Germany — but were careful to add that the United States should not be involved in the conflict. What would happen, however, if Germany should reject the demands? It was at this critical, this all-important, point that the editorial fury was apt to dissolve into the mists of ambiguity; it was here that a general tendency developed to 'stand behind the President' — and leave that problem to him. Only by inference could the *Literary Digest* distinguish some papers here and there which were apparently willing to accept war as an alternative. The overwhelming consensus appeared to be that the President should instantly compel Germany to disavow, to make reparation and to abandon her submarine war, though taking care not to get the United States into trouble while doing so. 'The American people,' as the Savannah *News* rather plaintively observed, 'don't want to become involved in the war and they don't want their government to be placed in the position of retreating from any position it has taken.' That was it exactly.

In justice to the editors, however, one important element in the situation should not be overlooked. While Marse Henry, for example, would not go to the length of demanding instant war against 'these barbarians,' he was the more ready to accept such an eventuality because 'actual war is not possible — Germany having no fleet we can sweep off the briny deep, nor army near enough to be exterminated.' It was a circumstance which seems to have lent fuel to more than one fiery pen. Several papers noted that adding our Navy to the already overwhelming fleets of the Allies could in practice mean but little; while few in the spring of 1915 seriously imagined, considering our relatively tiny standing army, that more than a color guard of American youth could ever stand in the blood-filled trenches of Northern France. To our editors, participation in the war seemed an unusually safe undertaking, and they fanned the flames — unaware that when their words were at last to take effect two years later the preparedness campaign would have fulfilled its historic mission, and prepared the national mind for a military effort upon a scale that would have been almost unthinkable in 1915.

Such was the furnace of seething and irresponsible emotionalism in which President Wilson now found himself — with the lives, the welfare and the national destiny of one hundred million human beings in his hand. That Saturday morning he made a point of taking his usual round of golf — less for the exercise, it was thought, than as an example of calm in crisis — and thereafter retired to the White House to wrestle alone with his responsibility. What was he to do? The advice was conflicting. On Sunday, May 9, there arrived a long and bellicose cable from Colonel House. There should, he thought, be an immediate demand upon Germany for assurances against a repetition of the crime with a threat of war. 'If war follows, it will not be a new war, but an endeavor to end more speedily an old one. Our intervention will save rather than increase the loss of life' — though of whose lives he did not stop to ask. 'America has come to the parting of the ways when she must determine whether she stands for civilized or uncivilized warfare.'

Another letter on the same day urged a different course. Mr. Jacob Schiff — the great Jewish banker, who had one nephew in the British Army and another in the German — did not see why America should stand for war of any sort; he begged the President to make an earnest effort, using 'the singularly impressive language you are capable of,' to bring both sides to make peace. Between these two extremes Mr. Bryan was taking a far more practical view. 'Germany,' he urged, 'has a right to prevent contraband going to the Allies and a ship carrying contraband should not rely upon passengers to protect her from attack.' This pointed toward a common-sense acceptance of the facts and the arrangement of the best practicable *modus vivendi* for safeguarding those Americans who had real business in the war zone. Unfortunately, that this would be intensely unpopular was obvious from the press comment; while it must involve an implied sanction of the submarine war and a tacit invitation to the torpedo to do what it could against the new tide of exports now flowing out to the Allied battle lines. We had permitted the Allies to destroy our trade with the Central Powers. If we now permitted the Central Powers to destroy our trade with the Allies, we should be risking a real and final economic collapse. No political administration could face that prospect; in particular President Wilson's could not, for the President had bound himself by that rash declaration that he would hold the Germans to 'strict accountability.'

Count Bernstorff was at the State Department on Monday morning to express his 'deep regrets' for the loss of so many American lives. Mr. Bryan spoke to him 'very seriously,' and the Ambassador was under no illusions. He advised Berlin that the Secretary of State would throw his influence for peace, but that 'Roosevelt, on the other hand, is beating the patriotic drum in order to win over the Jingo elements.' Berlin must take some action; they must show themselves ready to accept an American mediation or at least make motions toward reviving the proposed American compromise between the submarine and the blockade. 'The position is in any case *very serious;* I hope and believe that we shall find a way out of the present crisis, but in the case of any... recurrence no solution can be guaranteed.'

The Ambassador did not see the President. For three days the President saw no one except the rather belligerent McAdoo, who dined at the White House on Sunday. He had been scheduled, however, to address a gathering of newly naturalized citizens at Philadelphia that Monday evening, and the engagement was not

cancelled. The Convention Hall was packed with fifteen thousand people when the President entered; a nation was hanging
upon his words for the first indication of the policy to which he
was about to dedicate it. The long jaw was set; the now familiar
voice rolled on:

> America must have the consciousness that on all sides it touches
> elbows and touches heart with all the nations of mankind. The
> example of America must be a special example, and must be an
> example not merely of peace because it will not fight, but because
> peace is a healing and elevating influence of the world and strife is
> not. There is such a thing as a man being too proud to fight. There
> is such a thing as a nation being so right that it does not need to
> convince others by force that it is right.

The crowd burst into tumultuous applause, and the thousands
of little American flags with which the new citizens had been
provided fluttered bravely as the famous phrase (universally mis-
quoted ever since) was added to the language. It was the high
moral concept which the President had proclaimed in the first
bright days of his New Diplomacy; it was simply a rewording of
his appeal, in the Mexican problem of nearly two years before,
for 'the self-restraint of a really great nation which realizes its
own strength and scorns to misuse it.'[1] The crowd cheered; but
the editors and patriots, from their loftier sancta, regarded this
declaration of faith without enthusiasm. Mr. Roosevelt was heavily sarcastic about it to the reporters. The New York *Times* expressed the solemn opinion that 'this utterance of the President
does not respond to the feeling of the people.' The White House
was flooded instantly with telegrams of condemnation; and before
the swift storm of elegant disapproval the President was weak
enough to announce that the speech had been made without
reference to the Lusitania. The loyal *World* hastened to express
its relief at this disavowal. 'We have a pride that will make us
fight,' it said. 'Let there be no illusion on this score in Berlin or
elsewhere.' And the *Herald* regretted that Mr. Wilson should have

[1] Page 12.

used 'an expression so susceptible to misconstruction.' In London, Colonel House, who had gone to war already, first saw those dreadful words, 'too proud to fight,' on the newsboys' placards in Piccadilly. 'I feel as though I had been given a kick at every lamp-post coming down Constitution Hill,' he told Page when he reached the Embassy; and as the British and French press turned unanimously to load the President with their bitterest jibes and contumely, it doubtless only confirmed him in the feeling.

President Wilson had attempted to bring his countrymen to their senses. Apparently he now had his answer. He did not want war. He never fully accepted House's naïve faith that an American intervention would guarantee a peace 'for the lasting good of humanity'; on the contrary he clung, with a much surer instinct, to the idea that once the United States were involved upon one side of the quarrel, the nation's influence toward creating a stable world system would be largely at an end. He believed he had no mandate to enter the war. But he did not want or did not dare to face the now appalling difficulties of avoiding that eventuality; and besides, he was a stiff-necked moralist who had announced that he would hold the Germans to 'strict accountability.' Mr. F. I. Cobb, the celebrated editor of the *World*, was a caller at the White House at about this time, and long afterward he recorded the dangerous chain of reasoning with which President Wilson evaded his central problem:

I do not know [Mr. Cobb quoted him as saying] whether the German Government intends to keep faith with the United States or not. It is my personal opinion that Germany has no such intention, but I am less concerned about the ultimate intentions of Germany than about the attitude of the American people, who are divided into three groups: those who are strongly pro-German, those who are strongly pro-Ally, and the vast majority who expect me to find a way to keep the United States out of war. I do not want war, yet I do not know that I can keep the country out of war. That depends on Germany, and I have no control over Germany. But I intend to handle this situation in such a manner that every American citizen will know that the United States Government has done everything it could to prevent war. Then if war comes we shall have a united country... and there need be no fear about the result.

'That depends on Germany' — about whose attitude the President was not concerned. President Wilson would now do what the editors were shrieking for; he would send a stiff note to Berlin and leave the problem of what might happen in the event of its rejection to the future. It is in just that way that every modern war has been made 'inevitable.' It is an element of President Wilson's greatness that he realized instinctively the profound futility and irrelevance of force; it is an element of his weakness that he sought to find its substitute in the treacherous bogs of 'morality' rather than in the firmer ground of practical psychology and statesmanship.

After that, it was all over. The Cabinet was summoned on Tuesday morning; and the President began by reading them House's cable. The comment was favorable, and the President passed on to outline the note in which he proposed to follow this advice. They were all eager for the strong hand — except the Secretary of State. Mr. Bryan was 'appalled.' He showed his agitation, and angrily suggested that there were some members of the Cabinet who were less than neutral. At that *lèse majesté* the President turned upon him 'and said, with a steely glitter in his eyes, "Mr. Bryan, you are not warranted in making such an assertion."' It was outrageous to hint that Mr. Wilson could be biased, and the Secretary apologized. Yet he insisted upon pointing out the noose in which they were placing themselves; he urged strenuously that something be done to prevent the nation being plunged automatically into the war in case the Germans should not yield. The President was at first inclined to accede; later on he rejected the idea. There was no way of softening the note without encouraging the Germans to resist. The Cabinet approved; and Mr. Bryan, doubtful but uncertain of himself, signed. The die was cast; the first Lusitania Note was despatched on May 13, 1915.

It was impossible to use submarines against merchantmen, we declared, without an 'inevitable violation of many sacred principles of justice and humanity'; the 'indisputable' right of American citizens to travel where they would upon the high seas was reasserted, and the Imperial German Government was formally called upon to disavow the acts of its commanders, make reparation and 'take immediate steps to prevent' their recurrence. 'The Imperial German Government,' the Note concluded, 'will not expect the Government of the United States to omit any word or any act necessary to the performance of its sacred duty of maintaining the rights of the United States and its citizens.'

What we demanded was total surrender under the threat of war. Yet the really extraordinary aspect of the matter is that no one, throughout the whole time that the Note was being prepared, seems even to have thought of analyzing the chances of getting a surrender. No one called upon Mr. Gerard for an estimate of the real military, psychological, and political forces which they had to deal with. No one tried to calculate the real importance of the submarine to Germany. When they agreed upon their vigorous Note to Berlin, neither the President nor his emotional Cabinet can have had any adequate idea as to whether they were in fact preparing a diplomatic victory or plunging the people of the United States into the bloodiest war that history had known.

iv

Yet if the Administration was unwise, it was unquestionably representative. In New York, a brilliant dinner was given to the composer Saint-Saëns when he arrived on May 12 from France. Among those who welcomed him at the pier was Mme. Katscherra, the Wagnerian singer. 'No! no!' the old man exclaimed in horror. 'Away! You are a German.' At the University Club that evening the 'atmosphere of intellectuality was pervaded by a sentiment that was nothing if it was not ardently pro-Ally,' and Dr. Nicholas Murray Butler, earnest servitor of peace as well as of the intellect, delivered himself of the rather curious comment that 'while we here express no opinions, all of us take part in condemnation of the happenings of the past week.' 'France,' as another speaker put it, 'has made no propaganda in this country.'

There was a rush to join the Navy League — devoted proponent of preparedness and big shipbuilding contracts — and the National Security League found itself swamped in business as the distinguished contributions rolled in. In London Colonel House was meeting Lord Kitchener for the first time. The British soldier was deft:

> He said the war was one of attrition and the moment we entered, the Germans, unless they were totally mad, would know that the end was a certainty and would endeavour to make the best terms they could. . . . If we entered and I would let him know, he would at once put his mind upon the problem and would aid us not only as to organization but in any other way we desired. He paid a magnificent tribute to American valor and said, 'With American troops joined with the British, we will not need French troops on the West Front, but can keep them as a reserve.'

And House was only charmed by such frankness, such tact, so generous an offer to substitute American infantry for French in the fearful slaughter-house of 'attrition' — where they could fight for peace and humanity in a manner far more amenable (if House and Page were any guide) to the purposes of British imperialism. Lord Kitchener 'said no word to hasten' an American entry; he merely 'repeated time and again that the war would be shortened enormously' if the United States came in. 'How could he know,' was House's ecstatic comment, 'what would or would not influence me? He doubtless realizes, as the King does, that my advice to the President will be a potent influence in this crisis, but there was nothing of eagerness or urging in his remarks.' How could he have known?

Apparently it was only by a coincidence that on this same day, May 12, when the boiling indignation against Germany was at its height, the celebrated Bryce Report should have been

dropped into the maelstrom. The Belgian atrocities, if not precisely forgotten, had been sinking into the background under the
weight of an accumulating skepticism. The whole thing had been
rather overdone. But with the Bryce Report, published at just
that emotional moment, every doubt was obliterated. There was
no name in England which could have inspired more confidence
in an American public than that of Lord Bryce; his six colleagues
were only less impressive. 'Proof,' cried the New York *Times*,
'now comes to hand.'

The similar utterances of no less sincere and eminent Germans
had been frequently, and of course rightly, dismissed by our press
as valueless propaganda; but it was impossible for our editors
to imagine that the war could have the same effect upon Allied
minds which they observed it to have upon the German. Our
public not only believed all the findings of the Bryce Report,
which were worded with some restraint; they also believed all the
other atrocity stories they had ever heard. They not only believed
that the Germans had adopted a systematic campaign of atrocities
in the last weeks of August (the period covered by the report);
they also assumed that the campaign was still going on; they were
prepared to believe everything which they might hear thereafter.
Much of what followed is unintelligible unless one remembers
that innumerable sensible Americans were from that time onward
genuinely, seriously convinced that Germans were a peculiarly
fiendish and brutal race, quite beyond the pale of ordinary hu-
mankind. Even twenty years later the belief has not fully worn
off; and its persistence attests the magnitude of the service which
Lord Bryce rendered to the Allies — if not, perhaps, to his own
intellectual integrity.

One wanders today in amazement through those fantastic
mental climates. The *Times* was inundated with a flood of letters
to the editor which 'exceeded all previous experience with that
kind of spontaneous expression.' It had room to publish barely
one-twentieth of them. St. Louis produced 'the first translation in America of Edmund Rostand's "The Song of the

Stars," ' which had just been published in *L'Illustration*. The translation ran:

> 'Sir,' said the Man of Frightfulness, 'I've found it —
> These six months past, I have made up to look
> Like an American citizen, to find a way
> To make his Flag wave in the air for us,
> And never could I get the Flag to stir.'

The poem went on 'to link our national heroes with the cause of the Allies' — the heroes including, in rather odd assortment, Poe, Lincoln, William James, Franklin, and Washington. In Brooklyn, the 'regular weekly mobilization of General J. Hungerford Milbank's Army of Columbians, otherwise known as the International Order of Military Women' was delayed because the General herself (in her winter uniform of brown mohair, black velour campaign hat and silver eagles tacked to the shoulders) was making an airplane flight at Mineola. She said the flight would 'prove of immense benefit to the Allies.' At a dinner given by the Pilgrim Society in New York to Mr. Alfred Noyes and Sir Walter Raleigh, the eminent poet solemnly warned his hearers that Germany was contemplating establishing colonies in South America in contravention of the Monroe Doctrine. 'I have in my possession,' said the author of 'The Barrel Organ,' 'an atlas published in Germany.... This contains a map of South America upon which twenty-five or thirty places are inscribed in red as German colonies'; and the listeners were amazed at this crushing proof of the perfidy of the Teuton. As Dr. Butler (he was again presiding) gracefully put it, Americans who had long striven to be neutral though intelligent had gathered there that day 'to show how to be intelligent though neutral.'

In the midst of all this the first Lusitania Note was given to the public. It was received, except in the German-language press, with an all but universal enthusiasm. A small minority who had gone to war already, like Mr. Roosevelt or the emotional Mr. Whitney Warren, were heard to damn it as too weak; but the Allies were kindness itself. British papers dropped their scorn for the 'too proud to fight' speech with an interesting suddenness. 'Nothing less than the conscience of humanity,' said the London *Times*, 'makes itself audible in his measured and incisive sentences'; while the *English Review* caught an inspired vision of 'the President wrestling with the Wilhelmstrasse for the soul of Germany.' Mr. Page cabled his joyous relief. Such great men as Lansdowne, Balfour and Bonar Law were generous in their approval. Sir Edward was good enough to express to House his distinguished approbation — not forgetting to lime the twig a little more thickly as he did so. Had the United States taken any other attitude, he said, she 'would have been totally without... influence in the concert of nations, either now or hereafter'; and 'I am sure,' House dutifully added in his report to the President, 'that this is true.'

London, like Colonel House, not unnaturally assumed that the United States was now practically one of the Allies. It was to learn with something of a shock that Washington did not share this opinion. To its astonishment, Mr. Wilson had barely exploded his bombshell in the Wilhelmstrasse before he began exploding lesser ones in Downing Street. Mr. Page, to his rebellious disgust, was ordered to press the trade controversy, and on May 16 the President even tried to revive the submarine-blockade compromise. To imagine that the British, after the Lusitania Note had brought us to the verge of war, would assist in removing the issue was the acme of futility; but there was another flutter of cables and the last fortnight of May was devoted to this quaint project. It came to nothing, but the negotiations were enlivened by the subsequently famous episode of the Dumba telegram, in which Mr. Bryan apparently stands convicted of having at least intimated to the Austrian Ambassador that the United States did not wish to go to war over the Lusitania. For this black treason the Secretary of State has often been reproved, and his indiscretion has even been held up as the sole reason why the Central Powers did not at once accede to all our demands, scrap their submarines and resign themselves to strangulation. Yet this is not a very convincing theory; while, when one recalls the confidential relations between House and Page and the British statesmen, even the treason seems less than heinous. It was only a few days after Mr. Bryan's conversation with Ambassador Dumba that Colonel House, lunching with his friend Sir Edward, actually read him 'all the telegrams that have passed between the President, Gerard and myself since we last met.'

On the 29th of May, Ambassador Gerard put the German reply to the Lusitania Note upon the cables. It was simply a rebuttal of our argument and a play for time. On the next day, Sunday, May 30, Colonel House noted in his diary: 'I have concluded that war with Germany is inevitable, and this afternoon at 6 o'clock I decided to go home on the S.S. St. Paul on Saturday.' He was going, he told Plunkett, 'to persuade the President not to conduct a milk-and-water war, but to put all the strength, all the virility and all the energy of our nation into it.' The Colonel's sole justification for preparing such a bath of blood for his countrymen was his hope of establishing a new world order of peace and security as a result. Yet Colonel House, after all his negotiating, had not received even a shred of valid assurance that the Allies would support such a new order. He had no treaty; he had no guarantees; he had nothing but the altruistic though necessarily ulterior generalities of Sir Edward Grey — who had himself told House that he did not speak for his Cabinet, that he could speak much less for the French and not at all for the Russians! House sailed on the 5th of June.

But war depended on the Germans; and as a matter of fact it was not until the day after the Colonel had decided it to be 'inevitable' that the responsible German authorities even brought themselves to face their problem. Already it was confused in the three-cornered feud in progress between the Army, the Navy and the Foreign Office. The nation had naturally hailed the Lusitania sinking as a brilliant success. There were triumphant editorials, poems and postcards; and in Munich an obscure artisan struck off the famous medal which (after it had been reproduced in enormous quantities by a London firm and scattered by the British all over the world) was to prove so powerful an instrument of Entente propaganda. The sailors, of course, were all against surrender. Why waste time with the United States? The Germans, like Colonel House, knew that we were already in effect a partner of the Entente, and many readily convinced themselves, with Marse Henry, that an American declaration of war would mean little. But the Chancellor and the Foreign Office wavered; and when on May 31 the Kaiser finally summoned a general council on the subject at his G.H.Q. at Pless, Falkenhayn, speaking for the Army command, agreed with the civilians. The submarines were not, he felt, achieving results commensurate with the risk.

The Chancellor refused to take responsibility for a continuation of the campaign unless it were modified. Von Tirpitz and the naval people countered by insisting that it had to be all or nothing. This was basically sound, for it undercut the fatal instinct of the politician for half measures; but it was also a shrewd maneuver. In the end the Kaiser left it to Bethmann — unless he would accept responsibility for abandoning the submarine war altogether, it must go on. The Chancellor yielded, as Tirpitz knew he would, and thus lightly was another fateful issue determined.

In Washington on the following day, much the same sort of thing was happening. At his Cabinet meeting Mr. Wilson presented the draft of a second Note — strenuous, but not too strenuous. The belligerent Garrison was frank enough to call for a flat yes-or-no demand upon Germany; Mr. Bryan, who seemed 'under a great strain,' pressed the opposite objection. Someone said that if there was to be a strong note to Germany there should be an equally powerful protest against the British trade restrictions; but several rose in outrage at this suggestion that a mere question of commerce should be 'considered at the same moment when we were discussing a grave question of human lives.' At this folly Mr. Bryan not unreasonably 'got excited' and bluntly told them that they were all pro-Ally. Again he was sternly rebuked by the

President, while the others kindly explained to the ignorant Secretary that the British trade regulations had really been drawn 'to expedite the shipment of non-contraband goods and not to delay them.' In the end the President dismissed them by saying that his own mind was not made up anyway.

After the meeting Mr. Bryan told Mr. Wilson that he could not sign this second Note. Perhaps it checked the imperious President. On June 2 Count Bernstorff gained a personal interview with him. There was a long conversation. The Ambassador found the President 'animated solely by a desire to preserve peace' and privately concluded that Mr. Wilson would never actually fight of his own motion, but that the country might force him into it. Perhaps even so shrewd a man as Bernstorff did not quite realize the extent to which the political mind will juggle profoundly contradictory policies within itself. Again and again the President stressed the 'humanitarian' aspect — he didn't want civilians endangered on the high seas, yet could not face the basic practical issues which such a desire raised. The way he put it was that it behooved Germany 'by giving up the submarine campaign to appeal to the moral sense of the world.' Count Bernstorff, who was no moralist, saw himself confronted by the practical problem of managing both these romantics in Washington and his own romantics in Berlin; and he finally thought he saw the solution. It was to urge upon Berlin, not the dangers of American intervention, but the advantages which Washington might be induced, through a voluntary surrender on the submarine, to extort from the Allies.

President Wilson seems unintentionally to have misled Count Bernstorff as to the possibility of getting Great Britain to relax the blockade, and Tirpitz not unreasonably dismissed the Bernstorff policy as 'Utopian.' Yet the Chancellor continued to waver; the submarines were not stopping British imports, and a compromise idea again suggested itself. Armed with Bernstorff's cables, Bethmann on June 5 secured a secret order from the Kaiser forbidding any further submarine attacks on large passenger liners.

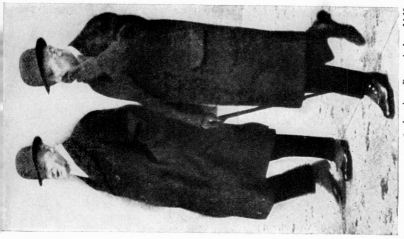

COUNT JOHANN VON BERNSTORFF

German Ambassador to the United States

CAPTAIN BOY-ED AND CAPTAIN
VON PAPEN

The German naval and military attachés, recalled in December, 1915, at the request of the
United States Government

Outwardly he would continue to defend the U-boats. It was a wonderfully characteristic example of the temporizations of statesmen. After partially curbing the submarine as a concession to the United States, the fact was kept secret even from Bernstorff as a concession to the Navy, thus largely throwing away the only political advantage to be gained from the military sacrifice.

In Washington they were also temporizing. A 'confused and somewhat tiresome' Cabinet discussion on June 4 got nowhere; it wearied the President 'perceptibly' and 'did not help him.' And on Saturday, June 5, a fresh blow fell. Mr. McAdoo was at lunch when Secretary Bryan unexpectedly called upon him. Mr. Bryan's 'face was haggard. He was visibly nervous and remarked that he had not slept well.' He believed, he told McAdoo, that the second Lusitania Note would 'surely lead to war with Germany, and that as a profound believer in peace he could not conscientiously follow the President in the proposed course.' Mr. Bryan, who had taken an immense pride and satisfaction in his great office, had concluded that his usefulness as Secretary of State was at an end. Mr. McAdoo hurriedly thought up arguments; to them all the Secretary of State replied that he must abide by his own feeling and his own conscience. He must resign. Mr. McAdoo carried him back to his own home; there he found that Mrs. Bryan looked as jaded as her husband; there 'was an air of fatigue about each of them.' It was the silent evidence to the exhausting emotional struggle they had fought out with themselves. But the victory was complete, and Mr. McAdoo saw that argument was of no use.

It was a bombshell. The President realized at once that it would tend to undermine the whole theory that the Administration's policy was a purely pacific one. It would create a 'mistaken' impression that we were forcing the issue. What the President did not see was that Mr. Bryan was essentially right. A sudden check had come which might have led Mr. Wilson to re-examine more carefully the precise bases of his own action. Instead, he merely overrode it; his advisers told him that the public would

probably side against Mr. Bryan, and the President let him go.
On Monday, June 8, the resignation was announced to the
Cabinet. The ex-Secretary was invited to a last sitting with his
colleagues, and was present while the Note received its final
discussion. It was a mildly worded but complete rejection of the
German thesis. They talked about it for a time, and the meeting
broke up. Mr. Bryan invited the others to a final luncheon;
six of them accepted. The meal passed in generalities, until
just as they were finishing Bryan spoke out with a brief and simple
explanation of his act. 'Each of us said some pleasant things to
him along conventional lines' until it came to Lane, who, perhaps genuinely touched by Bryan's obvious sincerity and nobility
of purpose, said: 'You are the most real Christian I know.' The
other was moved. 'I must act,' he began, 'according to my conscience. I go out into the dark. The President has the Prestige
and the Power on his side ——' Then suddenly he broke down
completely, stopped, and finally added: 'I have many friends who
would die for me.'

That evening the extras were on the street, and those who had
guessed that the public would side with the President were confirmed in their judgment. 'When I told Bryan that his action
would be criticized,' Mr. McAdoo has since said, 'I had no idea
of the hurricane of abuse that was to howl around him. His
resignation was denounced as a disloyal, traitorous act by many
newspapers and public speakers. The New York *World* declared
that his resignation was "unspeakable treachery, not only to
the President but to the nation," and the *World's* criticism was a
fair sample.' Thanks to the passionate newspapers Mr. Bryan's
heavy sacrifice for his conscience was to be of no effect. He never
had a detailed understanding of the intricate issues by which he
was surrounded; his mind was too slow and too unfamiliar with
the office to make effective the attitude to which his instinct
compelled him. But the instinct was so much surer than that of
the bemused intellectuals, lawyers and politicians who decried
him as to clothe him now with a homely nobility that they were

never to attain. It led him to a failure, but a failure which enshrines him in one of the more honorable niches of our history. Mr. Bryan was gone. The process which he so clearly felt must lead on to war, with all its suffering for the common man whom he represented, ground ominously forward.

VI. DEEPENING ENTANGLEMENT

i

YET it did not come to war — not then. What really saved Mr. Wilson (and destroyed Mr. Bryan) in the summer of 1915 was neither the strength nor the astuteness of our diplomacy. It was the limited capacity of the German dockyards — a factor which our diplomatists had scarcely even considered.

When the submarine campaign was launched in February the Germans had but sixteen completed U-boats and only eleven more under construction. With so small a force success had to depend, not upon actual sinkings, but upon their effect in terrorizing merchant shipping from the seas, and in this respect the campaign was a flat failure. The destruction achieved, on the other hand, was remarkable. At the opening of the war the German surface raiders in their best month had accounted for not quite 100,000 tons of enemy shipping, and as these cruisers were tracked down, Allied losses had fallen rapidly. With March, however, the first full month of the submarine war, they rose again to 80,000 tons; by May they reached 120,000 tons, and the average losses through the next twelve months were to come to about 133,000 tons monthly.[1] Yet these results were achieved by a few hundred men in a handful of small vessels, at a cost in life and effort hardly equal to the price of a day or two of futile

---

[1] The figures include Entente losses from mines and surface raiders, but the U-boats were of course the principal agents of destruction.

fighting in the land war. It was tempting evidence as to what might be done with U-boats — as soon as there were enough of them.

To build a submarine fleet, however, took time. The active force did not pass thirty boats until July; there were casualties to contend with, and another year was to pass before the effective strength could be maintained at much beyond this figure. The Navy admitted that the flotilla could not be brought to decisive numbers before 1916. Under the circumstances it was not worth while to risk too much for the U-boat — until 1916. Count Bernstorff was distressed by his inability to discover whether in the last analysis Berlin's real policy was war rather than surrender or surrender rather than war, and was finally forced to the conclusion that Berlin did not know itself. In this he was doubtless right. All that Berlin wanted was to avoid a war with the United States at the time, but to make no surrender that would foreclose an intensive use of the submarine later on.

In this simple desire to escape the necessity either of fighting or of giving way, Washington closely resembled Berlin. The Note of June 9, which Mr. Bryan had been unable to sign, was presented on the 11th. Mr. Wilson's periods were sonorous; the United States, he declared, 'is contending for something much greater than mere rights of property or privileges of commerce. It is contending for nothing less high and sacred than the rights of humanity.' Assiduously Mr. Gerard, as a practical diplomatist, set himself to translate this into some kind of working compromise — safe conducts for American ships or for specific belligerent passenger vessels. He was severely suppressed by Mr. Lansing, now Acting Secretary of State. Mr. Wilson and the State Department sternly entrenched themselves behind the rights of humanity, and then waited patiently for nearly a month while the Germans were considering their reply to this second Note. 'The tide of anti-German feeling,' Count Bernstorff reported on June 9, 'is still running pretty high, but it now may be regarded as certain that neither the President nor the American people want a war with Germany.' His British counterpart agreed with him. 'Nothing is more certain,' Spring Rice reported to his own government, 'than that the people of the United States are ready to accept any reasonable excuse for accepting Germany's contention,' or at any rate, for doing little more about it than they had done about the many damaging contentions of the Allies. The Germans refrained, more or less, from torpedoing large passenger vessels; in the succession of Notes which continued to pass between Washington and Berlin neither government abandoned its position, but the crisis sank imperceptibly away. The truth was that the situation in both countries worked admirably toward a simple evasion of the issue for the time being — but also toward a hardening of the conflicting policies in such a way as to guarantee that the issue, whenever it should arise again, would be doubly acute.

Just as the submarine, moreover, had helped to save the British at the crisis of the controversy over their trade restrictions, the trade restrictions were now in turn to hasten the relaxation of the tension over the submarine. In June our Consul General in London was reporting that the British authorities, although they had never even put cotton on the contraband list, had in effect 'interposed a veto' upon the American cotton trade, not only with Germany, but with the European neutrals. Yet 'enormously increased quantities of cotton, and American cotton principally, have been exported from Great Britain to the same destinations from which our own trading ships are excluded.' Toward the end of June Great Britain at last got around to answering our energetic protest, in March, against the offshore blockade; the New York newspapers loyally defended the British case, but the cotton country and the exporters were vociferous, while even the general public began to realize something of the true extent of British control over American commerce. 'About the middle of June,' as Mr. Arthur W. Dunn remembered, 'our people learned that Great Britain was rifling our mails, and that our commerce had been detained.'

The pressure declined. Mr. Roosevelt perceived the 'hideous' truth that the President was actually managing to talk out the Lusitania crisis, and was of course furious. 'The iniquitous peace propaganda of the last fifteen years,' he wrote to Senator Lodge, 'has finally had its effect. I think we can offset it, and will offset it, finally; but it will be a work of years unless there comes a catastrophe such as Wilson and Bryan are preparing us for.' Sir Edward was no less alarmed at the turn affairs were taking, and sent off a skillful letter after Colonel House:

> The dilemma I foresee is that the desire of the people of the United States to keep out of war with Germany may lead to burying the Lusitania issue inconclusively, in which case Germany will disregard, and the other belligerents will hope for little from, American influence in the future and the tendency will be to discount it.

Sir Edward had been careful to give Colonel House a naval convoy through the submarine zone. But though preserving him from the U-boat, Sir Edward could not preserve the Colonel within the radius of his own gracious charm; and House was by this time back in the United States. He had retired to a summer place at Roslyn, Long Island, for rest and meditation; and it soon appeared that the man who had come home to urge war with all the strength the nation could command had suffered a sea change. On June 16 he was writing out a long summary of the situation for the President. Several remarkable truths had begun to dawn upon the Colonel. He now realized that the war was 'a war of munitions, rather than one of men' and that the Allies were desperately dependent upon the American supply — though, when the Germans had told him as much three months earlier, he had thought it 'nonsense.' But this was not all. A really ominous thought had come to him. With the failure of the Dardanelles campaign he realized that the military position of the Allies was in fact a serious one, and 'I need not tell you,' he went on, 'that if the Allies fail to win it must necessarily mean a reversal of our entire policy.'

Perhaps the Colonel might have thought of that before dedicating the United States to a policy of 'neutrality' which required an Allied victory. As it was, he seems to have felt that it was too late to do much about it, and he believed that we must probably 'drift into' war with Germany. But he now regarded that eventuality without enthusiasm. Sir Edward's anxious bait brought little response from the Colonel; and on June 23 Spring Rice reported the sad truth that, although they could still count on House's 'hearty co-operation,' it must after all be 'with the proviso that America comes first.' That same day there was a minor comedy at the State Department. Mr. Page had cabled asking whether the great John Singer Sargent might return a German decoration through Department channels. There was a distinct note of asperity in Mr. Lansing's terse retort:

> Not matters with which the Department or its officers abroad can have any connection. Sargent should reimburse Embassy for your telegram and this reply, five dollars.

Patience with the pro-Allies was clearly wearing thin. It was also on June 23 that Mr. Roosevelt was again pouring out his despair (with a better command of invective than of Greek derivatives) over the outrageous Wilson:

> A true logothete, a real sophist. . . . I feel particularly bitter toward him at the moment because when Bryan left I supposed that meant that Wilson really had decided to be a man and I prepared myself to stand whole-heartedly by him.

That monumental effort had been in vain, for the only real issue had been 'one as to the proper dilution of tepid milk and water.' But since this was precisely what the nation at bottom wanted, Mr. Roosevelt's rage was of no account. President Wilson had triumphed.

On June 24 the President left Washington for his summer capital; and according to Secretary Houston's memoirs, from that time until the middle of December 'in the field of foreign relations there was no departure in policy which caused or demanded much discussion or consideration at the hands of the Cabinet, or which I felt it particularly necessary to note.' The situation, Count Bernstorff reported on July 2, 'has returned to normal'; and he even felt that the Lusitania incident might on the whole prove to have exerted a 'favorable influence' because 'the Government... now fully realizes the importance of these questions of sea warfare.'

ii

Unfortunately, nothing had been settled, nor could any amount of reason now undo the irrationalities of the past or much affect the underlying forces working day in and day out to confirm our entanglement in the Allied cause. The President did reject the remarkable suggestion that Mr. Page be brought home and made Secretary of State; instead, the appointment went to Mr. Lansing, who, though at bottom pro-British, was also an obstinate and capable legalist. And it was mainly as a technical adviser upon international law that the President selected him. Mr. Wilson had decided, as he told Mr. McAdoo, to be his own Secretary of State.

It was time. But what could even Mr. Wilson do now to alter the basic situation in which he had permitted the nation to become enmeshed? In May the British Government had placed a $100,-000,000 order for lyddite shell and shrapnel with the Bethlehem Steel Company. The 'shell scandal' in the spring had finally aroused Great Britain to the fact that it was a modern war which she was fighting; the munitions supply had been wrested from the feeble hands of the soldiers and transferred to the volcanic energies of Mr. Lloyd George, and the intensive exploitation of the vast resources of America was one of his first cares. With June our total exports for the fiscal year reached a new record, while the New York hotels were swarming with the eager competitors for the unparalleled profits of death. The Morgan purchasing bureau 'immeasurably broadened the field of production,' calling new businesses into existence and enormously expanding old ones to meet the insatiable needs of the Entente. In July, Mr. Whitlock, touring the German trenches in Northern France, found the ultimate consumers methodically labelling and photographing dud shells exported to them from America through French and British guns. But who cared for that? From the middle of 1915 the full war demand of the Entente began to develop, and the great tide of wartime prosperity, generated by that tremendous suction, began to flow in earnest just as Mr. Schwab had cheerfully predicted.

The evangelical pacifists persisted in their extraordinary notion that the way to peace was to stop the export of war material, even to stop the war; and Jane Addams had led a large delegation to The Hague that spring, hoping to found a women's peace conference that would call the governments to their senses and end the conflict. As the golden stream of war orders spread through our economy, such efforts by visionary females were regarded with an only more scornful amusement. The more cultivated peace movement was careful to avoid entanglement in anything so 'impractical'; it clung to the more popular objective of organizing peace only after the current war should have ended in victory for the Allies. It was on June 17 that the League to Enforce Peace, the flower of this altruistic agitation, was formally launched at Philadelphia. Ex-President Taft was at its head; Dr. A. Lawrence Lowell was chairman of its executive committee; and many other eminent and high-minded men were enlisted in its ranks. A powerful propaganda engine had been created to add the military strength of the United States to the guarantee of a 'permanent' peace system, once the Allies should have safely destroyed 'Prussian militarism.'

But could it stop there? Mr. Roosevelt, that distinguished peace-lover, pro-Ally and militarist, had early been attracted to the movement; and it was now to acquire an almost equally disconcerting recruit. Senator Henry Cabot Lodge was a bitter political enemy of Mr. Wilson; he was a close friend and confidant

of Sir Cecil Spring Rice; he was the most ardent Congressional
advocate of preparedness and had long been the shrewdest leader
of the new militarist-imperial industrialism rapidly developing
in the United States. In a commencement address at Union
College on June 9, Senator Lodge, under the flaming title 'Force
and Peace,' now suddenly enrolled himself among the Utopists.

> Nations must unite as men unite in order to preserve peace and
> order. The great nations must be so united as to be able to say to
> any single great country, you must not go to war, and they can only
> say that effectively when the country desiring war knows that the
> force which the united nations place behind peace is irresistible. ...
> It may seem Utopian at this moment to suggest a union of civilized
> nations in order to put a controlling force behind the maintenance
> of peace and international order, but it is through... the search for
> Utopias that the real advances have been made.

Thus the Senator, like Mr. Roosevelt, sacrificed Washington
and Jefferson in the interests of world peace, clearly perceiving
that a first requisite would be a huge program of military preparation in the United States — for the greater aid to the Entente and
the greater discomfiture of Mr. Wilson.

Preparedness was making noble headway. General Wood had
conceived the idea of extending his voluntary training camps to
include not merely immature undergraduates but influential
younger leaders of the community. The War Department cruelly
denied him funds for this inspired engine of publicity, but the
manna suddenly fell from Mr. Bernard Baruch, of all people in the
world, who sent a check for $10,000 and levied upon his wealthy
friends for more. From the middle of June onward the recruiting
for the 'business men's Plattsburg' was rapid and spectacular.
Mr. Roosevelt journeyed all the way to California that summer in
order to preach the gospel of 'National defence' at the Panama-
Pacific Exposition — which was making its pathetic attempt to
conserve the glories of peaceful industry amid the blood-soaked
world which that industrialism had largely assisted in producing.

The newest Utopian, Senator Lodge, was 'preaching and reiterating this doctrine wherever I go.' But for what were they preparing? At the end of June Mr. Page was writing in a very gloomy tone to Colonel House:

> The position in France is essentially the same as it was in November, only the Germans are much more strongly entrenched. Their great plenty of machine guns enables them to use fewer men and to kill more than the Allies.... I find more and more men here who fear that the Germans will never be forced out of Belgium. And the era of the giant aeroplane seems about to come — a machine that can carry several tons and several men and go great distances — two engines, two propellers and the like. It isn't at all impossible, I am told, that these machines may be the things that will at last end the war — possibly, but I doubt it.
>
> At any rate, it is true that a great wave of discouragement is come.... More and more people are getting their nerves knocked out.... It's got hot in London — hotter than I've ever known it. It gets lonelier... and sadder.

For all our new war industries, for all the military agitation in America, it was still hard for these men to realize that it was war with which the United States was dealing, or to grasp the colossal human agony and passion which that involved. On July 2 a strange little drama was enacted in a great country house on the north shore of Long Island — in that same peaceful terrain where Mr. Roosevelt had happily played at toy soldiers. Sir Cecil Spring Rice was visiting Mr. J. P. Morgan. In the evening he was sitting with Mr. and Mrs. Morgan, surrounded by the secure luxury into which there could penetrate no sound or hint of the ceaseless slaughter, three thousand miles away, which the banker and the diplomat were doing their utmost to maintain. Abruptly the butler came into the room and said 'in a most *fearful* voice,' 'Mr. Morgan, go upstairs!' They rushed out, thinking of a fire or something of the sort; but there was nothing upstairs, and Mr. and Mrs. Morgan were coming down again when they were suddenly confronted by a strange figure with a revolver in either hand. 'So you are Mr. Morgan,' the man said; the weapons rose, and for an instant the great financier was faced, in his own peaceful country home, by that death which he had been exporting in such quantity.

Courageously Mr. Morgan leapt upon the stranger; they went down, but in the scuffle the revolvers were discharged and the banker was twice wounded slightly. The man was taken. He said afterwards:

> I went to the Morgan home in order to force him to use his great influence to stop the shipment of explosives. That is why I took some explosives with me, in order to be able to demonstrate to him, *ad oculos*, what the use of machines of murder means, but I did not wish to hurt anyone. I wanted him to be in the same danger (him and his family) that we are imposing on Europe.... I tried to shoot in the air, but some one grabbed my hand.... He was the very last one that should have been hurt; he was to go out and do the work I could not do.

The man was identified as bearing the name of Erich Münter. Was it impossible, perhaps, for America to munition one side in a world conflict without being brushed by the struggle? That the banker should suffer a few minutes of peril and some days of discomfort as his share of the titanic suffering which he was helping to promote seemed quite dreadful at the time. 'It was an awful business at the Morgans',' Spring Rice wrote to Mrs. Cabot Lodge, 'except that they behaved so well.' The perhaps equally awful business on the European battle lines had claimed that day its average of some five thousand lives, more or less, with its countless others hurt or mutilated or ruined; and it was to claim one more when Münter committed suicide in prison. It was generally agreed that the man was insane; no doubt he was, and the fact remains as its own commentary upon the sanity of those fantastic years.

He had, however, borne a German name. Was there any truth

in the swelling tide of allegation as to vast German conspiracies in the United States — conspiracies against our peace and public order, against the munitions supply, against the purity of opinion? Unfortunately for the Germans, there was. With the Lusitania their official propaganda was brought to an end, and in June Dr. Dernburg sailed for home, his mission a disastrous failure. Count Bernstorff attended a farewell dinner to him in the roof-garden of the Ritz-Carlton at New York; and a party for whom the next table had been reserved declined to sit down in a spot defiled by the presence of Germans. The collapse of the open propaganda effort, however, only drove the agents who remained into the more dangerous method of clandestine subsidy. They appreciated, no less than Sir Gilbert Parker, the importance of getting native Americans to present their case; but where the Allies could command their thousands of devoted American propagandists, the Germans could find scarcely a handful. A list they drew up of possible native spokesmen contained only thirty-three names — a pitiful showing. The Allied propaganda, moreover, enjoyed the inestimable advantage of being self-financing. Our public clamored for the books, articles and motion-picture films which conveyed it. Old-established American publishing houses found it profitable, and did not think it unpatriotic, to enter into agreements with the Entente governments for the distribution of propagandist war books, and there was a huge trade in volumes on trench life from the French and British standpoint. Those who voiced the German side of the case found no such markets. The German representatives in the United States were led, not unnaturally, to supply them secretly with assistance.

Dr. Albert, who had originally come out with Dernburg, remained as the directing head of these activities. Mr. William Bayard Hale, a well-known American publicist and foreign correspondent, was retained to assist in a work which, if but little more reprehensible than what was everywhere being done for the Allies, exposed the Germans to far greater risk in case of discovery. Two of the most objective studies of America's relationship to the war published at that time were Frank Harris's 'England or Germany —?' and Edwin J. Clapp's 'Economic Aspects of the War.' Unfortunately, Mr. Harris was on Dr. Albert's payroll. Mr. Clapp was a professor of New York University who attracted the attention of Dr. Albert by some lectures on the British interference with American trade. Dr. Albert induced him to expand these into a book, and paid him some twenty thousand dollars in all to cover costs of preparation, publication and advertising. The quality of the work is indicated by the fact that the Yale University Press gave it its imprint. Even so, the sale was disappointing; while Mr. Clapp's really useful study remains tarred today by this ulterior aid.

Such paid propaganda was dangerous enough, but insensibly it led them further. About some of their efforts there is a certain touch of quaintness. Mr. Hale was at one time deep in negotiations with some 'ladies of Baltimore' who claimed that their League of American Women for Strict Neutrality had gathered two hundred thousand signatures to a petition to Congress. Mrs. Hale plunged into a humanitarian propaganda against the export of horses to the Allied battle lines; and it was decided to prepare a touching film scenario in this connection, the heroine to be a retired fire-engine mare who, after her years of noble service to humanity, was despatched to a miserable end upon the fields of Flanders. In their prolific organization of ostensibly native American peace societies and arms embargo movements the Germans were getting upon more devious ground. The American Truth Society, headed by Mr. Jeremiah O'Leary, poured forth German propaganda under seemingly domestic auspices. The American Humanity League, the American Independence Union, and many other devotedly pacifistic organizations of dubious parentage were very active that summer. On June 19 they held a great mass meeting in New York with Mr. Bryan himself as principal speaker, with Representative Frank Buchanan, member of the House Committee on Naval Affairs, as another, and with diplomatic representatives of the Central Powers on the platform, including Captains Boy-Ed and von Papen. A vast throng appeared and extra speakers harangued the overflow in the streets. Yet it did not help the embargo movement; and had anyone learned that it was Captains Boy-Ed and von Papen who supplied the funds, it would probably have destroyed it.

The Arms Embargo Conference, established in the Middle West later in the summer, long concealed its real inspiration; it secured the support of various prominent politicians and 'forced the papers to believe,' as it complacently reported to Mr. Hale, 'that it is, as it claims, an American movement.' No one knew at the time how far the German Government might be connected with these spontaneous manifestations of pacifism; but it was inevitable that they should fill the air with doubt and rumor. The *Providence Journal*, a responsible, conservative newspaper whose editor, Mr. John R. Rathom, happened to be an Australian, was leaping into national prominence with the first of its long series of sensational 'revelations' of German propaganda and conspiracy. Mr. Rathom claimed to have his secret agents planted everywhere, even in the German Embassy itself; he produced damning code messages (of a curiously detective-thriller character) said to have been plucked from the ether by his own wireless operators. The possibility that Mr. Rathom might be making propaganda himself apparently occurred to no one; and it was not until afterward that he was brought to confess that most of his revelations were the figments of a romantic imagination. The nation read, trembled and half believed; and a first-class spy scare was clearly in the making.

Few were ever scandalized by the *Providence Journal*, even though at least one Cabinet member, Mr. Lane, believed its Australian editor to be 'running the spy system of the British Embassy'; but when the Germans' clandestine purchase of the New York *Mail and Express* later came out, it caused a terrific furor. What subterranean activities the Entente agents may have engaged in is not known, for they were never investigated; they were probably few, for the Allies had little need of secrecy. The representatives of the Central Powers, on the other hand, were driven to try everything. Count Bernstorff and his attachés had started to buy up munitions factories and raw materials; the Austrians now set up an employment agency in order to take their sympathizers out of the munitions factories by finding them jobs elsewhere; the foreign-language press was subsidized to agitate among munitions workers, and the idea of fomenting strikes and sabotage soon took shape.

The most spectacular activities of this whole campaign, however, appear to have been those of Captain von Rintelen, who had arrived at the beginning of April to do battle single-handed against the munitions supply. Count Bernstorff has disclaimed all knowledge of or responsibility for Rintelen's achievements; the Captain himself (in whose memoirs truth seems not wholly unadorned by art) declares that he worked throughout with Boy-Ed and von Papen. However that may be, he began by organizing a conspiracy for planting incendiary bombs in the holds of munitions ships, and had some slight success with it. As early as June 5, Spring Rice was complaining to the State Department about the mysterious fires in such vessels; and the New York police department was duly stirred to a feverish activity in the matter, which yielded the results only too often produced by feverish police activity. Rintelen was never apprehended until he made the mistake of leaving the country in the fall, when the British secret service (which must have been very well organized in the United States) promptly gathered him in.

After the bomb conspiracy, his greatest achievement was to be Labor's National Peace Council. Into this work of art Captain Rintelen poured his government's money, much of which would seem to have been absorbed in passing by David Lamar, the obscurely celebrated 'Wolf of Wall Street' whom Rintelen enlisted as his agent. The council was set up in May, ostensibly as an organization of those union labor leaders who demanded an arms embargo. In June it held its first convention at the St. James Hotel in Washington, where it elected Representative Buchanan (a former president of the structural iron workers) as its head, consumed lavish supplies of cigars and comestibles, and passed formidable resolutions summoning the President to embargo munitions as an aid to peace.

The following month it held another meeting, this time in the still more impressive surroundings of the New Willard, and it passed still more formidable resolutions offering to support strikes in munitions factories. This might, conceivably, have been serious. On that rising tide of profits and prosperity, large-scale strikes would have been only natural; while it is difficult to think of a better moment in which union labor might have struck, if it was ever to do so, for a larger share in the proceeds of its industry. But this move to take over the American Federation of Labor at once brought the great Sam Gompers, whose private property it was, hurrying into the field. In that overwhelmingly pro-Ally atmosphere, Mr. Gompers clearly perceived which side of the bread carried the butter. He sprang to the defence of the munitions contracts and the established order.

He was 'much concerned,' as he put it in his memoirs, at thus finding 'a number of valuable labor men' caught in the Teutonic net. Mr. Gompers by this time knew all about the Teutonic net. He sternly excommunicated his friend, Dr. Rumely, for taking the editorship of the *Mail and Express* in the German interest, but he was proud to record that Mr. Rathom of the *Providence Journal* 'reposed confidence in me and gave me much information,' and with the aid of such distinguished and disinterested counsel Mr. Gompers set himself to reason with the erring brethren. When a big munitions strike did break out in the Bridgeport factories, Mr. Gompers rushed off at once to stop it and so 'protect the good name and safety of the labor movement.' The British did not have to combat Rintelen's machinations. Mr. Gompers did it for them. Later on, there were some long-shoremen's and munitions strikes of considerable proportions; but it seems rather doubtful that Labor's National Peace Council could rightly claim much credit for them.

The German conspiracies in the summer of 1915 appear in the upshot to have been of very small practical effect. It was one grossly disproportionate, certainly, to the increasing cloud of rumor and suspicion which they served to spread. As early as May President Wilson directed the Secret Service to take up the trail of hidden violators of our neutrality. By July the artless efforts of Rintelen and the others had reduced Spring Rice to one of his periodic panics. The attack on Mr. Morgan, he had now convinced himself, was simply a part of a vast plot; the Germans, he reported to Grey, 'expect any measures [by the United States] against Germany to be followed immediately by explosions on board United States ships and at all arsenals, by the crippling of means of communication, by the appearance of submarines and by armed demonstrations by large bodies of well-disciplined men.... Extraordinary measures of precaution have now become necessary in all arms factories, at the docks and on board vessels, even vessels of the United States Navy. It is probable that German agents are everywhere and excellently organized.' Many high officers of the Administration took a similar view; the public, under the diligent efforts of Mr. Rathom and other editors, was manifesting a 'universal feeling of fear and suspicion'; the air was ripening for an explosion.

Such was the position of affairs when on the afternoon of Saturday, July 24, Dr. Albert left the Hamburg-American Line offices in New York City on his way home for the day. Mr. George Sylvester Viereck, a devoted worker in the propaganda bureau, accompanied him, and the doctor's brief-case was stuffed with papers relating to the bureau's multitudinous activities. The two settled themselves in a Sixth Avenue Elevated train, and when presently Mr. Viereck got off the doctor immersed himself in reading. The peculiarly jerky yet monotonous progress of New York elevated trains seems almost designed to lull the inattentive passenger into forgetfulness; and Dr. Albert, like so many others before and after him whose brief-cases were not stuffed with the fate of nations, failed to realize that the train had halted at his

station, Fiftieth Street, until it was almost too late. He sprang —
with how human an impulse! — for the door; he was already upon
the platform when it flashed over him that he had left the brief-
case on the seat. Frantically, the burly doctor fought his way back
into the car. A young woman told him that another man had
snatched the bag. Dr. Albert came 'pouring out in a hurry.'
A desperate survey of the people on the platform yielded nothing;
he raced down the stairs and into the street, panic written upon
his face. A moment later he caught sight of the brief-case under
the arm of a stranger, but just as he gave chase an open type
street car came along. The thief leapt to the running-board;
the wild-eyed doctor was in hot pursuit, but the man whispered
something to the conductor and the car rapidly passed the next
corner and disappeared.

On Monday there was a modest advertisement in the classi-
fied columns: 'Lost — brown leather bag containing documents.
... $20 reward.' Nothing came of it. The propaganda bureau,
anxiously checking back to discover just what that brief-case had
contained, resigned itself to the faint hope that the stranger had
been only a common sneak-thief.

iii

While the propaganda bureau waited and trembled, history
was not standing still. The preparedness movement rolled on to
ever greater triumphs — not wholly unassisted, perhaps, by more
complex motives than those of pure patriotism. Mr. Hudson
Maxim's fat and gory volume, 'Defenceless America,' was now
flooding the country. 'The main object of this book,' as the patriot inventor of high explosives exclaimed in his first sentence,
'is to present a phalanx of facts upon the defenceless condition of
this country and to show what must be done and done quickly
to avert the most dire calamity that can fall upon a people —
that of merciless invasion by a foreign foe.' The arrival of war —
which of course meant the Germans — was 'inevitable.' The

quaint fact that it was Mr. Maxim's now British brother, Sir Hiram, who had armed the Germans with the machine-guns before which young Englishmen were daily being laid in windrows as they sought to repel the merciless invasion of Belgium was a fact which somehow did not appear in Mr. Maxim's 'phalanx.' His simple object was but to 'lessen a little the effect of the pernicious propagandism of the pacifists,' to 'place a few more men upon the firing line' and to 'help Congressional appropriations for defence'— which could hardly fail to include large sums for high explosives and machine-guns.

Diligently the new preparedness groups, subsidized by a patriotic industry and finance, spread the gospel; more and more clearly the effects began to appear. No one could accuse Mr. Wilson or his Administration of a vulgar interest in the profits of munitions manufacture; but they were not blind to the fact that patriotism might have advantages of a different sort. Preparedness was becoming a political issue. As early as July 1 an observant Washington newspaperman was warning Mr. Roosevelt that 'it is the intention of the President to recommend an increase in the Army and the Navy for the purpose of "drawing your tooth,"' and a day or two later General Wood heard that the conversion of Colonel House was complete. House, he was told, had decided that the President 'was lost unless he got on the band-wagon of preparedness.' Mr. Tumulty, the President's secretary, had turned his practical mind to the problem. 'In my opinion,' he advised his chief, 'there is left to the Republican party but two available issues for the campaign of 1916 — the tariff and the question of national defence.' Six months before the President had been cold to the militarists, but now, on July 21, a White House press release announced that Mr. Wilson was planning to submit a program of military and naval increases to the coming Congress. It would be 'reasonable' but also 'adequate' — adequate, at any rate, to the defence of the nation against the Republicans.

It was time. The muster rolls at Plattsburg, when General Wood's 'business men's' camp opened there at the beginning of

August, sounded like 'Who's Who' and 'The Social Register' combined. The Roosevelts were there, of course; so were the adventurous Chanlers from their patrician fastnesses in Dutchess County; so were the Fishes and Milburns. Mr. Richard Harding Davis appeared in the gathering twilight of his glory; Mr. Robert Bacon, a former Secretary of State and Ambassador to France, packed the humble rifle; so did John Purroy Mitchel, the gallant young reform Mayor of New York, whose life was to be one of the sadder sacrifices two years later. Arthur Woods, his Police Commissioner, accompanied him; George Wharton Pepper, Pennsylvania's pure light of legality and morals, offered himself to his country; so did Dudley Field Malone, Willard Straight and (it is perhaps necessary to add) some hundreds of humbler clay. 'The butterflies of Newport and Bar Harbor,' according to General Wood's devoted biographer, 'complained that life was desolate, since the best of their young men were at Plattsburg. Once more, as seventeen years before, the public read of millionaires doing "kitchen police," digging ditches, and caught the message behind the incongruity.' It was all very strange, very fascinating and very democratic. For 'this was no play soldiering.' Although one might have thought that the total absence of hostile bullets, of gas, shellfire or bloodshed might have damaged the verisimilitude, they really did dig trenches.

On August 25 Mr. Roosevelt made a royal progress to Plattsburg to address the patriotic millionaires and business men. Since Plattsburg was, after all, an Army post; since the General's political ambitions were pretty well known and it would have been unwise to have given his great lesson in patriotism the appearance of a personal electioneering scheme, he induced his famous friend to eliminate from the address the hottest parts of its sizzling attack upon Mr. Wilson. But Mr. Roosevelt thoughtfully supplied them to the reporters afterwards. Secretary Garrison, torn between his own belief in preparedness and his distaste for seeing the Army converted into an instrument of politics, raised a fearful row; it convinced the insubordinate General that he was 'skating on thin

THE BUSINESS MEN'S CAMP AT PLATTSBURG, AUGUST, 1915
In the left foreground is Robert C. Bacon, former Ambassador to France

ice' but confirmed his resolve that 'I am going to skate.' General Wood knew that he had now finally forfeited the confidence of the Administration; he had in effect declared war upon the President, who was also his constitutional commander-in-chief. 'I am out for national preparedness,' as he said, 'and I am going to get it.'

To get preparedness one must of course build up a menace against which to prepare; the German Menace was developing rapidly under all this bellicose enthusiasm, and it scarcely smoothed the way of the Lusitania note-writing which had been going on in the meanwhile. Our Note of June 9 had convinced Grand Admiral von Tirpitz that 'America is so shamelessly, so barefacedly pro-British that it is hard to credit that we shall eat humble pie.' The German reply of July 8 left Secretary Lane indignant at the idea of having 'a damned army officer, filled with strutitudinousness, spit upon the American Flag — a damned, goose-stepping army officer!' It was, indeed, unpleasant; but it was also war. Secretary Lansing decided that the German Note must have been framed for 'home consumption' rather than in a 'sincere desire to reach an understanding' — exactly as were our own, that is to say. Colonel House hovered full of nobility above the scene, but Mr. Wilson, laboring to solve the problem of 'how to keep us out of war and at the same time maintain our dignity,' showed that the situation 'weighs heavily upon him.'

The result was another Note on July 21, stiffer than the earlier ones. The astute Bernstorff saw that matters were threatening to get out of hand. With skill and subtlety he worked at his own idea of utilizing a frank surrender on the submarine issue as a means of purchasing drastic action by the United States against the British blockade. On the one hand he applied himself to Colonel House, and soon the two were on 'very friendly and intimate terms.' He worked upon his own government with promises of what they could get if only they would yield on the Lusitania issue. Tirpitz and the Navy raged, but the Foreign Office told Bernstorff to continue, and even the Kaiser agreed to withhold another Note until it was seen what the Ambassador could accomplish.

Then, on August 19, there came disaster. The White Star liner Arabic was torpedoed and sunk without warning in the Irish Channel, with the loss of forty-four lives, two of them American citizens. 'My laboriously constructed diplomatic edifice,' as Bernstorff afterward put it, 'came tumbling about my ears, and things looked blacker than ever.' To President Wilson it must have seemed to be the end. Desperately he appealed to Colonel House. What could they do now? The Colonel answered hotly that they could either break diplomatic relations on the spot, summon Congress and lay the facts before it, or else tell Bernstorff privately that this time it was a choice between complete backdown and war. House favored the first course, which he knew would mean war at once; and when the President failed to act immediately upon that flaming advice, he told his diary that he was 'surprised' at the lengths to which Mr. Wilson seemed willing to go just to keep the peace.

For the second time the Colonel had gone to war with Germany. Fortunately, President Wilson's was a less reckless statesmanship, and presently it was to be vindicated. In the press there was another cry of outrage, but it was outrage not unmixed with caution. The Lusitania had broken the force of so relatively minor an incident as this; and ironically enough the Arabic case, over which House wanted to fight, actually precipitated a kind of settlement. Mr. Gerard called upon von Jagow; he was told that the sinking of the Arabic had been contrary to instructions. 'What instructions?' the Ambassador quickly asked, and the cat was out of the bag. Jagow confessed to the orders not to sink large passenger steamers. At the same time Bethmann-Hollweg, supported by Falkenhayn, decided to make a frontal attack upon Tirpitz and the submarines. At G.H.Q. at Pless on August 26 and 27 there was a confused battle for the wavering mind of the Kaiser. There seems to have been no clear decision, but the relative inefficacy of the submarine fleet at that time was a fact too obstinate to be overcome, and in the main the Chancellor and the Army were victorious. On September 1 Count Bernstorff, stretching his actual instructions to the limit, gave Mr. Lansing his Government's formal assurance that passenger liners would not thereafter be torpedoed except with due warning and provision for the safety of non-combatants.

The tension relaxed. Unfortunately, three days later the large British liner Hesperian was apparently torpedoed off the Fastnet, with the loss of half-a-dozen lives. None of the few Americans on board was injured, however, and the Germans managed successfully to confuse this issue by alleging that the Hesperian had struck a mine — something almost impossible either to prove or disprove. The Hesperian, moreover, had been armed; while the State Department's wrath was probably tempered as well by the celebrated Baralong case. The Baralong was one of the first of the British 'Q-ships' or submarine destroyers disguised as merchantmen. On August 26 the Baralong had trapped and sunk the U-27, with all her crew, while falsely displaying the American flag. Only as her guns were unmasked did the Baralong strike her United States colors and break out the white ensign. It was a misuse of the American flag which lent considerable weight to the German contention that the submarine must be permitted, in view of the methods adopted against it, to operate upon the war-zone theory.

When at the end of September Count Bernstorff was able formally to disavow the act of the submarine commander who had attacked the Arabic, the danger seemed over. The disposition of the specific cases, from the Lusitania down, continued to exacerbate the correspondence; but in the meanwhile the United States had forced Germany publicly to relinquish an important use of her new weapon, and the State Department had reason to be pleased with itself. Count Bernstorff basked in a new atmosphere of official friendliness. Opinion in America, he thought, 'was once more favorable to us.' But perhaps Count Bernstorff was too optimistic.

Dr. Albert, spluttering, wild-eyed and panic-struck, had last seen his brief-case vanishing with a Sixth Avenue streetcar on

July 24. On August 15 the first installment of its contents reappeared — spread in a great exclusive story across the front page of the New York *World*. The worst fears of the propaganda bureau were confirmed; the sneak-thief, obviously, had been a British agent. But as it happened, he was not a British agent in reality. Only after the war was over did the Germans discover that it was not the Allies who had struck this blow. It was the Government of the United States.

Since the President in May had directed his Secretary of the Treasury, the pro-Ally Mr. McAdoo, to put the secret service on the trail of violators of our neutrality, American agents had been shadowing the Germans. It was one of these, Mr. Frank Burke, who had snatched the doctor's bag. Mr. McAdoo was immediately notified at his summer home in Maine; and the Secretary himself spent a long Sunday afternoon going over the 'captured' documents. They revealed a good deal about the workings of the propaganda bureau, the subsidies to writers and speakers, the plans to buy up American munitions factories. 'The more I saw of them,' as Mr. McAdoo later put it, 'the more clearly I realized their immense importance.' It was evident that their publication would serve magnificently to discredit the German cause. Yet an unfortunate difficulty was involved. In the first place, the papers had simply been stolen, without a shadow of legal warrant, by an official agent of the United States. In the second place, they contained nothing whatever upon which to base legal action. To buy munitions factories, even to subsidize propaganda, was no violation of the law. The nearest thing to criminal conspiracy was a letter offering, for a fee, to foment strikes, but this was written to Dr. Albert and not by him. The only criminal element in the affair had unfortunately been contributed by the secret service. It was a quandary which Mr. McAdoo finally solved by turning the juiciest of the documents over to Mr. F. I. Cobb, the editor of the *World*, for publication on condition that the source be kept an absolute secret.

Fifteen years later Mr. McAdoo explained this curious proceeding on almost equally curious grounds. He was 'morally convinced' that the Allies were doing the same things that the Germans were doing, but of this he had 'no documentary proof.' Instead of trying to get it, however, he simply published the German documents in order 'to throw a reverberating scare into the whole swarm of propagandists — British and French as well as German.' It was a very odd way of going about it, for Mr. McAdoo could not, of course, have rendered a greater service to the British and French propagandists if he had been one himself. At a stroke, every subsequent utterance favorable to the German side had been tainted before-hand with a suspicion which the Germans were never to overcome. Along with the documents the *World* proclaimed its editorial indignation. 'Nothing,' said the New York *Evening Sun*, 'could be more fortunate than the exposure of this system of corruption and distortion of American opinion, American sentiment and American politics.... With the foul play of the opposition made plain as noonday, there is no excuse henceforth for any division of our people in the front we present to Germany.' On his own initiative, Mr. McAdoo had generously presented to the Allies the worth of at least an army corps — of one of those American army corps, indeed, which we were later to despatch to their assistance.

The Germans, failing to perceive the ultimate effects, were inclined to think that the disclosures had fallen flat because they proved nothing criminal. But fresh disaster followed immediately in their train. Another American writer on the German payroll was Mr. James F. J. Archibald. Beginning as a correspondent with the Central Powers he had drifted into the more equivocal position of propagandist and, in his passages back and forth, of an agent for running despatches through the British blockade.[1] On August 20 he sailed from New York for Germany; at Falmouth ten days later the British authorities calmly removed him from his ship and went through his luggage. The haul was rich. They

---

[1] Mr. Archibald at the time denied that he had any knowledge of the character of the papers he was carrying.

found a long report from Ambassador Dumba to his Government outlining proposals for a 'very strong agitation' among Austro-Hungarian munitions workers against 'the indescribably degrading conditions' in our arms factories, and calling for large funds wherewith to subsidize it. They found a report by Captain von Papen on the Albert disclosures, and a jovial personal letter from the Captain to his wife:

> They unluckily stole from the good Albert in the Elevated a whole thick portfolio.... Well! one must after all have things go like this.... How splendid on the Eastern Front! I always say to these idiotic Yankees that they should shut their mouths and better still be full of admiration for all that heroism.

But if the Captain had perpetrated *lèse majesté* against the American people, Ambassador Dumba had committed an even greater enormity. In another report he had suggested that American foreign policy might be influenced by domestic political considerations and had even allowed himself to speak of 'the self-willed temperament of the President.' The British thoughtfully published the correspondence; they were even good enough to supply Mr. Page with photostatic copies of the documents.

It was a sensation. On September 8 the State Department arose in outrage to demand the recall of the Austro-Hungarian Ambassador as *persona non grata*. His Foreign Office squirmed hard; but the Department was unyielding. The Austrians had to give in, and on September 30 Dr. Dumba's mission was brought ingloriously to its end. It was not quite eighteen years since the recall of the Spanish Minister, Dupuy de Lôme, in a closely parallel passage, had carried us one long step nearer to the War with Spain.

Mr. Archibald's sensations must have been peculiar. Few of those who now execrated him as a traitor paused to remember that he had served in 1898 as one of the embattled war correspondents in the cause of Cuban freedom. He had, indeed, accompanied the first landing of American troops upon the soil of

Cuba, emerging from that brief operation as its sole casualty (he got a bullet-graze on the arm) and thus one of the first to shed his blood for country.

The public which devoured these exposures of the Teutonic system 'of corruption and distortion of American opinion' was but dimly conscious of the many systems operating to the same end on behalf of the Entente. When in September a motion picture made up of war films collected from within the Central Powers was released in New York it offered the American public practically its 'first chance... to see anything on the screen that admitted there were two sides to the war.' But it was also in September that another and far more moving product of the cinematographic art received its first showing. This memorable addition to the pictorial backgrounds of the war years sprang from a marriage of two great minds. Into the hands of Commodore J. Stuart Blackton, a leading motion-picture producer of the spectacular school, there had fallen a copy (it seems to have fallen into the hands of nearly every literate person in the United States) of Mr. Hudson Maxim's 'Defenceless America.' The Commodore read it in a night and sprang for the motion picture rights; the result was 'The Battle Cry of Peace.'

Hundreds of thousands of Americans were to witness this gory piece of incomparable propaganda for preparedness. They were to be thrilled and horrified by its portrayal of an unprepared America overrun by the brutal and licentious soldiery of a foreign power which, though unnamed, uniformed its troops in a strangely close imitation of the Germans. Assisted by tons of smoke powder and regiments of supers, Miss Norma Talmadge and Mr. Charles Richman personified the nation in the agonies of an invasion far more horrible — and more exciting — than anything depicted in the censored films of the real war in Europe. Commodore Blackton's masterpiece, according to an historian of the motion picture, won, 'warm endorsement from the belligerently minded, most conspicuously from Colonel Theodore Roosevelt.... National exploitation of the picture began'; and it was soon inculcating an enthusiasm for big armament appropriations and fears and hatred for the Germans in theaters throughout the length and breadth of the United States.

While Mr. Roosevelt was thus patronizing the arts, his friend Senator Lodge, the disciple of neutrality and non-entanglement, was addressing, at Canobie Lake, the Club Republicaine Franco-Américaine du Massachusetts. As he reached his peroration, the Senator (who always polished up his perorations) was swept from halting English into the tongue of philosophers and statesmen. Pointing to the people of France he exclaimed:

> Contemplez-les bien. Au-dessous de leur têtes... vous voyez flotter le drapeau qu'ils aiment. Les couleurs en sont pareilles aux nôtres... C'est sous ce drapeau que les légions de Napoléon ont ébranlé l'Europe. C'est le drapeau de liberté, d'égalité et de fraternité. Le drapeau! Le drapeau! Découvrez-vous! Sous ce drapeau marche la France. Vive la France!

Coming from the ranking minority member of the Foreign Relations Committee of the Senate, did it hint, perhaps, at a neutrality (and a sense of public responsibility) less than absolute? But another voice was remarking an impairment of our neutrality that might run even deeper than emotional speeches by aged and embittered opposition politicians. Senator Robert M. La Follette, Wisconsin's knotty-minded, idealistic radical Republican, was not on the Foreign Relations Committee, but he could take a rather more penetrating view of foreign affairs than his colleague from Massachusetts. The September issue of his *La Follette's Magazine* carried a caustic editorial:

> With the first clash of the great European War came President Wilson's solemn appeal.... 'The United States must be neutral in fact as well as in name.'... But when you can boom stocks 600 per cent in manufacturing munitions — to the Bottomless Pit with Neutrality! What do Morgan and Schwab care for world peace when there are big profits in world war?... The stocks of the Schwab properties which stood at a market value of seven millions before they

began supplying the Allies... are today given an aggregate 'value' of forty-nine millions. And now we are about to engage in furnishing the Allies funds.... We are underwriting the success of the cause of the Allies. We have ceased to be 'neutral in fact as well as in name.'

It was true — even though nobody, of course, paid any attention to Senator La Follette. Throughout the summer prosperity had been rising in an ever dizzier curve; by September the steel trade had 'never seen demand so overwhelming and at the same time its output expanding on such a scale under steadily rising prices'; by October the railway terminals, both east and west, were beginning to break down under a greater jam of traffic than had been witnessed in the most prosperous years of the past. But how was that bubble to be sustained? How were the Allies to go on paying for it?

They could not buy without dollar credits and they were reaching the end of their dollars. It was a difficulty foreseen by our own patriotic bankers even before it was observed by the Allies, and as early as June J. P. Morgan & Co. had begun to be alarmed by a situation so menacing, as Mr. Lamont has since put it, 'to the British Treasury and American agricultural and manufacturing interests.' J. P. Morgan & Co. were not a firm to forget their responsibilities to American agriculture and manufacturing interests; and the patriotic idea occurred to them that the flotation of a war loan would solve the problem. The American people could thus continue to enjoy the profits of supplying the Allies by also supplying the money wherewith to pay them. The bankers prepared not only to sustain but to expand the bubble — on the winds of credit inflation. In June, when they had first opened the idea to the Allies, the latter had been uninterested; by September, however, their crisis was already acute. On September 10 an Anglo-French Joint High Commission, headed by Lord Reading, landed in New York with the purpose of selling to the American people their first big Allied war loan.

Not until some years later, unfortunately, was it to occur to

J. P. Morgan & Co. that the economic process which they thus initiated might be a fundamentally irreversible one, and that war loans, while easy to advance, are by nature incapable of repayment.[1] Not until long afterward were they to sense some of the still deeper abysses which they were helping to dig for American agriculture and manufacturing interests. They were not, of course, all-wise; and since they were only the greatest financial experts in the United States perhaps they may be forgiven for having had no real idea of the financial and economic consequences of their actions. The political consequences, however, could scarcely be overlooked. A year before the State Department had correctly foreseen how gravely American neutrality must in practice be compromised by any flotation of war loans. It might be well enough to sell goods to one side; to finance their sale with American capital was a very different matter. In August, 1914, the State Department discouraged loans in a statement amounting to a prohibition. The bankers generally observed this prohibition; and at the same time devoted themselves to calling forth a war industry of enormous volume which without loans could not possibly continue. Under pressure from a depressed industry thirsting for profits and with at least the benevolent acquiescence of the Administration, the sole point of the prohibition was thus circumvented. The Administration, the pro-Allies and J. P. Morgan & Co. between them had managed to make war loans next to unavoidable.

As Spring Rice put it in one of his reports: 'When it became apparent that a loan was necessary in order to give a credit for American exports to Europe, many secret forces began to act in its favor. The Government itself undoubtedly wished it, mainly because a continuance of American trade depended on a credit.' The Morgans signed a contract with the Reading commission on September 25. The loan was for $500,000,000, and it was issued with a 2 per cent 'spread' through a syndicate of sixty-one New York houses with 1500 members throughout the country.

[1] The Morgan loans themselves were all repaid. For a further discussion, see pp. 334–35.

Chicago, the financial capital of the Middle West and with a considerable German sentiment, remained cool; the only serious attack upon the loan, however, was on grounds not of national policy but of financial safety. This was met by proving that the Allies did not really need money but only foreign exchange, and on October 14 the books were closed. The somewhat ticklish operation had proved a success.

The Anglo-French loan of 1915 was of course only the forerunner of later and much larger operations. What it meant was that the last difficult hurdle had been taken; the device had been provided which permitted the Entente to call without restraint upon an American market which, by that very fact, became dependent upon the Entente demand. The two economies were for the purposes of the war made one; each was now entangled irrevocably in the fate of the other. To allege that J. P. Morgan & Co. brought the United States into the World War to save their investments (which for the most part they passed on anyway, of course) is to take a very romantic view of such affairs. All they did was simply to facilitate — in accordance with their own sympathies, their own interests and business philosophies — the erection of the machinery which made us a vital part of the World War. Our neutrality was at an end. After that, our actual military participation was largely a question of chance.

iv

Against such backgrounds, Count Bernstorff's optimism over the Arabic settlement may seem to have been a very feeble candle. Yet superficially he was not without grounds for hope. Curiously enough, as the economic alliance with the Entente tightened, as war prosperity tended more completely to remove the economic basis for our demands upon Great Britain, the more diplomatically acute did the controversy become. Berlin's partial yielding on the submarine issue exposed the Allies (just as Bernstorff had intended) to the undivided force of our righteous insistence upon principle.

And the British were excessively irritating. They had an annoying way of hinting that they quite understood that our protests didn't really matter because they were of course for home consumtion. To our appeals to international law and justice they replied by gently pointing to the fact that we were making more money out of the war than we had ever made before. In August, as the new cotton crop approached the market, Sir Edward quietly announced that they would probably have to make cotton absolute contraband — a step which they had bound themselves not to take. Mr. Lansing despatched a hot rejoinder through Page; but to Colonel House, Spring Rice 'spoke in the kindest terms of the cotton farmers and thought they were being misled by demagogues and speculators who were acting under German direction.' From such errors the British were good enough to preserve these misguided men; cotton was declared absolute contraband. However, the British also agreed to buy the surplus themselves. The 1915 crop was actually disposed of at a good price; the result was the final confirmation of American business recovery, and linked the last important branch of our economy to the military success of the Entente.

Yet even the cartoonists were beginning to sharpen their pencils with a new, though still friendly, asperity; and John Bull's rotund form began to appear in our papers, often with a string of stolen American cargoes under his arm, in attitudes less than heroic. 'Thousands of American importers,' as Mr. Lansing wrote Mr. Page, were clamoring to the State Department against the British stoppage of cargoes from Germany. They were threatening to hold mass-meetings 'to denounce the dictatorial and illegal policy of Great Britain toward the United States' and lobbying for an export embargo as long as Great Britain continued to treat them 'with contumely and contempt.' In the new flood tide of war prosperity such plaints from minor interests were not, perhaps, of serious importance, but they were embarrassing to a statesman who in one solemn Note after another had summoned the British to accept and obey the legal principles on which they were based.

House finally warned Spring Rice that a really stiff Note to Great Britain was this time in preparation; and on October 14 (the day, as it happened, that the books were closed successfully on the Anglo-French loan) the two met at 'Billy' Phillips's house to discuss the matter. It was the same rendezvous to which Colonel House had hurried, eleven months before, to show Spring Rice Mr. Lansing's first protest against the British trade restrictions, and anxiously to water it down with the Ambassador's kind advice.[1] This time the scene was to be a very different one. Spring Rice arrived 'in one of his highly nervous states,' and began at once in a 'very disagreeable way.'

> Among other things he said, he supposed I knew the record would forever stand that when the laws of God and man were violated there came no protest from us, but that when our oil and copper shipments were interfered with, a most vigorous protest came.... I did not like the tenor of his talk, and, as is my custom, became more and more silent. In the course of the conversation he said: 'At one time this country was composed of pure rock, but now it is composed of mud, sand and some rock; and no one can predict how it will shift or in what direction.'

The Colonel, after all, had only himself to blame if Sir Cecil confused the United States with a dependency of the British Empire; but even for the Colonel this was too much. He lost his temper and tried, at last, a touch of the iron hand. The effects were remarkable. At once Spring Rice 'became apologetic and asked me to forgive him'; and a few days later the State Department people told House that Sir Cecil had 'changed his attitude entirely... taking the American side almost more strongly than we do ourselves.' This time, at all events, the Note was not watered down.

Despatched on October 21, it was a long review of the whole controversy, of all our flouted principles and unanswered protests — which we might never have had to send if Colonel House

[1] See p. 87.

had not been in such a hurry to temper that first one eleven months before. It concluded with the most ominous language we had yet adopted toward an Entente Power. The rules of evidence upon which the prize courts determined enemy destination were 'without justification'; the blockade order was 'ineffective, illegal and indefensible'; the judicial procedure for granting reparation to injured American shippers was 'inherently defective,' and the jurisdiction asserted was 'in violation of the law of nations.' The United States could not submit 'to the curtailment of its neutral rights by these measures.'

But we did submit. The Swedish Government congratulated us on this powerful blow for neutral rights, 'not being able to imagine that the Note... should have only academic interest.' Yet as it turned out, that was the sum of all the interest it ever did have. For this result there were doubtless many reasons. But an important one can perhaps be discovered in a letter which Colonel House, three days after his interview with Spring Rice and four days before the despatch of the American Note, had himself addressed to Sir Edward Grey.

The insults of the British Ambassador cannot have lessened the dissatisfaction with which House, since his return in June, had been surveying the fruits of his conduct of American foreign relations. Between the untrustworthy yielding of the Germans and the embarrassing obduracy of the British, his policy—whether or not he quite realized it himself — had in fact reached the point of bankruptcy. It had been founded upon the hasty assumption that the Allies must of course win the war. It had uncritically adopted the Allied rationalization of the war's origins, the corollary thesis that permanent peace could be achieved through an international association to abolish 'militarism' and suppress any future 'aggressor,' and the further corollary that Allied victory would provide conditions favorable to the institution of such a system. At every point this estimate of the situation was, as we now know, thoroughly unsound, but for over a year the Colonel had made it the basis of his diplomacy. At all costs we must keep on good terms with the winning side. When it had won — when the devoted soldiery of the Entente had saved civilization for us with their blood — we would then be in position to enter into the new world thus made possible. With the 'territorial objectives' of the Allies, of course, we had no concern; but if only we could retain our moral 'influence' over them we might use it to assist them in establishing that permanent peace for which they were fighting. We might even, when the war was safely won, help to guarantee it.

Such had been the general policy. By the late summer of 1915 even Colonel House could no longer conceal from himself the fact that it was full of holes. First, and most important of all, the Allies were not winning. More than that, it became increasingly doubtful, as the war strain deepened, whether it really was world peace and the destruction of militarism for which they were fighting, or only the destruction of Germany. To secure a peace system might require a greater exertion of American 'influence' than had originally been supposed; yet this influence for which we had sacrificed so much was not proving notably effective. As long as we left the winning of the war to them, the Allies, strangely enough, seemed disinclined to pay any attention to us whatever; while the developing irritations of the trade controversy constantly threatened to end in a quarrel in which that precious influence would vanish for good.

Finally, there were the Germans. At the moment, embarrassingly enough, it was the ogres of Prussian militarism who (because they were still generally victorious) were putting out all the peace feelers; it was in the pacific democracies of the Entente that the very mention of the word 'peace' was becoming a crime against the state. This put us into an equivocal position; the submarine, on the other hand, put us into a position not only equivocal but dangerous. We had curbed the submarine, but had we curbed it for good? Unless we got them some return for their sacrifice, the Germans were likely at any time to break the fragile reins which our diplomacy had imposed, and thereby precipitate us into the war — upon an issue, unfortunately, of relatively minor importance. We would then be in the Entente but not of it. We would be exposed to all the risks of an Entente defeat, but with little claim to control the uses it might make of a victory. War on the submarine issue held out the unattractive prospect of a maximum of sacrifice for a minimum of advantage.

From every point of view it was a debacle. The Colonel's own excuse for this unhappy result was in an appeal to that first refuge of incompetent statesmanship — a big army and navy. If only Mr. Wilson had taken his advice when (upon the astute promptings of General Wood) the Colonel had first urged the President to go in for a big program of preparedness! If only he had a huge military and naval force in his hands, then he would not be surrounded by this tangle of thorny diplomacy. If we were 'fully prepared' then the Germans 'would not provoke us.' Considering the mighty levers of economic and political power already at the Colonel's disposal, and which he had failed to use to any effective purpose, one cannot be much impressed by this retreat into the easy fallacy of force. It is the function of the statesman not to bewail a lack of means but to utilize whatever means are available.

However, the Colonel did not have a huge army and navy. 'Shall we ever get out of this labyrinth?' the President asked him in despair at the beginning of September. 'Only by adopting a positive policy,' Colonel House replied. It was obvious. But what policy? In general, there were two possible courses of action. They could confess the failure of the whole pro-Ally orientation and retreat into an effective neutrality. It should then be possible to play off the submarine controversy against the trade dispute in such a way as to avoid actual military entanglement on either issue, and to rely upon our own strength and skill to conserve our best interests in the wracked and ruined world which peace must bring. Unhappily, retreat was hard, if not now impossible. There remained the more reckless, but the always more alluring, possibility of advance. Already a plan was taking shape in the Colonel's mind — materially assisted by careful and far-sighted promptings from Downing Street. In July Colonel House had received a reflective letter from Sir Edward Grey:

> The more I have meditated on past events, the more continually I have come to the point that the refusal of a Conference [by Germany] in July last year was the fatal moment that decided the question of peace or war.... If neutral nations and the opinion of the world generally had been sufficiently alert to say that they would side against the party that refused a Conference, war might have been avoided.

But if war could have been avoided in this way might the war not be ended through a similar device? As military failure accumulated with the summer, as the United States disappointingly failed to fight over the submarine, as the dangerous new note of independence began to appear in Colonel House's communications, the thought recurred with a greater urgency and a subtler application to present exigencies. On August 10 Grey spoke of 'some League of Nations' as a 'pearl of great price' — it would compel the settlement of future disputes between powers by 'conference' and in strict accordance with that international law which Germany was at the moment flouting so outrageously. On August 26 (the subsidence of the Arabic crisis was again bitterly disappointing Allied hopes) Sir Edward addressed another communication to his friend:

> There is, I think, disappointment that the feeling in America is not more combative.... People here become less hopeful of the United States in taking a hand.... If I could feel that your people were sure to say, sooner or later, 'though we have no concern with territorial changes between the belligerents themselves, who must settle things of that kind by themselves, there can be no peace till the cause of Belgium is fairly settled in the interest of public morals and future peace,' I should be content.

It would have been pleasant; and today one gasps a little at the mental climate which could permit a British Foreign Minister quite seriously to propose that the people of the United States should grant him that magnificent free hand while placing their lives and fortune at his disposal. As to a league of nations, Sir Edward delicately observed, 'you have a great body of reflecting public opinion so disposed that it can give a great impulse and guidance to this idea.' Perhaps the Colonel was the more receptive because it all hinted at too inviting an exit from his own difficulties. One evening in September, as he was sitting chatting in the White House study, he was startled to hear the President casually remark that 'he had never been sure that we ought not to take part in the conflict, and if it seemed evident that Germany and her militaristic ideas were to win, the obligation upon us was greater than ever.' It was an unexpected but most useful cue; the amateur diplomatist seized upon it as the key to 'his idea of a positive policy.' Again Sir Edward was helpful; on September 22 the Foreign Minister was writing once more:

> To me, the great object of securing the elimination of militarism and navalism is to get security for the future against aggressive war. How much are the United States prepared to do in this direction? Would the President propose that there should be a League of Nations binding themselves to side against any Power which broke a treaty?

When Mr. Wilson presently visited New York, the Colonel, now armed with this direct query, opened the great plan which he had been formulating. We had, he argued, lost our 'opportunity' to break with Germany over the submarine; now if Germany should win 'our turn would come next; and we were not only unprepared, but there would be no one to help us stand the first shock.' Why an exhausted Germany should want to attack us and how the 'shock' was to be delivered across a 3,000-mile line of communications which would be closely flanked along most of its length by desperate and embittered enemies were alike questions which the Colonel did not pause to explore. He was convinced our turn was coming; therefore 'we should do something decisive now — something that would either end the war in a way to abolish militarism or that would bring us in with the Allies to help them do it.'

The Colonel's proposal was Machiavellian. He would first privately reach an understanding with the Allies. Then, whenever they were ready for such a step, the United States would publicly demand, as the impartial spokesman of the neutral world, that the war be brought immediately to an end on the basis of 'both military and naval disarmament.' In this manifesto we could be as severe upon the Allies as upon the Germans, since the former would be parties to the trick. The Allies, perhaps with some artful show of hesitation, would accept our mediation. If the Germans fell into the trap and accepted too — presto! the war would be over and we would have achieved (as Colonel House complacently described it) a 'master-stroke of diplomacy.' If the Germans should refuse, then the United States would be in the war — for the noblest of motives and in a manner giving us some guarantee that we would actually get something worth while in return for saving the Entente from defeat. The 'whole force of our Government' could then be exerted to win the war — and also, though the Colonel did not put it that way, to conceal and to retrieve the follies of the House diplomacy. For the whole position would then be regularized. The danger of German victory would be averted; our 'influence' with the Allies would be re-established; we might even manage to realize some of those dreams of disarmament and perpetual peace which British statesmanship had been astute enough to cultivate in Colonel House's mind.

Not unnaturally, President Wilson was 'startled' by this naïve proposal in international adventure and double-dealing. Did he agree? He did not say so, and House had no time to press the matter, for 'the entire conversation did not last longer than twenty minutes.' But House decided that Mr. Wilson had 'seemed to acquiesce by silence,' and it was enough for the eager master of diplomacy. A little later he hinted at the plot to Mr. Frank Polk, the Solicitor of the State Department, and found him favorable; in Washington in the second week of October he received encouragement from Secretary Lansing. Rapidly the scheme matured; and presently House got Mr. Wilson's authorization to initiate it in the form of a reply to Grey's communication of September 22. 'This,' the Colonel told his diary, 'is one of the most important letters I ever wrote.'

It must certainly be one of the most extraordinary letters in the history of diplomacy. 'It has occurred to me,' he began, 'that the time may soon come when this Government should intervene between the belligerents and demand that peace parleys begin upon the broad basis of the elimination of militarism and navalism.... What I want you to know is that whenever you consider the time is propitious for this intervention I will propose it to the President.' The full scheme was then outlined. The Colonel explained that he would try to mislead Berlin into thinking that the Allies would reject the proposed mediation, and might thus induce Berlin to accept it. 'But if they did not do so, it would nevertheless be the purpose to intervene [diplomatically]. If the Central Powers were still obdurate, it would be necessary for us to join the Allies and force the issue.'

Clearly, there was a great deal that was imprecise in this project. House assumed that the Allies would not set it in motion unless it seemed the only alternative to defeat, and that the United States could therefore largely dictate the terms of that preliminary 'understanding.' But just how much would the Allies demand in the way of those 'territorial changes,' just how much 'elimination' of militarism and navalism would they agree to? All that was vague; the letter was exact on one point only — that if Germany was obdurate it would be 'necessary' for the United States to enter the war.

House took his draft to the President. Mr. Wilson read it and at once approved, with, however, a single textual correction. He inserted just one word, to make the sentence read: 'It would *probably* be necessary for us to join the Allies.' Mr. Wilson himself regarded this as merely an 'unimportant verbal change.'

Under the American Constitution war cannot be declared by unofficial emissaries of the President negotiating in secrecy, and Mr. Wilson may have thought his emendation unimportant because it merely stated what should have been obvious. Yet as he laid down his pen, a slight and evidently unnoticed rift had in fact appeared between those two minds which functioned so often as very nearly one. That word was far more important than either man realized.

Scarcely six weeks before the President had declared that two things were 'plain' to him:

1. The people of this country count on me to keep them out of war; 2. It would be a calamity to the world at large if we should be drawn actively into the conflict and so deprived of all disinterested influence over the settlement.

Patently, the House scheme might work in either of two ways. It might bring a peace through forcing a conference, which would then necessarily be dominated by the more or less 'disinterested' influence of the United States. Or it might bring a peace through drawing the United States into the war to help the Allies conquer one. President Wilson, it seems clear, thought of the scheme as directed primarily toward the former result. The possibility of an American participation in the war would be used merely as a lever with which to force the conference; naturally, this involved some risk of an actual participation, but the President must have regarded that as a remote and problematical contingency. Colonel House, on the other hand, had little real confidence in the conference idea. He appears to have regarded the scheme as primarily a means of putting the American people definitely upon the Allied battle line. The President, it is reasonable to suppose, inserted his 'probably' assuming that this was what House had really meant; House accepted the correction assuming that it was but a verbal safeguard which the President didn't mean. Subsequent history leads one to the inference that both men were mistaken.

The letter went off in two sections on October 17 and 19, on

the eve, as has been said, of Mr. Lansing's strenuous protest against
the illegalities of the British blockade. It is not difficult to imagine
the emotions with which Sir Edward must have examined this
latest effort of the incredible Americans. As it stood, the whole
project was too fantastic to be of much practical importance,
yet its future uses might be considerable. Its obvious (though
clumsily concealed) hint, moreover, that the United States no
longer dared to let the Entente lose must, when laid beside Mr.
Lansing's vigorous periods, have been a source of great comfort
to Sir Edward Grey.

VII. COLONEL HOUSE'S POSITIVE POLICY

i

TODAY it is impossible to regard the mild figure of Colonel House, thus secretly dedicating his country to the slaughter, without a certain astonishment. One must not, however, forget the curious temper of the times. His project, had anyone known of it, would unquestionably have enlisted distinguished support, not only from the new men of peace but even from the men of God. Was not the Rev. Charles A. Eaton making the singular discovery that 'this war is the greatest blessing that has ever fallen on mankind since the German Reformation'? Yet Mr. Gerard at the same time was jotting a terser summary of the blessing into his diary: 'Feel the war more — deaths and prices. 680,000 killed to October 1 and many crippled. Food way up.' And Mr. Page, in his more polished style, was writing home to the President:

> The war crowds itself on us sensibly more and more.... Death is so common that it seems a little thing.... This sort of thing all day every day must have some effect on any man.... More widows, more mothers looking for lost sons!...

And there was no visible end to it. Before them all there stretched that remorseless vista of more savagery piled upon savagery, more horror and illimitable destruction, slaughter and starvation — 'deaths and prices' — with 'annihilation,' in Mr. Page's phrase, as the only outcome.

In the United States there were those who could consider other solutions. From the platform and from the editorial columns of his *Commoner* Mr. Bryan fought resolutely on for genuine neutrality and peace. From his citadel in Wisconsin Senator La Follette fought likewise with an accumulating cold bitterness. He was gathering around him other Northwestern radicals. One of them was Representative Charles Augustus Lindbergh of Minnesota — but it was not for that reason that a playful fate was to preserve Mr. Lindbergh's name to history.

As early as August the untutored business common sense of Mr. Henry Ford had been aroused by the incredible folly and waste of this continuing savagery. With the limitless millions at his disposal perhaps it might do to finance a great plea for education as a means to peace? There was a queer little 'peace-conference' that summer composed of Mr. Ford, Mr. Wanamaker and Mr. Thomas A. Edison; the three titans of industry and commerce put their heads together over the idea in the strange, simple-minded way of practical business men, but nothing came of it — not then. A more scholarly pacifist, Dr. David Starr Jordan, called on Colonel House only a week after he had perfected his own bellicose peace plan. Dr. Jordan was easily cowed by the Colonel's loftier knowledge of such matters, but the ladies were made of sterner stuff. Jane Addams came in November, with Lillian Wald and Rosika Schwimmer, to demand that the President summon a conference of the neutral powers to sit continuously at The Hague, presenting concrete peace proposals to the belligerents until something was accepted. This would, at least, have been genuine mediation, but House thought it the vaporing of idle females. 'As usual,' he complacently recorded, 'I got them into a controversy among themselves, which delights me.'

Doubtless Jane Addams realized that it was no use wasting time on the Colonel. She saw that her movement was at an 'impasse' unless she 'could bring to bear a tremendous pressure of public opinion upon the officials in Washington.' Levying upon Mrs. Henry Ford for the funds, she telegraphically summoned the thousands of women's clubs throughout the nation to bombard Mr. Wilson himself with demands for a neutral conference; and for some days there were extra telegraph clerks at the White House to struggle with the deluge which resulted. But what could one woman do against the universal lunacy? When a New York newspaper actually printed a few letters defending the execution of Edith Cavell (one of them pointed out that even the United States had once hanged a woman, Mrs. Surratt, on perhaps more dubious evidence), Marse Henry Watterson arose to denounce the outrage with all the power of his remarkable vocabulary:

> What shall we think of those pervert Americans, few indeed but wantonly defiant, who rush into print to excuse and even to extol the crime of the butcher of Brussels?... The New York *Sun* lowers its standard of patriotic duty... by giving in a recent issue space for a number of these reptiles... to deface its columns and disgrace the human species by such screeds... This insensate brute [the one who had cited the Surratt case] is equally disloyal to his country and his kind — assuming him to be a man and not an animal — and at the same time he is as ignorant as he is treasonable.

It does seem a slight overstatement; but it suggests the flavor of the times. That fall a questionnaire sent out to ministers of a score of denominations in the East came back 151 to 14 for preparedness; another distributed nationally from Chicago likewise showed the clergy in an overwhelming majority for peace by military preparation. The great bandwagon to which General Wood had set a prophetic shoulder so long before was at last beginning to roll in earnest. The younger business men and millionaires, back now from their bloodless trenches at Plattsburg, were organizing the Military Training Camp Association to put more powerful pressures than the General himself could exert upon the Congress about to convene. In the academic sphere (which as a rule is only less sensitive than the clergy to the winds of novelty) 'one university after another was adopting military training.' And when presently even Mr. Gompers was discussing with the General a training camp 'for laboring men,' it was clear that the conquest of the United States by Prussia (as a William Graham Sumner would have put it) was already much farther advanced than it was ever likely to be by Prussian bayonets.

Jane Addams might call upon the Ford millions; it was nothing compared to the financial artillery which the General and his colleague navalists could muster. In November, Senator La Follette's *Magazine* was acidly commenting — unjustly, perhaps, but by no means irrelevantly — upon this aspect of the crusade:

> If a man dares to intimate that he is unwilling to swallow the whole program for preparedness — a Big Army, a Big Navy, Big Contracts for Munitions of War — that man is a fool or a coward or a traitor. Who are the real Patriots of the Country?... They are the Morgans, the Rockefellers, the Schwabs, the Garys, the DuPonts and [those]... who are back of the thirty-eight corporations most benefitted by war orders.... They are the dollar-scarred heroes who organized the Navy League of the United States!...
> Shades of Lincoln! What a band of patriots!

So patently jaundiced a view as this, however, could hardly be expected to check the mounting glamours of militarism. In both the War and Navy Departments, by this time, the eager experts were busy. Secretary Garrison had reached the curious conclusion that 'those who dread real militarism should be the strongest advocates of reasonable preparation'; and as his own idea of what was reasonable had prepared a program calling for a thirty per cent increase in the regular establishment, backed up by a wholly new 'Continental army' of 400,000 trained militiamen. This represented a sensational change of policy; yet one may doubt its adequacy as a protection against 'real militarism.' In private, its War College authors regarded it as useless in itself, and only valuable (like Wood's training camps) as a device for 'beginning something in the way of preparedness.'

Secretary Daniels had in the meanwhile been busy with the

Naval General Board. Between them they had concocted not simply a recommendation for new ships in the following year but a continuing five-year program of naval construction — the first in the history of the United States. Against just what eventuality, however, were all these plans being devised to prepare us? In the latter part of October Mr. Gerard had a strange audience with the Kaiser. The Ambassador found him 'careworn and nervous' in his handsome new uniform; he was very bitter against the United States and talked rather wildly about 'standing no nonsense from America after the war.' Mr. Gerard was so alarmed that he dared to report this only in a single cryptic sentence upon a separate sheet of paper slipped in with another despatch. In Washington, perhaps, they really were seeing strings of German transports riding off Sandy Hook and New York lying in the ruins so realistically depicted by 'The Battle Cry of Peace.' Yet when, on November 4, President Wilson himself formally announced his conversion to the new cause, it was in language of a curiously baffling character.

His address was delivered at a dinner at the Biltmore Hotel in New York. 'It is due,' said the introducing speaker, 'to the great mind and patriotic heart of Woodrow Wilson that this country was not plunged into war.' The President had kept us out of war. He now arose to make the pronouncement which must plunge us at least into militarism. Mr. Wilson, however, did not think of it in so crass a way:

Force everywhere speaks out with a loud and imperious voice in the titanic struggle of governments, and from one end of our dear country to the other men are asking what our own force is, how far we are prepared to maintain ourselves against any interference with our national action or development.... We have it in mind to be prepared, but not for war, but only for defence; and with the thought ... that the principles we hold most dear can be achieved only in the kindly and wholesome atmosphere of peace, and not by the use of hostile force.

Upon this somewhat contradictory foundation, the President then went on to describe a program calling for half a million trained troops and the second most powerful navy in the world. Yet as he went on, the uses to which this presumably unhostile force were to be put became only more vague and more perplexing:

> No thoughtful man feels any panic haste in this matter. The country is not threatened from any quarter.... There is no fear amongst us.... The only thing within our own borders that has given us grave concern in recent months has been that voices have been raised in America professing to be the voices of Americans... but which spoke alien sympathies, which came from men... who were partisans of other causes than that of America.

This stern reference to the pro-Germans (which, as neither the President nor his cheering audience perceived, so exactly fitted the great pro-Ally majority now thirsting for preparedness) remained about the nearest approach to an explanation of what it was that Mr. Wilson wanted to prepare for. To at least one mind it was less than satisfactory; and in a public statement next day Mr. Bryan broke formally with the President:

> The plan which he proposes... is not only a menace to our peace and safety, but a challenge to the spirit of Christianity.... The European rulers... thought they were contributing toward the maintenance of peace when they were making elaborate preparations for defence. It is a false philosophy, and being false it inevitably leads into difficulties.... If we are not threatened by any nation,... if there is no fear among us, why is this time chosen to revolutionize our national theories and to exchange our policy for the policy of Europe?

Why, indeed? Mr. Bryan was profoundly right; but everybody knew that Mr. Bryan was just a woolly sentimentalist with no knowledge of foreign affairs. Besides, he had neglected the Republicans. The program had scarcely been announced before

Mr. Roosevelt was denouncing it as a mere 'shadow' and calling for a regular and reserve army of 1,500,000 men to be raised by nothing less than conscription. Congress was about to convene, in a more than usually uncertain temper, and beyond there loomed ever more insistently the Presidential election of 1916.

In preparedness the President had detected one of the major issues of the coming campaign; he had now distinguished another in what was already being referred to as 'the hyphen.' [1] Promoted by Mr. McAdoo's helpful disclosures, by the Archibald papers and by the imaginary sleuthing organization of the Providence *Journal*, the 'crimes of the hyphenates,' as House called them, were indeed becoming political material of the first importance. Captain von Rintelen, finding the climate growing too hot, had slipped out of the country at the beginning of August, and Bernstorff was now telegraphically imploring Bethmann-Hollweg for the 'complete suppression of propaganda.' But the summer's sowing was coming to harvest; the papers were in full cry and a first-class spy scare was now under way.

In October the police had at last managed to make an arrest. They picked up the luckless Robert Fay — supposed to be a lieutenant in the Austrian reserve — while he was experimenting with an infernal machine of his own design in the innocent publicity of a wood on the New Jersey shore of the Hudson. Fay seems to have been strictly a free lance, and the engaging character of his invention — a bomb intended to be attached to the rudders of munitions ships and ultimately detonated by the action of the helm — suggests at least a trace of feeble-mindedness. But there were columns about him in all the papers. He was remembered as a frequent visitor to powder factories; there was a report from Hartford that he had been seen in the heinous act of inspecting the 'Colt Arms Company and other munitions establishments with a telescope from the dome of the Capitol,' and presently he

---

[1] This concerned, it is scarcely necessary to note, only the hyphens carried by German-, Austro-, and Irish-Americans. The hyphens worn by English-, Franco-, Italo- and other kinds of Entente-Americans seemed not to count.

was indicted with four alleged co-conspirators by a Federal grand jury and a sensational trial was under way.

At the same time a succession of fires and explosions in munitions plants began to occur. A blast at a DuPont plant in Delaware took thirty-one lives at the end of November and there were numerous lesser catastrophes. The natural hazards of munitions manufacture, especially in a suddenly expanded boom industry, might conceivably have accounted for a good deal of this; but a public now fully aroused to the German Menace could accept no such pedestrian explanations. The fire marshal of the State of Pennsylvania announced his conviction that 'all' fires in munitions plants were incendiary; and the Mayor of Philadelphia proclaimed 'the Hyphen' as 'our greatest foe.' When a fire (happily fatal to no one) swept a new industrial town built by the DuPonts in Virginia, the 'Richmond Light Infantry Blues and two companies of the Richmond Greys' were rushed by special train to repel the Teuton, while the local citizenry promptly and patriotically hanged a Negro. And when the Providence *Journal* announced the discovery of a German plot to immobilize the United States North Atlantic Fleet in New York Harbor by sinking a Hamburg-American liner in the channel, no one doubted.

To make everything worse, it was just at this moment that Tirpitz's inventive sailors planted a new and an exasperating barb in the flank of the Wilson submarine policy. In the Mediterranean on November 7 the Italian passenger liner Ancona was first shelled and then torpedoed by a submarine with a loss of 208 lives. A hurried cable from our Ambassador at Rome announced that a score of them were 'believed' to be American citizens. It seemed at first glance a direct violation of the undertaking not to torpedo passenger liners, but it was not. Examination revealed that the submarine was one which had been officially transferred to the Austro-Hungarian flag — and the undertaking had been given only by Germany.

Here was an unsuspected joint in the armor of our triumph. The press, it is true, took the affair with a relative calm, the New

York *Times* only mildly characterizing the act as 'one of wanton savagery, a continuation in the Mediterranean field of the policy of frightfulness and of butchery of innocent persons so long pursued by Germany's Navy in waters about the British Islands.' Where the Germans were concerned this had become no more than the conventional language of journalism. Nevertheless, the incident appeared to re-open the whole submarine problem — just as the State Department was hoping to get some satisfaction out of the British — and a stiff note was despatched to Austria.[1] At the same time Mr. Lansing wearily summoned Count Bernstorff, to bring up again the question of an indemnity for the lives lost in the Lusitania; while House, full of the 'crimes of the hyphenates,' thought they ought to break relations with Austria and in the meanwhile dismiss 'some of the obnoxious underlings of the offending Embassies.'

The Fay trial, the new energy of official investigation, the torrents of rumor and emotion, were all bringing the names of Captains von Papen and Boy-Ed, the two German attachés, into a bad eminence. Already compromised by the Albert and Archibald documents, they were now being mentioned in the court proceedings and were beginning to appear as shadowy figures in the background of all the plottings, real and alleged, against the munitions supply. On December 1 Secretary Lansing abruptly demanded their recall as *'personae ingratae* on account of their naval and military activities.'

So still another blow had fallen. 'The great event of this week,' Spring Rice triumphantly reported, 'has been the German trials and the action taken against the German naval and military attachés.' Bernstorff sought out House. The Colonel had never seen him so disturbed; for the first time in Bernstorff's long and anxious mission he appeared 'visibly shaken.' He was afraid that his own turn must be coming next, and after that ——? The

---

[1] *Punch* had a savage cartoon, in Bernard Partridge's best style, showing Mr. Wilson remarking: 'This calls for a Note — Mr. Secretary, just bring me in a copy of our usual No. 1 Note to Germany, "Humanity" series.'

United States, he told House, was 'gradually drifting into an alliance with the Allies.' Coming on top of the Dumba recall, and at a much worse moment, it was the most serious catastrophe which the German cause had yet sustained in the United States.

Bernstorff thought that the Administration, facing the impending threat of Congress, had lost its nerve, and that the recall was 'intended to serve as a safety-valve — lest Congress should break off diplomatic relations with us.' Was that actually the temper of the gathering statesmen? Bernstorff did not know whether there was a real danger of this, but 'Lansing thinks there is.... They have not the courage to swim against the stream.' The attachés went home in disgrace.

ii

On Saturday, December 4, an extraordinary scene was being enacted upon a pier in Hoboken. To understand it one must remember that behind all the emotional storms of spy-hunting, patriotism and preparedness there was a real war in Europe, now dragging on to its second bloody and futile Christmas. There was war weariness in the air. The peace talk was now seeping through all the censorships and even into the American press. 'The losses on all sides,' as Mr. Lloyd George noted, 'had been beyond anything the students of war had ever contemplated'; and the question of what, in fact, all that agony was about would not down. Started in an accident, it was simply running upon its own momentum; the peoples were continuing to fight because their ideas and their institutions had provided them with no means of stopping. Those Americans who felt that the United States, as the one great neutral remaining, might really exert an influence to cut through this insane and tragic impasse may have failed to think through to the bottom of their appalling problem. But today one can only admire the soundness of their instinct and the courage of their convictions.

Jane Addams had appealed to Mrs. Henry Ford; Rosika

Schwimmer, with a cooler boldness, had gone straight to Henry Ford himself, and in November had taken him by frontal assault. The automobile manufacturer had the haziest notions about the war; he possessed, however, an enormous fortune, he wanted to do something, and Madame Schwimmer brought him to see her pacifist colleagues in New York. Her project of a continuous peace conference at The Hague seems to have meant little to his rather bewildered mind, but when someone suddenly suggested that a ship be chartered to take over American delegates to such a conference, he sprang to life. There, at least, was something concrete.

Impetuously he stormed the White House, to be met only with elegant and cautious generalities that seem to have confused and angered him. Mr. Ford could not understand (and many today find it a little difficult) why, with so much talk of humanity, altruism and peace, nothing definite was ever *done*. He returned to New York, chartered the Oscar II of the Scandinavian-American Line, summoned the reporters and, on November 24, announced his project. He would himself take an expeditionary force of all the most distinguished American pacifists to Europe, and he would 'get the boys out of the trenches by Christmas.' Thus the story broke; and it was, as Madame Schwimmer had disastrously failed to realize, 'a beauty.'

> It was the answer to an editor's prayer. It had everything — humor, pathos, big names, a political angle, international complications, the golden glow of Ford's millions. The reporters did their duty.... Madame Schwimmer was prepared for violent attacks upon the peace project.... But there is no defence against a loud and unanimous burst of laughter from every important organ of public opinion.

The famous 'Peace Ship' had been launched, to the undying shame of American journalism, upon one vast wave of ridicule. As Jonathan Norton Leonard points out, Madame Schwimmer had forgotten the Ford joke, then at the height of its popularity. She had failed to calculate upon the peculiarly homespun quality

of Ford's immense reputation. She was unprepared for the on-
slaught of American crankdom which ensued. The important
people whom she hoped to enlist scrambled frantically for safety
as the 'wild men' and the pro-Germans poured in. Jane Addams
suddenly discovered that she was too ill to go; David Starr Jordan
denied indignantly that he had accepted an invitation; even Mr.
Bryan felt that he could be of greater usefulness by remaining to
fight preparedness at home. The whole thing was a disaster —
but the ship had been chartered, the announcements made, the
sailing date set for December 4. It was impossible to withdraw.

'Hoboken has always been a crazy town, but it never witnessed
a crazier scene than the sailing of the Ark of Peace.' Long before
sailing time the ship and pier alike were jammed with reporters,
photographers, brass bands, fanatics of every sort, pro-Germans,
pro-Allies, publicity-seekers and the delegates. When Mr. Bryan
fought his way through the mass someone thrust a small cage
containing a grey squirrel into his hand, and the former Secretary
of State, not realizing what it implied and not knowing what to
do with it, solemnly carried it thereafter. Presently Mr. Ford
himself arrived and the crowd 'went entirely mad,' but the manufacturer bravely faced the uproar. In the saloon one of the newspaper reporters, who had brought along his bride but had forgotten to marry her, was being joined in last-minute wedlock by
one of the many ministers before a battery of news cameras.
Ford and Bryan (still holding the squirrel) were pressed as witnesses while the flashlights went off; and as the crowd closed in
Mr. Bryan at last escaped down the gangplank exclaiming that he
had *not* kissed the bride. Sailing time approached:

> On the promenade deck near the gangway was Ford, leaning over
> the rail and shouting with the rest. Someone handed him a huge
> bunch of American Beauty roses which he threw one by one to the
> crowd.... At the rail near the stern the Lieutenant-Governor of
> North Carolina was delivering a speech on the beauty and purity of
> Southern women. Governor Hanna of North Dakota, a delegate,
> was explaining for publication that he believed in preparedness, but

HENRY FORD AND CAPTAIN HEMPEL ON BOARD THE PEACE
SHIP

wanted to visit some relatives in Sweden. Judge Ben Lindsey, a delegate, was telling the press that he was a patriotic American even if he *was* on the Oscar II. His last words were reported as: 'Oh God, why am I here!'...

All this time the whistle had been droning overhead.... At last the Oscar II began to move amid an uproar of cheers, pacifist hymns, patriotic songs, whistles and mere noise. When she was fifty yards out in the river a small but intense disturbance appeared in the outskirts of the crowd and worked its way towards the edge of the wharf. Someone was trying to reach the spot where the gangway had been. Finally he reached the water's edge, hesitated a moment, then dived into the river and swam frantically after the ship. It was Urban Ledoux, the famous Mr. Zero.

After that, of course, it was all over. In Europe as well as in America the peace conference idea had received a blow as tragic as it was irreparable; and one of the few really generous and rational impulses of those insane years had been snuffed out with a cruelty and levity which are appalling. Today the joke is less enjoyable, and posterity will remember that it was not the fault of Mr. Ford that his crusade was a catastrophe. Yet its actual effect was to cloud the whole neutral peace movement with an imbecile buffoonery, just three days, as luck would have it, before Congress was to reassemble in Washington.

Three days after the Oscar II had departed, trailing her clouds of ridicule behind her, the statesmen were gathered to hear President Wilson's annual message upon the state of the nation. It was a repetition, in even loftier and even less logical terms, of his address in New York a month earlier. But it left no doubt as to the President's strategy. 'Defence and allegiance,' as Spring Rice happily summarized it, was to be his platform. The Ambassador thought that there had been a 'great change' in the situation, and that more and more the public was being educated to perceive that in the war 'the principles of democracy are at stake' and that America was menaced. Nothing could be more satisfactory. But was the Ambassador — was even the President himself —

rightly estimating the Congressional attitude? Tumulty had
already privately reported to Mr. Wilson that, whatever the
vociferous Northeast might think of the German Menace, he was
hearing 'from all sources that there is no enthusiasm on "the hill"
for preparedness.' Count Bernstorff shrewdly guessed that in reality 'no man can say what Congress will do.' He remembered the
West, with its large German population, its relative detachment
from Entente war orders and its disproportionate representation
in the Senate. He remembered the cotton South, the foundation
of Democratic power and the one section that had felt most
bitterly the effects of the British blockade. The Administration
was expecting revolt against its leniency toward the Germans;
but the Ambassador had his doubts, and almost immediately they
were justified.

On the first day of the session Senator Hoke Smith of Georgia
was introducing a resolution demanding a Congressional investigation into British interference with American trade. Senator Lodge leapt at once to the defence with an amendment including the crimes of the submarine and of the hyphenates in the
scope of the investigation. The Senator was pained at the idea
that the nation should act upon anything so vulgar as a merely
material interest. 'To me,' he exclaimed in a moving passage,
'American lives are more important than American dollars.
The body of an innocent child floating dead upon the water, the
victim of the destruction of an unarmed vessel, is to me a more
poignant and a more tragic spectacle than an unsold bale of
cotton.' And perhaps this righteous contempt for material considerations was understandable. The Senator's constituents did
not have to sell cotton to keep themselves alive; on the contrary,
they were reaping enormous profits on the bursting cargoes which
they were sending, along with the innocent children, into the war
zone, while low prices for cotton could only benefit their great
textile industry. In the end the resolution was not adopted and the
investigation (to posterity's loss) was never made.

The whole blockade controversy, however, had been publicly

raised again — and the American protest of October 21 was as yet unanswered. Mr. Page was plaintively satisfied that if only it could be 'generally understood beforehand that our fleet and the British fleet shoot the same language,' all issues of peace and war would be forever settled. Unfortunately, the British faced the embarrassing fact that the American arguments were legally (in the words of the British Admiral Consett) 'most difficult to refute.' Strangely enough, Sir Edward, as he now confessed to his friend Colonel House, had finally concluded that the real question after all was 'not one of legal niceties.' If they admitted all these legal points they might be unable to 'prevent Germany from trading... as freely in time of war as in time of peace.' The United States, unintentionally of course, might in effect 'strike the weapon of sea power out of our hands and thereby ensure a German victory.' Since we had already struck 'the weapon of sea power' out of Germany's hands on grounds of strict legality, thus helping to ensure an Entente victory, the argument might well have suggested an equal strictness against Great Britain. But long practice upon Colonel House was by this time making Sir Edward very nearly perfect; besides, Sir Edward now had House's extraordinary proposal secure in his safe, and he knew where he stood.

With impatience Colonel House had been awaiting the Foreign Minister's reply to this great project, sketching in the meanwhile the happy futures which were to flow from his master-stroke of diplomacy. In the interests alike of 'civilization' and of 'our own welfare' they must, as he wrote the President, 'throw the influence of this nation in behalf of a plan by which international obligations must be kept.' Mr. Wilson was upon the verge of playing 'the noblest part that has ever come to the son of man.' It was a thrilling prospect. Yet the days went by, and Sir Edward seemed strangely tardy in accepting this high collaboration. Was anything wrong? Not until the end of November did Grey's reply appear. One can picture House's excitement as he scanned it; one can believe that he was indeed 'frankly disappointed' at what he saw. House believed that he was offering to the Allies what must amount to the active intervention of the United States to impose upon the Central Powers that peace of righteousness, disarmament and democracy which the Allies had been demanding since the first days of the war. Yet Sir Edward revealed only the most tepid interest in the project. He was so certain that the other Allied governments would reject the scheme that he had not even discussed it with them. 'I do not see how they could commit themselves in advance to any proposition,' he wrote, 'without knowing exactly what it was and knowing that the United States was prepared to intervene and make good if they accepted.' The greater part of the letter was devoted to the trade controversy.

Such stupidity was incomprehensible to the amateur diplomatist. 'The British,' he wrote to the President, 'are in many ways dull.' These extraordinary people seemed not to understand what he was offering to them; and he went to work at once 'to impress upon Lansing the necessity of the United States making it clear to the Allies that we considered their cause our cause and that we had no intention of permitting a military autocracy to dominate the world if our strength could prevent it.' One sometimes wonders whether Sir Edward's skill was not rather thrown away upon the Colonel, but one can only applaud the masterful delicacy and precision of his effects.

Evidently, Grey had paid a closer attention to that little word 'probably' than either House or Wilson. The one thing which the Entente governments could not possibly afford to do was to get themselves into a peace conference while the Germans were still substantially victorious in the field. Should the fighting actually stop it would be impossible to drive the war-weary peoples back into it again, and the best they could hope for would be a peace on terms more or less in accordance with the military position, which was everywhere favorable to Germany. But the Allies had to have total victory. They were a looser coalition than the Central Powers, held together only by mutual promises of spoils; and a mere hint that one of them was ready to stop without making good the promises to the others would alone be enough to fracture their alliance. A peace conference, save with a beaten enemy, would almost certainly end in dissension among the Allies, rout and complete disaster. Only an ironclad guaranty by the United States to fight unless Germany accepted the full terms dictated by the Entente could justify the latter in risking even the thought of a conference; and House's letter fell very far short of offering that. Yet it opened great possibilities. One skillful show of indifference had already sent House scurrying to blunt the point of Mr. Lansing's embarrassing protests. With careful handling, the United States might even be drawn forward ultimately into the kind of alliance which the Entente could make use of.

Colonel House, however, entertained no such unworthy suspicions, nor, apparently did the President. The two had a long conversation over Grey's letter. Mr. Wilson felt that they must 'let the Allies know how our minds are running'; and the idea of still another Odyssey of personal negotiation began to form. They had another conversation on December 15, and plans for a new mission were farther advanced. House asked the President to tell him again what Gerard had said about that alarming interview with the Kaiser. Mr. Wilson 'went to the safe and got it out and read it to Lansing and me.... The upshot... was that the Kaiser said "he would attend to America when this war was over; that President Wilson's attitude regarding Germany eliminated him from any possibility of acting as mediator."' In the end they decided that the Colonel had better not go to Germany at all unless he was asked; but perhaps they failed to realize how completely this would destroy the neutral character of the mission. The whole affair, at any rate, was to be very clever and secretive, and was to be represented as simply a personal survey by the Colonel to place the Administration in more intimate contact with events. On December 22 Mr. Lansing announced the third coming of the peacemaker in a circular telegram to the Embassies, instructing each to 'impress upon the Foreign Office that Colonel House is not on a peace mission.'

The day this warning was despatched Count Bernstorff called upon the Colonel in New York with a somewhat disconcerting announcement. He had, he said, just heard from his Government; they would like the Colonel to go 'directly to Berlin to discuss peace upon the general terms of military and naval disarmament.' It had never occurred to the Colonel to try to put an end to militarism with the aid of the Germans. The amateur diplomat was not to be trapped, however, by such Teutonic guile. They must be careful, he advised Mr. Wilson, not to let the Germans get them into a 'disagreeable position with the Allies.... I am always suspicious of their diplomacy.' Colonel House was of course right to suspect the Germans — or at any rate Bernstorff, who was far too intelligent a diplomatist not to try to capitalize upon the Colonel's altruism in the same way that the British were doing. Unfortunately, however, House was suspicious of the Germans only; while Wilson, puzzled and worried by this inescapable 'labyrinth,' was still leaving it all to his 'dearest friend.' On Christmas Eve the President sent off a final letter to New York. He was tired of both sides; Spring Rice was a 'highly excitable invalid' and he had no confidence in Bernstorff's offers. Congress was threatening to make damaging trouble over the British blockade. House simply must go abroad. He needed no instructions, for their minds were in accord. 'The United States [in Professor Seymour's paraphrase] was interested only in the future peace of the world and in its guarantees' — military and naval disarmament, and a league of nations to suppress aggression and maintain the freedom of the seas.

With this, the Colonel again packed his trunks as the Christmas season descended upon the Christian world. In London Mr. Page was sending home the season's greetings to some of his old friends:

They're killing one another all right.... When there's 'nothing to report' from France that means the regular 5000 casualties that happen every day. There isn't any way of getting rid of men that has been forgotten or neglected.... And the worst is to come....

A member of the Cabinet.... told me so much bad military news which they prevent the papers from publishing or even hearing, that tonight I almost share this man's opinion that the war will last till 1918. That isn't impossible....

It was but a faint echo from the awful hurricane which Colonel House (assisted only by his private secretary, Miss Denton) was again setting forth to quell over the coffee-cups. On December 28 he took ship for the third time — now with a whole battery of cameras snapping and an army of half a hundred reporters surrounding him upon the pier. Discreetly the discreet Colonel said nothing. At Falmouth, where he arrived on January 5, the British joyfully seized him, rushed him through the controls, gave him taxis, gave him a special sleeping car to London, gave him everything.

iii

Behind him, the year 1916 was dawning upon his countrymen with all the radiance of an unparalleled prosperity. For the statesmen it was dawning also, though less happily, as the harbinger of a Presidential electoral campaign. The political situation, they observed, was decidedly 'confused.' The Wilson Administration was 'fortified by a brilliant record' of domestic reform; worse than that, the country 'was getting very prosperous and the people were in a money-getting rather than a heroic mood.' It left the Republican politicians facing a bleak absence of issues at a moment when they were also without a man. The party was still divided by the great schism of 1912. Mr. Roosevelt had long since forgotten his battle for the Lord and social reform in his consuming hatred for Mr. Wilson, and was now indistinguishable from the orthodox Republicans. But many of his followers were not. Besides, the Republican leaders were in a quandary for which the simple, blood-thirsty bellicosity of Mr. Roosevelt offered no solution.

It was obviously upon the field of foreign policy that their assault would have to be delivered. Like Mr. Roosevelt, the Republican chieftains had earnestly sought to capitalize the martial ardors and pro-Ally enthusiasms of the populace against Mr. Wilson. They had denounced his Mexican policy not for its recklessness but for its timidity; they had tried to undermine his conduct of European relations not by pointing to its adventurous altruism and dangerous bias toward the Allies, but by holding Mr. Wilson up as a cold-blooded pacifist and a base pro-German. Powerfully assisted by Mr. Roosevelt they had themselves established the myth that Mr. Wilson was a devoted neutral and his policy an ignoble one of peace at any price. It seemed an obviously politic course; was it possible that they had been too hasty? Daily the horrid truth was now becoming more apparent: The nation, however quick it might be to applaud the 'strong hand' or respond to the glamours of preparedness, really wanted peace; while, far worse than that, in a close election the relatively small pro-German element might decide the result!

It was a baffling problem. One broad and absolutely basic issue in national policy was at that moment confronting the people of the United States. Should they abandon the tradition of a century, definitely link their fate with one side in the European quarrel and so take a conscious position in the international system with all which that must imply? Or should they entrust themselves in the future as in the past to a genuine policy of genuine neutrality and non-entanglement? From the presentation of this issue the Republican opposition, unfortunately, had debarred itself. The Republicans' delicate task was now to prove themselves more martially patriotic than Mr. Wilson, stronger in the defence of American right and more hostile toward Germany, while at the same time annexing the German vote and convincing the nation that they were the genuine party of peace. It was not precisely a noble or even a statesmanlike maneuver, nor was it an easy one. Patriotism, preparedness and a skillful vagueness upon everything that really mattered was the one possible solution; and even here the reprehensible and slippery Wilson was actually threatening to beat them to it. Marse Henry had forcefully summarized their unhappy state:

There is not even an essential issue.... The tariff? Absurd! Economy? Tell it to the Marines! The flag? Does anyone imagine that at the psychic (the new name for opportune) moment Wilson will not wrap it around him, march down to the footlights and fire the traditional hosspistols?

Indeed, he was doing so already. Yet, politically shrewd and secure though the Wilson position might appear, it was identical with that of the Republicans and so exposed to the same pitfalls. Both sides were proposing to give the country what it wanted and both suffered from the basic fact that what the country wanted was impossible of attainment. The country wanted peace. It also wanted military preparedness, full protection of Americans in Mexico, no truckling to the Germans, a continuation of war prosperity and ultimate victory for the Allies. These objectives were profoundly incompatible.

The Republicans, moreover, had only to promise; the President had concurrently to perform. And at the outset he faced a special difficulty in Congress. If, as Bernstorff had guessed, the anti-British, pro-German and neutral elements were overrepresented in Congress, they were even more heavily overrepresented in the Democratic majorities upon which the President had to rely. Senator Stone, chairman of the Foreign Relations Committee, represented the state of Missouri, which contained a large German population in its chief city, St. Louis, and which had suffered in its rural areas from the British blockade on cotton. In the House there were a number of Southern Democratic Congressmen as determinedly pacifistic as the Northwestern Progressives and quite as bitter against the British. In constructing his foreign policy to appeal to a majority of the whole nation (necessary if one is to win a Presidential election) Mr. Wilson was risking a revolt in his Congressional following which might lead at any moment to the most damaging consequences; and it imposed upon him a special evasiveness.

Such are the peculiar beauties of our ingenious Constitution. The American people happened to be confronted by their most serious issue of national policy since the South Carolina batteries had opened on Fort Sumter fifty-five years before; consequently, this was the one issue which it was not practical politics to raise. On a basis which corresponded only remotely if at all to the fundamental question of the hour, the Presidential campaign of 1916 now opened, as usual, in the debates of the short session of Congress.

Preparedness was the chief battleground. At the Capitol the military and naval bills were flooding the committees and General Wood was soon in his element. Elsewhere Mr. Howard E. Coffin was now quietly at work with his fellow titans preparing the industrial mobilization of the United States in the event of war. Mr. Hudson Maxim was among those working with him; and when presently the egregious Ralph Easley brought Mr. Gompers along, the labor chieftain was 'interested' and gave valuable assistance. Everywhere the nation was preparing. Yet when Mr. Frederick Palmer, the war correspondent, came home from first-hand experiences abroad to undertake a lecture tour for preparedness, he was surprised to find that 'even the strongest advocate of a large army never breathed a word suggesting that a single soldier should ever be sent to Europe.'

He discovered General Wood solemnly putting his staff to work surveying the Atlantic seaboard, noting every harbor and beach where hostile troops could be landed and selecting artillery and trench positions for their repulse. Mr. Palmer knew that the idea of a German invasion, 'until the British and German navies should make common cause against us,' was the most fantastic folly. It was apparent to him that if the national safety required us to prepare against Germany the only rational course was to prepare to join the Allies in defeating her while the war offered the opportunity; and he wanted frankly to advocate the creation of an expeditionary force for the Western Front. His friends were shocked. That was not the idea at all. Senator Lodge told him that such a proposal would not have the slightest chance of success. The proper course, it was explained to him, was to 'throw a scare into the masses' by picturing the Germans sacking New York or violating middle-western farm girls. Mr. Palmer was too honest to act upon the advice, but when he got into the South and West he understood the reason for it. There he found not only 'more genuine neutrality'; he also found that people were actually 'pondering the restraining idea that if we got into the war we should have to send soldiers to France and some of them might be killed or maimed.'

Undoubtedly it was a restraining thought; and along with the flood of armament bills in Congress there began to appear a flood of bills of a different character — bills to deny clearance papers to passenger vessels carrying munitions, to defray the costs of all new defence measures by taxes upon munitions-makers, to embargo the export of munitions to nations that interfered with American foreign trade, to create a commission to go to Europe and make peace. Along with the admirals and the generals, the pacifists were trooping into the committees. The sentiment against militarism and for neutrality, though confused, was unexpectedly impressive. And then on December 30 the sinking (either by mine or torpedo) of the armed British passenger liner Persia in the Mediterranean, with the loss of 334 lives, two of them American, added fresh fuel to the controversy. It was the greatest disaster since the Lusitania; again our newspapers flamed, and the crisis brought the President hurrying back from the wedding journey which had followed his marriage to Mrs. Norman Galt.

Yet many were at last beginning to realize that for the submarine problem there were two possible solutions. One was to fight Germany; the other was to prevent American citizens from imperilling their own lives, and those of their countrymen who would have to do the fighting, by travelling in war zones. On January 5 Senator Gore of Oklahoma, a cotton state Democrat, introduced a bill to deny passports to Americans taking passage in belligerent vessels; and a few days later he backed it up with another demanding the protection of the non-contraband com-

merce of the United States against the Entente restrictions. A
Republican from Ohio was voicing the suspicion that 'there is a
vast array of continental liars in this preparedness game.' Senator
Lodge was 'feeling very depressed' about national defence. 'The
reports that come to me,' Mr. Bryan wrote hopefully to Jane
Addams, 'all indicate a growing sentiment against preparedness';
and on January 13 Spring Rice sent home an alarming report:
'The spirit of Congress is somewhat menacing.'

Secretary Garrison's great 'Continental army' of 400,000
trained militiamen had run into an absurd difficulty. In Congress
it was being opposed not only by the anti-militarists, who thought
it went too far, and the patriotic Republicans, who damned it
for not going far enough, but also by the vested interest of the
National Guard — the existing state-controlled militia force
which now saw itself in danger of being swallowed up by this vast
Federal competitor. In alarm Mr. Garrison appealed to the
President. 'In my judgment,' he wrote on January 12, 'we are
facing a critical juncture with respect to the military part of the
national defence program'; and he summoned Mr. Wilson to
preserve the nation's new army from the National Guard. But
the President, to Mr. Garrison's not unreasonable pain and surprise, refused. It was an issue, he felt, which must be left to Congress to decide.

In the upshot, Congress was to decide for the National Guard;
Mr. Garrison was to resign in anger and dismay; the Continental
army was to die, and the actual increases finally voted for the
military establishment were to be of slight importance. With a
singular adroitness the President thus retained his standing as an
anti-militarist, yet without sacrificing his new leadership of the
preparedness mania. For just as Mr. Garrison was rising privately
to the boiling point over the President's defection from the cause
of militarism, the President himself was launching, in New York
City, a sensational personal speaking tour in preparedness's behalf. The defence enthusiasts, 'thoroughly outwitted, were left
bewildered and sputtering.' So were the pacifists.

The precise motives which underlay President Wilson's famous plea for preparedness in January and February, 1916, are now forever lost in the impenetrable confusions of those years and in the rationalizations subsequently invented to explain them. Did he believe in the German invasion? Or was he thinking of Colonel House, at work in Europe at that moment upon the scheme which might so easily land American infantry upon the Western Front? Did he really believe that the German element within the country had been drilled and armed by Berlin, and that the religious fervors of militarist patriotism were psychologically necessary to unify the people? Or did he think of a great army and navy as simply an abstractly useful force which would free his hands in dealing with both belligerents? Was it actually, at bottom, simply an electoral maneuver — or were all these contradictory considerations perhaps mingled in the President's mind? It is impossible to say; it is certainly impossible to discover from the substance of the speeches themselves.

It was in New York on January 27 that he wrapped Marse Henry's flag more firmly about him and drew the hosspistols. Their first detonation was unexpectedly heavy. Mr. Wilson gave warning of the gravest perils. But from whom? It was a point which the speech neglected to make clear, and when Mr. Bryan asked he got no reply. The East was left to assume that it was of Germany that the President was thinking; yet as he carried the campaign westward his tone softened somewhat, and as he approached the pro-German centers it even began to appear that England might be the real enemy. And as his tour ended in St. Louis on February 3 one might have begun to wonder at first whether there were any enemy at all. At a gathering in the afternoon the President stressed, rather, the horror of war itself. Pointing to the fearful conflagration in Europe he went on:

> We must keep our resources and our strength and our thoughts untouched by that flame in order that we may be in a condition to serve the restoration of the world, the healing processes. The world will not endure, I believe, another struggle like that which is going on now.

At the great evening meeting in the Coliseum, however, his subject was defence. In St. Louis he was supposedly on Germanophile ground, and the audience at first seemed rather hostile. But it warmed to him as he made an ever stronger and stronger plea for preparedness; until at last, perhaps carried away by the emotional response, he cried that the American Navy 'ought, in my judgment, to be incomparably the greatest Navy in the world.'[1] To assist in the 'healing processes' and prepare us for a time which would not see another major war, President Wilson had announced a program of navalism surpassing anything ever advocated by American navalists in their wildest propaganda. Whatever this was, it was not precisely logic.

Mr. Roosevelt, perceiving his own most private thunder being thus appropriated once more by the New Jersey schoolmaster, resigned himself to a bitter probability:

> Wilson, with his adroit, unscrupulous cunning, his readiness to about-face, his timidity about any manly assertion of our rights, his pandering to the feelings of those who love ease and the chance of material profit, and his lack of all convictions and willingness to follow every gust of popular opinion, will be supported by the mass of our fellow-countrymen.

It was very likely; and though it convinced the Rough Rider that Wilson was 'the demagogue, adroit, tricky, false, without one spark of loftiness in him, without a touch of the heroic in his cold, selfish and timid soul,' that did not help much. The true issue, as Mr. Roosevelt may dimly have understood, lay between the President on the one side and the La Follette progressives and Bryan on the other — a circumstance which left both the Rough Rider and the great army of orthodox Republicanism with singularly little reason for existence. Their opportunity to play a really great and serious role at one of the decisive moments of

---

[1] So it was reported in the newspapers and generally understood at the time. In later published versions the phrase has become 'incomparably the most adequate Navy in the world'; the context, however, would still make this mean the same — if it means anything

American history had been squandered in petty partisanship. The President was in command of the situation.

Yet even so, the President himself was still a long way from the election.

iv

For nearly a month now, quiet, sensational cables had been filtering back into the White House recording the secret progress of an extraordinary negotiation. Colonel House had reached London on the 6th of January. On his first day he had made the happy discovery that the minds of both Grey and Balfour (then First Lord of the Admiralty) were running 'parallel with ours.' The whole position seemed unexpectedly bright. 'Grey is now in favor of the Freedom of the Seas provided it includes the elimination of militarism, and further provided we will join in a general covenant to sustain it'; and this appeared so promising that the Colonel hoped immediately to formulate with Grey and Balfour 'some plan which I can submit to you and which they can recommend to their colleagues.'

This glowing report went on January 7, and Mr. Wilson at once cabled back that he would be glad to co-operate in a policy of permanent peace. 'This cable,' says Professor Seymour, 'may well be regarded as historic,' for it marked President Wilson's first definite commitment (on the urging of Sir Edward Grey!) to a future League of Nations. Thus by another step was Sir Edward's far-sighted policy advanced. But the commitment was a future one. The use which Colonel House was now to make of it can scarcely have been anticipated by President Wilson.

The Colonel was in his element — and plainly having a magnificent time. The whole atmosphere appears to have been suffused with cordiality and Anglo-American friendship. On January 11 he lunched with McKenna, Chancellor of the Exchequer, and Runciman, President of the Board of Trade. Bryce dropped in afterward and Page brought in Lloyd George, Austen Chamberlain and Lord Reading. In the end they asked him what it was that the United States wanted Great Britain to do; and House's reply was: 'The United States would like Great Britain to do those things which would enable the United States *to help Great Britain win the war.*' [1] Thus at the very outset he again gave away his hand and offered his country up upon the altars of Allied victory. Yet, strangely enough, both Grey and Balfour continued to prove elusive. They doubted whether their colleagues would agree to too many 'concessions' to American opinion in the way of peace leagues and the ending of militarism and navalism. Vainly the Colonel tried to make them see that these wouldn't be concessions to the United States. It was 'quite the other way around.' It was the United States which was making the concessions. But somehow they seemed incapable of grasping this idea. Perhaps it was just another case of that British stupidity which the Colonel had already noted.

On the 12th there arrived a cable which the Colonel might well have pondered. There was a more and more pressing demand, the President suggested, for some satisfaction from Great Britain in the blockade matter; and this demand the President felt to be only just. Mr. Page detected a 'certain fierce, blue-bellied Presbyterian tone' in this communication, and it should have warned House that the President's policy was not primarily, perhaps, to 'help Great Britain win the war.' But it failed to deflect the Colonel. He continued his 'propaganda' with the British. He saw the King. On January 14 he dined with Lloyd George and Reading.

The energetic Welshman was in a mood of startling frankness. He told House plainly that the war could alone be concluded by the neutral intervention of President Wilson; that this should come, he thought, in September (when the slaughter then in preparation for the new year would have again proved ineffective), and that 'terms could be dictated by the President which the belligerents would never agree on if left to themselves.' It was in

[1] Italics mine.

general just this kind of intervention to force a peace which the President must have supposed that his emissary was preparing. But House's own comment was:

> Fantastic as this may seem, there is some truth in it; and if the President had taken my advice and increased the army... in the early months of the war, as I strongly urged him to do, he would be in a position today to do what George wishes him to do.

The subtle Grey had no desire to invite the United States into a commanding position in a post-war Europe which the Allied armies would have conquered with their blood. What he wanted from House was not simply the guarantee of a future peace system but a guarantee of Allied victory. Yet just at this rather delicate juncture, Mr. Lloyd George had very nearly upset the apple cart. In a conference with Grey and Balfour on the afternoon of the 15th, House repeated what Lloyd George had said to him the night before. Balfour and Grey hastened to explain to the Colonel that all this must have been just Lloyd George's own idea. They had never thought of such a thing. Lloyd George had never breathed a word of that kind to the Cabinet. Apparently the danger was averted; and they went on to discuss the Freedom of the Seas. Balfour was strangely skeptical about this important item in the House-Wilson project, for he was, House noted, 'unalterably distrustful of the Germans.' But House accepted the objection without difficulty. It didn't matter after all, he decided, because the proposed league of nations would attend to all such matters 'under the lead of Great Britain and the United States,' and in this Sir Edward 'strongly' supported him!

A few days later the Colonel had been enticed still farther. House had originally intended to leave all territorial and indemnity questions to the belligerents; but after all, it was not very easy to discuss peace in a vacuum. By the 19th Colonel House had been induced to confess his ideas of what would be 'reasonable' in this respect. A 'reasonable peace,' he thought, would have to include the restoration of Belgium and Serbia, the cession of

Alsace-Lorraine to France and of Constantinople to Russia. Sir Edward must have breathed a sigh of relief. That Germany, still winning in nearly every theater, would agree to cede Constantinople (which the Allies had just failed disastrously to take) to say nothing of her own territory of Alsace-Lorraine was patently impossible. The British statesmen could at least conclude that there was no fear of Germany's exploiting the Colonel's innocent activities, and Grey and Balfour now 'thoroughly approved' his idea of going on to Germany. On January 20, House departed to explore the situation in Berlin.

As in 1914, as in 1915, now for the third time in 1916 the British had skillfully parried the House menace, captured the Colonel and sent him onward to Berlin as an emissary of the Entente cause.

Between the President at the White House and the Colonel in Europe there were now the beginnings, at least, of two different American foreign policies. Two days before House's departure from London Secretary Lansing, to the further confusion of posterity and the diplomats, had contributed a third. While the President and his emissary had been concentrating on the larger questions of peace, the State Department had been struggling, as usual, with the more immediate issues of the war; and after the sinking of the Persia it was sufficiently apparent that they were issues of a serious character. The tenuous nature of our victory over the submarine could no longer be denied; and it was the fear that the Germans might at any moment plunge us into war over the submarine which lay at the bottom of all three policies. Where Mr. Wilson, however, sought to escape the 'labyrinth' by bringing the war to an end, and Colonel House by bringing us into it anyway, Secretary Lansing now sought an exit through regularizing our position toward the war itself.

A new difficulty, moreover, had by this time arisen. The Allies had adopted the practice of arming their merchantmen and instructing the captains in methods of destroying an attacking submarine. The Germans naturally claimed that this made every

Allied merchantman a war vessel and therefore legitimately subject to being sunk without warning; more than that, the 'Q-ships' — actual men-of-war disguised as merchant vessels for the entrapment of submarines — made it impossible for a U-boat captain to distinguish the merchantman (bound by international law to offer no resistance to capture) from the war vessel which was free to sink him on sight. For the U-boat under these circumstances to observe the rules of visit and search upon which the United States was insisting was equivalent to suicide.

The legal argument on all sides was of an intricacy which it is useless to follow. The British of course cheerfully contended that if the legal use of the submarine was equivalent to suicide, the Germans would just have to stop using submarines. Unfortunately, this was not a very realistic argument, nor did it meet the fact that we had for many months permitted the British to violate the rule of visit and search precisely because to observe it in the presence of submarines would have been suicidal. [1] But in the course of the discussion Mr. Lansing thought that he discerned a path out of the whole imbroglio. On January 18 he presented a memorandum to the Allied Ambassadors in Washington, outlining a *modus vivendi* for the regularization of the whole sea war. The submarine, he proposed, should be bound by the rules of visit and search; but in return it was only reasonable that belligerent merchantmen should be disarmed and required to stop immediately upon being ordered to do so by a submarine.

At once the Entente Ambassadors were filled with dismay and despair by such gross pro-Germanism in the American Government. Gently Ambassador Jusserand pointed to the insoluble 'difficulties' of any such arrangement. To Sir Edward, fresh from the comforting assurances of House, it must have come as a severe shock. He summoned Mr. Page, and presently the latter was

[1] In the diversion of ships for examination in harbor. See pp. 117–18. When the Germans presently sent out disguised surface raiders, closely analogous to the Q-ships, the British simply announced that a new modification of the visit-and-search rule was 'necessary,' and must be 'instantly' obeyed, otherwise their patrols would open fire, regardless of possible peril to neutral lives.

cabling in anguish that 'I have only once before seen Sir Edward so grave and disappointed, and that was when [in August, 1914] he informed me that the British had sent the German Government an ultimatum.' The Foreign Minister 'indulged the hope that the Department had not foreseen the results of the proposal, which was wholly in favor of the Germans... and wholly against the Allies.'

It was, and for that reason the proposal never had the slightest chance of success. Bernstorff, indeed, believed that the President could not have read it, or at most could only have glanced through it without sensing its implications. Today, one cannot be so sure; but however that may be, the idea came far too late, and was in the end to be of no effect. But it raised a fearful row.

While Mr. Lansing was thus reducing the Entente Ambassadors in Washington to a cold sweat, Colonel House, in a very different frame of mind, was surveying the scene in Berlin. He met various leaders, though he drew the line at Tirpitz, that monster of 'German frightfulness upon the sea.' One trouble with Colonel House as a negotiator was his inability to allow for the curious German belief that winning the war was just as important to the Germans as the Allies felt it to be to the Allies. On his third day, however, he saw the Chancellor and von Jagow at a formal dinner at the Embassy. With the Chancellor he managed to get about an hour and a half of private conversation, though much of it was wasted in generalities. Bethmann explained the 'scrap of paper' speech; he went on to deplore the war and to insist, quite truthfully, that up to that moment he had been the sole responsible statesman on either side to speak in favor of peace. But Colonel House had spent far too much time in London. Never once did he seize this opportunity of finding out what the Germans, on their side, might be prepared to offer in the way of permanent peace and disarmament. He did not even try to get something which he might use to bid up the Allies. Instead, he frittered away the chance trying to convince Bethmann that the British were going to win — until the Colonel finally grew 'weary' and broke off the discussion!

The Chancellor drank copiously of beer.... I contented myself with mineral water.... The beer did not apparently affect him, for his brain was as befuddled at the beginning as it was at the end. Into such hands are the destinies of the people placed.

Possibly the same might have been said of the mineral water as of the beer. House next found Jagow and went over the same ground with him until midnight, when he went to bed, feeling with some justification that 'not much had been accomplished.' Next day Zimmermann, the Undersecretary for Foreign Affairs, likewise proved to be a disappointment. Unable to convince the obtuse Germans that they had lost the war and should therefore place their destinies in his hands, the negotiator abandoned Berlin four days after he had arrived there.

He was in Paris on February 2, busy interviewing Briand, the Prime Minister, and Jules Cambon. Since his trip of the year before Colonel House had remembered the existence of the French; and upon them he now tried the sally which had gone so well in London: 'I have told them all that what we wanted most was for them to do those things which would help us to help them best.' It is not surprising that Cambon was 'pleased'; and he must have been even more so when the Colonel went on to explain that although he hoped to patch up the submarine controversy for a time, he was sure that the break could only be deferred. Curiously enough, it was on the day after this assurance was given that President Wilson, many thousands of miles away at St. Louis, was declaring that 'we must keep our resources and our strength and our thoughts untouched' by the flames of the European War, in order to serve 'the healing processes.'

Clearly, the rift between the two minds was widening. It was at this juncture that the repercussions of Mr. Lansing's *modus vivendi* proposal began to roll in upon Colonel House. Lansing cabled him Page's report that Sir Edward was 'seriously disturbed.' His English friends hastened to reveal themselves directly in a state of even more serious disturbance. The air was full of serious disturbance; and House, seeing his great scheme of an American-

Entente alliance jeopardized, was seriously disturbed himself.
He rushed to the cables to suppress Mr. Lansing. The idea, as
he kindly put it, 'seems fair taken by itself, but there are many
collateral questions....' The coils were tightening around the
negotiator. He again told the French 'that the lower the fortunes
of the Allies ebbed, the closer the United States would stand by
them.' This left the French very little to worry about, and they
agreed readily enough to the final conclusion: If the Allies felt
that they could win unaided, the President would stand aloof
and they could dictate their own terms to Germany; if they felt
they were losing ground, the President would intervene to save
them and guarantee a settlement based on 'justice.' There would
seem to have been very little in this to which the French could
not have agreed. House took ship for England.

As he did so, Mr. Gerard was cabling from Berlin the text of a
new German memorandum on the subject of the armed merchantmen. Both the French and the British had by this time formally
rejected Mr. Lansing's *modus vivendi* on the ground that it would
'insure the effectiveness' of the submarine campaign; the Germans
now closed the issue. After a long recital of alleged attacks by
merchant vessels on submarines, the memorandum concluded:

> Enemy merchantmen armed with guns no longer have any right
> to be considered as peaceable vessels of commerce. Therefore, the
> German naval forces will receive orders, within a short period, pay-
> ing consideration to the interests of the neutrals, to treat such vessels
> as belligerents.

A belligerent vessel may legitimately be sunk on sight. Considering the large number of Entente vessels which had now been
armed, and the practical impossibility of distinguishing the others
through a periscope, it amounted almost to a declaration of
unrestricted war on Allied commerce. Crisis again appeared.

Would the United States accept this theory and leave the British and German navies to fight it out, or would we again inter-
pose the shield of our moralistic humanitarianism between the

war supply business and the torpedo? The President, thoroughly committed, at the beginning of a campaign year and with the country rolling in a 'blood-soaked boom' (as one Congressman called it) of war industry, neither wished nor dared to recede. At the other end of Pennsylvania Avenue, however, many Congressmen were taking a different view. They saw that to insist on visit and search under the conditions which had grown up would be to give the armed merchantman quite as unfair an advantage over the submarine as the latter would otherwise have over the merchantman. It was impossible for them to understand why the United States should fight the Allies' battle on the sea, or why the willingness of a few American travellers to risk their lives in a declared war zone should be permitted to drag the hundred million people of the United States into the most frightful war in history. Rapidly there developed in Congress a strong sentiment in favor of accepting the German contention, warning American citizens off belligerent passenger vessels and leaving it to the warring powers to fight out their war.

Suddenly, the basic issue had been drawn between a policy of genuine and effective neutrality, and one of silent partnership with Entente. The President perceived the seriousness of the Congressional revolt. Did he fully understand what it implied? It is not clear; his actual course was to be, like that of so many other strong statesmen under similar circumstances, one of stern and uncompromising evasion. In the House, Mr. McLemore, a Democrat of Texas, was preparing a resolution warning American citizens against travelling in armed ships of the belligerents; the first of the similar Gore resolutions had already been introduced into the Senate. After a Cabinet meeting one day about the middle of February, two members of the Cabinet remained to advise the President that 'it would be a hopeless task on his part to attempt to stem the tide now running' in favor of such a declaration. To fight it 'might result in a disastrous defeat to his leadership.'

It was, indeed, a difficult moment. The Republicans had brought in a stirring counter-resolution: 'There should be no acquiescence in the order of the German Admiralty on the part of this or any other neutral Power'; and Senator Lodge was doing his best with a long, a learned and legalistic defence of the armed merchantman. To support the Gore-McLemore movement would mean the reversal of the President's whole European policy; to oppose it would be to risk his repudiation by his own party. For Mr. Champ Clark, the Speaker of the House, was presently bringing a delegation to announce that the Gore-McLemore resolution must pass two to one. The issue hung, for a time, in suspense.

As it hung there, the unofficial ambassador was arriving again in London. He came, according to Mr. Page, 'full of the idea of American intervention.'

> First his plan was that he and I and a group of the British Cabinet … should at once work out a minimum program of peace — the least the Allies would accept, which, he assumed, would be unacceptable to the Germans; and that the President would take this program and present it to both sides; the side that declined would be responsible for continuing the war. Then, to end the war, the President would help the other side — that is, the Allies.

It is to Mr. Page's credit that he was skeptical of this ingenious statesmanship. 'Of course, the fatal moral weakness of the foregoing scheme is that we should plunge into the war, not on the merits of the cause but by a carefully sprung trick.' But House had no hesitations. He had left France on Wednesday, February 9, with the understanding that if the Allies found themselves hard pressed they would consent to the President's calling for a peace conference. On Thursday morning he had a long talk with Grey, and in the end it was 'understood though not definitely agreed upon' that the President should issue his call for a conference 'within a very short time.' The Colonel's eager report continued:

> The Allies will agree to the conference, and if Germany does not, I have *promised for you* that we will throw in all our weight in order to bring her to terms.

You will see that we have progressed pretty far since I left Paris — further than I had any idea it was possible to do. I am to meet the Prime Minister, Balfour and Grey tomorrow at lunch ... *to endeavour to get their approval.*[1]

'We' had indeed come far. Yet at the luncheon approval was not clearly forthcoming. Once more there arose that old difficulty which the Colonel seemed always to encounter as he approached the point. The truth was, of course, that all the British statesmen recognized the dangerous character of the game Grey was playing. It was vital to humor the Colonel in order to protect themselves against the ominous insurgencies of the American Congress or of Mr. Lansing. It was valuable to develop the House scheme as a means of retaining the United States for a last-line defence, should their case become desperate; and it was even possible that the project, fantastic though it was, might serve to bring the United States to the military support of the Entente. Until the United States had been irrevocably committed, however, not only to the war but to the full Entente war aims, the peace conference idea might backfire disastrously at any moment; while they entertained a by no means unwarranted doubt as to just how far Colonel House was really empowered to make these sensational promises for the President. 'Do not count upon purchasing effective help from [the United States] by any concession,' Spring Rice had warned them. 'You would build on sand.' It was the delicate task of Grey and his colleagues to encourage the Colonel, to involve him as deeply as possible, and to commit themselves to nothing.

The conferences were numerous and skillful. The British wanted the United States to come in on the submarine issue — so much simpler an arrangement and involving no embarrassing questions of peace terms. Solemnly House reasoned with these men — now experts in buying the support of neutrals — to show them the error of their ways. Giving ground here, the British tried outflanking him and entangling him in a definite commit-

[1] Italics mine.

ment as to territorial settlements. On Monday, February 14,
Lord Reading gave a dinner at his home. Asquith was there and
Grey, Lloyd George, Balfour and House. Mr. Lloyd George
pressed for assurances, and they proceeded to discuss the terms.
House himself recorded in his diary that 'we cheerfully divided
up Turkey, both in Asia and in Europe,' and spent a long time
over Constantinople and Poland. They finally agreed, according
to Lloyd George, upon the restoration of Belgium and Serbia,
the cession of Alsace-Lorraine, 'adjustments' of the Italian frontier
so as to 'liberate' Italian communities in Austria (the innocent
Colonel seems never to have probed very deeply into the secret
commitments of the Treaty of London) and the cession of Constantinople to Russia. In compensation for Alsace-Lorraine,
however, Germany was to get concessions 'outside of Europe'
— where the great principles of self-determination and freedom
for small peoples apparently did not apply. Did House realize,
as he thus complacently remade the map of Europe, just how much
American blood it might take to validate such armchair decisions?
Perhaps he thought it did not matter, for there were also, of
course, to be those 'guarantees against any future recurrence of
such a catastrophe as this World War.'

As the evening wore on, House tried to bring them back to
these higher spheres, but at midnight Asquith broke up the meeting. As to the precise character of the peace system nothing very
definite seems to have been said. However, as House noted in his
diary, 'there was at least a common agreement reached in regard
to the essential feature; that is, the President should at some time,
to be later agreed upon, call a halt and demand a conference.'
The question of when this should be — absolutely vital from the
American standpoint — was the most indefinite of all. The
British statesmen had reason to feel satisfied; and it is not surprising that when House called upon Sir Edward next morning
he found the Foreign Minister 'visibly pleased with the result.'
Sir Edward proposed to write out a 'memorandum of our understanding.' It was not even necessary, he skillfully suggested, to

have another general meeting. 'He and I could button up the details better alone. This also met with my approval.' That afternoon the Colonel went on for a social call at Buckingham Palace. He pleased the King greatly by showing him 'a 50-mark piece upon which was stamped *"Gott Strafe England und Amerika"* ' and the monarch reciprocated with the unexpected confession that he had been a reader of *Life* for a quarter of a century. Thus were the bonds of Anglo-American amity confirmed.

Rapidly the tragi-comedy was now rising to its climax. The Colonel had rashly told the French that 'the lower the fortunes of the Allies ebbed, the closer the United States would stand by them.' Toward the end, the tactical weakness of this policy of backing the losing horse more heavily the more he fell behind began to dawn upon Colonel House, and he sedulously sought to 'correct' it. 'I am trying,' he slyly noted, 'to force early action by making both England and France feel that they run the risk of losing our support entirely unless they act quickly.' The attempt would have worked better had it been made six months before; however, Sir Edward at least went forward with his draft memorandum of their 'understanding.' It is the document now celebrated in history as the House-Grey Memorandum of February, 1916. As agreed upon by House it read:

Colonel House told me that President Wilson was ready, on hearing from France and England that the moment was opportune, to propose that a conference should be summoned to put an end to the war. Should the Allies accept this proposal, and should Germany refuse it, the United States would *probably* enter the war against Germany.

Colonel House expressed the opinion that, if such a conference met, it would secure peace on terms not unfavourable to the Allies; and, if it failed to secure peace, the United States *would leave the conference as a belligerent on the side of the Allies*, if Germany was unreasonable. Colonel House expressed an opinion *decidedly* favourable to the restoration of Belgium, the transfer of Alsace and Lorraine to France, and the acquisition by Russia of an outlet to the sea, though he thought that the loss of territory incurred by Germany in one place would have to be compensated to her by concessions to her in other places outside Europe. If the Allies delayed accepting the offer of President Wilson, and if, later on, the course of the war was so unfavourable to them that the intervention of the United States would not be effective, the United States would *probably* disinterest themselves in Europe and look to their own protection in their own way.

I said that... I must inform the Prime Minister and my colleagues; but that I could say nothing until [the matter] had received their consideration. The British Government could, under no circumstances, accept or make any proposal except in consultation and agreement with the Allies....[1]

As to the character of the peace guarantees, the military and naval disarmament and the freedom of the seas for the sake of which the United States would thus be committed to the war, there was not one word in the whole of this extraordinary document.

On Monday, February 21, House saw Grey once more at his home in Eccleston Square and learned that the Memorandum had been circulated to Asquith, Balfour and Lloyd George. The Colonel spent some time reassuring Grey that 'the President and I were in earnest' and the proposal genuine; and as they were strolling away from the house together, the Foreign Minister gave the amateur diplomatist his photograph. The happy Colonel was unaware of another conference, taking place that same afternoon, perhaps at that identical moment, in the White House at Washington.

V

On the evening of February 21 Mr. Wilson summoned Senators Kern and Stone and Representatives Kitchin and Flood — respectively the leaders and the chairmen of the foreign relations

[1] Italics mine.

committees of the two Houses — to discuss the Gore-McLemore resolutions warning American citizens from armed belligerent liners. Precisely what happened is not known. According to the best account [1] Mr. Kitchin was unable to be present; when he heard from Mr. Flood, however, what the President had said he was so startled that he asked immediately for another conference. This was arranged for 7:30 on the following morning, in order to escape the newspaper men; and in the early sunlight of February 22, Washington's Birthday, the Congressmen, now accompanied by Speaker Clark of the House, reconvened at the White House. The President hinted to them, apparently, that he was at that moment arranging the intervention of the United States in the European War.

It is certain that he told them that he was opposed to the Gore-McLemore resolution; that he hoped Great Britain would not reject the Lansing compromise but that she would be within her rights in doing so, and that in event of this happening he believed the United States should neither bar armed merchantmen from her ports as war vessels nor prevent Americans from taking passage in them. Furthermore, in case Germany should attack one of these ships with American citizens on board he would consider it his duty to hold her to strict account. This, it seemed obvious to Stone and to the others, meant war.

At once, however, rumors of even more sensational statements made by the President ran through the Congressional cloak-rooms. Senator Gore declared publicly a few days later that he had been told [2] that Mr. Wilson not only explained the imminent probability of war over the submarine but went on to say that 'war might not be of itself and of necessity an evil, but that the United States by entering the war now might be able to bring

[1] Furnished by Senator Gore, who was not there, to George Sylvester Viereck, and printed by the latter in 'The Strangest Friendship in History,' p. 182.

[2] He had talked with Stone, Kern and Kitchin. Stone did not tell him what had been said but admitted that his 'gravest apprehensions' had been aroused. Kern repeated the conversation. Kitchin much later told Senator Dill about it. Viereck: 'The Strangest Friendship in History,' p. 183–84.

it to a conclusion by midsummer and thus render a great service to civilization.' Senator Stone at once denied that any such statement had been made; but a denial would have been so obviously imperative, for every reason both of foreign policy and domestic politics, that this cannot be taken too seriously. It seems incredible, moreover, that even the stubborn and self-willed President could have permitted Colonel House to continue his negotiations abroad without seeking to give some hint of them, at least, to the leaders of Congress — where there resides the sole constitutional power to declare war.

If this was the purpose of the gathering, however, the results could scarcely have been encouraging. Senator Stone was shocked and angry; the President is said to have become angry in turn, until Speaker Clark at last interposed: 'Neither of you is in a frame of mind to discuss so serious a question,' and the conference broke up. It was on the following day, February 23, that Grey gave House what they intended to be the definitive draft of the House-Grey Memorandum; and two days later the unofficial envoy sailed, eager and important, to lay it before his principal.

It was also on the 23d that the Congressional revolt at last broke out into the open and it was announced that the Gore-McLemore resolution would be called up for a vote. The precipitant was a formal letter from Senator Stone to the President:

Since Senator Kern, Mr. Flood and I talked with you on Monday evening I am more troubled than I have been for many a day. I have not felt authorized to repeat our conversation, but... I have felt that the members of the two Houses who are to deal with this grave question were entitled to know the situation we are confronting as I understand it to be.

I think I should say to you that the members of both Houses feel deeply concerned by what they read and hear. I have heard of some talk to the effect... that, after all, it may be possible that the program of preparedness, so called, has some relation to such a situation as we are now called upon to meet....

On the 24th Mr. Tumulty was in a state of agitation. 'In the last hour,' he advised the President in a hurried memorandum, he had been talking to the Congressional leaders; he was convinced that the Gore-McLemore resolution could no longer be smothered and that behind it was a 'purpose to discredit your leadership, for the forces that are lined up for this fight against you are the anti-preparedness crowd, the Bryan-Kitchin-Clark group and some of the anti-British Senators like Hoke Smith and Gore.' To repel this political threat from the rear, Mr. Tumulty urged an answer — taking, of course, the loftiest ground of humanity and public policy — to Senator Stone's letter. The President accepted the advice; a reply was at once composed and given out the same evening:

My dear Senator:

... You are right in assuming that I shall do everything in my power to keep the United States out of war.... Through many anxious months I have striven for that object, amid difficulties more manifold than can have been apparent upon the surface, and so far I have succeeded.... The course which the Central Powers have announced their intention of following in the future with regard to undersea warfare seems for the moment to threaten insuperable obstacles, but its apparent meaning is so manifestly inconsistent with explicit assurances recently given... that I must believe that explanations will presently ensue which will put a different aspect upon it....

But in any event our duty is clear...; and if the clear rights of American citizens should very unhappily be abridged or denied by any such action we should, it seems to me, have in honor no choice. ... The honor and self-respect of the nation is involved. We covet peace and shall preserve it at any cost but the loss of honor. To forbid our people to exercise their rights for fear we might be called upon to vindicate them would be a deep humiliation indeed.... It would be a deliberate abdication of our hitherto proud position as spokesmen... for the law and right. It would make everything this Government has attempted and everything it has accomplished during this terrible struggle of nations meaningless and futile.

What had we accomplished? How far had we defended honor, national self-respect and 'the law and right' against the Entente? How frank was all this in view of the House negotiations? Such are some of the questions which occur today as one re-reads that lofty manifesto. But Senator Stone, at any rate, had his answer, clear and unequivocal. The answer was war — unless the Germans wished to avoid it by a complete backdown. On that basis only was the President striving 'to keep the United States out of war,' and those who blame him for his later entry into the conflict upon the specific issue of the submarine cannot accuse him of having failed to make plain his exact policy. The nation, moreover, shrieked an approval which the editors of the *Literary Digest* recorded as 'unanimous.' 'Have we an American Congress?' demanded the New York *Times* in a blazing editorial in support. 'Shall the foreign policy of the United States Government be determined in Washington or Berlin?' cried Mr. F. I. Cobb from the editorial page of the *World*, and the echoes rolled through the country's press, while the *Journal of Commerce* paused for the comforting thought that 'taking the situation at large, war with Germany could not be a very serious matter to the United States, and if it hastened peace would be distinctly beneficial.'

But it was possible that we did still have an American Congress, for this unmistakable announcement of the reckless path down which the President was steering the nation to an alliance with the Entente only added power to the Congressional revolt. To the nervous eyes of Spring Rice it seemed that there was a 'panic' at the Capitol like that which had swept the French Chamber in 1904 when Delcassé fell; and perhaps there was a panic at the White House, for the President's advisers were urging him to make a final effort to suppress the Gore-McLemore resolution in committee. Unfortunately, Mr. Wilson, having staked everything on the strong hand, now felt that he must make it strong in fact; and in a letter on February 29 he demanded that the House Rules Committee let the resolution come to a vote:

The report that there are divided counsels in Congress in regard to the foreign policy of the Government is being made industrious use of in foreign capitals.... So long as it is anywhere credited it cannot fail to do the greatest harm and expose the country to the most serious risks. I therefore feel justified in asking that your Committee will permit me to urge an early vote... in order that... all doubts and conjectures may be swept away and our foreign relations once more cleared of damaging misunderstandings.

Under the full steam of Administration pressure upon the recalcitrants the resolution came up for action. It failed in the Senate on March 3. In desperation Senator Gore offered an ironic substitute declaring that the death of another American citizen in the sinking of an armed liner without notice 'would constitute a just and sufficient cause of war between the United States and the German Empire.' It was no use; the final impossibility in politics is to make either peoples or statesmen understand and face the consequences of their own acts. The substitute, like the original resolution, was tabled; and there remained only the final test in the House. It was at just this critical moment that the unofficial envoy, bearing his masterstroke of diplomacy in his pocket, stepped from the train at Washington.

The Colonel lunched at the White House on March 6; afterward he, the President and the new Mrs. Wilson took a long automobile ride, during which 'I outlined every important detail of my mission.' They dropped him at the State Department and he went over it all once more with Lansing; he then returned to the White House and that evening showed the President the full text of the House-Grey Memorandum. According to House the President approved everything he had done; they agreed to write out a cable for Grey on the following morning, and at the end Mr. Wilson placed his hand upon the Colonel's shoulder, saying: 'It would be impossible to imagine a more difficult task than the one placed in your hands, but you have accomplished it in a way beyond my expectations.'

Yet President Wilson, strangely enough, did have just one little correction to make. It was nothing less than the insertion of the word 'probably' in the second paragraph of the text [1] to make it read: 'The United States would *probably* leave the conference as a belligerent.' Once more, as had happened when the President made precisely the same correction in House's letter of the preceding October,[2] both men appear to have regarded this as an unimportant verbal change. Once more, however, it materially altered the bearing of the scheme — or rather, indicated that the President's conception of the scheme was not the same as that of his emissary.

British statesmanship is heir to a long tradition of meticulous care in the wording of important documents. British diplomatists will fashion an ambiguity or shape a pledge with all the precise, unapparent artistry of a Japanese print maker. It can hardly have been by accident that there was a slight discrepancy in Grey's text of the Memorandum. The first paragraph stated that should the Allies accept and Germany refuse a conference, the United States would 'probably' enter the war; the second paragraph, however, dealt with the very different case of a conference actually being convened but failing of agreement, and there Grey had introduced no qualifying word. In the first instance the Allies would risk nothing, in the second, they would be risking everything, and an absolute, inescapable guaranty from the United States was essential before they could even consider it. Not even a House could really have missed the significance of this little point — and House had been specifically warned upon it by the President in October!

They must do 'something,' the Colonel had said when he was first developing his 'positive policy,' that would 'either end the war in a way to abolish militarism or that would bring us in with the Allies to help them do it.' Throughout the President seems to have assumed that House was working for the first objective, but it was the second which the negotiator had actually achieved. With one word the President now restored the plan as a device

[1] See pp. 271-72   [2] Page 230.

primarily directed toward the first. Neither man perceived the difference between them at the time. There is evidence that the President was soon to awake to it.

Next morning, March 7, they met again to draft the definitive cable to Grey. The immediate menace of the Memorandum had been withdrawn; but with its several dangerous ambiguities it was still scarcely a safe document. In the House of Representatives that same day the forces were marshalled for the final battle over the Gore-McLemore resolution. The debate was long, confused and impassioned, but at the end of the day the vote was reached and the President and the 'strong hand' triumphed by 276 to 142. The resolution was tabled. The Democratic leaders voted against the President and for peace; so did an important element of the party. The Republicans, on the other hand, were split almost evenly; and without the 93 Republican votes against the resolution it must have carried in spite of the President. The nation had been dedicated to the intransigeant patriotism which was to end almost exactly a year later in the declaration of war upon Germany. It was a result for which the two parties were about equally responsible, and one applauded by nearly the whole press.

That evening Senator Stone was at the White House again. 'I had,' he assured the Senate next day, 'another very frank talk with the President.... So far from the President desiring to involve this country in this disastrous European war, his supreme wish is to avoid that calamity.' Even as the Senator was speaking, the cable was on its way to Sir Edward announcing the President's acceptance of the Memorandum with the one indicated change. In beating the Gore-McLemore resolution, House added in effect, the Administration had done its part; 'it is now squarely up to you to make the next move, and a cable from you at any time will be sufficient.' But no cable came. Again, Sir Edward took note of the 'probably.'

Perhaps actually it did not make much difference. The whole scheme was too indefinite at best for the Allies to have put much confidence in it; but the President's emendation was a clear warning that their doubts about America and the Colonel were well justified. The document, of course, might have a future usefulness.

We believed and the French believed [as Sir Edward later put it] that defeat of the German armies was the only sure overthrow of Prussian militarism.... [But] the chances seemed that things might get worse rather than better in 1916. If this happened it would be most valuable to bear in mind what sort of a peace could be obtained by the mediation and influence of the United States, and also to know that these would be forthcoming.

Or, as he explained a trifle more bluntly to Lloyd George at the time: 'It has always been my view that until the Allies were sure of victory the door should be kept open for Wilson's mediation.' Sir Edward Grey laid the paper away for possible future reference. By a striking irony, the date which had been appended to it was that of February 22, 1916, the anniversary of Washington, who has been canonized as the patron saint of the opposition to entangling alliances.

The House-Grey Memorandum slept peacefully in the files of the Foreign Office, while President Wilson and Colonel House impatiently awaited the Allies' call to end the war — or participate in it. The call never came. Instead, in the countryside around Verdun the guns were soon to open for another summer's massacre — the bloodiest and most futile of all. The soldiers were in command once more; and the 'master-stroke,' with which House had frittered away whatever chance there was to impose peace on Europe in the winter's lull, was to fade wraith-like in the smoke of their artillery.

VIII. THE END OF THE MONROE DOCTRINE

i

OF the existence of the House-Grey Memorandum — which, while without direct result, was nevertheless to lead on indirectly to such vast consequences — the nation, of course, remained in complete ignorance. As to the submarine, however, the cartoonists were outdoing themselves with depictions of a craven or a traitorous Congress being held to its duty by an iron-jawed President (when the drawings were for Democratic papers) or an equally iron-jawed Uncle Sam (in the Republican journals). Rollin Kirby in the *World* showed the Kaiser slinking hastily out of the Capitol; Jay Darling in the Des Moines *Register* represented the President ramming a huge roll of paper labelled 'Wilson's Submarine Policy' down the throat of the peculiarly imbecile figure with which he has long delighted in personifying the Legislative Branch. The editors glowed with the sentiment of 'No surrender.' Yet with affairs brought to this stirring and decidedly dangerous juncture, it was not after all the U-boat which now suddenly drew the lightning of our new martial enthusiasm. It was the Mexicans.

In the whole history of those grotesque years, there are few passages more grotesque than that which was about to ensue. With the possibility of involvement in the most horrible war the world had ever known now quite clearly before the nation, the last risk, it would seem, which anyone would care to take would be the risk of a military entanglement in Mexico. Unfortunately, the Republicans had never forgotten that Mexico was one of the weakest spots in the Wilson policies. In October, 1915, the President had finally recognized the government of General Carranza; the bandit General Pancho Villa, the principal opposition chieftain, had agreed to retire to the United States, and it had seemed that Mexico's long turmoil was at an end. But the Villistas continued to harry the two northwestern states of Mexico with guerilla warfare, and the Republicans and Mr. Roosevelt continued to keep the issue burning against the coming election. On January 6 Senator Albert B. Fall — the patriotic Republican from the Southwest whose incarceration in a Federal penitentiary as a result of his imprudent relations with the oil industry was still many years away — secured the passage of a resolution demanding full information upon the problem. The Villistas were now threatening to kill any Americans they might find in order to bring on intervention; and four days later — as if encouraged by the Fall resolution — they did so. They held up a train at Santa Ysabel, near Chihuahua (an area from which the State Department had already warned all Americans to withdraw) and massacred eighteen of our citizens in cold blood.

Instantly the Republicans in the Senate sprang to arms. A resolution was brought in commanding the President to intervene with the military and naval forces of the United States for the protection of life and property. Senator Fall fanned the flames; so did Senator Henry Cabot Lodge and others. Senator Stone received these warlike proposals with a puzzled alarm. 'The world has gone crazy about war,' he exclaimed, and perhaps he was right. Demands for action began to echo through the press, side by side with the bellicose expressions upon the submarine.[1]

---

[1] Administration statistics showed that from the outbreak of the Mexican revolution in 1910 up to the Santa Ysabel massacre 143 American civilians had lost their lives in the country, in addition to the military losses at Vera Cruz and along the border. The death roll was thus quite comparable to that exacted by the submarine.

Thus Mexico was again taking a firm place in the headlines when, early on the morning of March 9, the residents of the little town of Columbus, New Mexico, were suddenly awakened by a wild uproar of popping rifles, clattering hoofs and bursting flames, as a torrent of armed riders swept through their streets. Pancho Villa, with an estimated force of some 1500 men, had crossed the border and descended upon the gringo. The 13th United States Cavalry, stationed at Columbus, was caught badly off its guard. Though Villa had to cross a considerable stretch of American territory he was not discovered until he was in the town. When the cavalry finally got up, their machine guns jammed in the darkness, and before the bandits were driven out, much of Columbus had been laid in ruins. Seventeen Americans were killed, nine of them civilians, and many others wounded.

That afternoon the headlines blazed throughout the nation. The Administration, declared the Washington despatches, was at last 'thoroughly aroused.' 'High authority' announced (just two days after the defeat of the Gore-McLemore resolution) that 'the United States Army will be utilized in the present crisis regardless of the attitude of the Carranza government.' At the War Department on that day, as it happened, Mr. Newton D. Baker — the liberal-pacifist lawyer at that time known only as a reform Mayor of Cleveland — was being sworn in as Secretary of War to fill the place left vacant by Mr. Garrison's resignation. As he took the oath, the editorial pencils in a hundred newspaper offices were sizzling with the heat of vengeance.

The private and political pressures behind a Mexican intervention have often been stressed. But there was more to it than that. For too many months our papers had been filled with the horror and heroism of the European slaughter, with the pictorial glamours of war and with the fascination that war irresistibly exerts. Too long a strange, haunting feeling had been growing that the United States was missing something. Pancho Villa had suddenly provided us with a chance to have a war of our own. Could we fail to take it — more especially since it wouldn't be a real war and promised to be all but bloodless? Again, as in April, 1914, President Wilson made a snap decision.

On March 10 it was officially announced from the White House that 'an adequate force will be sent at once in pursuit of Villa.' It would be a 'punitive expedition' of approximately 5000 regulars and would 'endeavour to capture Villa by a swift surprise movement.' It was not until three or four days later that the Army command on the border seemed to realize that in order to effect 'surprise movements' it would be necessary to suppress the eager reporters; but this was ultimately done, and before the strange veil of censorship the nation impatiently awaited news. The punitive force, it learned, would be commanded by Brigadier-General John J. Pershing — an officer dimly remembered as having distinguished himself in the conquest of the Moros in the Philippines a decade before. In the meanwhile the Army recruiting stations in the great cities were opened to receive the expected flood of volunteers; in Chicago a huge banner, 'Help Catch Villa,' was paraded behind a brass band to stimulate enthusiasm, and in Washington an emergency bill authorizing the recruitment of the regular establishment to full war strength was rushed through Congress. On March 15 Pershing's column moved out from Columbus. In Washington at ten o'clock the same evening Secretary Baker gave out the brief announcement that American troops had, for the second time in two years, invaded the territory of Mexico.

Was it war? Nobody precisely knew. The editors cheerfully explained that Pershing was on 'police duty, pure and simple'; or even evolved the happy theory that our troops were merely assisting the recognized Mexican government to put down an 'international outlaw' and so in reality were helping to bring a 'sane self-government' to Mexico. Unquestionably this made the adventure square better with our moral outrage over the invasion of Belgium. But would it stop there? Mr. William Randolph Hearst, who disliked the British and who also had large interests in the Southwest, was shrieking through the multitudinous voices of his newspaper chain for 'real intervention.' Did Mr. Hearst recognize the possible value of a Mexican entanglement in diverting us from the battlefields of the Entente? He was soon spreading even brighter visions before his public:

> California and Texas were part of Mexico once.... What has been done in California and Texas by the United States can be done ALL THE WAY DOWN TO THE SOUTHERN BANK OF THE PANAMA CANAL AND BEYOND. And if this country really wanted to do what would be for the best interest of civilization,... the pacifying, prosperity-giving influence of the United States would be extended south to include both sides of the great canal.

Perhaps it would be before we got through — after all, even Mr. Page and Colonel House had once dreamed of something of the sort.[1] As a matter of fact, Pershing's orders did not even direct him to capture Villa, but only to pursue and disperse his band. Unfortunately, however, the publicity (as so often happens) had far outrun the orders. Secretary Lane was advising the President that a failure to capture Villa himself would 'ruin us in the eyes of all Latin-Americans,' while the newspapers and the Administration between them had managed to implant the idea of getting Villa 'dead or alive' too deeply in the public mind for it easily to be eradicated. That, it began to seem, might carry us far — more especially as the attitude of the Carranzist forces toward this altruistic exportation of 'sane self-government' became increasingly uncertain. Two days after Pershing's departure, Spring Rice was reporting to Sir Edward that there was 'considerable anxiety' about the end of the adventure. 'A check might mean a general attack, and this, of course, would mean a serious war.'

As it was, practically the whole of our regular Army was now being concentrated in the Southwest; merely to protect the border, in other words, it had been necessary to denude the country of its first-line troops. Spring Rice himself was in a state of considerable anxiety:

[1] pp. 21–22.

The Germans have threatened aggressive movements against the Dominion [of Canada]. Opposite New York are the towns of New Jersey, Hoboken and Newark, through which all the southern railways debouch upon the Hudson. These towns are almost entirely occupied by Germans, and it is believed that the Germans have many trained men among them and are under military orders.... Scattered through the country are solid blocks of Germans who have been organized for the last thirty years.

It was alarming to contemplate. But luck, by some very narrow margins, was momentarily with the President.

All through February Bethmann-Hollweg had been fighting with his back to the wall against the ambitious propaganda of Tirpitz and the navalists, now reinforced by the conversion of Falkenhayn. The destruction of armed merchantmen had already been promised; but the Grand Admiral, wielding a propaganda machine quite as powerful as General Wood's, was going on to promise his countrymen victory in six months with a completely unrestricted U-boat war on 'English freight-space.' He had his own bloc in the Reichstag and such powerful industrialists as Hugo Stinnes on his side; and toward the end of February Mr. Gerard was convinced that the slightest thing might suffice to tip the balance. Yet the Chancellor retained both his healthy fears of the United States and his skepticism of the naval calculations. The unrestricted war, he argued, must be postponed at least until he could effect a settlement of the various outstanding controversies with the United States.

It was half an issue of grand strategy and half a personal and political intrigue. Mr. Wilson's fiery letter to Senator Stone on February 25 was no help to the Chancellor, but he was getting some support from one faction within the Navy. The crisis was reached on the 6th of March, in a conference before the Kaiser at G. H. Q. in Charleville. The strings were pulled to exclude von Tirpitz, and the upshot was a definite decision to defer unrestricted warfare. It was the day Colonel House arrived with his diplomatic master-stroke in Washington; the day before the failure of the Gore-McLemore resolution; three days before Pancho Villa was to create his diversion. Would the decision have been different had the Germans known that the United States was on the verge of plunging into guerilla warfare in Mexico? One cannot say. As it was, the Tirpitz policy was rejected; and ten days later the Grand Admiral's resignation as Minister of Marine had been accepted.

Von Tirpitz was out. It was received in the United States as a sensational triumph for Wilsonian statesmanship, as perhaps it was. The unrestricted campaign had been averted for the time and its proponents weakened; unhappily, the sea war question had not been regularized. An arrangement under which the Chancellor would address himself to settling past controversies while the U-boat captains were authorized to create new ones by attacking armed liners was in reality 'quite useless,' as Falkenhayn has dryly observed, 'because the inevitable mistakes of the submarine commanders in deciding whether a particular ship was armed or not would lead to complications.' Von Tirpitz had barely left the Ministry of Marine before the first 'complication' duly arose.

On March 24 — with Pershing now deep in northern Mexico but getting no results and with even the New York *Times* demanding that more troops be sent after him — the French cross-Channel steamer Sussex, unarmed and carrying over 300 passengers, was torpedoed without warning. She managed to reach port, but about eighty persons, including a number of American citizens, were killed in the explosion. Once more crisis had arrived; and we faced the startling possibility of simultaneous war on two fronts — for the eradication of banditry from Mexico and of the submarine from the English Channel. For diplomatically, the whole submarine problem was back again precisely where it had been on the morning after the Lusitania.

ii

So was Colonel House. In the press, as a matter of fact, the Sussex was less than a first-rank sensation. There had been too many submarine sensations, all the adjectives had been used too often and Mexico was for the moment more engrossing. But on March 27, before any of the details were clear, the Colonel's mind was made up:

> It looks as if we should have to act this time without further parley. I am hardly well enough to make the trip to Washington, but I feel I ought to be there to advise the President during these critical hours. I am afraid he will delay and write further notes when action is what we need.

One cannot help noticing a new tone of patronage in the adviser's attitude toward his chief. Conquering his illness, he was in Washington next day, breathing fire and vengeance. He found Lansing no less bellicose; a brief interview with the President, however, served only to confirm the Colonel's fears. 'I am inclined to believe that he intends making excuses for not acting promptly in this new submarine crisis.' Was it possible?

In a long conference with Mr. Wilson on the 30th the Colonel demanded blood — or at any rate a severance of diplomatic relations, which under the circumstances would amount to the same thing. Yet Mr. Wilson manifested a distressing reluctance for such a course. The President reminded House of the latter's own argument that a break on the submarine issue would ruin the great scheme of intervention to establish permanent peace. Should he break relations now, 'the war would go on indefinitely,' we would be involved in it and there would be no one to lead the peoples out. This was something of a poser; quickly, however, the Colonel recovered:

> I told him.... I had thought of another way by which we could lead them out even though we were in. I suggested that, when he sent von Bernstorff home, he should make a dispassionate statement

of the cause of the war and what the Allies were fighting for. I suggested that he should say nothing unkind of the German people, but should strike at the system which had caused this world tragedy. ... Then I thought at the right time — which would perhaps be by midsummer — I could go to Holland and, after a conference with the Allies and with their consent, I could open negotiations directly with Berlin, telling them upon what terms we were ready to end the war.

According to the House diary, Mr. Wilson seemed 'pleased' with this remarkable inspiration. Yet it was the Colonel himself who, going over his papers nine years later, appended the marginal comment: 'My suggestion now seems like nonsense, and not even good nonsense.' One may let it go at that.

At the moment, the President had apparently accepted the idea. But he failed to break off relations. Back in New York once more, Colonel House was displeased by his chief's strange 'penchant for inaction.' The Colonel fired fresh broadsides by mail: 'Our becoming a belligerent would not be without its advantages, inasmuch as it would strengthen your position at home and with the Allies.' Nothing happened. Perhaps Count Bernstorff had a more accurate finger upon the pulse of opinion than the agitated Colonel when, on April 4, he reported:

Except for the surprises that are usual over here things are at present quite calm. This is due, in the first place, to the desire for peace shown by the population, ... and secondly to the development of the Mexican question.... It seems to be increasingly probable that the punitive expedition against Villa will lead to a full-dress intervention.... So long as the Mexican question holds the stage here we are, I believe, safe from an act of aggression on the part of the American Government.

Possibly Colonel House had forgotten about Mexico. Nevertheless, it was true that the President was now at an *impasse* with his submarine policy. Something had to be done. The impatient adviser hurried back again to Washington to find that a Note severing diplomatic relations with Germany had already been drawn up. Yet the President still hesitated; and on April 6 the two went into another long conference. Before committing themselves irrevocably on the submarine issue, should they not give the Allies a last chance to avail themselves of the House-Grey Memorandum? In the end the President sat down at his portable typewriter and drafted the following communication for Sir Edward Grey:

> Since it seems probable that this country must break with Germany on the submarine question unless the unexpected happens, and since, if this country should once become a belligerent, the war would undoubtedly be prolonged, I beg to suggest that if you had any thought of acting at an early date on the plan we agreed upon, you might wish now to consult with your allies with a view to acting immediately.

This must stand today as the strangest of all the jewels of confusion which the House-Wilson diplomacy produced. Here, also, it was to occur to Colonel House nine years afterward that the move might have been a 'mistake.' By 1925 he realized that the best method of forcing the Allies to give us their guaranties and allow us a free hand in making peace was not, perhaps, to assure them that they were about to have us in the war anyway on their own terms. The thought did not occur at the moment, however; and with an almost child-like confidence in the high purposes of Sir Edward Grey and the sincerity of the Entente war propagandas, the cable was solemnly typed out.

It was on April 6, 1916, that Colonel House thus went to war. One year later to the day both House and the American people would be going to war in earnest; the sands were running faster now, the end was nearer and less evitable. But for a last time President Wilson was to preserve us from the impatience of his adviser.

On April 8 House was back again in New York; and the first thing he found was a letter from Sir Edward (written on the day of the Sussex disaster) acknowledging the final draft of the House-Grey Memorandum. Sir Edward was polite, encouraging, and as evasive as possible. Putting the scheme into operation must depend upon the decision of France, and Grey felt that they simply could not ask the French 'to consider a conference' while their territories were held by the invader and the fate of Verdun was in doubt. This communication was forwarded immediately to the President. It is possible that it suggested to him the absurdity of the cable which he and his adviser had just despatched; it may have opened his eyes for the first time to the serious defects in the Colonel's diplomatic technique. Returning to Washington on April 11, House discovered that Mr. Wilson had thrown away the original Sussex Note and drafted another. It was strongly worded — but it failed to break off relations. Indeed, one cannot help feeling today that the cable to Sir Edward on April 6 marked a climax in the first period of the House-Wilson collaboration. One can detect only the slightest of changes in the personal relationship of the two men; but from that moment onward President Wilson can be seen more and more definitely freeing his own policy from the influence of his adviser.[1]

Colonel House did his best over the new draft; he induced the President to sharpen up the phraseology in some respects, but after two hours of discussion, the most Mr. Wilson agreed to was to submit the draft, as a tentative version, to the Cabinet. Mr. Wilson had many reasons to hesitate. There was Mexico. There was the fact that the country had taken the Sussex with relative calm. There was the uncertain temper of Congress. And there were the British. If Sir Edward was evasive about peace, the Admiralty and the Foreign Office were growing steadily more callous, and more exasperating, about the blockade. Our long, categorical protest of October 21, 1915, was still unanswered after

[1] After our entry into the war the Colonel's approach again became useful to the President, for obvious reasons, and the collaboration was resumed. It is perhaps for this reason that the evidences of an earlier break have not received more attention. Viereck notices them, but connects them with Mr. Wilson's remarriage — a dramatic but hardly necessary interpretation.

the lapse of over five months. At the end of March there had come fresh indignities and new devices for the control of our commerce; and on April 8 — just three days before — Mr. Lansing had been sending off a sizzling communication to Mr. Page:

> The action of the British Government in thus treating with indifference the contentions of the United States by... making still more rigorous the practices... to which the United States is objecting cannot be regarded here as otherwise than an act which appears to be intentionally discourteous.

Mr. Lansing denounced the new restrictions as 'entirely opposed to the fundamental principles of international justice for which Great Britain and the United States have stood in the past,' and demanded an immediate reply to the Note of October 21. Were our harassed statesmen, one begins to wonder, preparing for war on *three* fronts?

It must have added to the new caution with which the President was now receiving Colonel House's advice. But at this critical juncture, the Germans were unwise. On the 13th there arrived their own explanation of the Sussex incident. It was true, von Jagow granted, that a submarine had torpedoed without warning a vessel very much like the Sussex, on the same day and near the spot where the Sussex had come to grief, but this could not have been the Sussex herself since the U-boat captain had 'gained the definite impression that he had before him a war vessel, a minelayer of the newly-constructed English Arabic class.' The evidence, unhappily, from which the captain had gained this convenient impression seemed strangely nebulous. This preposterous explanation was, as Bernstorff has put it, 'probably the most unfortunate document that ever passed from Berlin to Washington. Mr. Wilson thought he detected a direct untruth'; and before that 'mixture of uneasy conscience and clumsiness' the President's always rather tenuous patience snapped. He did not declare war. He did not break relations. But he took the Colonel's advice to the extent, at least, of couching the Note in the terms of a flat and unequivocal threat:

Unless the Imperial Government should now immediately declare and effect an abandonment of its present methods of submarine warfare against passenger and freight-carrying vessels, the Government of the United States can have no choice but to sever diplomatic relations with the German Empire altogether.

The Note was sent on April 18. Before the applause had died from the embattled editorial pages, Ambassador Bernstorff was receiving secret instructions to prepare for the disabling of the interned German liners, as the first step when war should come.

iii

The British naturally seized this opportune moment for sending in the reply which we were demanding to the October protest. The 'Memorandum' which appeared on April 24 was a massive document. Taking up our arguments point by point with patient reasonableness, it now occupies no less than twelve pages of fine print in the war supplement to 'Foreign Relations.' But what it actually said would seem to be sufficiently summarized in the paraphrase of the British Admiral Consett:

[The British Government] are disposed to show a friendly disposition toward America: they do not contradict, nor are they rude: they simply tell America that they understand her complaint to be something quite different from what America herself understands it to be and what, to the best of her ability, she states it to be; and that they are going to argue on this understanding.

That was, for all practical purposes, the end of the October protest. In the autumn of 1914, when the country was really suffering, we might conceivably have made good our appeals to international law. Now, about all that we could argue was that Great Britain was using her blockade measures to prevent our making money as rapidly out of the war as we might otherwise have done. It was not a strong argument. Everybody knew, no matter what the business forecasters and the 'fundamentally sound'

men might say, that our rushing prosperity was not only a war
prosperity but an Entente war prosperity. A mere rumor of peace
negotiations was enough to shake a four or five point drop out of the
stock market; and even in Chicago, which had remained far more
cool toward the Allied cause than the Eastern commercial centers,
the business men were said to be unanimous in believing that a
German victory would be a disaster. Nor can it be forgotten that
our great war industries machine was running more and more on
credit, and the Allied bonds which J. P. Morgan & Company had
peddled for the good of American industry were now beginning
to operate as a powerful propaganda for Allied victory.

The more conscious forms of propaganda were not, of course,
neglected. With the collapse of the German propaganda effort,
that of the British became only more conscious, better organized
and more far-reaching. A friend back from the United States
was complaining to Colonel Repington about the lack of co-ordi-
nation between the three chief agencies — the Press Bureau, the
industrious Sir Gilbert Parker and the 'Pilgrim section' under Mr.
Harry Brittain. The Pilgrim Society was a most useful device.
It was Mr. Brittain who 'took charge of the Hon. James Beck'
when that great legal mind arrived in England in the summer of
1916, and 'gave him so good a chance to do great work for the
cause of unity between the two nations.' The author of 'The
Evidence in the Case' was throughout of the utmost value. So, of
course, was the outgoing tide of British lecturers — ranging all
the way from Mr. Arthur Guy Empey to Mr. John Masefield —
now rising toward its height.

The steady approach of the Presidential election did nothing to
lessen the mental confusions of the time. Mr. Wilson would of
course lead the Democratic hosts on an appeal to his record —
which he had now managed to broaden so as to invite almost every
shade of sentiment, from the social reformers of 1912 through the
preparedness fanatics to the anti-German war hawks. To the
Republicans it presented an ever more difficult problem, and they
were still without a candidate. The Colonel of the Rough Riders

seemed clearly to be maneuvering his Progressive party to its extinction and himself into position to receive the Republican nomination. On the last day of March there was a luncheon gathering that caused something of a stir. 'T. R.' and General Wood sat down with Elihu Root and Henry Cabot Lodge; apparently the prodigal was being received at last into the fold of 'old guard' regularity. 'First meeting in years,' General Wood jotted into his diary. 'All passed off well.... Roosevelt cussed out Wilson as did Root and Lodge. Opinion that the country never so low in standing before. Much talk about Mexico, what they would have done had they been in power.'

That was the position exactly. Yet the great glamour of the Rough Rider had been too far dissolved in the acids of age and bitterness. The country feared his bellicosity and no longer trusted his judgment. Besides, there were those inconvenient but essential pro-German votes. Mr. Charles Evans Hughes, Associate Justice of the Supreme Court, a less colorful politician and less deeply committed to anything, seemed a more likely chance. Or possibly the ambitious General himself? General Wood was identified only with preparedness, which was politically strong everywhere; he had all the martial romance of his friend, Mr. Roosevelt, and practically none of the disadvantages. 'The shadow of the White House,' as Mr. Roosevelt observed, 'rests heavily upon him'; and as the General's star arose, an American Boulanger episode seemed actually within the realms of the possible. In May the Wood boom was openly launched under the rather odd aegis of Mr. Gutzon Borglum, the sculptor.

Congress, in the meanwhile, was grinding on to the end of the Army bills and beginning upon the Navy. As the defence legislation progressed the preparedness mania only mounted. The new Secretary of War, Mr. Baker, was supposed to be a pacifist, but in April he was suggesting to the President that this militant enthusiasm 'ought not to be allowed to cool and pass away as a fruitless agitation, but rather should be captured and capitalized into a policy tending to strengthen and consolidate our national life.'

Thus did Mr. Baker accept what had always been the basic philosophy of Prussian militarism.

Such were the atmospheres of the moment — politics, propaganda and preparedness, Mexico, the submarine, the new war wealth rolling out into every corner of our economy; and behind everything the thought of that long, grey curtain stretching from the Channel to the Alps, where all thought stopped, where the world, it seemed, came to an end. Such were the backgrounds against which President Wilson had now brought his countrymen to a crisis of a gravity which few of them — which not even the President himself, perhaps — could really have understood. With the arrival of the Sussex Note Mr. Gerard had felt that the 'situation was almost hopeless.' Von Jagow thought the same; he said that it was 'fate' and that there was nothing more to be done. Mr. Whitlock in Brussels began to pack his trunks. Throughout Germany there was intense bitterness against the United States. Progressively our demands had become more exacting. We had forced an agreement not to torpedo large passenger liners (Lusitania); we had forced its extension to the Austrian flag (Ancona); we had rejected the armed ship theory and extended our protection to vessels ready and able to destroy intercepting submarines on sight; now we made the flat demand that the rules of visit and search must be applied to all vessels, armed and unarmed, liners and freighters alike. To yield would largely end the effectiveness of submarine activity. Was technical American neutrality worth it?

The Army General Staff under Falkenhayn no longer thought so; the soldiers calculated that an American declaration of war would be of small military importance and might even help to dislocate the Entente munition supply. From his retirement von Tirpitz bombarded the Kaiser with appeals for a clean break. But the Chancellor and the Foreign Office still believed that an American entry would be disastrous. It might bring in all the remaining European neutrals and it would of course end all hope of achieving anything through an American mediation. What, after all, could the Navy really offer? In April, 1916, the active flotilla amounted to only forty-three U-boats, with but nine more under construction, and the force still looked very inadequate. Bethmann-Hollweg set himself to find out how much he could get from the United States, in the way of possible diplomatic action against the Entente, with which to outbid the sailors.

On April 25 Count Bernstorff called upon Colonel House with a cable from his government. If Germany, it said in substance, acceded to the American demand, would the United States put pressure on Great Britain in regard to the blockade? According to Colonel House, his reply — perhaps slightly disingenuous — was that he thought 'acquiescence... would bring peace nearer.' What Bernstorff reported [1] was that House had assured him, speaking for Wilson, that if the American demand were accepted the President would 'take in hand measures directly against England' — not toward raising the blockade, however, as the President now believed this to be impossible without war or an arms embargo. Either would have had too disastrous an effect on American domestic economy. The 'measures' would therefore be directed toward forcing a peace.

Count Bernstorff, a convinced opponent of the submarine, may have been embroidering the conversation a little; on the other hand, the Colonel seems to have been benefiting by reflection. Colonel House's statesmanship was too variable a quantity to follow with ease; but in the next day or two he was actually finding the President too belligerent toward Germany, too stiff-necked in his refusal to negotiate our demand, and was trying to cool an ardor which only a short time before he had been doing his best to enflame. The truth was, perhaps, that even Colonel House was at last beginning to realize upon what sands the great House-Grey Memorandum had been founded, and on April 30 one finds a curious note in his diary:

[1] According to a message printed by Hendrick, in his life of Page, as 'an unpublished despatch which is found in Page's papers' — presumably having been supplied to the Ambassador by the British secret service, which freely intercepted the German despatches.

What the Allies want is to dip their hands into our treasure chest. While the war has become a war of democracy against autocracy, not one of the democracies entered it to fight for democracy, but merely because of the necessity of self-preservation. If we go in, it will be because we believe in democracy.

Colonel House was all at once very friendly with Count Bernstorff.

But whatever assurances he actually gave to the Ambassador, all this at least provided the Chancellor with something to hold up against the problematical results of the U-boat. It was the old battle for the Kaiser's verdict, and in the course of it the civilians played one interesting move. They arranged to bring Ambassador Gerard to the G.H.Q. at Charleville for a personal audience — the first in many months. Mr. Gerard made a visit of two or three days. The Chancellor always came back to the idea of making 'any settlement of the submarine question contingent on our doing something against England,' but Mr. Gerard was discreet. At last the Kaiser received him, before lunch, in a garden on the hillside below the Chateau of Charleville. His Majesty was in full uniform.

As I drew near the Emperor he said immediately, 'Do you come like the great pro-Consul bearing peace or war in either hand?'...

I said, 'No, Your Majesty, only hoping that differences between two friendly nations may be adjusted.'

They went all over the old ground — the munitions, the American hostility, all the rest of it. The Kaiser was particularly aggrieved because the American notes accused Germany of 'barbarism.' Nothing definite resulted, of course, but perhaps it eased the tension. Just before Gerard returned to Berlin the Chancellor said to him: 'I hope now that if we settle this matter your President will be great enough to take up the question of peace.' Apparently the Ambassador said nothing to this, but did not try to disabuse them of the idea.

Mr. Gerard's audience took place on May 1. On May 3 he

heard that an answer to the United States had been prepared.
That day House had been lunching with the President, discussing
not war but Democratic electoral strategy. Mr. Wilson was in a
curious mood. He would stand for re-election only as a matter of
duty; he did not desire to be President any longer and he believed
that a second term might prove an 'anti-climax.' For a statesman
awaiting the word which might plunge his country into history's
greatest conflict it seems a singularly detached attitude. Perhaps
even yet the idea of war had not become an imaginative reality to
President Wilson, any more than to the embattled editors. As for
the political campaign, he would stand upon a policy of neutrality,
backed up by a willingness to enter a world peace league when the
war should end. That would fix the Republicans.

Would it fix the Germans? Next day, May 4, the long cipher
telegram began to come into Count Bernstorff's Embassy. As the
first paragraphs were decoded the staff read them solemnly.
'Then it is war,' they told each other. The text continued in a
harsh rebuttal of the American contentions, and not until the
final paragraphs arrived some time later did they see that Berlin
had ended in an all but complete surrender. 'In accordance with
the general principles of visit and search and destruction of merchant vessels recognized by international law, such vessels... shall
not be sunk without warning and without saving human lives,
unless these ships attempt to escape or offer resistance.' It yielded
everything which the United States had asked. But then the Note
went on:

Neutrals cannot expect that Germany... shall for the sake of
neutral interest restrict the use of an effective weapon if her enemy
is permitted to continue to apply at will methods of warfare violating the rules of international law.... The German Government is
confident that... [the United States] will now demand and insist
that the British Government shall forthwith observe the rules...
as they are laid down in the Notes presented by the Government of
the United States to the British Government on December 28, 1914,
and November 5 [October 21], 1915.

If such insistence proved without effect, Germany would recover her liberty of action. This, one is bound to grant, was fair enough. We could not reasonably force our interpretation of international law upon one side while allowing our interpretation to be flaunted by the other. Nor could the great argument that the blockade affected only property while the submarine involved human life be very well used with the Germans, since the blockade and the munitions trade very directly affected German life, both on the battle fronts and at home. The German condition was reasonable. What made it particularly irritating was the fact that it was now politically and economically impossible for the United States to meet it.

'The situation here,' Secretary Lane wrote on May 8, 'is tense. Of course, nobody knows what will be done. I favor telling Germany that we will make no trade with her.... I am getting tired of having the Kaiser and Carranza vent their impudence at our expense.' But Colonel House, under Bernstorff's able management, had now swung full circle and was in eager cry after the new idea of a peace mediation with German acquiescence. After all, he argued with the President, the Germans had instituted 'cruiser warfare'; even his friends in the British Embassy reluctantly agreed that until this concession was actually withdrawn the United States could not well break off relations. Bernstorff worked hard both on House and on Berlin. In the upshot a final American Note was despatched on the 8th of May. We noted and accepted the agreement to abide by the rules of cruiser warfare; we explicitly rejected the idea that this could be in any way contingent upon the action of the British.

There the matter rested. The Germans made no formal reply, and a new calm settled after crisis over both Washington and Berlin. The submarine had been completely curbed; the laurels of smashing diplomatic victory lay upon Mr. Wilson's brow, while he had at the same time kept us out of war. But once more nothing had really been settled; and in winning his victory, Mr. Wilson had at the same time built an iron trap for himself and his countrymen. The issue had been defined so sharply that no further flexibility was possible. There was no further room for such useful compromises as the protection only of large liners or only of unarmed ships. The victory was good only so long as the Germans were content to wait upon American action against the Entente; and the moment they decided that the U-boat was worth more to them than American neutrality, Mr. Wilson would be helpless. Almost anything, at any time — a military failure, a new stringency in raw materials, the delivery of more submarines — might suffice to reverse the delicate balance of their calculations; and whenever that happened, the United States would be almost automatically at war. From that danger there remained but one avenue of escape — the end of the war itself. President Wilson now had to bring peace to Europe, or war to the people of the United States.

On May 9 there was ominous news from Mexico. The Carranzist forces were threatening to attack the Pershing column; and that day the National Guard of Arizona, New Mexico and Texas was called out to reinforce the border. The day after, Colonel House despatched a long cable to Sir Edward Grey:

> There is an increasingly insistent demand here that the President take some action toward bringing the war to a close. The impression grows that the Allies are more determined upon the punishment of Germany than upon exacting terms that neutral opinion would consider just.... If the President is to serve humanity in a large way, steps should be taken now....

But that transparent appeal could scarcely have alarmed Sir Edward — who could follow the submarine controversy quite as well as Colonel House. The answering cable was back in two days. To act under the House-Grey Memorandum now, Sir Edward felt, would be 'premature'; while if the President should summon a peace conference of his own 'without any indication of a basis on which peace might be made,' he would merely be helping Germany to win the war. For the Colonel, who really seems to have believed that Grey was more interested in ending 'militarism and navalism' than in beating Germany, it was a bitter disillusionment. On May 13 he noted:

> I am disappointed that he does not rise to the occasion. For two years he has been telling me that the solution of the problem of international well-being depended upon the United States being willing to take her part in world affairs.... A situation may arise, if the Allies defeat Germany, where they may attempt to be dictatorial in Europe and elsewhere. I can see quite clearly where they might change their views on militarism and navalism.

Indeed, it was very likely; and one can only regret that the Colonel's clairvoyance had not descended upon him two years before — in that far-off winter of 1913–14 when he had first started out to regenerate the European under the kindly tutelage of Sir William Tyrrell.

iv

At the very moment that Colonel House, in the seclusion of his apartment in East Fifty-Third Street, was thus confronting the strange fallibilities of men and governments, the avenues beyond his windows were echoing to a sensational demonstration of militant patriotism. His diary entry was on May 13. All that day New York City's monster 'preparedness parade' — the first of a great series of such manifestations throughout the country — had been flowing on through cheering throngs. The bursts of applause and band-music must have penetrated even to his quiet study; did they convey just a hint, perhaps, that even the American people 'might change their views on militarism and navalism'?

Preparedness, to be sure, had not yet completely triumphed. In Congress there remained a little group of determined opponents, who retained an obstinate skepticism both as to the military necessity of preparation and the disinterestedness of some of the preparedness fanatics. Jane Addams and Lillian Wald refused to

THE END OF THE MONROE DOCTRINE 303

surrender, and on April 6 — the day that Colonel House was going to war against Germany — they had filled Carnegie Hall in New York with an anti-preparedness mass meeting. The reprehensible Professor Scott Nearing was arguing in the Socialist 'Rip-Saw' pamphlets that preparedness was simply a device of American munition makers to provide themselves with a cushion of domestic orders against the time when peace should calamitously abolish the European demand. Of course, nobody who mattered read Socialist pamphlets; but it was less easy to avoid the full-page advertisements which appeared in the metropolitan papers during April under the signature of Mr. Henry Ford. The automobile manufacturer had long since escaped from the disastrous Odyssey of the Oscar II; but he had now recovered sufficiently to lend his name and wealth to a slashing attack upon the 'defence' enthusiasts:

HUMANITY — AND SANITY

By Henry Ford

For months the people of the United States have had fear pounded into their brains by magazines, newspapers and motion pictures. No enemy has been pointed out. All the wild cry for the spending of billions, the piling up of armament and the saddling of the country with a military caste has been based on nothing but *fiction*....

It was largely true; but when Mr. Ford's ghost-writer went on to hint that 'The Battle Cry of Peace' was an advertisement to sell stock in Mr. Hudson Maxim's new munitions corporation, the producers of the film promptly clapped a libel suit on him. 'Why War?' asked a new book by Frederic C. Howe — the old reformer who in 1913 had seen so bright a sun arising with the inauguration of Mr. Wilson — and went on to argue that the real war danger was never from without but from within. That was true, too; but where Mr. Howe and the radical Progressives were mistaken was in supposing the internal danger came only from the machinations of 'powerful financial interests.' 'Consult the People!' cried Senator La Follette through his *Magazine*:

The day is coming when the people... are going to have the final
say over their own destinies.... They themselves shall decide what
questions of 'defence,' of 'aggression' or of 'national honor' may be
involved, compelling enough to make them desire to kill and be
killed.

Yet of what use was that, when the Senator himself was so obviously only crying in a wilderness of popular enthusiasm and
frenzy? Through these radical pacifists there was speaking with
its last breath (had they only known it) the voice of an older
democratic ideal, already perishing in the forge fires of a new and
harsher world. And when May brought the New York demonstration, it must have been very hard for even a Progressive to
retain his faith in the pacific foresight and self-restraint of the
people.

But one word can adequately describe the preparedness parade
of May 13, 1916 — it was stupendous. From the preliminary
announcements one might have felt, perhaps, that the idea was
just tinged with something other than pure patriotism. To prove
its non-partisan inspiration, Mr. Roosevelt was not invited, and
neither was the President. Mrs. Roosevelt, however, was to
march in the Independent Patriotic Women's Division, under the
command of her daughter-in-law, Mrs. Theodore Roosevelt, Jr.;
in the great reviewing stand at Fifth Avenue and Twenty-Fifth
Street, the chief place (next to Mayor Mitchel) was to be occupied
by Major General Leonard Wood himself — an arrangement which
could scarcely injure the General's own Presidential ambitions.
And although an American flag was to be placed in every one of
the 9000 grandstand seats to 'insure patriotic demonstrations,'
there was somehow a curious absence of any participation by the
Democratic Administration in Washington, which happened at
the moment to be the government of the country. It is true that
General Wood was counterbalanced by Admiral Usher, appearing
as a representative of the Navy. But no one seems to have paid
much attention to Admiral Usher.

All such carping thoughts, however, must have vanished when

AN AMERICAN AT BAY

From the motion picture *The Battle Cry of Peace*

WOMEN MARCHERS IN THE PREPAREDNESS PARADE IN NEW YORK
CITY, MAY 13, 1916, WHICH CONTINUED UNTIL LONG
AFTER NIGHTFALL

the great day itself arrived. Two hundred brass bands and fifty drum corps had been mobilized to play forward 'the greatest civilian marching demonstration in the history of the world,' as the New York *Times* ecstatically announced it.⌉ Sixty-three marching divisions, men and women together, poured into lower New York for the start at the City Hall. The American flags flying from every window along the way were beyond enumeration, but one reporter made it half a million and let it go at that. On the William K. Vanderbilt residence at 666 Fifth Avenue there appeared the one word 'PREPAREDNESS' in letters a foot and a half high, arranged for night illumination. Every church on Fifth Avenue displayed the national colors; but the great Union League Club at Thirty-Ninth Street — citadel of strictly Republican patriotism — outdid them all with an electric sign:

ABSOLUTE AND UNQUALIFIED LOYALTY
TO OUR COUNTRY.

At nine-thirty-five in the morning the head of the parade swung out from City Hall Park. Up Broadway the column marched, past General Wood, standing gloriously at salute, up Fifth Avenue, past the entrance to East Fifty-Third Street, where Colonel House sat alone with Sir Edward's procrastinations, and still on again, not to disband until it reached the plaza at Fifty-Ninth Street. As fast as one division cleared another took its place. All morning, all afternoon and onward into the darkness the marchers passed — '125,683 serious, earnest Americans,' according to the New York *Times* count. For twelve solid hours they flowed on without a break; for twelve hours the vast throngs stood and cheered upon the sidewalks. After night fell the whole scene was lit up with searchlights, until finally, at nine-forty in the evening, 'the last line went by the reviewing stand and a three-inch field gun trailing behind was wheeled and fired.'

It was, as a later, less reverent age might put it, a wow. The biggest division of all was that 'including the financial associations, the bankers and brokers of Wall Street, the Stock, Produce,

Cotton and Consolidated Exchanges.' Wall Street put 14,700 men in line. The lighting trades came next with 9000 and the insurance men were a good third with 8500. There were a hundred actors and writers from Broadway, led by John Drew, Irvin Cobb, Frank Tinney and the celebrated Eddie Foy. The greatest applause, however, went to the battalion of 130 clergymen, in clerical garb and American flags, under the command of the Rev. Herbert Shipman for the Episcopalians, the Very Rev. Mgr. James R. Connolly, for the Catholics, and the Rev. Charles A. Eaton, leading fire-eater, for the Baptists. As they passed the stand a voice arose above the din: 'Hurrah for the Church Militant!'

Everybody was there. Mr. Thomas A. Edison, who had incautiously flirted a year before with the pacifism of his friend, Mr. Ford, tramped along in his old brown hat; Mr. Hudson Maxim was in a prominent position; Mr. Elihu Root was in the Union League Club's private reviewing stand. The ladies were magnificent; thousands marched, while the New York State Committee of the Women's Section of the Movement for National Preparedness sold a handsome preparedness medal in the crowds. But General Wood was superb. He remained for eleven hours in the reviewing stand, sitting down only in the rare intervals when a gap appeared in the column, and religiously standing to attention and saluting every national ensign that was carried past. It was a genuine feat of pluck and physical endurance.

Most of the marchers, the *Times* noted, were youngish men, from twenty to thirty-five years old, who 'showed in face and figure that they were intelligent, sturdy Americans of the kind who might do much more than march.' How many realized how soon they were to have the opportunity? Mr. Joseph H. Choate was a trifle more direct: 'They would make good soldiers,' he said. Mayor Mitchel, forgetting the strict non-partisanship of the demonstration, came near to striking a false note: 'You can say,' he told a *Herald* reporter, 'that this splendid showing ought to be almost enough to wake up the dead, even those at the national capital.' But then, Mr. Mitchel was himself an independent Democrat, so perhaps it was all right. The only really discordant moment of the day came when the Women's Peace Party tried to distribute pacifist circulars and even break into the line of march. A few arrests sufficed for them.

The effect upon the country was impressive. There were some skeptics, rather notably among the local trades union leaders, who were suspicious of standing armies, who had not taken part in the parade and one of whom was bold enough to denounce it as 'a hypocritical and diabolical invention.' 'Are we to enter the armament gamble,' asked the influential Rabbi Wise, 'in which every nation loses and hell alone is victorious?' But the Rev. William T. Manning, a rising Episcopal clergyman, could answer with severity that 'our moral sense as a nation is dulled,' due 'in part to a vast amount of well-meant but mistaken and misleading and really unchristian teaching about peace.' With unanimity the nation now turned to demonstrate its Christian virtue and imitate New York's example. The final field-gun had scarcely been fired before Chicago was planning a preparedness parade of its own; Baltimore was marching before the week was out; Lincoln, Nebraska, citadel of Mr. William Jennings Bryan, was soon announcing its plans; while the long and shocking martyrdom of Tom Mooney was to stand as a bitter memento through the years to San Francisco's patriotism.

In cities everywhere up and down the land the throngs were presently tramping the pavements to the glorious chant 'Prepare! Prepare! Prepare!' The enthusiasm was awe-inspiring. Yet one cannot help noticing a small but curious detail. To meet the Mexican crisis Congress in the middle of March had authorized the recruitment of the regular Army to full war strength, an increase of not much more than 20,000 men. By the middle of May, with the citizenry marching in their hundreds of thousands, the Army — despite the best efforts of a hired publicity expert, the blandishments of posters and advertisements and the 'most persuasive capitalizations of the adventures of Pershing's chase of

Villa' — was still about 20,000 men short. Perhaps the wages of prosperity were too high, or perhaps — was it possible? — the people who marched in preparedness parades were not those who ordinarily felt called upon to enlist for fighting.

No one noticed this detail at the time, however, and the chant 'Prepare! Prepare! Prepare!' continued to resound. But for what? Still no one knew; it didn't matter anyway and besides, that was presumably something for the Government to worry about. Silent behind the furore Mr. Wilson, at least, had reason to worry. Spring was slipping toward summer; at Verdun the bloodiest and most frightful battle ever sustained by armies roared on and on, without cease and without decision. Even the guileless Tumulty became alarmed, and on May 16 sent in a memorandum to his chief: 'It seems to me the time is now at hand for you to act in the matter of *Peace*.' The proper procedure, the secretary felt, would be for the United States simply to announce that it was meeting both sides at The Hague to mediate a settlement. One may regret that this idea had not been more cordially received when Jane Addams had been agitating it a year and a half before, or when Henry Ford had brought it to the White House in November. Now the President knew better than Tumulty that the United States had to have peace. The same day he wrote to House in New York that it was time to get down 'to hard-pan' with his friend Sir Edward.

Thus stirred to action, House drafted another cable to the Foreign Minister; the President approved it and it went on May 19. It was a repetition of the May 10 cable [1] but with an added sharpness — and a threat.

> America has reached the cross-roads, if we cannot soon inaugurate some sort of peace discussion there will come a demand from our people... that we assert our undeniable rights against the Allies with the same insistence we have used toward the Central Powers.

Here at last, for the first time in the long course of the House negotiations, was the threat of direct pressure upon the Entente

[1] Page 301.

— the sort of pressure without which the negotiations had never from the beginning had the slightest chance of success. As if to lend point to it, an exceptionally stiff note was handed to the British and French Ambassadors, protesting Entente interference with American mails — the latest exasperation of the blockade. At this, Sir Edward declared himself 'much disturbed'; Spring Rice was greatly 'exercised' and thought 'the same object might be accomplished by a softer tone.' But Colonel House, upon whom that approach had worked so well and so often before, was now disinclined to agree with him.

Yet Downing Street had slight reason for alarm. It was too obvious by this time that we were wielding only a stuffed club. Sir Edward continued his campaign of skillfully polite evasion. The more talk there was of peace, the more certain were the Allies that Germany felt herself the loser; the more ground she lost the sooner she would again resort to the submarine and so bring in the United States, and the more impatiently Colonel House appealed, the more plainly did he reveal Washington's fears that this result was imminent.

Nor was this all. The policy of the House-Grey Memorandum had been founded upon the assumption that the American people would support the future guaranty of world peace. In the general temper of that time it was not an unreasonable assumption; yet the President had omitted to verify it or even to hint to his country-men of the extent to which he was committing them. A meeting of the League to Enforce Peace, to be held at Philadelphia on May 27, now offered him the opportunity not only to announce the general policy of peace on the basis of future guaranties, but also to insist that the Entente accept his mediation to that end. The President and his adviser had already drafted the address — apparently as a forthright demand for immediate peace in Europe. But now, with the obduracy of the French, the persistent reluctance of Grey, how far dared they go? If the Entente should answer such a move simply by denouncing it as a German trick, the effect would be negligible abroad and at home politically disastrous. The President and his adviser faced the penalty of having failed to build any really sure opinion behind them.

On May 24 they were again in conference. They agreed that it would be wise 'to modify greatly' the projected speech; Mr. Wilson was 'not to do more than hint at peace.' On that same day in the House of Commons, Sir Edward, no doubt warned by House's innocent appeals, deftly neutralized whatever might be coming. He made a short but stirring proclamation of a finish fight. Mr. Page was in transports:

> No utterance by anybody has so stirred the people of this Kingdom for many months as Sir Edward Grey's impromptu speech... about Peace, when he called the German Chancellor a first-class liar.... The more sensational press intimates that any Englishman who uses the word 'peace' ought to be shot.

Any hope of forcing a peace conference at that time was dead. When, three days later, Mr. Wilson stepped upon the platform at Philadelphia he did not call for peace. Instead, he merely stated the attitude which, 'if it should ever be our privilege to suggest or initiate a movement for peace,' he believed the United States should adopt. The President founded it upon two proposals. First, the actual settlement of the existing war should be left wholly to the belligerents. 'Our interest is only in peace and its future guarantees.' But to assist the belligerents in reaching a settlement, the United States should be 'willing to become a partner in any feasible association of nations' thereafter; and therefore he made his second proposal:

> A universal association of the nations to maintain the inviolate security of the highway of the seas for the common and unhindered use of all the nations of the world and to prevent any war, begun either contrary to treaty covenants or without warning and full submission of the causes to the opinion of the world — a virtual guarantee of territorial integrity and political independence.

Thus was the League of Nations brought from the cradle of the House-Grey negotiations and formally given to the world as an official policy of the United States. It was by no means the birth of the idea; Mr. Wilson was even a tardy foster-parent. Long before he adopted it, it had been nursed by such partisan opponents as Lodge and Roosevelt, or by such highminded and honored leaders as Mr. Taft, Dr. Eliot, Mr. Baker. It had been fed by all the preparedness and pro-Ally propagandas; while its actual parentage can be traced past all these into the minds of the eminent British intellectuals who advised us from the first days of the war, and particularly into that of Sir Edward Grey — a man of honor, even of nobility, but also a skillful diplomatist whose sole loyalty was given to the interests of the great Empire which he served.

In the form in which Mr. Wilson now adopted it, however, it had two distinct faces. Mr. Wilson's League would prevent another war begun 'contrary to treaty covenants or without warning and full submission of the causes' to world opinion — which was what the Entente professed to be fighting for. It would on the other hand, however, preserve the freedom of the seas and so give Germany that guaranty against 'encirclement' by British navalism which she professed to be essential to her national existence. The Philadelphia speech was in fact a singularly fine effort of intellectual statesmanship, and should have been received with enthusiasm by all sides. It had but one defect. Nobody was really fighting for what they said they wanted. They were fighting for victory. The speech received a bad press.

The British were furious; the French were furious; the Republicans were furious, and even the loyal Democratic papers were surprised and uncertain. With 'the causes and objects of the war,' the President had said in a minor passage, 'we are not concerned.' It almost seemed to imply that President Wilson put Germany on the same moral plane with the Allies, or that he was ignorant of the fact that the Kaiser had started the war and that the Entente was fighting for humanity and the small peoples. The phrase was snatched up in the Entente and anti-Wilson press and made to overshadow the sensational significance of the pledge to support a world peace league. Mr. Page sent back a long lecture to the President upon the enormity of this sentence. In the columns of the New York *Sun*, Lord Grey (a cousin of Sir Edward and a former Governor General of Canada) informed the American people that 'you have failed.... Belgium has lost everything but her soul. What shall be said of America?'

Paris, like London, rejected the whole business out of hand as a patent German intrigue. But even the Germans were furious. In the Reichstag Stresemann, whose name was to live as one of those who honorably tried to pacify the post-war world, 'violently abused President Wilson and said he was not wanted as a peace-maker,' and all but the Socialists applauded. In the United States many newspapers rallied to the support of the President; but a really curious thing is the fact that neither his defenders nor his opponents seemed to grasp the profound importance of the address as a departure in American policy. Had too many of the editors made the departure already? The speech was without question, as Mr. Brand Whitlock saw, the most significant American state paper since the enunciation of the Monroe Doctrine nearly a century before. In effect, it directly reversed that greatest pillar of American foreign policy, and in doing so abandoned one of the most powerful traditions of American statecraft. One might suppose that upon this aspect of the declaration all the thunders of the opposition would have been concentrated. The point was, of course, raised. Yet the principal ground for attack was not that the new policy was wrong, but that it was so Utopian as to be impossible of achievement. The New York *Tribune*, one of the President's bitterest critics, did not quarrel with the aim; it merely dismissed the announcement of it as 'only another flagrant illustration of Mr. Wilson's instability as a statesman, his fluid sentimentalism, his servitude to winged phrases which carry him far beyond the boundary-lines of his matured thought.'

There was an obvious reason. The Republicans, like the belligerents, were not really fighting for what they said they wanted, but for victory; and the address had undercut a large part of their effort to work up the pro-Ally enthusiasm for the President's overthrow. House was delighted with the address, for he saw that 'it leaves the Republicans without a single issue either foreign or domestic,' and that 'Taft, Root, Choate and most of the Republican leaders are compelled to endorse it because of their previous position.' It was quite true. If Mr. Wilson had repealed the Monroe Doctrine, he had done so only upon the most eminent of advice and urging.

IX. HE KEPT US OUT OF WAR

i

SPRING was giving way again to summer; June was once more on the threshold with its straw hats and muslin dresses, with its crowds flocking to the beaches or the ball parks in the new silk shirts of prosperity. Wealth was flowing and the trees were green and the sun was bright — yet underneath it all there ran on and on that distant muttering of the guns which even American ears could never quite shut out. The war maps might retire to the inside pages; but there they still presented those long, black, unchanging battle lines across the face of Europe, where men were dying not in tens but in their hundreds of thousands. It had all gone on too long; it was too much, too futile, too fantastic. 'Great Heavens!' ejaculated Mr. Page in a queer aside in one of his facile letters, 'it's a crazy world — a slaughter house where madness dwells.' And a day or two later: 'They get more on edge as the strain becomes severer. There'll soon be very few sane people left in the world.' There were few enough as it was; and even in the United States that universal madness began to wear upon the mind, the fierce emotional pressures which it generated began to tell.

Count Bernstorff, as May ran out, was in a momentarily hopeful mood. 'The placation of American opinion,' he reported, 'is progressing. Hardly any mention is now made in the press of German-American relations.... Mr. Wilson's peace plans are becoming more and more tangible. The only question is whether he possesses sufficient authority to force our enemies to agree to negotiations. Colonel House is convinced that Mr. Wilson will succeed.' But Berlin did not think so; and Berlin was nervously impatient. On June 7 a long instruction was despatched to Count Bernstorff. 'More than a month,' von Jagow pointed out, had passed since the surrender on the U-boat, and nothing had happened. Mr. Wilson's 'complete passivity' toward England, if continued much longer, would mean resumption of the submarine campaign. As to peace negotiations, however, it seemed that what Berlin really wanted was merely to use the President as the Entente had been using him. House had arranged with Grey for an offer of mediation which would be rejected by the Germans and so bring the United States into the war on the side of the Entente. The Germans now thought it would be an excellent idea to have an offer of mediation which would be rejected by the Entente and so align the United States with Germany. Actual mediation — especially by 'a statesman so partial to England and at the same time so naïve as President Wilson' — was as little desired in the Wilhelmstrasse as in Downing Street. Indeed, von Jagow was explicit:

> As soon, therefore, as Mr. Wilson's mediation plans threaten to assume a more concrete form and there is evidence of an inclination on the part of England to fall in with them, it will be Your Excellency's duty to prevent President Wilson from approaching us with a positive proposal of mediation.

But how this was to be managed without 'endangering our relations with the United States' was something which von Jagow generously left to 'Your Excellency's diplomatic skill.' Count Bernstorff's skill was great; but the best he could do with this was to cable earnestly for patience, backing up the plea with the warning that any modification of the new submarine policy must mean war with the United States. For the moment, at all events it was useless even to attempt negotiations. On June 7, the date of von Jagow's instruction, the Republican national convention assembled at Chicago to write the platform and choose the candidate for the coming campaign. The 'keynote' speaker was Senator Warren Gamaliel Harding of Ohio; and as his massive periods rolled forth, domestic politics claimed the stage.

Simultaneously and in the same city the Progressives also opened their convention. There were but two questions of any interest: what would happen to Mr. Roosevelt and his party, and how successfully the Republicans would adjust their attacks on Mr. Wilson's 'weakness' with their need of the pro-German vote. The President's emphasis on the 'hyphen issue,' his leniency toward the blockade and sternness toward the submarine, had by this time reduced the pro-Germans to a state of such blind fury that they seemed ready to fight the Wilsonian devil with almost any kind of fire. According to Mr. Viereck, Professor Hugo Münsterberg had actually proposed to put the German vote behind the Rough Rider himself, but this strange plan came to an abrupt end in a meeting between the professor and the ex-President. The German-American Alliance arrived at Chicago promising the Republicans their full support, provided only that Mr. Roosevelt were not the nominee.

The Progressives, on the other hand, were making a last, feeble stand against extinction. The great vision of 1912 had faded; the mighty leader who had aroused it remained silent now in his tent at Oyster Bay. The Progressives' only hope was to exact as high a price as possible from the Republicans for their return to the folds of orthodoxy. But their threats to run Mr. Roosevelt again on a third ticket if the Republicans did not nominate him were empty; everyone knew that the Rough Rider's one passion now was the defeat of Woodrow Wilson and that there was no danger that he would repeat the diversion which had put the schoolmaster in office four years before.

The two conventions sweltered onward through the oratory and the intrigue, the tragi-comedy of the Progressives unfolding to an extraordinary climax. If the Republicans would not take their hero, might they not force some other liberal upon the orthodox managers? From Oyster Bay the hero himself at first gave no word, as he wrestled there alone with his conscience and his chances. But then at last the rumor ran that a message had been received, that Mr. Roosevelt had named an alternate candidate whom the liberal host might present as the price of their return to Republicanism. Secretary Houston, an onlooker at Chicago, heard it and hurried early to the Progressive galleries. There was a good deal of speech-making. There was a collection. Finally the chairman stepped forward and announced that the word had come at last. He read the message. It began in an appeal for national unity in the name of 'genuine Americanism and genuine Preparedness.' It adjured them to leave 'nothing undone to reach an honorable agreement with the Republicans.' It reminded them of their 'principles,' and went on to suggest the name — of Senator Henry Cabot Lodge!

Mr. Roosevelt had picked perhaps the one man whose long record of bourbon conservatism offered the greatest denial of every liberal tenet to which the party had been dedicated. 'A more stunned, whipped crowd,' Mr. Houston recorded, 'I had never looked upon. It was a pitiful spectacle. It had been hoaxed.' So Progressivism died miserably and ignobly at the hand of its creator. 'The radicals,' wrote William Allen White as the convention ended, 'stand on a lonely and rather dreary shore, looking at the ebb-tide and the wreck.'

The Republicans thereupon adopted a platform of stirring platitudes, deftly evading every important issue of the hour, and nominated Mr. Justice Hughes. They now had, they believed, the Progressive vote. Their candidate ought to be able to hold the pro-Germans; while their platform blazed with enough nationalistic fervor to escape the danger — it would have been calamitous — of their being regarded as a German party. On June 10 a colored messenger brought to the White House a curt note, barely polite, announcing Mr. Hughes's resignation from the Supreme Court. Republican hopes were high.

Four days later the Democratic convention assembled in St. Louis. The Democratic managers were no more anxious than the Republicans to draw any of those basic issues which, unfortunately, always risk the alienation of votes. They stood, like the Republicans, firmly against war and resolutely in favor of those things which normally lead up to it. Indeed, on the day the convention opened, as it happened, the city of Washington was having its preparedness parade; and this time President Wilson was very careful to place himself at the head of the procession. He led the column himself, trudging solemnly along the street to the cheers of the massed patriots before taking his place in the reviewing stand. The photographs show him still — a tall figure, in straw hat and white trousers, looking, with the toy American flag over his shoulder, rather like an impatient and uncomfortable small boy. For five hours he took the salutes of a devoted citizenry, and in an address afterward made a ringing attack upon the 'hyphenates.' Yet even as these events were taking place in Washington, a remarkable, and very different, scene was being enacted in the convention hall at St. Louis.

The Democratic 'keynoter' was former Governor Martin H. Glynn of New York. Governor Glynn had decided to stress the note of peace; and to show that peace was not incompatible with honor, he had compiled a long catalogue of instances in our history in which foreign outrage of one sort or another had been adequately met not by war but by diplomacy. It was dull, yet the huge crowd appeared to be absorbing it with interest. He started to skip; instantly shouts arose: 'No, no! Go on! Give us more!' It began to dawn upon the startled speaker that they meant what they said; they were devouring every word of it. With every case of a past indignity which we had failed to resent with the sword, there came only fresh roars of applause. The speaker hesitated over one particularly flagrant episode involving the hanging of some American seamen by the British. 'What did we do?' shouted the crowd. 'We didn't go to war,' answered Glynn; and the convention broke loose. 'Men jumped up in their seats and danced

about the aisles and waved American flags, shouting like school-
boys and screaming like steam sirens.' According to one hostile
account:

> What was going on in their minds was as easily read as if it had
> been printed.... Pacifism had been jeered at, made to seem in
> opposition to Americanism, until they had come to feel almost
> apologetic about it. Now they were told that they had been right all
> the time, that one could be patriotic and pacifistic, that it was the
> historic American policy to submit to great provocation and his-
> torically un-American to go to war over it; and they could not con-
> tain themselves.

It was a 'stampede'; it was also a revelation. The Democratic
managers themselves could not have realized the true depth and
power of the pacifist sentiment in the country — so long obscured
by the outpourings of the editorial war-hawks or the romantic
patriotism of the upper classes. Here, suddenly, was something
to conjure with. The Democratic keynote, soon to be summarized
in the famous slogan, 'He kept us out of war!' had been sounded
almost by accident.

Naturally, Governor Glynn did not make the mistake of assuming this sentiment to be universal. His appeal to the pacific on
the ground that the President had not gone to war was carefully
reinforced with an appeal to the bellicose on the ground that the
President was ready to fight if necessary. The Administration's
policy, as he put it, satisfied 'the mothers of the land, at whose
fireside no jingoistic war has placed an empty chair'; simultaneously it satisfied 'the fathers of this land and the sons of this land'
who might be prepared to 'die for our flag when Reason primes
the rifle, when Honor draws the sword!' It was the perfect combination, constructed upon the immemorial principles of political
oratory to catch them going and coming. As the applause re-
echoed, Senator Ollie James, a leather-lunged orator from Kentucky, sprang forward to seize upon that wave of emotion and give
it a still more impassioned and more adroit development. Pointing to the President, he exclaimed:

Without orphaning a single American child, without widowing a single American mother, without firing a single gun or shedding a drop of blood, he wrung from the most militant spirit that ever brooded above a battlefield the concession of American demands and American rights.

It was true; he had done so — until such a time as the militant spirit should withdraw the concession. At the German Embassy only two days before they had been decoding another impatient cable from von Jagow: 'The Army and Navy are again urging submarine warfare as the only weapon against England....' But Senator James and the other Democratic politicians naturally knew nothing about that. They had their keynote now: 'He kept us out of war!' and it solved all their difficulties.

The slogan, it is important to note, was quite honest. That was the principal trouble with it. It did not promise peace. It merely stated, what was a fact, that the President, while making the foreigner back down, had done it without going to war. That was what the nation wanted. The slogan failed to add that this policy was extremely likely to precipitate a war sooner or later; but for that aspect of the matter the nation was at least as much to blame as the President. Had the Democrats attempted to run upon a straight pacifist platform they would almost certainly have been defeated. It was easy enough to see at the time. Bernstorff, for example, was never for a moment misled into supposing that the Democratic oratory meant that the Democratic Administration would not fight should the submarine campaign be resumed. 'By condoning such a move,' he reported on June 19, 'Wilson would forfeit all hope of being re-elected and Hughes, who is already suspected of being the German candidate, could not afford to recommend a surrender.' But in the meanwhile the Democrats had found a safe means of tapping the powerful sentiment for peace without too far alienating the war hawks. A moment of gloom among the Democrats began to lift. Colonel House (who had a far surer touch in domestic politics than in international relations) was content; the Republicans could have the German vote, for

Mr. Wilson now had William Jennings Bryan back again. That sincere apostle of peace was, in fact, to do yoeman work for the Democratic cause.

As luck would have it, moreover, the Wilsonian policy of belligerent pacifism was almost immediately to receive a curious but in the end very useful test. Three days after Woodrow Wilson had been renominated for the Presidency by the St. Louis convention (the vote was 1092 to one lone recalcitrant from Chicago), Reason suddenly primed the rifle and Honor came extremely close to drawing the sword — not, however, against the submarine. Once more it was the Mexicans. For some time the Mexican situation had been taking on an increasingly ominous look. General Pershing had not yet succeeded in catching Villa either dead or alive, and the Carranzist forces had been more and more clearly manifesting their dislike of our altruistic, but apparently permanent, essay in international 'police duty.' Having so rashly got in, the Administration saw no very good way of getting out again; and matters were settling down to a rather embarrassing *impasse* when President Carranza abruptly precipitated the storm.

On June 18 he formally demanded that the punitive expedition be brought to a halt. On June 19 the Mexican state of Sinaloa was reported independently to have declared war upon the United States, while Mexican troops were massing all along Pershing's tenuous line of communications. On June 20, as Mr. Lansing was sternly rebuking President Carranza for his impertinence, the border command was wiring the War Department for 65,000 more National Guardsmen wherewith to repel a threatened invasion; and on June 21, at the town of Carrizal in northern Mexico, a Carranzist force suddenly fell upon a foraging party from Pershing's column. The American detachment, consisting of Troop C of the Tenth Cavalry, the celebrated Negro regiment, was overwhelmed; two officers and seven men were killed and twenty-three others were taken prisoner. On June 22 Secretary Baker telegraphically ordered General Pershing to stand his ground and directed the border force to seize the international bridges preparatory to a first-class invasion of Mexico. At the same time, the entire National Guard was summoned into the Federal service and directed to proceed to the border immediately upon being mustered in.

Considering the submarine danger, these fiery orders may seem a trifle surprising. But the cartoonists and the editorial-writers sprang to action; the 'treachery' of Carrizal was denounced in stirring words, while Uncle Sam advanced upon the Mexican border, in the cartoons, with a visage of stern nobility, bearing a rifle in one hand and 'education,' 'peace' and 'civilization' in the other. As the guardsmen were mustered in throughout the land there were scenes almost as impressive as those in which the youth of Europe had been mobilized for the slaughter in 1914; for a moment it seemed almost like the real thing at last.

The Pope appealed to the United States and Mexico to keep the peace. In Baltimore 'slackers' were decorated with yellow ribbons. It was rumored that the Allies were about to land at Tampico to conserve their naval oil supplies. Clergymen left their pulpits to enlist and Mr. Ford denied that he had threatened to dismiss any employee who joined the National Guard. The Socialists demanded peace; the interventionists declared that there was already war. Mrs. Cornelius Vanderbilt gave an ambulance train to the New York guardsmen. There was a great pacifist mass meeting at Cooper Union. And it was dramatically announced that in the event of a declaration of war Mr. Roosevelt would ask permission to put into the field a full private army of his own — two brigades of cavalry, a brigade each of infantry and artillery, with all auxiliary troops, a 'full quota of the most modern machine-guns,' 'high-powered armored aeroplanes,' everything complete. Where he was to get these things was not very clearly explained.

The martial dream which had inspired Mr. Roosevelt at every breath of war since a Mexican border incident far back in 1886, which had once come gloriously true at San Juan Hill, which had appeared again in the first months of the European War, now flamed brightly over Mexico. It was to flame once more before it was finally to be extinguished in bitterness and disappointment; this time, however, there was no war. Mr. Wilson did not want one; and the sudden show of force once more worked. The Carranzists were humbled and began to co-operate in the pursuit of 'bandits'; the troopers captured at Carrizal were ultimately released, and by the early days of July the worst of the crisis was over. The orders to the National Guard, however, were not countermanded, and it continued to mobilize (with an alarming slowness and inefficiency) along the Rio Grande. Many thousand young men were to get a long, healthy though undesired vacation that summer; they were also to get some real approach to military training. Mr. Wilson, on the other hand, had played the strong hand again with a dangerously complete success. Fresh laurels of nationalist victory were upon his brow — while his campaign orators were able to point to the complete safety of the splendid young American manhood on the border as compared with the bloody fate of European manhood 3000 miles away.

The Mexican tension passed; as it did so there only came more clearly the roar of that distant shell-fire which was tearing the vitals out of a continent. Throughout the whole last week of June the German trenches below Bapaume had sustained the most intense and prolonged artillery bombardment in the history of warfare. For one entire week the French and British guns had poured down an almost solid rain of shells; until at last, on the morning of July 1, 1916, the heroic Allied infantry rose out of the ground and plunged forward into the titanic Battle of the Somme.

The immense attack was a failure on its first day — yet it was to drag on for four and a half months thereafter before it died down at last in a horrible futility. Mr. Owen Wister has recorded the effect of that long and dreadful summer upon those Americans who watched:

The siege of Verdun began February 21, 1916, and lasted into November.... Four hundred thousand French were killed there.... To the roar of Verdun during the summer of 1916 the roar of the

Battle of the Somme was added. [That cost over 500,000 British lives.] We in the East heard nothing else any more. The destruction of Europe confined all our thoughts as if we were shut up in a mental prison. Concentration upon one's daily work was broken increasingly month after month. During the morning and afternoon hours there was never a minute when the bulletin boards were deserted. Men stepped out of their offices for a glance to see what later news might have been posted since their last look at them.

Once the Battle of the Somme was joined there was not much use in talking peace in England. Again the diplomats were powerless. House had made a final effort with Jusserand, only to find him confident of imminent and decisive victory. Guilelessly the Colonel advised Grey of this discovery: 'As far as I can see there is nothing to add or to do for the moment.' The statesmen were all abandoning Washington now, in the usual flight from the summer heat. Count Bernstorff went to Rye, on Long Island Sound; the President set up the 'summer White House' at Shadow Lawn, on the New Jersey shore; House picked a remote retreat in New Hampshire, 'nine miles from a railroad and four miles from a post-office,' in order that he might give himself uninterruptedly to 'rest and read and think.'

ii

'It is dreadful to think,' Mr. Roosevelt was writing to Senator Lodge in the July heat, 'that some millions of Americans will vote for Wilson.... They can't so vote without incurring moral degradation.' And to his friend the British Ambassador the former President of the United States burst out:

Your country is passing through the flame and will come out cleansed and refined to lofty nobleness. *Mine* is passing through the thick yellow mud-streak of 'safety first' and its high places are held ... by the men of little soul who desire only sordid ease; and perhaps we shall have to be shot over, and eat the bitter bread of shame, before we find again the spirit of high desire.

Nothing, unfortunately, could overcome the certainty that great numbers of his countrymen would vote for Mr. Wilson; but in Congress Senator Lodge was doing his best to awake the spirit of high desire — and militarist imperialism — with the preparedness bills. The Army's National Defence Act, as emasculated by the National Guard, had been signed on June 3; and almost immediately the border mobilization had revealed the lamentably unmilitary state of the National Guard. Weeks, even months, after the orders were issued guard units were still struggling painfully toward the border, devoid of training and equipment; and General Wood was soon writing of the 'tragic failure' of a mobilization which showed 'not more than twenty per cent' of the force even moderately efficient. Nor was that all. War was not, after all, without its inconvenient side. Under the stimulus of the preparedness enthusiasm many from the more eminent and important elements of the community had incautiously enlisted in the National Guard, just as they had gone to the Plattsburg camps. It was now discovered that 'large numbers of men of family and business responsibilities' had as a result been incontinently 'brought into action, while others who had not attained a high economic value were left at home.'

Clearly, 'adequate' preparedness, providing a great standing army and conscription to utilize those without 'a high economic value,' would avoid such *contretemps*. The deficiencies of the National Guard and the long weeks under the broiling border sun for men of business responsibilities only brought new fuel to the preparedness fires; and though further Army legislation now had to be deferred until the next session, it helped in speeding the vast naval building program to its passage.

One trouble about the naval bill was the great difficulty of finding any military needs in accordance with which to devise the proposed increases. This never worried Senator Lodge, who early resolved merely to 'move all the increases I can think of over what the Secretary recommends.' But in the House the peace men, the economizers and the opponents of the munitions makers revealed a stubborn insistence upon being shown. Plowing through masses of expert testimony, Representative Callaway arrived at the strange suspicion that naval experts 'consider only their desires and their fancies and not the real necessities of the government.' The five-year building program, calling for a large fleet of dreadnaught battleships and battle cruisers, was fantastic as a preparation against any possible exigencies of the war then in progress. We could not coerce the Germans by adding more battleships to the overwhelming fleets of the Allies; while a mere export embargo offered us at any time a much more effective weapon against the Entente than anything we could get after five years of naval building. Only as a post-war program could the project have any semblance of logic, and even here Mr. Callaway exposed the lamentable truth:

> Who is going to attack us?... Oh, they say, after the war is over those nations are going to come across the ocean and eat us. Germany,... going to come across 4000 miles of ocean, crippled, a bankrupt, horrified by the war through which she has just passed, crepe on every door for lost son, husband or brother, with an enemy at her back, and sweep from the seas, a navy... pass our forts... and levy tribute on New York, Boston and Philadelphia!

As for a post-war attack by the Allies, the program did not pretend to defend us from that; and in order to justify this circumstance its own supporters had spent hours proving that we need never fear any trouble from Great Britain. The House heartlessly slashed the program from eight capital ships to five and let it go at that.

But the Senate was in no mood for trifling. Senator Swanson of Virginia, the Democratic chairman of the Naval Affairs Committee, seems to have been putty in the hands of Senator Lodge and the Republican imperialists. Mr. Lodge explained it in a letter to Mr. Roosevelt:

> The bill was made by Swanson and myself, and I can say for Swanson that he worked without any regard for party. He got the

President and Daniels together and told them that we were going to stand on the floor for eight capital ships... whereupon they fell into line.

Mr. Lodge commanded that the building be compressed into three years instead of five; again the Administration humbly 'fell into line,' and it was so ordered.[1]

While Congress was still in the midst of its naval discussions, a rather striking episode had occurred. Early on the morning of July 9 the pilot-boat off the Virginia Capes suddenly found herself confronted by a startling apparition. That small conning-tower and long, low, wave-swept hull belonged unquestionably to a submarine; yet it was a larger submarine than any ever seen in American waters and it was signalling for a pilot like any commercial vessel. Was it possible that those half-joking rumors, then, were true? They were; the mercantile submarine Deutschland, of Bremen, had made her landfall, fourteen days out from Kiel with a cargo principally of dyestuffs. Solemnly the Deutschland took her tug in regular fashion, proceeded up Chesapeake Bay and before nightfall was duly berthed at Baltimore, where Captain Koenig entered his papers like any other merchant skipper.

The possible military significance of this spectacular voyage was largely lost at the time in a genuine admiration for the achievement. It was exactly the sort of exploit to appeal to Americans;

---

[1] Eight months later we were at war with Germany — the one most likely contingency at the time the act was passed — and the first thing we did was to scrap the 1916 program in its entirety. All the plans for the great capital ships upon which Senator Lodge had insisted were tossed aside, and we concentrated upon the huge fleets of destroyers and merchant ships which were what was actually needed. In the meanwhile, however, the nation had been successfully launched upon a project which was to serve in after years to make us one of the great militarist powers (in the naval sense) of the world. The program was revived immediately after the Armistice. In final form it authorized no less than sixteen superdreadnaughts and battle cruisers, only one of which was laid down during the war. The remaining fifteen, however, were taken in hand in 1919 and 1920. Though most of them were never completed, they provided the threat with which we wrested the principle of 'parity' from Great Britain at the Washington Conference and so established the policy of 'second to none' upon the seas.

while the startled flurry in the Allied Embassies was not without its amusing side. Upon inspection by American officials the Deutschland was found to be without armament of any sort, and was regularly admitted as a commercial vessel. The Allies were power-less to protest. Their own long, learned and indignant arguments proving that their armed merchantmen could not be regarded as war vessels now recoiled upon their heads. Sir Edward made a really heroic effort, discerning in the immoral 'quality of travelling under water' a peculiar illegality. This novel principle of inter-national law, however, failed to impress the State Department officials who had been so often browbeaten by the Allies' insistence that one could not 'change the rules in the middle of the game.' When the Allies presented an Identic Note, it was rejected with firmness; and there was a distinct note of malice in our polite observation that 'the Government of the United States [is not] aware of any circumstance concerning the use of war or merchant submarines which would render the existing rules of international law inapplicable to them.' The joke was much too clearly on the Allies.

It lost none of its savor from the fact that the Allies' own freedom with the rules and with our protests was becoming almost unbear-able. It was on the day after the Deutschland's arrival that they abruptly notified us of their intention to discontinue their ob-servance of the last remaining shreds of the Declaration of London — which they had originally declared that they would follow in all but one or two details. A French naval writer has dispassion-ately summarized the significance of this move:

> The Declaration of London had been used as a facade for all the measures taken [in establishing the blockade]; but the structure so raised by the Allies was only distantly connected with the monument of law erected by the Powers in 1909, and was in certain respects entirely out of keeping with it.... When a building is finished, the scaffolding which made its construction possible is removed, and the first idea of Lord Robert Cecil when he was appointed Minister of Blockade was to pull down the scaffolding.

It was now far too late, as has been said, to do anything about the architectural masterpiece thus revealed, but its exposure in all its oppressive massivity hardly lessened American irritation. And the publication a few days later of the first British blacklist of American domestic firms rather abruptly brought home to us just what this edifice of Allied trade control had come to imply. The blacklist system was its final and most humiliating capstone. The system itself was not open to legal attack, as all it did was to prohibit British subjects from trading with the listed firms. The effect, however, was that any American concern merely suspected of trading with the 'enemy' or even of 'enemy association' could be subjected at a moment's notice to a ruinous boycott. With the appearance of its name upon the list it was cut off at a stroke from all Allied contracts, denied shipping and insurance even to neutral countries, denied raw materials originating in Entente nations or their colonies, and cut off from business even with the 'good' American firms. The blacklist aroused 'intense feeling,' as the State Department advised Mr. Page, not only among the Department lawyers but in the country. Yet here the shoe was on the other foot; the blacklist was a matter wholly within the domestic jurisdiction of Great Britain. It derived its oppressive force, indeed, only from our own past acquiescence in measures that had bound up our economy so firmly with that of the Entente.

At the White House, however, there was an abrupt reaction. On July 23 President Wilson wrote to his adviser that the blacklist was the last straw. From the very beginning the President had been more skeptical of the British than Colonel House. It was the President who had reminded his emissary more than once that he must retain his neutrality. It was the President who had twice saved House from his reckless promises by inserting the word 'probably.' And it now appears to have been the President who finally realized the futility of House's patient waiting upon the military necessities of the Entente and the skillful procrastinations of Sir Edward. The President had to have peace in Europe. Secretary Lane was hearing that Germany might 'any day' resume her submarine warfare; Mr. Gerard was cabling almost weekly warnings of the developing strength of the submarine agitation; the Deutschland was visible evidence of the power of the submarine weapon — and the President was committed beyond the possibility of reversal on the submarine. He had to have peace; yet when he had offered it to the Entente on the terms they claimed to be fighting for, he had been excoriated by their press, ignored by their statesmen and subjected to fresh indignities in the matter of the blockade. The President announced that his patience was at an end; he suddenly ordered Mr. Page home in the hope that the Ambassador might acquire something at least of 'the American point of view,' and he informed House that he was at last considering applying to Congress for authority to prohibit further Allied loans and to embargo exports. In alarm, House hastened to discourage such rashness. But the foundations were being laid for a policy of peace which would involve putting pressure not simply on one belligerent but upon both.

It was in these same days that there occurred another dramatic event. Early on the morning of July 30 the people of New York and its surrounding cities were startled awake by the roar of a tremendous explosion. They looked out to see a great glow in the sky, as if the whole city were on fire. Many of them started for the downtown section to find the holocaust; as they went they passed block after block in which the sidewalks were covered with the shattered glass from the shop windows. All the time the glow rose or faded over the harbor as lesser detonations shook the city and as shrapnel shells burst in the sky or even bombarded lower Manhattan. The Black Tom pier in Bayonne — a chief loading point for the munitions traffic — had gone up.

Because it happened at the lucky hour of two in the morning the loss of life was almost negligible. But the shock, it was said, was felt as far away as Philadelphia and Baltimore. The huge East River bridges had trembled ominously under the blast; windows were smashed all over Brooklyn and as far north as Forty-Second Street in Manhattan; while in the offices of J. P.

Morgan & Co. (and it seems singularly appropriate) not a pane remained intact. It was some faint suggestion of what war and the munitions trade really meant. The State of New Jersey, within whose boundaries the pier was situated, clapped an embargo upon the transit of munitions through her territory. But that lasted a bare ten days. There was a good deal of editorial severity upon the negligence with which the explosives had been handled; there were next to no voices raised for the stoppage of a traffic which might be dangerous, but upon which our golden stream of prosperity now depended.

On the other hand there was singularly little disposition to blame the Germans. Much time and money have since been spent upon the effort (so far unsuccessful) to prove that the Black Tom disaster was the work of German agents. At the time it was generally accepted as an accident. The truth was that the spy scares had pretty well died away — not really to revive again until our own plunge into the struggle. Captain Koenig of the Deutschland even became something of a hero; and in Baltimore, where there were many citizens of German descent, there was a great welcoming celebration for him and his crew. Count Bernstorff went down for the occasion. The Mayor of Baltimore was taken through the submarine, despite the intense heat and his own corpulence; and in the evening he returned the courtesy with a banquet which 'passed off as in the good days before the war.' German flags were actually intertwined with the American colors which decorated the room; the band played 'Die Wacht am Rhein' along with 'The Star Spangled Banner' and 'many speeches were made on the good relations between the two countries.' For one queer, nostalgic moment those sloughs of passion, bitterness and calumny through which they all daily struggled seemed to have disappeared; for a brief hour the war could be forgotten and the Ambassador could recover that happy past when Germans were human beings and one could talk in cheerful platitudes about 'good relations' in a world at peace. For a moment only. The gathering broke up; the band went home.

The next day Count Bernstorff was at work again on House, trying to prod the Colonel into a peace move, and upon Berlin, where he sought to buttress the Foreign Office against the sailors with fresh hopes of early action by the President. With House he was not successful. In Berlin the results were better, due partly to the intransigeance of the sailors themselves. Von Tirpitz was 'practically demanding war with America' in statements so violent that Gerard was surprised that the government permitted their publication. It was in reality an attack not on America but upon the Chancellor. In Bavaria they were passing resolutions declaring that a principal object of the war should be to 'clean out the Anglophile Foreign Office.' 'It is impossible to conceive,' wrote Mr. Gerard, 'of the general breakdown of nerves among this people.' And again: 'As a son-in-law of a high official told me today, the break between the military and the navy on one side and the civil government on the other has widened almost into civil war.' Mr. Gerard knew that great new fleets of U-boats were being built, and he expected unrestricted warfare with September; but the Chancellor was now fighting for his own political life.

In June the Foreign Office had been warning Bernstorff that he must prevent anything that looked like an actual mediation. Now the tone was changing. On August 18 the Chancellor telegraphed that 'mediation by the President intended to lead to the opening of peace negotiations we are gladly ready to accept.' Mr. Herbert Bayard Swope, arriving in Germany as a correspondent of the *World*, could see at once that the Tirpitz faction, with its promise of quick victory, had an overwhelming popular sentiment behind it. The chief of the war press bureau in Berlin was receiving American correspondents at a desk adorned with three shells of American manufacture, and was careful to point out pleasantly that he himself had been wounded by one of them. The Chancellor was fighting a losing battle. But when Hindenburg replaced Falkenhayn as Chief of Staff in August it was thought to be a gain for Bethmann; and the Rumanian declaration of war on August 26 won him his reprieve.

On August 30 and 31 there was a long conference with the Kaiser at Pless, in which the entire U-boat problem was again canvassed in all its aspects. With relief the Chancellor shouldered all responsibility off upon Hindenburg. Hindenburg and Ludendorff postponed the decision. Until the Rumanian crisis had been met they could not risk entangling themselves in any further complications. But the impression which lingered was that at heart the new army command had been converted to the submarine.

Throughout his struggle the Chancellor had got very little help from the United States. Now, another effect of the Rumanian entry was to fill the Allies again with high hopes, and until these had been disabused mediation would be more difficult than ever. This, at any rate, was what Colonel House told Bernstorff when the two met at New London on September 1. Besides, the Entente would now pay no attention anyway to a President who might not survive an election but two months off. On September 2 there was another anxious cable from Bethmann. He was prepared by this time to guarantee the evacuation and restoration of Belgium if Mr. Wilson would initiate peace negotiations; otherwise, 'unrestricted submarine warfare would have to be seriously considered.' Count Bernstorff was obliged to reply that there was no possibility of mediation until after the vote had been taken on November 7. For the rest, unrestricted warfare would mean that 'the United States would inevitably be drawn into the war — no matter what may be the result of the election.'

iii

This was the only possible conclusion from the course which the campaign was taking. To the Democratic cry that the President had 'kept us out of war' the Republicans had no answer except to denounce Wilsonian 'weakness.' Embarked as they were upon a masterpiece of straddle, they were unable to point out that the Wilson policy was almost certainly calculated to get us into the war in the future. Instead, Mr. Hughes, in his opening speech at Carnegie Hall on July 31, had dedicated himself even more uncompromisingly than Mr. Wilson to 'the unflinching maintenance of all American rights on land and sea.' In his answer, delivered at Shadow Lawn on September 2, the President showed himself straddling almost as heroically as Mr. Hughes. On the one hand he evoked a vision of peace:

> We have been neutral... because it was manifestly our duty to prevent, if it were possible, the indefinite extension of the fires of hate ... and seek to serve mankind by reserving our strength... for the anxious and difficult days of restoration and healing which must follow, when peace will have to build its house anew.

On the other hand he wrapped the flag more firmly round him:

> The rights of our own citizens of course became involved; that was inevitable. Where they did, this was our guiding principle: That property rights can be vindicated by claims for damages, and no modern nation can decline to arbitrate such claims, but the fundamental rights of humanity cannot be.

It is true that a week later Congress (in the final hours of the long session) was at last granting the President discretionary powers to retaliate against the British blockade measures, and there was another angry flutter among the Entente diplomatists. Yet these acts failed to authorize an embargo on exports; their provisions were so weak as to be next to useless, while the Entente had little reason to fear that they would ever be put into operation. On August 1 J. P. Morgan & Co. had launched a large French loan, followed on September 1 by a $250,000,000 United Kingdom loan — the first publicly offered Allied financing since the Franco-British flotation of the year before, but only the beginning of a series of heavy issues which were quickly to follow. The American investor was now to undertake in earnest his financing of the Allied war effort.

It was in September that Mr. Alexander Dana Noyes, financial editor of the New York *Evening Post* and already a commanding authority on economic questions, published a little volume on war finance. Discussing the already staggering war loans, both domestic and foreign, Mr. Noyes felt that:

Nothing is more improbable than refusal of any great European Government after the war to pay interest on that debt or the principal at maturity.... On the Continental money markets discussion has been heard of the plan to pay in paper money the interest on war loans, so far as the bonds are held by the people of those countries. But nobody has suggested the payment of anything but gold for interest due to foreign creditors.

It reads a little curiously today. It is true that the new Morgan loans, unlike the earlier one, were fully secured; and all were paid off on maturity in gold value. Nor were any of the vast additional loans later supplied by the American Government applied directly to this purpose; it is arguable, however, that without them the operation might have proved very difficult, and on these loans the American taxpayer is still awaiting payment. But all that was far in the future; and besides, as Spring Rice rather airily remarked to Grey at the time: 'Who is to help us financially during and after the war if not the United States?' Who, indeed? Mr. Stillman, president emeritus of the great National City Bank, confessed to a friend that he was 'more interested in trying to be of some service to the French' than he was in business; but he felt that he might accomplish more in this direction in New York than in Paris, since 'we are doing all we can to finance loans to the Allies and to help in every way possible.'

Mr. Davison of J. P. Morgan & Co. was unwearied. He was abroad again in October. At the end of that month another $300,000,000 loan was to be floated in the American market, but even so he found Lloyd George and others 'anxious.' Lloyd George told him that it was 'absolutely necessary' for them to have $300,000,000 a month for the next five months — a billion and a half altogether. Could they get it from the American investor? McKenna (if one may believe Colonel Repington's report of a conversation he had with him at the time) felt that if only the United States would enter the war he could get it all from the American Government and his difficulties would be over. That would be easier; as it was, however, the patriotic banker (according to Mr. Lamont) told them that he would do his best with the private investor, and 'his unqualified advice was: "Proceed as though you were going to get the money."' The Chancellor of the Exchequer seems to have put it a trifle unkindly when he told the gossipy Repington that 'he had found that J. P. Morgan and others had learned a lot about finance and were now less provincial.'

At any rate, the money was forthcoming; the mighty stream of supplies flowed out and the corresponding stream of prosperity flowed in, and the United States was enmeshed more deeply than ever in the cause of Allied victory. In Washington Mr. Davison found that the Administration entertained its doubts about all this new lending. But what could they do? They dared not check those 'handsome returns' now being enjoyed by 'the American farmer and manufacturer' — particularly not upon the eve of an election in which they would need all the farmer and manufacturer votes they could get.

Perhaps there was really no necessity for Professor Gilbert Murray to give ten lectures that summer at Columbia University on the war, designed, as he said, 'to bring about better relations between the United States and Great Britain by smoothing away some of the complications which have arisen.' Those handsomely engraved smoothers-away issuing from 23 Wall Street were doubtless more potent than Professor Murray. Yet the 'complications' were steadily getting more complex. In August the State Department was again defending its lenience toward the British in long communications to irate Congressmen; the Senate actually passed a resolution reflecting upon Great Britain's suppression of the Easter Rebellion in Ireland, and Mr. Page, who had reached the United States in August for his bath of American opinion, was having a most unhappy time. Fresh from the scene of action, bursting with first-hand information from Sir Edward with which to instruct the ignorant, he found to his dismay that no one in the government paid any attention to him. There were a couple of perfunctory luncheons with the President and nothing more. Secretary Lansing received his lengthy messages from Sir Edward, Asquith and Bryce, but betrayed 'not the slightest curiosity about our relations with Great Britain' — not even when the Ambassador by main force 'rammed down him a sort of general statement of the situation as I saw it.' The press and public in the pro-Ally Northeast were kind; but official Washington was cold.

At last on September 22 Mr. Page did have a long morning with the President at Shadow Lawn. The Ambassador began by showing him the celebrated Lusitania medal; but strangely enough 'that did not especially impress him.' Mr. Page emphasized 'the high purposes of the British' and argued for war upon the Teuton; Mr. Wilson responded by reading his Ambassador a 'homily' upon the sins of the Entente. The President expressed the astonishing view that the war was the 'result of many causes'; he seemed to find 'no very great reprehensibility' in the Prussian system of government and even 'showed a great degree of toleration for Germany.' At the beginning of the war, Mr. Wilson said, 'he and all the men he met were in hearty sympathy with the Allies; but that now the sentiment toward England had greatly changed.' And when the Ambassador warned him that England would regard any proposal for an armistice in no friendly spirit, the President merely answered that he would use the powers of the new reprisals act if there were further British provocation, and would advance any German proposal for mediation which looked as though it would bring peace. It was more in sorrow than in anger that Mr. Page confronted this wreck of a once admired leader. 'Mr. Wilson at this meeting did not impress his Ambassador as a perverse character, but as an extremely pathetic one.' It is possible that the feeling was mutual. Evidently the American bath had been without effect. Mr. Wilson thought of Page as just another Englishman by this time; he was, apparently, now written off the books for good, and the two men, whose friendship had been so warm and long, never met again.

Colonel House tried his hand on the Ambassador a day or two

later. Again the meeting was without result as far as Mr. Page was concerned, but it left behind it not the least interesting of the entries in the Colonel's diary:

> Page thought good relations might have been brought about with Great Britain had we acted differently. This irritated me.... I ventured the opinion that if we sent Bernstorff home and entered the war, we would be applauded for a few weeks and then they would demand money. If the money was forthcoming they would be satisfied for a period, but later would demand an unlimited number of men. If we did it all, they would finally accuse us of trying to force them to give better terms to Germany than were warranted.

One must admire the complete accuracy of this prediction; at the same time one must regret that through two years of negotiation Colonel House had failed to foresee this quite obvious result.

Gradually, the iron logic of events was closing in. On September 10 General Ludendorff had a long conversation with a representative of the Admiralty. In the end the General was impressed; 'he attached great importance to the Navy's being told and fully realizing that the General Staff desired the U-boat campaign as soon as our military position was stabilized.' New and more powerful types of submarines were now coming to completion. With September the active force had reached fifty-seven boats, as against the puny sixteen of the February, 1915, campaign. To wait until the spring, the sailor urged, would be too late. Certainly, the Quartermaster General agreed, they did not wish to wait until the spring. Washington was of course ignorant of this conversation, but the warnings from our Berlin Embassy, from press reports, from the very character of the situation, were now coming thick and fast. And the one door of escape — peace in Europe — was now being hammered shut by the Allies.

As the great offensives of 1916 began to die away the Entente statesmen found themselves confronting a situation of the utmost difficulty. There was an immense war weariness everywhere. The first faint but ominous crackings of the Russian collapse were already being heard; and the submarine threat was far more dangerous than either the public or the Wilson Administration were allowed to know. A year of enormous effort had brought only another stalemate, with its ever more frightful toll of losses; after the expenditure of something like a million French and British lives alone, the whole task was still to be done over again. Could their peoples be nerved once more to repeat the colossal sacrifice — especially when the Germans were daily hinting at peace terms at least good enough to make small difference to the common men and women in most of the Allied countries? Within the British Cabinet there was already a strong peace group, and on the 19th of September a French Deputy arose in the Chamber to ask why peace negotiations could not be considered. M. Briand hastened to demolish any such dangerous thought under a barrage of patriotism; yet the question had been asked.

The British leaders were in a particularly delicate case. It was not easy to make those lofty war aims which they had avowed to Wilson, to House, and to their own as well as to the American public, square with a continuation of the war. It was even less easy to make them square with Great Britain's private arrangements with her Allies or her statesmen's practical objectives for Great Britain. When the peace talk came up at this time, the forthright Sir William Robertson submitted a memorandum in which he assumed that the three principal British war aims were: '(a) the maintenance of the balance of power in Europe, (b) the maintenance of British maritime supremacy and (c) the maintenance of a weak power in the Low Countries.' Here there was nothing about humanity, the rights of small peoples or international law; while even the reference to Belgium would seem to be severely practical. Could they hold out for such ends? On the other hand, could they hope to achieve them in any peace negotiations initiated at that time, under the influence, as they must be, of President Wilson?

Mr. McKenna was privately considering how the captured German colonies might be 'retained by us at the peace, and not used for bartering against Germany's conquests.' It was a nice point, remembering Mr. Wilson's altitudinous moralities, but Mr. McKenna solved it neatly with the suggestion 'that we should say that we refused to begin negotiations while any part of the territory of our Allies remained in German occupation. This would close the mouth of America and prevent all questions of haggling over our colonial conquests.' Yet there was one trouble about that. As Mr. McKenna realized himself, the Allies' power to continue the war for such objectives 'rested largely upon America' — and their power to continue in any event was not too clear. Should they, after all, cry quits and take what they could get through an American mediation?

But the Germans, too, were facing an ominous future. On September 25 Ambassador Gerard cabled the State Department:

> Germany anxious to make peace. I can state on best authority that if the President will make an offer of good offices in general terms... Germany will accept in general terms immediately and state readiness to send delegates to proposed peace conference. Today or tomorrow von Jagow will ask me to get cipher cablegram to you for Bernstorff.... Of course, utmost secrecy desirable as, if any hint augurs that suggestion comes from here and not as spontaneous act of the President, whole matter will fail and be denied.

When Mr. Gerard sailed three days later for a much needed vacation in the United States, it was partly on von Jagow's urgent insistence that he go to make in person 'every effort to induce the President to do something towards peace.' The message from Bethmann-Hollweg to Bernstorff, mentioned in the Gerard despatch, went on the 26th:

> The whole situation would change if President Wilson... were to make an offer of mediation to the Powers.... Such a move, however, would have to be made soon, as otherwise we could not continue to stand calmly aside and watch England... improving her military and economic position at our expense, and we should have to claim the renewed liberty of action for which we stipulated in the Note of the 4th of May of this year.

Should Mr. Wilson insist on waiting until immediately before or after the election, he would lose the opportunity for such a step.... A further prolongation would be unfavorable to Germany's military situation and would result in further preparations being made by the Powers for the continuance of the war into next year, so that there would be no further prospect of peace within a reasonable time. ... A peace movement... which bore the outward appearance of spontaneity would be seriously considered by us, and this would also mean success for Mr. Wilson's election campaign.

Unfortunately, however, for the millions who were to die in 1917 and 1918, the German Chancellor had but an imperfect knowledge of American electoral strategy. Unfortunately for those heroic and voiceless legions, Colonel House had failed to explore the possibilities of a House-Grey Memorandum with Germany. And again unfortunately for the fighting peoples, on the day the Chancellor's despatch was sent Mr. Lloyd George had chosen to call in Mr. Roy Howard of the United Press and give him, for the edification of the American public and the world in general, a fiery cry for a 'lasting peace' to be achieved with a finish fight and a 'knock-out blow.'

From the United States, the Munitions Minister explained, there must be no 'butting-in.' There could be 'no outside interference at this stage. Britain asked no intervention when she was unprepared to fight. She will tolerate none now that she is prepared, until the Prussian military despotism is broken beyond repair. ... The inhumanity and pitilessness of the fighting that must come before a lasting peace is possible is not comparable with the cruelty that would be involved in stopping the war while there remains the possibility of civilization again being menaced from the same quarter.'

Mr. Lloyd George had dedicated his countrymen to two years of war which were to be worse than futile; but he had at any rate stopped the mouths of the peace men in his own Cabinet and successfully undercut any embarrassing proposals which might come from President Wilson. In the long view Bethmann-Hollweg was right. The psychological moment had come. No especial credit here attaches to the Germans, who were certainly no less militaristic and no less selfish than their opponents. It was simply that events had so fallen out that a peace substantially without victory — which would have been saner, more stable, less harrowing for all the Powers than the calamitous settlement and the profound economic dislocations which the Entente peoples were actually to win two years later — was a possibility in September of 1916. It was never a possibility again. There was just one power in the world capable of seizing upon that moment and forcing such a peace upon the nerve-racked peoples and their war-maddened statesmen. Had the United States remained genuinely neutral, had our principal leaders tried to understand the European War rather than allowing their emotions to make them the dupes of its propagandas, had our party politicians risen only a little way toward the grave responsibilities which they pretended to discharge, it is just conceivable that the United States might have brought the war to an end in the autumn of 1916. But none of those conditions had been fulfilled — and besides, we were in the latter stages of a Presidential election.

Sir Edward was genuinely alarmed at his colleague's rashness. After so direct a slap in the face, he wrote Lloyd George, the President might refuse to act should the submarine war be renewed; he would certainly refuse now to offer his mediation should they need it to save themselves from defeat. That door 'is now closed forever as far as we are concerned.' For a moment Sir Edward saw two years of subtle diplomacy undone. But his fears were groundless. Spring Rice reported that the Lloyd George statement, 'which had an immense and instantaneous effect in this country, put a stop to the peace rumors which have for some time been prevalent here.' The Stock Market, which had been sagging badly under the dire threat of peace, at once happily revived. On October 5 Count Bernstorff was forced to repeat again that there was no chance of Mr. Wilson's intervening until after the election. In the Reichstag, Bethmann made a bitter speech against England; in England the cries for a finish fight, for no stopping, for a knock-out blow, re-echoed. The governments were committing themselves, as Bethmann knew that they would, to another year of slaughter; and in Germany the sailors were preparing at once to launch the submarine. The opportunity passed. When, two months later, President Wilson at last tried to seize it, it had gone forever.

iv

'The certain prospect [in the event of] the success of the Republican party,' declared Mr. Wilson in a speech at Shadow Lawn on the last day of September, 'is that we shall be drawn in one form or another into the embroilments of the European War.' As if to prove it, Mr. Roosevelt, campaigning for Hughes at Battle Creek, was shouting on the same day: 'President Wilson, by his policy of tame submission to insult and injury from all whom he feared, has invited the murder of our men, women and children by Mexican bandits on land and by German submarines at sea.' Mr. Roosevelt was a great help to the Democrats, who cheerfully reprinted this passionate effusion and spread it broadcast over the radical-pacifist Northwest. Unhappily, the fact that the Republicans were committed to war in the event of the submarine pledge being withdrawn did not alter the fact that Mr. Wilson was committed equally.

It was at about this time that the Chief of the German Naval Staff was reviewing the position in a memorandum for the Kaiser. The war was a deadlock. The Allies had shown themselves incapable of beating down the German resistance in the field; on the other hand, Germany no longer had the power to break the Allied lines and so free herself from their siege. With enormously greater resources and man power against her, this meant that she must inevitably be crushed in the end. At just this juncture the short world harvest of 1916 had fortuitously intervened. It 'gives us,' said the memorandum, 'a unique opportunity this year.

North America and Canada will probably hardly be able to send grain to England after February, 1917.' The British would therefore have to turn to the more distant sources in Argentina, India and Australia, which would compel them to devote to the grain supply alone 750,000 more tons of shipping than in 1915. It followed that 'if Germany by means of unrestricted submarine warfare succeeds in sinking 600,000 tons of shipping a month, and if we can count upon neutral traffic being stopped by the terror our methods inspire, British commerce must be reduced mathematically by 39 per cent in five months; the United Kingdom cannot stand this and will be forced to sue for peace. In a word, unrestricted submarine warfare is the best and only means of bringing the war to a victorious conclusion.' [1]

Neither Mr. Wilson nor Mr. Hughes could wield any lightnings capable of affecting such calculations as these. No military threats which the United States might make could possibly take effect within the indicated five months. The sole way in which the United States could influence the decisions of the German authorities was by promising to put pressure on the Allies — and that was impossible until after the election. Steadily the threat grew more ominous. Beginning with the 1st of October, Mr. Grew (our chargé in Berlin during Mr. Gerard's absence) sent off daily bulletins as the struggle between Bethmann and the U-boat wavered precariously back and forth. And if the American public was unaware of this, they were to receive, on October 7, a dramatic and unmistakable hint of it.

---

[1] It is interesting to note that at the moment the Allies, trampling on the neutrality of a small people at Salonika, were violating international law in a manner perhaps as reprehensible as anything involved in unrestricted U-boat warfare. Strategically, moreover, the proposed submarine campaign was simply the German version of the Salonika intervention or the Dardanelles campaign of the preceding year. All alike were efforts to turn the flank of the impregnable battle lines in France. From this point of view, the U-boat, which Mr. Wilson denounced for its barbarity, was actually a weapon of the utmost humanity. All the lives, both civilian and naval, lost in the whole course of the U-boat war were as nothing compared with the frightful slaughters of the West Front deadlock, which the U-boat sought to circumvent. It was humane because it was the one remaining means which promised to get a quick military decision at relatively small cost.

At Newport, Rhode Island, the summer palaces of the million-aires are skirted on their seaward side by the celebrated Ocean Drive, whence the commonalty may look out across the long Atlantic groundswells rolling in toward the harbor entrance. It was early on that Saturday afternoon that the passersby suddenly caught sight of the sinister form of a big submarine, calmly plodding in from the sea. At her staff there fluttered, unmistakably, the German naval ensign, and on the side of her large, squat conning tower the white number could be plainly read — U-53. An American submarine, dwarfed by comparison, piloted her up past the guns of Fort Adams and into the inner harbor. As she anchored off the United States Naval Torpedo Station, a crowd of small boats came hurrying out; her crew, lining the deck, received the curious with cheerful German smiles and bowings, but no one was permitted on board. The U-boat remained only a few hours. A package of newspapers was tossed on board; but her commander was careful to make it very clear that he required no supplies and still had ample fuel in the tanks to complete the voyage homeward. She took nothing; and at about five o'clock weighed anchor and departed. She passed Brenton's Reef Lightvessel at about seven o'clock; the people in the lightship noticed that she was already shipping her radio masts, and while they watched she slid under water and was gone, the brief trail of bubbles vanishing quickly in the dusk. Just off Nantucket Island next evening the U-53 sank six merchantmen. Three more were destroyed on the following morning, and the submarine then went safely back to Germany.

It was a very different sensation from that which had greeted the Deutschland. The Allied governments were appalled. Captain Guy Gaunt, the skillful and popular British naval attaché (so different from the reprehensible Boy-Ed!) rushed post-haste to Colonel House. House had 'never seen him so perturbed'; it was 'a little too much for even his staunch nerves.' The idea that the whole vital North American trade artery might be at the mercy of raiders operating immediately off the American coast

was sufficiently alarming, and it was made no less so by the fact
that the United States had if anything facilitated the U–53's
visit. In London there was a 'fierce public feeling' with bitter
allegations against the United States; while Mr. Rathom's Providence *Journal* promptly 'discovered' and published secret documents from the German Embassy proving that it was all a plot
against the nation's peace. Mr. Rathom even threw in two extra,
and quite mythical, U-boats for good measure.

But once more, nothing could be done about it. The sinkings
had been carried out in conformity with the pledge to give warning and assure the safety of life, and our naval authorities reported
after investigation that 'no rules or regulations governing neutrality were violated.' The Allies, whose own men-of-war had long
hovered off our coasts to the State Department's helpless annoyance, were obliged to fume in silence. American opinion, however, did not miss the fact that the U–53's visit had been addressed
to the attention of the United States quite as much as to that of
the Entente, and not a few saw that it was a warning that we were
going to have war with Germany. A cartoonist for a Nashville
paper showed a helmeted 'Germany' tramping up and down
before the swinging doors of a saloon, which bore the legend:
'Resumption of Submarine Warfare.' In one hand the unlovely
figure carried a paper labelled 'Pledge to the United States,'
and the caption was the one word: 'Backsliding?'

On October 10 Count Bernstorff was at Shadow Lawn. The
President spoke seriously to him about the U–53 and urged that
there be no repetition of the visit; but the interview as a whole
proved 'unusually pleasant.' By this time Mr. Wilson was plaintively remarking in private that he wished 'someone would tell me
what the Allies are fighting for' and the Entente had sunk in his
esteem very nearly to the lowest point. He now assured the Ambassador that his one desire was to maintain neutrality and bring
the war to a close. It gave Bernstorff something more, at any
rate, with which to bid against the sailors. With this encouragement and with the help of Hindenburg, the Chancellor did finally

A GERMAN SUBMARINE BOUND WEST ON WAR SERVICE

Courtesy of U.S. Navy Department

THE U-53 AT NEWPORT, RHODE ISLAND

manage to postpone the submarine war at least until after the election. On October 20 Mr. Grew cabled that the danger seemed for the moment to be over. In America by that time the U-boat had very nearly been forgotten. All thoughts were absorbed in the bitter Presidential race now sweeping to its climax.

It was early seen to be a close thing. What it all signified is less easy to discern. The American intellect is rarely at its best in a Presidential campaign; in the campaign of 1916 it was even less so than usual, and if those passionate floods of argument and propaganda made any sense at all it is difficult to detect it now. Mr. Roosevelt went up and down the land breathing fire and slaughter in support of Mr. Hughes; while Colonel House heard from the newspapermen that 'Hughes is becoming more irritable and that it is caused largely by Roosevelt's speeches.' General Wood (he had 16,000 patriots in his Plattsburg camps that summer) was laying down verbal barrages ostensibly in behalf of preparedness but 'in effect,' as his biographer says, 'campaign speeches against Wilson.' Mr. Wilson, now far more friendly to Germany than the Republicans, had nevertheless given them the pro-German vote, and consequently was pounding upon the 'hyphen issue' for all there was in it. When Mr. Jeremiah O'Leary (the Irish-American who had been so useful to Dr. Albert's propaganda bureau) assailed the President for 'truckling to the British Empire,' the President flashed back with a celebrated telegram:

> I would feel deeply mortified to have you or anybody like you vote for me. Since you have access to many disloyal Americans and I have not, I will ask you to convey this message to them.

It probably cost the President New York, where the Irish Tammany vote dominated the Democratic party, but House thought it 'the best thing so far in the campaign.' The remarkable situation developed of the pro-Germans moving heaven and earth to defeat Mr. Wilson while he was actually adopting the policy desired in Berlin, and while Bernstorff was desperately trying to hint to them that they were on the wrong tack.

The nation might properly ask, Senator Lodge granted, what the Republicans, if elected, intended to do. The Senator gave his reply:

No one can say what... complications may arise after the 4th of next March.... But this much can be said: We will take a position worthy of the greatest nation in the world; we will restore the country to the position of influence and respect which it held under McKinley and Roosevelt. We will if possible keep the peace and maintain neutrality.

Unfortunately, what the nation really wanted to know was whether that was possible. But the Democrats were no more enlightening on this point than the Republicans. They plastered the nation with posters — 'He kept us out of war!' Some of them were still on the billboards, it is said, in the following April. The Republicans hoped to hold the German vote and tried to damn the Democrats with the charge that the latter were angling for it. The Democrats excoriated the 'hyphenates' and played for the pacific citizens of the West, many of whom were of German descent. On November 2 a great Democratic rally was staged in the old Madison Square Garden in New York. Mr. Wilson himself arrived in imperial state in the Presidential yacht Mayflower; and Colonel House, who had arranged everything in advance, even down to the precise times allotted for each spontaneous burst of irrepressible popular enthusiasm, watched with a quiet satisfaction from a side street. It went off with the greatest 'precision,' but it failed to collect many votes from a surly and suspicious Tammany. Mr. Wilson thought New York 'rotten to the core,' and shook its immoral dust from his feet.

On the following evening Theodore Roosevelt arrived for the final effort of his campaign at the Cooper Union. There Lincoln had stood before him; there the Rough Rider stood now, primed for the blast which should shrivel and obliterate forever the Princeton schoolmaster. He had been primed, as a matter of fact, by Mr. John Wanamaker, who had appealed in a truly moving telegram:

It seems as though you might crown your splendid work for Mr. Hughes by the soul cry of a true patriot from Cooper Union, Friday night, November 3, awakening the people to the crisis of the hour....

The 'flower of Republicanism in the East was gathered there, Progressive mingling once more with the Old Guard.' Mr. Roosevelt rose heroically to the occasion. As he reached the end of his flaming speech, he tossed his manuscript aside and 'trembling with emotion' uttered that soul cry of the true patriot for which Mr. Wanamaker had called:

There should be shadows now at Shadow Lawn; the shadows of the men, women and children who have risen from the ooze of the ocean bottom and from graves in foreign lands; the shadows of the helpless whom Mr. Wilson did not dare protect lest he might have to face danger; the shadows of babies gasping pitifully as they sank under the waves; the shadows of women outraged and slain by bandits.... Those are the shadows proper for Shadow Lawn; the shadows of deeds that were never done; the shadows of lofty words that were followed by no action; the shadows of the tortured dead.

But the soul cry seemed not to affect the West much more than House's nicely timed applause had affected Tammany. On November 4 House concluded that 'the fight is won'; but if so, it could only be by a fearfully narrow margin. The Colonel had already conceived a striking idea. With defeat at the polls, the authority of an American President always comes abruptly to an end; at that time, however, it was still one of the beauties of our Constitution that his responsibility was continued until the inauguration of his successor four months later. With our European relations in the critical state which they had now reached, the prospect of such an 'interregnum' was more than dismaying. It occurred to Colonel House to suggest to the President that he should, in the event of defeat, immediately resign and install Mr. Hughes in his place.[1] One or two to whom the Colonel mentioned

---

[1] Through the device of appointing Mr. Hughes Secretary of State and then securing the Vice-President's resignation together with his own. This, it was believed, would make Mr. Hughes legally the acting President for the remainder of the Wilson term.

the idea were 'staggered' at the thought; but the President seized upon it at once and resolved to put it into execution. In order that it might not appear to have been an afterthought, he recorded his determination in a letter to Mr. Lansing.

The slight drift which was to prove decisive seems to have set in only with the final days. Count Bernstorff's carefully discreet hints had at last 'given pause' to Mr. George Sylvester Viereck, and toward the end he softened somewhat the blasts with which he had been summoning the pro-Germans (through his propaganda weekly, *The Fatherland*) to the destruction of Mr. Wilson. Perhaps more important was the famous and fatal blunder of Mr. Hughes in snubbing the Progressive Hiram Johnson in California. But on the morning of the election, Tuesday, November 7, such slight effects could not be estimated. Colonel House might still be confident, but the result to most was beyond prediction.

The day wore on in that strange and grateful calm which always soothes the mind still reeling from the last bursts of campaign oratory. Colonel House was in his apartment in Fifty-Third Street with Mr. Gregory, the Attorney General. Mr. Hughes and his entourage were installed at the Hotel Astor in Times Square; the Democratic chieftains were preparing for a banquet at the Biltmore; Mr. Roosevelt waited at Oyster Bay. The President and his family were at Shadow Lawn, while the faithful Tumulty sat in the executive offices which had been established in nearby Asbury Park. As evening fell and the New York polls were closed there rolled in the first waves of the deluge. By seven o'clock it was certain that New York had been lost, and lost badly; and as the other populous Northeastern states, with their heavy votes in the Electoral College, followed one after another in swift succession it seemed increasingly impossible that the Democrats could have won. At the Biltmore, where Lansing, McAdoo, Lane and the campaign managers had gathered, the banquet proceeded in a 'morgue-like' gloom. A few blocks away down Forty-Second Street the hearts at the Astor were beating high. At about nine-thirty Mr. Tumulty, sitting alone in his office by the sea, was aroused by excitement in the corridor; a flock of correspondents burst in, led by a reporter from the loyal *World* bearing the bulletin in which that paper conceded the election of Mr. Hughes.

To me the blow was stunning... and yet I had faith to believe that the news... would be upset. Steadying myself behind my desk, I quickly made up my mind.... Concealing the emotion I felt, I dictated the following statement: '... Wilson will win. The West has not yet been heard from.'

A few moments later the telephone rang; it was the President. 'Laughingly he said: "Well, Tumulty, it begins to look as if we have been badly licked"'; and when the Secretary spoke with hope the President only chuckled and called him an optimist.

At 10 o'clock Illinois went by an enormous majority for Hughes. Colonel House, sitting with Mr. Gregory, was imperturbable; but the two could not blind themselves to possible eventualities. Together they went down to the Lawyers' Club. Beyond the windows, the roaring election crowds were filling the streets of the whole nation; within, the two sat in the dignified silences of the club library, solemnly looking up the precedents bearing upon the proposed resignation of the President. Mr. Gregory reached the conclusion that the plan was 'legal and desirable'; they parted, and House went to bed. Wisconsin followed in the wake of the eastern states. The thing was certain now. In the Metropolitan Club, where the great magnates of Republicanism had gathered, there was 'jollification.' In one group a *World* reporter, arriving with his bulletin, found Mr. Frick, the steelmaster, Mr. Choate, pillar of the law, and Mr. Ogden Mills, pillar of patriotism. They authorized a happy statement:

It is a great constructive victory,... a national triumph.... America may again hold her head up among the nations of the world. It means preparedness that will make war impossible and it means the greatest era of prosperity that the country will ever have known.

At Oyster Bay the joy was almost too much, as Mr. Roosevelt expressed 'my profound gratitude as an American proud of his country that the American people have repudiated the man whc coined the phrase about this country that it is "Too proud to fight." '

The streets were filled now with the election extras bearing their huge portraits of 'The President-Elect — Charles Evans Hughes.' At Shadow Lawn Mr. Wilson had 'retired early'; but outside the Astor there were two immense brass bands, and the entire square was packed with 'wildly cheering thousands.' The management unfurled a huge American flag across the face of the hotel, with searchlights beating upon it; other lights 'flashed Hughes's name in gigantic illuminated letters,' and when pillars of red fire went up from the hotel roof a 'great roar of cheering... rose to the ears of the successful candidate and his family.' With a proper sense of his new dignity the President-Elect refrained from showing himself before the howling multitude. Instead, at one-thirty, he finally retired.

But he was not the President-Elect.

Shortly after Mr. Tumulty had dictated his heroic message there came over the telephone a mysterious, anonymous voice warning him 'in no way or by the slightest sign to give up the fight.' Who it was he never knew; perhaps it was a miracle. The tidal wave swept on. The Brooklyn *Eagle* conceded. The New York *Times*, last line of defence, conceded. Mr. Tumulty conceded nothing. And then at last, 'just about the break of day on Wednesday morning,' he was notified that Ohio had gone for Wilson by 60,000; and as the far Western states began to report it seemed — was it possible? — that the tide was turning.

When Mr. Hughes awoke that morning his photograph was still resplendent upon the front pages of the late editions. The *World's* banner headline stood as before — save for the addition of one small punctuation mark. It now read:

HUGHES ELECTED IN CLOSE CONTEST?

The *World* had recanted. The *Times* had recanted. Colonel House had awakened at about five o'clock in the morning, and had at once leapt back 'into the game.' He telegraphically advised headquarters to urge every county chairman in every doubtful state to the utmost vigilance. As Mr. Wilson was shaving that morning his daughter Margaret knocked on the bathroom door and told him of the *Times* extra. He thought she was joking and, advising her to 'tell that to the Marines,' went on shaving. But it was not a joke.

For the Democrats in that glorious dawn all hopes revived. That Wilson was carrying the West was clear; yet as the anxious managers totted up their electoral votes they still could not claim a victory. The long day wore on with no decision. By Thursday morning 'the result of the most confused and extraordinary Presidential contest ever held in the United States was still in doubt.' The indicated electoral vote was standing at 251 for Wilson to 228 for Hughes; the balance hung upon the 52 remaining votes which could not yet be assigned. The largest block of these were the thirteen votes of California, where United States marshals were standing guard over the locked ballot boxes while the excited managers raged around them. On Thursday evening Mr. and Mrs. Hughes went to the theater; the play, as it happened, was the farce 'Nothing But the Truth.' William Collier was playing the lead. At one point in the action he received some money from his sweetheart for investment, and her line as she handed it over was, 'Is it absolutely safe?' That night Mr. Collier hesitated, glanced at Mr. Hughes and replied: 'I can't tell until I hear from California.' Mr. Hughes joined in the laugh; and next morning the nation had heard from California. Woodrow Wilson had been re-elected President of the United States.

The popular vote was 9,128,837 to 8,536,380 — a scant plurality of less than 600,000 votes. The minor candidates got nearly 900,000. Thus the popular verdict was close enough; but a shift of less than 4000 votes in California would alone have sufficed to reverse the outcome in the Electoral College. In the Senate the Democratic majority fell from sixteen to ten; in the House it disappeared, leaving the two major parties exactly even with 214 members each, and a sprinkling of independents holding the balance.

X. THE TRIUMPH OF VON TIRPITZ

i

'NOW the burden upon me is heavier than ever,' the President wrote in the hour of victory to his friend, Mrs. Edith Reid. 'If we can escape entering the war and bring about a rational peace it is something worth living and dying for, and I believe the country feels that way or it would not have re-elected me.' Undoubtedly the President was right about the country; but how was it to be done? The result of the election had not been definitely ascertained until Friday morning. It was on the following Tuesday, November 14, that Mr. Wilson summoned his adviser from New York. The Colonel reached the White House that evening, and the two men plunged at once into a long discussion of the whole dilemma.

The weary road over which they had come so far was now winding to its end. Its beginning — in the happy spring of 1914 when House had first sought to make peace in Europe — belonged already to an almost forgotten past. It had carried them through the first strange months of the war, when the President had proclaimed neutrality and entrusted the nation's destiny to the established rules of international law. That had ended with the Lusitania. It had twisted on through the efforts to work out some new compromise between 'the prize court and the torpedo' adequate to preserving the United States from the conflagration. That had ended in the winter of 1915–1916. It had involved them in Colonel House's 'positive policy' and the futilities of the House-

Grey Memorandum. That instrument was already dead; but it had left them committed to the idea of a league of nations and a permanent world peace system. Now the road had brought them down at last to the point where guaranteeing a future peace was not enough; the immediate end of the war in Europe was the sole visible means of escape for the people of the United States.

'The President,' Colonel House discovered when he reached the White House, 'desires to write a Note to the belligerents, demanding that the war cease.... His argument is that, unless we do this now, we must inevitably drift into war with Germany upon the submarine issue.' Quite aside from the many warnings they had received that the May 4 pledge would be withdrawn, it was evident that the pledge was breaking down anyway. The ardent U-boat commanders were discovering all kinds of useful holes in it, and 'mistakes' were accumulating. On October 28 a horse-boat was torpedoed without warning, with the loss of six American horse-tenders. The Germans argued that she was a British government transport and hence of military character. The liner Arabia was sunk without warning on November 6; she was crowded with passengers, and though all were saved it seemed a flagrant violation of the pledge. But the Germans contended that she had been armed, had behaved suspiciously and had appeared to be a troop-ship. Many other excuses were discovered by the submarine captains, and a procession of protests was now issuing from the State Department.

What were the chances of compelling a 'rational peace'? Colonel House, who had for weeks shown himself very friendly toward the Germans, was now going back to his original ground. On the night before the election he had paused to drop a note to the President:

> At spare moments I have kept in close touch with the European situation, and I find indisputable evidence that Germany is not yet ready to agree to peace terms that this country could recommend to the Allies. They sneer at such proposals as a League to Enforce Peace and believe... that large military armaments are necessary to enforce peace.

The Colonel may have been right about the Germans; the trouble was that he had not a shred of firm assurance that the Allies were any more enthusiastic for a peace league or any less convinced that 'large military armaments' would be essential to their future safety. Indeed, at this moment Colonel House's admired friend, Mr. Balfour, was drawing up a thoughtful memorandum for the British Cabinet upon Allied war aims. It said nothing whatever about either a league of nations or disarmament. It did begin with the declaration that 'the principal object of the war is the attainment of a durable peace,' but Mr. Balfour's ideas upon this subject had little in common with those of Colonel House or President Wilson. The best means of attaining this end, he argued, was by 'diminishing the area from which the Central Powers can draw the men and money required for a policy of aggression, while at the same time rendering a policy of aggression less attractive by rearranging the map of Europe in closer agreement with what we rather vaguely call "the principle of nationality."'

With skill and realism Mr. Balfour then went on to weave into the framework of this theory the satisfaction of all the more mundane ambitions of Great Britain and her allies. From it he logically deduced the necessity of carving up Austria-Hungary for the benefit of the Italians and the Serbs, of ceding Constantinople and restraining Poland within the bounds of 'a large measure of autonomy' for the benefit of Russia, of annexing Alsace-Lorraine for the benefit of France and of requiring the replacement of the merchant fleet destroyed by the submarine for the benefit of Great Britain. The colonies, where the British expected to make their chief gains, he did not discuss.[1] It was, in short, simply a scheme

[1] The whole memorandum offers further interesting evidence upon the true authorship of 'Wilsonism.' It is striking to find Mr. Balfour, a strict realist and British patriot, embracing the principle of 'self-determination' which was later to be condemned as the folly of our President's impractical idealism. Mr. Balfour also proposed the granting of rights of way to the sea to countries which would be left landlocked by the settlement. He suggested it in connection with Austria rather than Poland (which was to remain an 'integral part' of Russia despite the 'principle of nationality') but it was the same principle as that embodied by Mr. Wilson in the Fourteen Points and finally applied in the creation of the Polish Corridor.

to assure a 'durable peace' by the short method of dismembering Austria-Hungary and reducing Germany to a complete subjugation. But Mr. Balfour was not blind to what this would really imply for post-war Europe. Bluntly, and prophetically, he observed that after the war 'the peace of the world will depend, as heretofore, on defensive alliances formed by those who desire to retain their possessions against those who desire to increase them.' The memorandum made a great impression in the inner circles of the British Government. As to whether it was representative of their views, one has Mr. Lloyd George's statement that it supplied 'the only concrete proposals as to peace terms' ever submitted to the Asquith Cabinet, and this at a time when the peace question was more urgent than at any other moment until the end.

Naturally, his British friends did not show the Balfour Memorandum to Colonel House. Yet the territorial ambitions of the Allies were no particular secret. Wilson and House may have been unaware of the precise terms of the 'secret treaties,' but they could not have been ignorant of their general tenor, while every reader of the newspapers knew that something of the kind existed. Broadly speaking, there were now but two ways in which the war could end. It could end in 1916 with a draw; otherwise it must go on indefinitely — at least for another year or two — to the complete destruction of one side or the other. In either result the United States would be compelled to participate. To achieve a draw, our diplomatic intervention would be required, with all the risks of embarrassment and of hostility from both sides which that would imply. In a bitter-end fight, our military entanglement on behalf of the Allies would be practically unavoidable.

In its widest terms, this was the character of the issue which confronted the two men as they met in the White House on the evening of November 14. Was the United States to attempt to force a peace at once, or let the war go on and accept the certainty of our own entanglement in the hope of salvaging a new world order out of Allied triumph at the end? President Wilson was in favor of the first course; his adviser strongly urged the second.

His reason was that the Allies would regard a peace effort as an 'unfriendly act' — in which, of course, he was quite right. The President was 'much worried' at this reply, and a long discussion ensued. What was best to do? For the submarine danger, House's only remedy was a bland insistence that 'we should sit tight and await further developments.... I argued again and again that we should not pull Germany's chestnuts out of the fire merely because she desired it, was unruly and was forcing us into war.' This passive statesmanship seems not to have satisfied the President. The two parted at last, and Mr. Wilson spent a bad night. Next day he put an end to the discussion. He would have to write his ideas out, he said, before they could make any further progress; and he dismissed his adviser.

Too much time had been lost already. Had the President seized upon Bethmann's offer when it came in September he might have forestalled to some extent the 'no surrender' campaign of the Allied statesmen. The delay had greatly intensified the resistance which would have to be overcome in the Entente countries. Guy Gaunt dropped by to tell House pleasantly that 'the feeling in Great Britain against the United States grows apace,' and that in the trenches the troops were nicknaming dud shells 'Wilsons.' Mr. Page was writing out his resignation in disgust. But in Germany, also, delay was foreclosing the opportunity. Berlin also had its 'no surrender' gentry and its fire-eating public to contend with, and it always had the sailors. Bethmann had to have results. The election, upon which he had been told to wait, had come and gone. The day after House and Wilson parted, von Jagow cabled the first hint to Count Bernstorff that if the President did not make a peace move, the German Government would.

On November 22 the Ambassador received definite word that his Foreign Office intended immediately to announce the German readiness to enter peace negotiations. Bernstorff hastened to discourage this disastrous idea with fresh promises of early mediation. But on November 23 von Jagow, who had throughout been one of the strongest opponents of the submarine, was relieved

only upon those who preferred to live in idleness upon the relief doles from America. But the American press did not agree with the Germans; and at this delicate juncture in Mr. Wilson's policy, the deportations came to revive all the alleged horrors of the earlier days and send a wave of anti-German sentiment through the United States.

The President delayed his move still longer, while the State Department entered a solemn protest at Berlin on November 29 against the deportations. It was coupled with a private hint that the matter was embarrassing the President in his peace move and that the latter would be initiated as soon as the deportations ceased; yet it served to touch the Germans on one of their rawest spots. They were particularly bitter at what they regarded as the utterly false and unwarranted accusations of slanderous enemies in regard to Belgium. This communication, raising a matter in which no American interest of any sort was involved, and implying that our government accepted these accusations at their face value, could only destroy their already waning confidence in any mediation by the United States.

On December 4 Ambassador Gerard sailed again for Germany, at the 'special request' of the President. 'Before I left I was impressed with the idea that he desired above all things both to keep and to make peace.... I think that the inclination of the President was to go very far towards the forcing of peace.' But at that moment the short session of Congress reassembled, and simultaneously the Asquith government in Great Britain fell. When the Cabinet was reconstituted with Lloyd George as Prime Minister, it seemed clearly to imply a bitter-end policy and a 'knock-out blow.' House's beloved Sir Edward was out of office; his place was taken by the practical Mr. Arthur James Balfour, who had written the Cabinet memorandum on peace terms.

ii

In his annual report as Chief of Staff, prepared to greet the new session of Congress, Major-General Hugh Scott frankly recommended to the American people a conscript military system like that of 'Germany, Japan and France.' Great numbers of our editors, strangely oblivious to the fact that the European War was being fought for the elimination of 'Prussian militarism,' earnestly supported this final step in the conquest of the United States by Prussia. It is true that conscription had now been renamed 'universal service,' and perhaps that made all the difference. For as even the liberal and democratic *World* argued, while 'universal service based upon German military theories' would be profoundly objectionable, 'universal service adapted to American theories of government' might meet with general approbation.

It might, indeed. The Scott report was one shadow of coming events; the first meetings of the new Advisory Commission of the Council of National Defence were another. The Advisory Commission, set up by the preparedness legislation of the summer, brought together a group of distinguished American industrialists to carry forward the plans for a large scale industrial mobilization upon which Mr. Howard E. Coffin had already begun.[1] Preparedness had not as yet done much for our actual military equipment; but it had gone far by this time in its greater task of preparing the American mind for that grand scale intervention upon the European battlefields which was so soon to come.

Yet Congress opened in the first days of December in a confused, uncertain temper. The pacifists were much in evidence. Representative Charles A. Lindbergh introduced a resolution calling for joint action by Congress and the President to bring the war to a close. Mr. Bryan appeared again in Washington; he was received upon the floor of the House, and at a banquet in his honor he spoke for peace. 'There was peace talk everywhere,' Mr. Arthur Dunn remembered; while the Women's Peace Party even

[1] Page 254.

stormed the White House. But the sands were running by this time with a fearful rapidity. On the 9th of December the State Department cabled six separate demands to our Berlin Embassy for investigation and report upon as many different cases of submarine attacks on merchantmen. And then, late in the afternoon of Monday, December 11, the Department received from Mr. Grew its first definite warning that the Germans were themselves about to make a peace proposal. It was to come on the following day.

Bethmann-Hollweg had refused to wait any longer. He had begun to angle for some kind of American action seven months before, with the conditional surrender of May 4. He had definitely asked for a peace move through both Gerard and Bernstorff on September 25 and 26 — two and a half months before — and had been told that he must wait until after the election. Even then he had only with difficulty restrained the sailors. The election took place on November 7. One week elapsed before the result was determined and the President (on November 14) finally faced the question of a peace move. House sought to dissuade him. Another week went by before the President actually began (on November 21) to draft a peace note. A third week passed before the draft was finished and submitted to House (on November 27), and House then tried to soften it and to defer its despatch. Through all this time, of course, Bethmann did not even know that a note had been drafted. More than that, Colonel House, whether intentionally or not, seems to have deceived Bernstorff into the belief that it was the President who was hesitating to make the peace move against the Colonel's own urgings that such a move be made. On December 4, four weeks after the election, Count Bernstorff cabled:

Everything is prepared for a peace move, but with Mr. Wilson still hesitating, it is still doubtful when he will take action. All the authorities here have now been won over to favor such a step.... In any case, so much is certain, that House is continually urging Mr. Wilson to take action; moreover, peace propaganda here is steadily increasing, notwithstanding that it is for the moment very seriously hampered by the Belgian [deportations] question. If Mr. Wilson — as is to be expected — finds a strong feeling for peace in Congress, he should at last make up his mind.

Count Bernstorff in these days was snatching at every straw to convince his Government that a peace note was really coming. Had Colonel House told him that a peace note was already in existence and that the hesitations were largely the Colonel's rather than the President's, the Ambassador might have succeeded. But if the President was now procrastinating in spite of his powerful adviser's urgings and in spite of the conversion of 'all authorities' in Washington — if he was now going to wait until he could find a 'strong feeling in Congress,' until British animosity could be assuaged, until Germany humbled herself in the deportations matter — what was the use? Bethmann-Hollweg could not wait.

At noon on December 12 the Chancellor handed to Mr. Grew a Note which he requested the Government of the United States to transmit to the Entente Powers; he then went before the Reichstag to announce and explain his action to the world. The Note read:

The most formidable war known to history has been ravaging for two and a half years a great part of the world. That catastrophe... threatens to bury under its ruins the moral and physical progress on which Europe prided itself at the dawn of the twentieth century. In that strife, Germany and her Allies... have given proof of their indestructible strength.... It was for the defence of their existence and freedom of their national development that the four allied Powers were constrained to take up arms. The exploits of their armies have brought no change therein....

They do not seek to crush or annihilate their adversaries. Conscious of their military and economic strength and ready to carry on to the end, if they must, the struggle that is forced upon them, but animated at the same time by the desire to stem the flood of blood and to bring the horrors of war to an end, the four allied Powers propose to enter even now into peace negotiations. They feel sure that the propositions which they would bring forward and which would aim to assure the existence, honor and free development of their peoples, would be such as to serve as a basis for the restoration of a lasting peace....

If the peace move ever had any chance of success, the chance ended at that moment. A neutral intervention by the United States might conceivably have been so managed as to mobilize the war-weary publics of all the belligerents against extreme demands by either side. For Bethmann to hope to do so was fantastic. To the Entente, of course, his offer seemed only proof that victory was at hand. President Wilson had delayed too long. The door had not only been shut, but was now bolted fast; and that being so, the President was now finally to spring to action. The peace note which had been deferred for four weeks was to be rewritten and sent off in six days. The Reichstag speech was on Tuesday. On Friday, December 15, Mr. Wilson came into the Cabinet meeting with the note in his hand.

The Cabinet, led by the violently pro-Ally McAdoo and Houston, seems to have reacted much as had Colonel House. They doubted the 'wisdom' of sending such a note at that time; they feared it might even 'be regarded as an act of friendship toward Germany'; they seized upon the implication to which House had objected, and wanted the President to make it 'absolutely clear that he was not asserting that he thought the belligerents were fighting for identical things.' The President cut it short. It would have to be either that note, he sensibly declared, or nothing. It could only be.

On Saturday afternoon, the 16th, Secretary Lansing transmitted the German Note to our Ambassadors for presentation to the Entente Powers. He sent with it a hint that an American peace move was to be expected shortly, entirely unconnected with the German offer. This communication was handed in at the Quai d'Orsay on Monday, the 18th. On Tuesday M. Briand spoke to the French Senate, Baron Sonnino addressed the Italian Chamber and Mr. Lloyd George stirred the House of Commons — all with the flaming rejections of the idea of peace negotiations. 'Any man or set of men,' Mr. Lloyd George exclaimed, 'who abandoned the struggle without achieving the high purpose for which they entered the war would be guilty of the costliest act of foolery ever perpetrated by any statesman.' The Czar's Government had already summoned his people to fight on for the high purpose of recapturing Poland and appropriating Constantinople, and the Duma had voted a categoric refusal to consider any German proposals. And it was with these speeches and votes filling the Entente press that President Wilson's Peace Note arrived at last in the Entente capitals.

The Note had been placed upon the cables at nine-thirty on Monday evening, December 18. Swiftly and intelligently, the President had altered his tactics to meet the new situation. House's advice against a demand for peace negotiations was adopted; but in place of the demand the President had resorted to a more ingenious device. He simply called upon all the warring Powers to declare what it was that they were fighting for:

> The objects which the statesmen of the belligerents on both sides have in mind in this war are virtually the same, as stated in general terms to their own people and to the world. Each side desires to make the rights and privileges of weak peoples and small states as secure... as the rights and privileges of the great and powerful states now at war. Each wishes itself to be made secure in the future... against the recurrence of wars like this and against aggression or selfish interference of any kind.... Each is ready to consider the formation of a league of nations to insure peace and justice throughout the world. Before that final step can be taken, however, each deems it necessary first to settle the issues of the present war upon terms which will certainly safeguard the independence, the territorial integrity and the political and commercial freedom of the nations involved....
>
> The President, therefore, feels altogether justified in suggesting an immediate opportunity for a comparison of views as to the terms which must precede those ultimate arrangements for the peace of the world.... Stated in general terms, [the objects of the war] seem

the same on both sides. Never yet have the authoritative spokesmen of either side avowed the precise objects which would, if attained, satisfy them and their people that the war had been fought out.... It may be that peace is nearer than we know; that the terms which the belligerents ... would deem it necessary to insist upon are not so irreconcilable as some have feared; that an interchange of views would clear the way at least for conference and make the permanent concord of the nations a hope of the immediate future....

It was a shrewd effort of genuine statesmanship; it was also one upon which Colonel House, for almost the first time in the tortuous course of Wilsonian diplomacy, had not been consulted. On the day after it had gone there arrived in New York a friendly little note from the White House, explaining that time had been too short for summoning the Colonel. But the Note, which had been read to the Cabinet on Friday, had not been cabled until Monday evening — and New York is only six hours from Washington by train! It is Professor Seymour who notes the interesting detail that from about this time the customary salutation of the President's letters, 'Dearest Friend,' sank to 'My dear House.' The tone of the letters remained the same; but the President apparently no longer agreed with Colonel House that he required the latter's 'guidance,' and the passages which followed were to be largely Mr. Wilson's own.

On Monday evening, as the Note was going upon the wires, a great protest meeting against the Belgian deportations was being held in Carnegie Hall in New York. The Rev. William T. Manning presided and there was a telegram from Archbishop Ireland. Thus sanctified by the Church, the meeting continued with telegrams from Mr. Roosevelt and Mr. Choate and addresses in which the Hon. James M. Beck, Alton B. Parker and Elihu Root fanned the flames of hatred against Germany. At the same time a private dinner of the Vigilantes, 'an organization of writers working for preparedness,' was also being held. As General Wood arose to the applause it was with a grave face. 'Gentlemen,' he said, 'I have just received word that the President has today despatched another

Note to the German Government. In this Note he states that, so far as he can see, the aims of Germany and the Allies are the same.' There were 'exclamations of consternation and disgust. "Gentlemen," he went on, "we have no leadership in Washington."'

It suggests something of the atmospheres into which, on the morning of Wednesday, the 20th, there fell the public announcement of the Note. The response was what might have been expected. The Stock Market and the produce exchanges immediately collapsed. The Republican newspapers damned the Note at once as 'certain to favor the German side' and therefore obviously calculated to abolish all 'American influence for real peace, for just peace.' The pro-Ally Democratic papers like the *Times* mingled doubts as to whether the move would be of any use with their tepid applause. Mr. Hearst's anti-British *American* was certain that this 'brave and manly and opportune appeal... ends the war.' Mr. George Wharton Pepper summoned the Christians of America to repel 'any attempt to promote a premature peace in Europe' and collected many Christian signatures upon a public protest. Mr. William Jennings Bryan wired his congratulations to the President and his personal appeal to Mr. Lloyd George to accede to the beginning of peace negotiations. But through it all there seemed curiously little realization by either side of the vital American interest involved.

Returned again to Berlin, Mr. Gerard found the Germans 'simply delighted with the President's peace Note'; but from every Allied source, of course, the cries of anger and dismay resounded. For the Allies, unfortunately, could not state their real war aims. Their own peoples would have refused to go on fighting for all the territorial spoils they had been compelled to pledge each other. 'That ass President Wilson,' the British soldier, Sir Henry Wilson, disgustedly told his diary, 'has barged in and asked all belligerents their terms.' Mr. Houston found Maurice Low, Washington correspondent of the *Morning Post*, 'very much disturbed and angry' at this suggestion that the Allies, who had been fighting for two and a half years for justice and humanity, should translate these ends into some practical statement of what they wanted. Sir William Wiseman, the head of the British Secret Service in the United States, applied himself at once to Colonel House. Lord Bryce wrote a personal letter of protest to Mr. Wilson against a Note in which he appeared to draw no distinction between the aims of the combatants; while in London Lord Northcliffe told Mr. Page that 'everybody is angry as hell.' Mr. Asquith refused even to talk about it — 'it is most disheartening' — and the King, Page heard, broke down and wept.

But the Entente leaders might have felt less anger, and much less alarm, had they known that on the day the Wilson Note was filling all the newspapers, General Ludendorff was writing from the G.H.Q. at Pless to Zimmermann, the new Foreign Secretary: 'After Lloyd George has refused our peace offer by his declaration in the House of Commons, I am convinced, in view of the impressions I have received on the Western Front, that the U-boat campaign must now be inaugurated in full force.' On December 23 General Hindenburg followed it up with a letter to Bethmann-Hollweg: 'Wilson's efforts can change nothing.... I regard Wilson's suggestions as being inspired by England in order to delay' the submarine campaign. And on Christmas Eve the Chancellor, though still playing for time, replied:

[Unrestricted submarine war] can only be considered when our military situation offers us the guarantee that European neutrals can be restrained from making an attack upon us. Your Excellency believes that that time will have come by the end of January. On that assumption, and so far as I can bring myself to Your Excellency's conviction that the advantages of a wholesale and ruthless submarine campaign outweigh the disadvantages of the entry of America into the ranks of our enemies, I shall be prepared to consider even the unrestricted U-boat warfare....

iii

The German 'peace offensive' had been turned; like the West Front drives, it was a failure in its opening days, and what really remained was only the tragic confirmation of the fact and the consolidation of the new positions. Yet the President could not realize that the case was hopeless. A sad, and ominous, Christmas came and went — the third Christmas of the war. On the 27th the first disappointment arrived — from Berlin. To the President's request for a statement of war aims Zimmermann replied with only a brief and barely courteous announcement that his Government preferred the method it had already proposed of direct negotiations between the belligerents. Then on December 30 the State Department received the Allies' collective answer to the German peace offer. It was a long and passionate denunciation of Germany and a reassertion of the complete purity of the Entente cause:

> The so-called proposal, devoid of substance and of precision, circulated by the Imperial Government, appears less as an offer of peace than as a maneuver of war....
>
> As to the past, the German Note ignores all the facts, dates and figures which prove that the war was desired, incited and declared by Germany and Austria-Hungary....
>
> As regards the present..., to conclude a peace ... would be to the sole advantage of the aggressors who, having believed they could attain their object in two months, perceive after two years that it will never be attained.
>
> For the future, the ruins caused by the Germans' declaration of war, the innumerable aggressions committed by Germany and her allies against the belligerents and against neutrals demand penalties, reparations and guarantees; Germany eludes one and all....

So it went on — a savage outpouring, clearly designed to end all idea of peace, not only in the United States but in Germany as well. The Entente press, of course, rang with applause — and with confidence. Mr. Page was convinced that the German

' "invincibility" legend is fading out' and that the war would be over in six months or perhaps a year at the longest. At the Quai d'Orsay M. Cambon was telling Ambassador Sharp 'quite emphatically' that the war would be finished within three months. Mr. Sharp, unlike his colleague in London, could see that such estimates were 'incredible'; but Entente journalists were demonstrating that it was a mathematical impossibility for Austria-Hungary to hold out beyond midsummer and that the Central alliance must collapse. Perhaps only a handful of soldiers, politicians and diplomatists in the warring governments really knew how desperate was the Allies' situation. A British agent at Archangel had already written that within three months there would either be a separate peace] or a revolution in Russia. Britain's allies 'ought to be told now,' Sir Edward had declared as he was leaving office, 'that our support in shipping or finance, one or both, has to be curtailed in a few months.' Even with what remained of restricted U-boat warfare, ship losses had more than doubled since the summer. With the new war loan to be floated in January, Great Britain alone would have borrowed more than $1,000,000,000 from the American investor, and she was beginning to see the end of her collateral. The mutinies which were to paralyze the French army throughout much of 1917 were already germinating. But naturally there was no hint of any of this in either the Entente or the American newspapers.

Mr. Wilson, in the meanwhile, had been discussing with House what was to be the President's last effort — and in the minds of many one of the noblest efforts he ever made. Could not the President force the issue by himself stating what he believed to be reasonable and practicable peace terms? House had already suggested something of the kind, and was at once in his element — rearranging the map of Europe, carving up the Central Powers and distributing their fragments among the Allies. 'Alsace and Lorraine we were not quite certain of, but we agreed that Turkey [in Europe] should cease to exist.' They would free Poland, but in return do something about a warm-water seaport for Russia...

Fortunately, the President was to discard all this as far as his immediate purpose went; but the plan of a broad appeal, not to the recalcitrant governments of the belligerents but over their heads directly to their peoples, rapidly matured.

Yet the sands, by this time, were run nearly out. This conference was on January 3. At the Adlon Hotel in Berlin three days later the American Association of Commerce and Trade gave Ambassador Gerard a dinner. It was made an impressive affair; it was, in fact, 'a last, desperate attempt to preserve friendly relations.' All the important people in the Foreign Office came; so did many from other branches of the government, including Helfferich, the Vice-Chancellor. Important financial and industrial leaders were there, as well as the Mayor and Police President of Berlin. The Germans made friendly speeches, and Mr. Gerard declared in a short address that 'relations between the two countries had never been better' and that he was sure they would so continue. Actually, all 'the reasonable men present' including the Ambassador himself knew that only a miracle could now avert the break. The press comment next day was 'very friendly' and the Chancellor sent the Ambassador his thanks. But the deep shadow of the submarine lay over the whole affair. It was just three days afterward, at the G.H.Q. at Pless on January 9, that the final decision, so long delayed, so momentous in its consequences, was taken at last.

'Recorded' is perhaps a better word. When Bethmann-Hollweg, Hindenburg and Ludendorff met for the decisive audience with the Kaiser on January 9, the issue had all but settled itself. Bethmann no longer held any cards. After the Entente reply to his own peace offer he could advance no hope of direct negotiations. They all profoundly distrusted Wilson, and the failure of the Wilson Note in any way to shake the Entente determination left the Chancellor nothing to promise in the way of diplomatic action by the United States. That reduced the question to a purely technical military calculation. Bethmann declared his distrust of the Navy's promises; but that was a matter beyond the competence

of the political arm, and the military men were committed. So
the fateful decision ¹ was ratified at last. 'In about half an hour
the audience... came to an end.' When at two-thirty on the following afternoon M. Briand in Paris handed to Ambassador Sharp
the joint reply of the Entente Governments to President Wilson's
request that they state their war aims, the whole affair was already over.

A large part of the Allies' reply was devoted to another denunciation of the 'series of crimes perpetrated [by the Germans] without regard for universal reprobation.' It repeated the formula already being echoed and re-echoed in the Entente press: what
they wanted was 'reparation, restitution and... guarantees' against
another 'aggression' by the Central Powers. For the rest they
were fighting not for 'selfish interests, but above all to safeguard
the independence of peoples, of right and of humanity.' Having
laid this foundation, however, the Allies did permit themselves
to be a little more specific than Zimmermann had been. Their
demands included:

> The restoration of Belgium, of Serbia and of Montenegro, and the
> indemnities which are due them; the evacuation of the invaded
> territories of France, of Russia and of Rumania with just reparation;

¹ The decision was by no means the monumental folly it is often represented as
being. The Navy's estimate of probable sinkings was more than borne out. The Germans were correct in believing themselves safe from action by European neutrals, and
if anything rather overestimated the military effort which they calculated on from the
United States. They believed a 'considerable time' would be required before our
troops would appear in the field; actually it was not until a year and a half after the
Pless conference that we came into the battle line in any significant strength, and the
whole submarine calculation rested on the assumption that the U-boat would end
the war long before the summer of 1918.

All warfare is a gamble, but as long as the Germans believed victory in the land war
no longer possible to them, the submarine was a good gamble. Their real mistake,
perhaps, was less in overestimating the submarine than in underestimating their
chances of victory without it. They were blind to the imminence of the Russian collapse and the enormous advantage it would give them; they failed to appreciate the
desperate financial straits of the Allies or the disaffection in the French Army. The
American entry, repairing the Entente finances and preventing the disaster of morale
which might have followed on the Russian peace and the French munities, destroyed
these chances. Would the United States, however, have permitted Germany to win in
any event?

the reorganization of Europe, guaranteed by a stable régime and
founded as much upon respect for nationalities and full security and
liberty [of] economic development, which all nations, great or small,
possess, as upon territorial conventions ... ; the restitution of provinces
or territories wrested in the past from the Allies by force or against the
will of their populations, the liberation of Italians, of Slavs, of Rumanians and of Czecho-Slovaks from foreign domination; the en-
franchisement of populations subject to the bloody tyranny of the
Turks; the expulsion from Europe of the Ottoman Empire.

It is clear that these great (if still slightly vague) principles would
take in about all the 'selfish interests' that might occur to the
Allies as well as avoid any commitment as to the 'independence
of peoples' which happened to be subject to the Entente Powers.
After stating them, the Allies added that they had never desired
the 'extermination of the German peoples,' and there rested their
case, confident that their paramount wish 'to insure a peace upon
the principles of liberty and justice' would be apparent to all.

It seemed to be apparent, at any rate, to our own greatest and
most influential newspapers. The New York *Herald* proclaimed
these Carthaginian terms as 'a new Declaration of Independence
in behalf of civilization.' The New York *Times* applauded the
President for having elicited 'from the Allies this full and candid
statement of their purpose.' The *World* did feel that in 'at least
two minor respects' the terms were 'wholly immoral' (since they
offered to 'bribe' the Italians and Rumanians with territories
which had never belonged to those Powers); but elsewhere the
World felt that the reply 'touched the highest point of idealism
that has been reached in the international politics of Europe.'
It is true that there were, perhaps, a greater number of dubious
voices than in the earlier days of the great crusade; and Mr.
Hearst's *American*, with a somewhat more prophetic insight than
the others showed, could observe:

> The avowed object... is to completely destroy the political and
> commercial and industrial existence of the Teutonic and Magyar
> peoples and erect upon the ruins a Slav empire and minor Latin

states, which among them shall rule continental Europe, while England destroys German trade competition and asserts a complete lordship of the oceans of the world.... Instead of establishing permanent peace in the world, the program of conquest and division of spoils... makes another great war in the near future not only probable but ABSOLUTELY NECESSARY to the reasonable freedom of all the nations not included in this gigantic coalition.

But no one except the pro-Germans agreed with Mr. Hearst any longer — no one, that is, with the possible exception of Mr. Wilson. On the evening of January 11 the President, in a two-hour session with Colonel House, was going over his own draft outline of practicable peace terms. Mr. Wilson was not convinced of either the adequacy or the soundness of the Entente reply.

It was arranged that he would deliver his proposals in an address from the impressive forum of the Senate Chamber on January 22. Whether it was megalomania, as has so often been charged, whether it was the recluse's inability to understand the real power of the passions, ignorances and pettinesses that were everywhere arrayed against him, whether it was sheer, Presbyterian obstinacy or only his own sense of public responsibility — whatever the reason, Mr. Wilson went forward with his resolve to force a viable peace if it was humanly possible to do so. But on Friday, January 19, Count Bernstorff had received the official notice that unrestricted warfare would begin on February 1. When President Wilson stepped to the Senate desk on Monday to read one of the greatest of his state papers, the Germans had already reduced it to an academic issue.

The address of January 22, 1917, was an ingenious and powerful effort of constructive statesmanship. What it did was simply to take the idealist and propagandist rationalizations of the belligerent war aims and give them a practical application in the real world of men and nations. It established the necessary conditions to a viable peace conceived in such terms. Completing the address of May 27, it clearly and for the first time related the American people to such a peace, and distinguished — as our various Entente sympathizers and peace league men had never done — just what were our rights and our responsibilities in participating in its establishment:

> In every discussion of the peace that must end this war, it is taken for granted that that peace must be followed by some definite concert of power which will make it virtually impossible that any such catastrophe should ever overwhelm us again.... It is inconceivable that the people of the United States should play no part in that great enterprise.... But we owe it to candour and to a just regard for the opinion of mankind to say that, so far as our participation in guarantees of future peace is concerned, it makes a great deal of difference in what way and upon what terms [the war] is ended. The treaties and agreements which bring it to an end must embody terms which will create a peace that is worth guaranteeing and preserving, a peace that will win the approval of mankind, not merely a peace that will serve the several interests and immediate aims of the nations engaged....
>
> The question upon which the whole future peace and policy of the world depends is this: Is the present war a struggle for a just and secure peace, or only for a new balance of power?... Fortunately, we have received very explicit assurances on this point. The statesmen of both of the groups of nations now arrayed against one another have said, in terms that could not be misinterpreted, that it was no part of the purpose they had in mind to crush their antagonists. But the implications of these assurances may not be equally clear to all....
>
> They imply, first of all, that it must be a peace without victory. It is not pleasant to say this.... I am seeking only to face realities.... Victory would mean peace forced upon the loser, a victor's terms imposed upon the vanquished. It would be accepted in humiliation, under duress, at an intolerable sacrifice, and would leave a sting, a resentment, a bitter memory upon which terms of peace would rest, not permanently, but only as upon quicksand. Only a peace between equals can last, only a peace the very principle of which is equality and a common participation in a common benefit.

Upon this, the absolutely essential basis for the sort of peace in hope of which the millions were alone being nerved to sustain their suffering, President Wilson then established the broad conditions which would be necessary to the making and maintaining of it. All were deduced directly from the ideas which the Allies, and to a lesser degree the Germans, had been fostering for two years. The first was acceptance of 'the principle that governments derive all their just powers from the consent of the governed.' It was a combination of the Entente hatred for 'autocracy' with Mr. Balfour's useful 'principle of nationality.' The second was acceptance of the principle that every great Power should 'be assured a direct outlet to the great highways of the sea.' Again the President merely agreed with Mr. Balfour. The third condition was that the sea should 'alike in law and in fact be free' — an idea originally contributed by Sir Edward Grey and developed by the British and Germans alike in the long course of the submarine controversy. It was linked with the 'limitation of naval armaments' which in turn led on to the fourth condition: 'There can be no sense of safety and equality among the nations if great preponderating armaments are henceforth to continue here and there to be built up and maintained.' That was all.

That was all; yet the President had embraced in these few paragraphs nearly all the fundamental military, political and economic causes around which modern wars develop. The very simplicity of his four conditions reflected their far-reaching character; and today one can understand the extraordinary difficulty — perhaps the impossibility — of establishing them in the Western capitalistic world. Yet one can also believe that they were in fact the only conditions under which the kind of peace for which all the belligerent powers claimed to be fighting could conceivably have been established. They implied the end of modern imperialist nationalism. But if the nations wanted what they said they were dying for — if the United States wanted what its leaders of opinion said that it must have — this was, in fact, what all must accept to get it. The alternative was that so clearly perceived by Mr. Balfour — an armed truce dependent upon 'defensive alliances formed by those who desire to retain their possessions against those who desire to increase them.' Unfortunately, it is this alternative which we are today witnessing in operation; Mr. Wilson's address came far too late at best, and besides, it had already been cancelled by the German G.H.Q.

iv

The curt telegram already reposing in Count Bernstorff's safe, instructing him to announce on the last day of January that unrestricted warfare would begin on February 1, lends a rather grim irony to the explosions with which the 'Peace Without Victory' speech was received. Discretion modulated the first response of the Entente press, where the President was duly applauded for the nobility of his sentiments even as doubt was expressed concerning the practicability of ever putting them into effect. But the bitter anger did not fail to peep through between the lines of such diplomatic expressions. Mr. Page had cabled to the President in advance urging him to cut out the one little bit about 'peace without victory.' As this was the heart of the whole speech the President naturally could not, but Mr. Page was correct in his prediction that the phrase would give 'great offence in England, since it puts each side in the war on the same moral level.' Mr. Balfour was 'not much impressed.' Sir William Wiseman told House that although 'on the surface and officially' the address had been accepted with cordiality, 'underneath there was a deep feeling of resentment.' And the surface was very thin.

The American reaction was one of almost indescribable confusion. Secretary Houston studied the speech in bewilderment, finally deciding that what the President was really trying to do was only to caution the Allies to use their victory moderately. Senator Borah denounced the peace league idea as 'perfectly vicious, perfectly heinous and indefensible in morals.' Senator Lodge, no longer a Utopist, was working the Monroe Doctrine for all it was worth together with some die-hard Republican

papers. Other leaders of pro-Ally sentiment were working Belgium (on grounds the antithesis of the Monroe Doctrine) with equal vigor. Senator Tillman, a Democrat, thought the speech the 'most startling and the noblest utterance that has fallen from human lips since the Declaration of Independence'; while the Providence *Journal* felt that Mr. Wilson 'beckons the bleeding and suffering nations of the world toward him with his schoolmaster's cane and delivers a prize-oration on the millennium while civilization and the liberty of the world are battling for life in the shambles of a hundred fields.' The Bethlehem Steel Co. — and was it a reminder that the battling was not without its uses? — chose the day after the President's speech to announce a stock dividend of 200 per cent and an increase of the dividend rate. Ex-President Taft, one of the organizers of the League to Enforce Peace, expressed a curiously cautious and tepid approval; Mr. William Jennings Bryan, who opposed the league idea altogether, gave his support to much of what the President had said. Faced with such comment, Mr. Wilson seems to have felt no exultation; and he waited anxiously for the response from Germany, ignorant of the time bomb sleeping in Count Bernstorff's safe.

The telegram which announced the end of two and a half years of devoted labor had reached the Ambassador on January 19. That gave him just twelve days in which to work. He immediately fired one cable at Berlin:

> War inevitable in view of the proposed action.... I shall have to give the password for unnavigable German steamers [the orders to disable the interned liners] on February 1, as effect of carrying out my instructions here will be like declaration of war, and strict guard will be kept. In any case, an incident like that of the Lusitania may be expected soon. If military reasons are not absolutely imperative ... postponement most urgently desirable. Wilson believes he can obtain peace on the basis of our proposed equal rights of all nations....

And then, knowing how little hope there was in Berlin, he applied himself to Colonel House. The Senate speech three days later gave him something; he seized upon it and hurried off another urgent telegram to stay the fatal submarine. The same day there was a wire from Colonel House asking him to come to New York; not until the 26th, however, with only five days left, did this meeting take place. Then the Ambassador found that the Colonel had, not merely his own ideas to offer, but a memorandum from the President himself. This document (it was read, but not delivered, to the Ambassador) was a definite offer to act as mediator in bringing about a peace by negotiation. Mr. Wilson wanted the Germans to submit peace terms which he might publish; he was confident that if the Germans could only trust him he would be able to bring about a conference. It was so strong as to leave Bernstorff 'in no doubt whatever that Mr. Wilson was certain of being able to achieve this end'; the President, indeed, thought the Allied reply to his peace offer was a bluff and that a conference could be achieved in time to stop the spring offensives.

Realizing the immense possible importance of this, Count Bernstorff rushed it upon the cables, imploring Berlin to hold off the submarine if only for a few days — if only until some offer to negotiate from the German side could at least be got upon the record in order to soften somewhat the American reaction to the U-boat. This cable was at Pless on January 29, with only two days left. Perhaps by that time it would have been impossible to halt the U-boats anyway, as many of them must already have been at sea with their orders. Perhaps the responsible German authorities had really interpreted the Wilson speech (as they afterward claimed to have done and as many Americans had done) to be a maneuver inspired by the Entente. Hindenburg declares that he never even heard of the new message from Bernstorff until months afterward. Ludendorff, on the other hand, has recorded the meeting at Pless on the 29th, when Bethmann and Zimmermann produced it before the Kaiser:

The whole discussion took place in one of the Emperor's rooms and occupied but little time. The Emperor's birthday presents were still lying about, and I remember in particular a fine picture of the cruiser Emden....

It had no effect. On the same day Bethmann cabled Bernstorff his reply. He thanked the President politely for the proposed mediation, and professed Germany's readiness to accept the offer. Where the President had asked, however, for dramatically moderate terms with which he might undercut the Entente governments with their own and with the American people, the Chancellor sent only a diplomatist's list of outside demands. Though perhaps slightly more moderate than those which had been announced by the Entente they were of a character which no American President could possibly have supported; while to make the rebuff more complete, they were supplied for the President's private information alone. It amounted simply to a flat rejection of the idea. Count Bernstorff was at the same time ordered to carry out his instructions in regard to the submarine war. It was the end.

The short winter's day closed down upon a peaceful Washington. Count Bernstorff, sitting in the Embassy he had so long and so skillfully defended, duly transcribed the answer and prepared to mail it through Colonel House. He drew his bombshell from the safe where he had hoped to stifle it:

'Germany [he was instructed to announce] will meet the illegal measures of her enemies by forcibly preventing after February 1, 1917, in a zone around Great Britain, France, Italy and in the eastern Mediterranean all navigation, that of neutrals included, from and to England and from and to France, etc. All ships met within that zone will be sunk. The Imperial Government is confident that this measure will result in a speedy termination of the war.

As a concession, one American passenger ship was to be permitted to go to and from Falmouth, England, every week, provided that she carried no contraband and was marked with 'three vertical stripes one meter wide each to be painted alternately white and red' and displayed at each masthead 'a large flag checkered white and red,' all these marks to be fully illuminated at night. Otherwise, American citizens could avoid injury by remaining outside the war zones. After that, there was certainly no hope whatever.

On the morning of Wednesday, January 31, Count Bernstorff telegraphically ordered the German liner crews in New York and other ports to disable their ships; he dropped the Chancellor's reply to Colonel House in the mails, and then, as the afternoon lengthened, he collected his documents and set out for the State Department.

XI. ARMED NEUTRALITY

i

IT was a little after four o'clock when Count Bernstorff entered Mr. Lansing's office at the State Department for his 'last political interview in America.' Solemnly the Ambassador handed to the Secretary of State his official communication. 'We both knew that the end had come, but we did not admit the fact to each other. The Secretary of State contented himself with replying that he would submit my communication to the President.' The Ambassador bowed himself out. No hint of his business had been given to the reporters at the State Department. But before five an Associated Press 'flash' was in the newspaper offices and the rumor was running through the streets. It was the A.P. bulletin which first brought the news to the White House. In the Executive Offices the President had just concluded an interview with Mr. Herbert Hoover, chairman of the Belgian Relief. Mr. Tumulty at once took the bulletin in to Mr. Wilson. 'As I entered, he looked up from his writing, casual enquiry in his eyes. Without comment I laid the fateful slip of paper on his desk, and silently watched him as he read and re-read it.' Quietly Mr. Wilson handed it back. 'The break,' he said, 'now seems inevitable.' The text arrived a few minutes later; so did the newspapermen. It was announced that there would be no statement and that the President would see no callers; Mr. Wilson then retired from the Executive Offices to the White House proper, to spend the rest of the evening alone with the German Note in the seclusion of his study.

Outside, excitement seethed. The extras were on the streets in the early evening. Ex-President Taft refused to comment. Ex-President Roosevelt shrilly called upon Mr. Wilson to pay no attention to the German threats. 'If he had acted as he should have acted at the time I asked him to act — at the time of the Lusitania affair — Germany would now have something besides notes to fear!' In his apartment in East Fifty-Third Street Colonel House was at once in a furious whirl of business:

> As the afternoon grew late, the excitement became intense, for the different press agencies had begun to receive the news. Wiseman, Gaunt, newspapermen, etc., etc., called me up to discuss it. We had a dinner engagement at the Plaza with Frank Trumbull, and the confusion of dressing, of receiving visitors and of answering telegrams and telephone calls was something beyond endurance.

Sir William Wiseman thoughtfully warned him that the Germans were planning to do something to their interned ships. This, of course, the Germans had a perfect right to do; but without troubling with such details the Colonel at once telephoned Dudley Field Malone, the Collector of the Port. Mr. Malone was likewise on his way to a dinner, but he broke the engagement and turned immediately 'to take such precautions as seemed necessary.' House finally got off to the Plaza, where he dined with 'Mrs. Henry Redmond, Stuyvesant Fish and an Englishman, Mr. Askwith.' Even there he was 'constantly interrupted by telephone calls'; and he tore himself away early, for he had arranged to take the midnight train to Washington. Mr. Malone called at about eleven to drive him to the station, and when they got there the Colonel 'could see that there was a good deal of suppressed excitement' among the railway officials 'who knew of my departure.' He was at the White House in time for breakfast.

In Washington that morning it was being 'taken for granted' that a break of relations was inevitable. In Wall Street the market opened with a flood of selling orders under which even U.S. Steel Common staggered, while the rest of the list was plunged for an hour or two into a 'complete demoralization' amounting almost to a panic. Not until later in the day did the more long-headed speculators, with a sounder appreciation of the effect of war on stock prices, come heavily into the market to arrest the decline. It was rumored that Mr. 'Barney' Baruch, on his way to his southern shooting preserve, had jumped from the train at a way-station and begun 'pouring in covering orders,... thus offsetting the public's wild delirium.' Now that their cause was wholly lost, the pacifists were galvanized into a desperate activity. Miss Lillian Wald's American Union Against Militarism telegraphically demanded of the President (over the signatures of Oswald Garrison Villard, Henry W. L. Dana, Carlton J. H. Hayes, George Foster Peabody, John Haynes Holmes, Max Eastman and others) that he be not 'dragooned into war.' The American Neutral Conference Committee called a mass-meeting in Madison Square Garden for the following evening, with William Jennings Bryan as chief speaker. But if the pacifists were rallying, so were the war-hawks. Senator Lodge devoted the afternoon to tearing the 'peace without victory' speech to ribbons for the edification of the Senate, at the same time perfecting his own transition from a believer in Utopia to chief *saboteur* of what had now become the President's peace league. In the cloakrooms and 'wherever members of Congress spoke privately with one another, there was no attempt to conceal the gravity of the situation.... Congress is merely waiting for the President's word.' The break everywhere 'seemed only a matter of hours'; and Count Bernstorff, pausing merely to deny that he had already received his passports, went to a moving picture show.

In the White House, strangely enough, the President and his adviser had been playing pool. From the first there seems to have been little question about breaking relations. House breakfasted alone; and when Mr. Wilson presently came in, it appeared that Secretary Lansing was already at work drafting the papers for Bernstorff's dismissal. House gave the President Bethmann's reply to the offer of mediation; Mr. Wilson read it through, and 'saw at once how perfectly shallow it was.' After all their talk of peace, the Germans had not only kicked him in the face; they had made a dupe of him as well. The President felt 'as if the world had suddenly reversed itself... and that he could not get his balance'; he seemed 'sad and depressed,' and all the Colonel's cheery efforts failed to restore him to 'a better frame of mind.' The point over which there was most discussion was whether Bernstorff should be sent home at once or not until an 'overt act' had been committed. House, who had throughout been convinced that a diplomatic break must lead to war, was in favor of the first course; but he was alarmed to find Mr. Wilson still refusing to accept an American participation in the slaughter:

> The President was insistent that he would not allow it to lead to war if it could possibly be avoided. He reiterated his belief that it would be a crime for this Government to involve itself in the war to such an extent as to make it impossible to save Europe afterward. He spoke of Germany as 'a madman that should be curbed.' I asked if he thought it fair to the Allies to ask them to do the curbing without doing our share. He noticeably winced at this, but still held to his determination not to become involved if it were humanly possible.

But the Colonel could well bide his time. There could be little doubt now about our ultimate involvement. The whole discussion lasted barely half an hour, and there 'was nothing further to say.' They sat about listlessly waiting for Mr. Lansing. 'The President nervously arranged his books and walked up and down the floor. Mrs. Wilson spoke of golf, and asked whether I thought it would look badly if the President went on the links. I thought the American people would feel that he should not do anything so trivial at such a time.' Consequently, they tried pool instead; and the balls solemnly rolled and clicked across the table until, toward the end of the second game, Mr. Lansing at last arrived. The Secretary proved to be 'so nearly of our mind' that again there was little discussion. They did agree, however, to make the break at once — for the rather naïve reason that this might possibly bring the Germans 'to their senses.' The President was bound by a promise to Senator Stone that he would not actually sever relations without telling him; the Senator happened to be in St. Louis and it was therefore necessary to wait until he could be brought back to Washington. But the decision, if it can be called a decision, had been taken. House left for New York again the same afternoon.

Next morning, Friday, February 2, the headlines still flamed; the editorial pages flamed more passionately than the headlines. 'Piracy' and 'a return to murder' were 'favorite expressions of the American press in describing Germany's move.' Mr. Hearst still sounded a note of caution: 'I think that the President fully realizes that advice from blusterers like Roosevelt is not either serious or sincere.... Notes are better than bullets; ink is cheaper than blood, and if there had been more writing in Europe there would have been less fighting.' But even Mr. Hearst was already maneuvering to be on the patriotic (and profitable) side if war should come; while if there was any really important or influential journalistic voice raised to counsel directly against a severance of relations, it was not audible in the impassioned East.

When the Cabinet gathered for its regular Friday meeting, it was, according to Secretary Redfield, with 'a certain sense of relief that we need hesitate no longer and that the matter was settled by forces whose weight was beyond all doubt.' Secretary Lane thought it was simply a case of Germany's being about 'to turn "mad dog" again.' Secretary Houston felt that the Note, especially the part about one American ship being allowed to sail under a checkerboard flag, 'was the last word of a mad war-lord — the farthest limit of dictation.' The President asked them what they thought he should do. One man countered, very sensibly, by asking which side the President wanted to see win the war. Mr. Wilson answered that he wanted neither to win. This led to a discussion of the world problem, in the course of which the rather startling idea cropped up that the United States should take no action against Germany, but should preserve her neutrality in order to be in a position in later years to defend the white race from the coming menace from the yellow. At that, 'several of us immediately began to speak.' Mr. Baker and Mr. Daniels — the two war secretaries! — seemed impressed by this 'long look ahead'; but Mr. McAdoo was all for 'prompt action' and 'did much talking,' while Mr. Houston, the martial spirit who ruled over the Department of Agriculture, was firm 'for asserting our rights, for standing with the Allies, for doing our part for our sake and for humanity.'

> The President said: 'Very well. That does not reach far enough. What is the proposal? What is the concrete suggestion?'...
> I replied: 'Do not wait to set out a full program. Immediately sever diplomatic relations and let come what will....'

If Mr. Houston's report of the discussion is a fair one, it is not hard to understand why the President soon broke it off. At the Capitol that afternoon he held another conference with the leading Democratic Senators, but it can hardly have been of much importance, since no one troubled to close the doors, and the reporters in the corridor could watch the group as it talked. Everywhere the break was a foregone conclusion. Spring Rice, who only a short time before had been seeing visions of the United States turning into an ally of the Germans, was now cheerfully astonished 'to observe how greatly sentiment has changed within a few weeks'; and he could speak in almost kindly terms of the country. And Spring Rice's friend, Mr. Roosevelt, was preparing to humble himself at last before the Administration which he hated. It was on February 2 that he wrote to the Secretary of War:

> I have already on file... my application to be permitted to raise a Division of Infantry... in the event of war (possibly with the permission to make one or two of the brigades of infantry, mounted infantry).... If you believe that there will be war, and a call for volunteers to go to war immediately, I respectfully and earnestly request that you notify me at once.

That same evening, on the other hand, a crowd of 5000 men and women were making Madison Square Garden rock with their applause as Mr. Bryan cried that the United States should never 'get down and wallow in the mire of human blood.' Mr. Bryan refused to be bound by those rash ultimata of the President. War was not the only possible issue from the submarine imbroglio. We could keep our ships out of the danger zone or our citizens off the ships. We could arbitrate the question when the war was over; or at least submit the issue of war to a direct popular vote. The American people, Mr. Bryan urged, were not willing to send American troops to fight 'under the banners of any European monarch, or to die on European soil in settlement of European quarrels.' He implored them to wire their Congressmen: 'A few cents now may save many dollars in taxation and possibly a son.' From the mass-meeting there sprang a new organization, the Emergency Peace Federation. It was to spread throughout the country in the next few weeks; its Keep-Us-Out-Of-War committees were to fill the land with meetings. But the cause was buried now, under the accumulated history of two and a half lunatic years. The papers which reported Mr. Bryan's speech next morning also carried the announcement that President Wilson would address the two Houses of Congress at two o'clock that afternoon, Saturday, February 3.

It gathered an enormous crowd. Long before two o'clock the corridors of the Capitol were jammed with people importuning Congressmen for admission to galleries already overflowing. Thousands milled about outside the building, though it was before the day of the loudspeaker. Awaiting the President in the chamber of the House there was 'probably the most impressive audience' that had gathered there 'in many years.' Every Representative was in his seat, some with their 'little sons on their knees.' In the diplomatic galleries the Allied Ambassadors were conspicuous. Mrs. Wilson was in the executive gallery, equipped with an opera glass. Shortly before two the Chief Justice of the Supreme Court entered, followed by the Associate Justices; behind them there came every member of the Cabinet — save the Secretary of State, who had, as they all knew, other business to attend to — and finally the Senate, marching two by two down the center aisle in all its majesty. All took their seats; the hush fell, and then was shattered in a great burst of applause as the President of the United States was escorted to the rostrum. 'Gentlemen of the Congress: The Imperial German Government on the 31st of January ——'

Briefly the President rehearsed his Note of April 18, 1916, with its declaration that unless unrestricted submarine war was abandoned, the United States could 'have no choice but to sever diplomatic relations with the German Empire.' He read the answering pledge of May 4; and the firm interpretation which he had put upon it in his reply of May 8 and to which, as he stated, Germany had made no answer.[1] He then read the recent Note. 'I think you will agree with me,' he said, 'that, in view of this declaration, which suddenly and without prior intimation of any kind deliberately withdraws the solemn assurance... of the 4th of May, 1916, this Government has no alternative... but to take the course which in its Note of 18th of April, 1916, it announced that it would take.... I have, therefore, directed the Secretary of State to announce to his excellency the German Ambassador that all diplomatic relations —' As he reached the words there was a thunderous burst of applause from Democrats and Republicans alike. Senator 'Pitchfork Ben' Tillman of South Carolina was the first to give way to the intense emotion; Senator Henry Cabot Lodge of Massachusetts was the second; and the whole chamber, floor and galleries together, joined in. '— are severed,' the President concluded when it died. But then he went on: 'I refuse to believe that it is the intention of the German authorities to do in fact what they have warned us they will feel at liberty to do.... Only actual overt acts on their part can make me believe it even now.'

So it was not war, after all — not yet. If American ships or

[1] See p. 293 and pp. 299-300.

lives should actually be sacrificed, the President promised, he would again come before Congress to ask authority 'to use any means that may be necessary for the protection of our seamen and our people in the prosecution of their peaceful and legitimate errands on the high seas.' Did that mean that there would never be a real war at all? Not, perhaps, if the President could help it; but the thread by which he thus left the nation's peace still hanging was an extremely slender one.

As the President had begun to speak, Mr. Lansing had handed his passports to Ambassador Bernstorff, while the cable had already gone to Ambassador Gerard, instructing him to request his own. All diplomatic representatives in neutral countries were directed to announce that diplomatic relations between the United States and the German Empire were at an end.

ii

By breaking off diplomatic relations — a step which seemed so natural, so necessary and so little decisive that it was taken almost without discussion or opposition — President Wilson had deprived himself of all further command over the situation. There were three primary factors in his problem, and at a stroke he had lost control of each of them. Obviously, nothing was now to be expected from the Germans. The Entente statesmen, on the other hand, now had no further fears of American action on behalf of Germany; consequently, nothing more was to be got from them except, possibly, as the price of an active American participation in the war. But finally, and perhaps most important of all, the President had lost control over his own public. As he broke relations with Germany he automatically strengthened each of the many forces which were hurrying the nation into the holocaust; he swept opinion into martial patterns which gave those forces their freest rein, and he disqualified himself from the task, had he wished to attempt it, of mobilizing a counter sentiment. It was apparently to take him some weeks fully to realize the fact, but as the reverberations of the break resounded through the world, the President was fairly launched upon the whirlwind.

The nation met the crisis with a noble resolution, and a thrilling conviction that war was certain. 'Without Fear and Without Reproach' Mr. F. I. Cobb headed his solemn editorial in the New York *World* that Sunday morning:

> The national conscience is clear. In all the records of history there will be found no other example of a great and powerful nation exerting such effort and making such sacrifices to keep the peace as the United States has done.... If all our efforts have come to naught and we, too, must be plunged into the crater of calamity, let us at least thank God that we shall enter the war on the right side.

St. Luke's Episcopal Church in New York staged a 'big military service,' with the choir marching in behind an immense American flag and with the rector, the Rev. G. Ashton Oldham, announcing from the pulpit his readiness to 'lay down my life, if my country needs it, for the rights of humanity and what I believe to be the cause of God.' Other churches were quickly to imitate this inspiring example. Mr. Sam Gompers peremptorily cabled Carl Legien, the president of the German trades union federation, demanding that he put pressure on his government to halt the submarine; and when the German presently responded with the suggestion that Mr. Gompers put pressure on England to raise the food blockade, the great American labor leader felt that this answer was a patent 'evasion of duty.'

In London that Saturday evening the enthusiasm could but with difficulty be restrained. Mr. Page and his staff had been waiting anxiously all day in the Embassy. Not until nine o'clock did the first news arrive, when Admiral Hall, the head of the British Naval Intelligence, came dashing in. An aid met him; he 'stopped abruptly and uttered just two words: "Thank God!"' So then they knew. The Admiral hurried in to the Ambassador, and laid before him a code message from Captain Guy Gaunt:

> Bernstorff has just been given his passports. I shall probably get drunk tonight.

To Mr. Page, to all of them, it was the great dream come true — or almost come true. Even before the news arrived Colonel Repington had been at work upon an article for the London *Times* on the American Army. At the War Office he had got some information on the subject and had been given the interesting idea 'that if America comes in we could more rapidly absorb American volunteers in our Army than the U.S. can in hers.' This thought, however, was not among those which Mr. Lloyd George poured out in rapid fire upon Mr. Page when the Ambassador reached 10 Downing Street promptly on Sunday morning. The Prime Minister 'hoped that in no event would our supply of ammunition be curtailed, and that a much larger supply of steel could be got from the United States, and he asked earnestly about our merchant shipbuilding activities.' Were the Great Lakes shipyards doing all they could? Might the British be in any way of help? 'I have already directed our Army Chief of Staff and the First Sea Lord,' Mr. Lloyd George ran on, 'to give you all possible information out of our experience that you may ask for.' Could other departments be of service? 'If so, come and see me at any time, and I will open the way.'

The Prime Minister was full of the idea that the break meant war. Mr. Page, to his credit, met this with officially correct discouragement — though hardly, one may imagine, with conviction. In the House of Commons Mr. Asquith was publicly polite; so was Mr. Bonar Law. To Lord Bryce an American entry not unnaturally appeared both 'practically unavoidable' and 'desirable in the interests of mankind'; and he now turned to at once 'trying by letter and pamphlets to make neutrals in Switzerland and your Western states realize these supreme moral issues.' With the British public, keyed to an angry contempt for the President's peace moves, the transition was perhaps a trifle too abrupt; but in the first days Mr. Page could report to Mr. Wilson that 'public as well as official opinion continues to become more cordial.... It was becoming fearful lest we should wander from the road of practical action. Now both the Government and the press understand and heartily appreciate your whole wise and patient course. I think the expectation is general that the Germans will force war on us.'

The news was at Berlin with the noon papers on Sunday. Herr Stresemann, who had always been bitter against the United States, was finishing a speech before a conservative gathering in which he had argued that America would take no action, when someone arose in the audience with the newspaper in his hand. The papers reached the Embassy just as Mr. Gerard was going in to luncheon, with two Foreign Office officials among his guests. 'The lunch was far from cheerful. The Germans looked very sad and said practically nothing, while I tried to make polite conversation at my end of the table.' Now that the long tension had been broken at last, the hostility was to dissolve in a queer afterglow of the old friendship. A police guard was promptly furnished for the Embassy, but there were no disturbances. On Tuesday afternoon Mr. Gerard went alone for a long walk through the Berlin streets — was it to take a regretful farewell of the city in which, on the whole, he had had such a gorgeous time? — and no one offered to molest him.

In Brussels Mr. Whitlock was learning to his annoyance and almost to his surprise that with the severance of relations he could no longer enjoy the forms and advantages of diplomatic status. Our public was much angered to hear that the authorities had asked him to haul down the American flag which had floated for so long above the Legation; but the Germans were not impolite about it, and readily agreed that Mr. Whitlock and his staff might remain as private officials of the Belgian Relief. In Berlin as in Brussels there were some embarrassments, it is true; but when Mr. Gerard was finally ready to leave he had 'a pleasant farewell talk' with both the Chancellor and Zimmermann. It was on February 10 that he got off at last from the Potsdammer station with his flock of over a hundred diplomatic and consular officials and American citizens. The Foreign Office sent down four of its people to see them off, and a couple of Army officers were detailed as a formal escort to the border. The Ambassador had ordered 'plenty of champagne and cigars to be put on the train' for the entertainment of these gentlemen; and so they all rolled pleasantly down to Switzerland. At the frontier the Ambassador gave to each escort a gold cigarette case engraved with the recipient's name. They shook hands; and Mr. Gerard passed out of Germany, his role in world history honorably and intelligently fulfilled.

The break had come; as yet, however, Mr. Wilson (like the editors who were so enraged about the flag on the Brussels Legation) had scarcely realized its full consequences. At the Cabinet meeting on Tuesday, the 6th, there was a good deal of talk about the protection of American ships in the war zones; nothing much was decided, however, while the President (according to Mr. Lane) declared himself 'passionately' resolved to avoid the smallest aggressive act or violation of punctilio in dealing with Germany. 'If we are to have war, we must go in with our hands clean.' Yet this, perhaps, was not the only reason for Mr. Wilson's determination. On the verge of war already, the President was about to launch his last 'peace offensive.' He had broken with Germany, but Austria-Hungary — as few stopped to remember — remained.

It was on February 8 that President Wilson initiated this final effort. Mr. Page was instructed to take up, directly and informally with 'the leading members of the Government,' the possibility of working for peace through Austria. Mr. Wilson pointed out that the one great obstacle to getting peace in this way was the Allies' own announcement that they were fighting for a 'virtual dismemberment of the Austro-Hungarian Empire'; what he wanted was a guaranty from the Entente which would remove this fear of dismemberment, at least so far as the 'older units of the Empire' were concerned. The British, bound by their treaties, could not give such assurances, of course, and Mr. Lloyd George held out no encouragement. But the Prime Minister did not conclude his interview with the American Ambassador without taking care to soften its effect. At the end he spoke 'with warmth and admiration' of the President and 'substantially as follows':

We want him to come into the war not so much for help with the war as for help with peace. My reason is not mainly the military nor naval nor economic nor financial pressure that the American Government and people might exert in their own way against Germany; grateful as this would be I have a far loftier reason.... The President's presence at the peace conference is necessary for the proper organization of the world which must follow peace. I mean that he himself must be there in person....

Most of the present belligerents will have suffered so heavily that their judgment also may have suffered, and most of those that win will want some concrete gain, old wrongs righted or boundaries changed. Even Great Britain, who wants nothing for herself, will be prevented from returning the German colonies.[!] South Africa and Australia will not permit the giving back of lands that would make them neighbors to German subjects and give Germany secret submarine bases throughout the whole world.

The United States wants nothing but justice and an ordered freedom and guarantees of these for the future. Nobody therefore can have so commanding a voice as the President. Convey to him this deep conviction of mine. He must help make peace if the peace made at that conference is to be worth keeping. American participation in the war would enable him to be there and the mere moral effect of this participation would shorten the war, might even end it very quickly.

As the Prime Minister of Great Britain spoke these remarkable words — so rich in suggestion, so skillfully bare of commitment, so flattering and so vague — what is one to suppose that he was really thinking? Even as one reads and re-reads them they seem to change their shape and color and significance. One cannot say what was in Mr. Lloyd George's mind; but as Mr. Page committed the interview to the cables it is evident that another foundation had been laid for that 'de-bamboozling' trouble which Mr. J. M. Keynes was to record two years later at Versailles.

On February 12, two days after this interview, Colonel House complacently noted in his diary that Mr. Wilson's declaration that he would not go to war 'seems unlikely to be verified, for we are drifting into it as rapidly as I expected.' A resolution endorsing the break with Germany was introduced into the Senate at Mr. Lodge's instigation. It passed with but five dissenting votes. One was that of Senator La Follette; two were supplied by Senators Gronna and Works, both Progressively inclined Republicans, and the other two were from Bryanite Democrats. Senator Lodge seems to have been rather surprised by the negative vote from Senator Works. The latter, Mr. Lodge wrote, was not only 'a high-minded, conscientious, upright man,' he was also 'a soldier of the Civil War'; yet in spite of all that he was 'perfectly unreasonable about peace and there is no doing anything with him.' It was very curious.

The wheels of the great engine of preparedness were turning already of their own motion, as lesser officials within the government or enthusiasts outside it sprang to demonstrate their readiness in the hour of need. At the War College the experts were 'putting in sixteen hours a day to meet the influx of requests for recommendations from the Secretary and the Chief of Staff.' Just before the crisis General Pershing had at last been ordered out of Mexico. There were still some 50,000 National Guardsmen on the border, but the Mexican menace was now forgotten, and as these troops were brought home, that possible embarrassment to the prosecution of a major war in Europe seemed finally liquidated. At Washington, the military men were drafting the bill to establish 'universal service,' thus making possible (and, therefore, inevitable) the raising and despatch of a conscript mass army to Europe. 'Drastic measures' were being framed 'for dealing with spies'; they were the basis for the later famous Espionage Act which, though it never caught any spies, served very usefully for the suppression of the Constitutional guaranties and for dealing with domestic war-resisters and pacifists. On February 13 the House voted 353 to 23 for the largest naval appropriations bill in the nation's history. On the same day Secretary Lane, as a member of the Council of National Defence, was galvanizing the industrialists of its Advisory Commission into instant activity, urging them to plan 'for the mobilization of all our national industries and resources,' and helping to set up the nation-wide committees of business men from which the dollar-a-year people were later to be recruited.

The church, of course, was already mobilized. The Rev. George A. Gordon of the Old South Church in Boston was soon winning an immense reputation for his sermon: 'Was Jesus a Pacifist?' It is true that a neighboring clergyman found difficulty in imagining the Saviour clad in khaki and a gas mask and hurling a hand grenade or unloosing a machine gun 'to spatter wounds and death among his fellow men.' But even after two and a half (censored) years of it, there were few who could picture war in such harshly realistic terms as these; and even the pacifists were now giving way. Mr. Henry Ford went over with a resounding splash. He was reported to have given not only his factory but his fortune to the Government, offering to build '1000 small submarines a day and 3000 motors a day' without profit. Mr. Schiff, the great banker who had honorably stood out for a rational and impartial attitude toward the war, was discovering that his viewpoint had 'undergone a thorough change,' and was to wave flags and sell bonds with the rest. Even Mr. Bryan was preparing to 'support the Government' should war actually come.

Count Bernstorff and his Embassy staff at last left Washington on February 14 and sailed from New York next day — 'inexpressibly sad,' as the Ambassador wrote in his farewell letter to Colonel House. So that link was broken. Everywhere the ground was simply slipping out from beneath the President's feet. On February 20 one glimmer of hope appeared — in the shape of a telegram from Page announcing that Mr. Lloyd George had now 'completely changed' his views as to peace negotiations through Austria. However, the Prime Minister still withheld those guaranties against dismemberment for which the President had asked. The most the Entente could do was to offer up the Czechs as a sacrifice. They were willing to leave Bohemia to the Empire and would not seek to separate Austria from Hungary. It was little enough to work with; but on February 22 Mr. Penfield at Vienna was instructed to dangle these very 'limited assurances against dismemberment' before the hard-pressed Government of the young Emperor Karl. Again it was the birthday of George Washington, and the first anniversary of the House-Grey Memorandum. This telegram was President Wilson's last, belated effort to preserve his countrymen from the bloody embrace of the 'entangling alliance' into which the Lodges and the Roosevelts, equally with the Tafts and Roots and Eliots, the Pages and Houses and McAdoos and, to a large extent, the President himself had combined to thrust them. The cable was to bring no results. Before the fact was apparent, however, other events had already taken command.

iii

The one element now rapidly emerging as the dominant factor in the situation was, strangely enough, the submarine campaign. In the moral satisfaction of bringing retribution down upon the faithless Teuton, few had paid much attention to the submarine itself. It was widely assumed that the Germans had resorted to the U-boat either from sheer lunacy or merely to gratify their innate lust for crime; and the sobering thought that they might also have taken it up because it was a militarily powerful instrument occurred to almost no one. The French Minister of Marine assured the world that the U-boat, though 'horrible,' was quite 'ineffective'; and Mr. Winston Churchill even let Mr. Page know that he had 'had a careful mathematical study made of the whole problem which demonstrates conclusively to him that the submarines must fail to embarrass shipping very seriously for any considerable period.'

Unfortunately, the ship-owners failed to appreciate the beauties of mathematics. It was soon observed that almost no merchantmen were being detained for examination at Kirkwall, for the simple reason that Scandinavian shipping was remaining 'to a large extent in home ports.' Mr. Frost, our Consul at Cork, was noting that the U-boats, despite the destruction wrought upon them by the Admiralty, were sinking a dozen ships a week off that port alone. Oddly enough, Mr. Frost's conclusion was the exact opposite of the French Minister's; the U-boat war, it seemed to him, was not only very effective but noticeably lacking in horror. He was struck by the 'exceedingly few lives... lost in proportion to the number of vessels sunk.' In general there was no doubt that 'when they can safely do so, except in the rarest cases, the submarines take pleasure in extending every courtesy and consideration to the vessels which they destroy.'

But they missed no opportunity to destroy them, and they were doing so at a rapid rate. In January, the last month of the restricted war, the Germans sank 368,000 tons; in February they destroyed 540,000, and the figures were to rise all through March and April. British merchant ships and crews continued to sail with stolid courage; but worse than the actual sinkings was the fact that in the first weeks, at least, neutral shipping was terrorized from the seas, just as the Germans had hoped. American-flag vessels, like the Scandinavian, were remaining in port and clamoring for protection, for convoy, for naval guns and gun crews. As early as February 6 this was the chief topic of discussion in the Cabinet. Mr. Wilson agreed that American ships might arm themselves if they wished, but refused to offer them any governmental assistance. Yet at each succeeding Cabinet the subject recurred. At the Cabinet meeting on Friday, the 16th, the situation seemed 'more embarrassing and critical' than ever. American ships were simply 'interning' themselves. So great a congestion had now accumulated in the export terminals that the railroads were forced that day to declare an embargo on further shipments to the seacoast. The President was unmoved. At the meeting of the Council of National Defence on the 17th Secretaries Houston and Lane agreed that action was imperative — though for rather mixed reasons. 'We should side with the Allies,' Mr. Houston felt, 'promptly and wholly.... I would rather see this nation side with the Allies, go down to destruction with them if necessary and disappear from the map as a nation, than see it exist and prosper subject in the slightest degree to the dictation of an arrogant mediæval tyrant and his supporters.' Their emotions were running away with them all, and the armed ship question had already become, in reality, the question of a full-scale participation in the war.

Sir Cecil Spring Rice was praying for 'the destruction of an American ship with American passengers.' Unfortunately, this was impossible as long as American passenger ships did not sail; but Mr. P. A. S. Franklin, 'a very energetic man,' as the Ambassador called him, and head of the one American-flag transatlantic passenger line, was ready enough 'to send his ships in the danger zone with passengers on board' if only the Government would give him guns. He applied pressure by announcing that he was unloading his ships and discharging their crews until such a time as the guns should be forthcoming.[1] Then on February 20 a remarkable occurrence took place in New York City. Thousands of women poured out of the East Side tenement districts in a riotous protest against the enormous increases in the price of food. 'They upset pushcarts and barrows of food peddlers and in some cases threw kerosene on the stock. They improvised boycotts and drove away intending purchasers. Hundreds of women marched to the City Hall shouting "Give us food!" "Feed our children!" And later a mass meeting adopted resolutions calling upon the Government for relief.' A public which had been reading so cheerfully about starvation in Germany and Austria was astonished to discover itself confronted by an actual food riot in the richest city of the United States. It was charged at once to the work of German agents; nevertheless, the hard fact remained that

[1] Mr. Franklin's American Line was the American-flag division of the International Mercantile Marine, the Anglo-American merger promoted by J. P. Morgan & Co. and enjoying close relations with the British Government. In the case of large passenger liners, guns as a matter of fact were probably quite as much a menace as a protection to the lives of those on board. They compelled the submarine to torpedo without warning, if she was to attack at all, rather than to follow the usual course of halting the victim, evacuating her company, and then destroying her afterward by gunfire or explosive.

there was ample reason for the demonstration. Prosperity, as too often happens, was proving very hard upon those who needed it most, and the cost of living was rising to outrageous heights.

It could all be turned to account, however. The Cabinet meeting on Friday, February 23, was the most 'animated' that Secretary Lane had ever attended. The beginning was curious. 'It all arose,' according to Mr. Lane, 'out of a very innocent question of mine as to whether it was true that the wives of American Consuls on leaving Germany had been stripped naked, given an acid bath to detect writing on their flesh and subjected to other indignities.' From this interesting topic Mr. Lane went on to ask 'about the bread riots in New York, as to whether there was shortage of food because of car shortage due to vessels not going out with exports. This led to a discussion of the great problem which we all had been afraid to raise' — the arming of merchant ships. Mr. Lane's account (written two days afterward) continues:

> The President said that the country was not willing that we should take any risks of war. I said that I got no such sentiment out of the country, but if the country knew that our Consul's wives had been treated so outrageously that there would be no question as to the sentiment. This the President took as a suggestion that we should work up a propaganda of hatred against Germany.

But Mr. Lane hastened to disavow any such idea as that. He merely thought that 'in a Democracy the people were entitled to know the facts.'

> McAdoo, Houston and Redfield joined me. The President turned on them bitterly, especially on McAdoo, and reproached all of us with appealing to the *Code Duello*. We couldn't get the idea out of his head that we were bent on pushing the country into war.

After the Cabinet Mr. Houston announced his intention of resigning, and Mr. Lane thought that McAdoo would go as well. But there was another factor in the situation. The short session of Congress would reach its end on the 4th of March — now little more than a week away. Normally, the new Congress would not meet until December, and Mr. Wilson would thus be free for nine months from the interference of the Legislative Branch and from the uses which partisan politics knew only too well how to make of it. Some of the vital appropriations bills, however, were still lagging, and if they should fail to pass in the ensuing week Mr. Wilson would be compelled to summon an extra session. The Republicans, who were now belaboring the President for his refusal to arm the merchant ships, were also maneuvering to block these bills, and so chain him to his Congress. As Mr. Lane put it:

> The Republicans fear that he will submit to anything in the way of indignity or national humiliation without 'getting back,' so they are standing for an extra session. The President believes, I think, that the munition makers are back of the Republican plan. But I doubt this. They simply want to have a 'say'; and the President wants to be alone and unbothered.

This Republican threat to force an extra session upon him was doubtless to have something to do with the President's sudden decision to yield on the armed ship issue. For the moment, however, this Cabinet on the 23d broke up with no action taken. In the country at large the situation, as Spring Rice reported that day, was 'much that of a soda-water bottle with the wires cut but the cork unexploded.' The failure of shipping to sail had produced 'a stoppage of trade, a congestion in the ports, widespread discomfort and even misery on the coast and inland, even bread riots and a coal famine.' All this, nevertheless, was not 'spectacular enough'; the West was still against war and the President was still fighting for peace. But on Saturday, the 24th, the British themselves were able to supply something 'spectacular.' Mr. Balfour deftly gave the unexploded cork a push.

At eight-thirty that Saturday evening there arrived in the State Department a sensational cable from Mr. Page. Mr. Balfour had just handed him, the Ambassador reported, the text of a cipher telegram from Zimmermann to the German Minister in Mexico

City, which had been transmitted on January 19 through the German Embassy in Washington itself. The damning text was then given in English translation:

> We intend to begin on the 1st of February unrestricted submarine warfare. We shall endeavour in spite of this to keep the United States of America neutral. In the event of this not succeeding we make Mexico a proposal of alliance on the following basis: Make war together, make peace together, generous financial support and an understanding on our part that Mexico is to reconquer the lost territory in Texas, New Mexico and Arizona. You will inform the [Mexican] President of the above most secretly as soon as the outbreak of war with the United States is certain and add the suggestion that he should, on his own initiative, invite Japan to immediate adherence....

There is no doubt that President Wilson was profoundly shocked by this revelation of the fact that one could not go to war with Germany without having the Germans fight back. It did not even occur to him to question the authenticity of the document or the motive for the production of a month-old telegram at just that moment.[1] At once the President cabled back his thanks for 'information of such inestimable value' and his 'very great appreciation of so marked an act of friendliness on the part of the British Government.' No suspicions crossed his mind. The cable arrived on Saturday evening. It was some time on Sunday that President Wilson abruptly concluded that an appeal to Congress for authority at least to arm American merchant ships was unavoidable. On Monday he went again before the joint Houses of Congress. 'Since,' he told them, 'it has unhappily proved impossible to safeguard our neutral rights by diplomatic means... there may be no recourse but to armed neutrality.'

---

[1] Mr. Balfour, it is true, had been careful to tell Page that the telegram had only just been received. Actually, if one may believe Mr. Page's biographer, the British intelligence service had intercepted and deciphered the document even before it had reached Mexico City, and had been holding it since then for the time when it would have the maximum effect.

Even so he still sought to keep the situation in his own hands.
He went on:

It is devoutly to be hoped that it will not be necessary to put armed
force anywhere in action.   The American people do not desire it....
I am not now proposing or contemplating war or any steps that may
lead to it. I merely request that you will accord me... the authority
to safeguard in practice the right of a great people who are at peace.
... I can make no definite proposals or forecasts of action now and
must ask for your supporting authority in the most general terms....

But the applause which greeted his concluding words was
noticeably confined to the Democratic side. Senator Lodge felt
such moderation to be 'deplorable.' The Republicans 'generally
showed no sign of approval'; and the reporters found the Republican statesmen in 'no mood to permit the enactment' of a bill
which would allow Mr. Wilson to escape their clutches. Mr.
Wilson's request was 'too vague.' A witticism went round: 'The
President wants to declare war in confidence'; and the movement
for an extra session received only a fresh impetus.

Did the people want war or not? Mr. W. C. Durant, another
philanthropic and pacific automobile manufacturer, returned from
a trip across the continent to tell Colonel House that 'he met only
one man between New York and California who wanted war.'
It is probable that the great mass of Americans did not know what
they wanted, did not understand what was happening and did not
perceive the consequences of their own emotions; but whatever
they may have wanted they were now to be swept quickly forward
to the end which great numbers of them had combined to render
unavoidable.

In the grey seas off the southwest of Ireland, only a few hours
before the President arose to speak, a German submarine had fired
a torpedo without warning into the Cunard liner Laconia. Twelve
lives only were lost (out of nearly 300 on board) but among them
were those of two American women, Mrs. Mary Hoy and her
daughter, who died of exposure in the small boats on the way into

Bantry Bay. The news blazed in the same headlines which announced the President's appeal for authority. In London a New
York *Times* correspondent found Mrs. Hoy's son — a British resi-
dent and the head of a machinery firm 'of London and Chicago.'
'As an American,' the distracted man exclaimed, 'whose mother
and sister were drowned in the torpedoing of the Laconia I feel
I have a right to ask President Wilson, "What is America going
to do?"... I am going to telegraph President Wilson asking him
as an American citizen that the death of my mother and sister be
avenged.' He actually did so; and the cable stirred the quick passions of multitudes who did not stop to ask how many thousands
of other lives were to be expended in exacting a barren vengeance
for those two. The same day the President let it be known that he
regarded the Laconia sinking as the 'overt act' for which he had
been waiting; the armed ship bill was revised in more explicit
terms, and Senator Stone, who still believed in peace but who regarded it as his duty to support the President, reported it out of
the Foreign Relations Committee with a heavy heart.

But there was another Senator who also believed in peace, and
who saw that with the armed ship bill the final crisis had come.
As the bill was reported out that Tuesday evening, Senator La
Follette launched his one-man 'filibuster' to prevent its passage
before the session's end. Next day, Wednesday, the 28th, the Administration leaders professed themselves confident that the measure would pass, but Mr. La Follette was still grimly throwing every
available parliamentary obstacle into its path. The Republicans
suddenly began to realize that it might now be unnecessary for
them to filibuster the supply bills in order to force an extra session;
the bitter pacifist from Wisconsin was doing the work for them —
and saving them from the onus of it. But Mr. Polk at the State
Department knew of the waiting bombshell so kindly supplied by
Mr. Balfour. The Zimmermann telegram, he believed, would
produce a blast of popular emotion that would sweep the armed
ship bill through against everything. So did Colonel House, who
had now seen the text, and who was urging the President to 'pub-

lish it tomorrow.' So, no doubt, did the President — to whom it
must have been plain enough that the first effect of Senator La
Follette's pacifism would be to deliver Mr. Wilson himself into
the hands of the intransigeants. On Thursday, March 1, the headlines were shouting from the morning papers:

GERMANY SEEKS AN ALLIANCE AGAINST US;
ASKS JAPAN AND MEXICO TO JOIN HER;
FULL TEXT OF PROPOSALS MADE PUBLIC

It was a stupendous sensation. The headlines, it is to be observed, were not always precisely accurate. Germany had not
actually sought an alliance as yet; the text of the telegram expressly
instructed the Minister in Mexico to initiate the move only in the
event that the United States should declare war, which the German Government would itself endeavour to prevent. It was not
a proposal for an aggression against the United States, but merely
a conventional, though rather blundering, diplomatic preparation
against a probable American attack upon Germany. This, however, was far too fine a point for the hot passions of the moment;
and the telegram was everywhere seized upon as final proof of the
complete and fathomless treachery of the German.

What made it particularly shocking, of course, was the suggestion that the Japanese (with whom we were about to become
allied) should be invited into the American continent, or that the
principle upon which many Americans had demanded the restoration of Alsace-Lorraine (because they had been acquired by force)
should be applied to California and Texas, which we had forcibly
detached from Mexico. Informed Americans understood perfectly well that the Allies had bribed Japan, Italy and Rumania
into the war with the promise of slices from the enemy carcass;
but they were sincerely and profoundly horrified by the thought
that Germany could be so base as to bribe Mexico and Japan with
the promise of slices from the flanks of the United States. The
Zimmermann telegram became a major German disaster. Not its
least useful aspect, moreover, was the fact that it gave the North-

eastern fire-eaters their first direct lever upon the pacific sentiment of the Southwest. If a German triumph threatened the annexation of California and Texas to Mexico ——! The German Foreign Secretary's innocent cablegram had exploded with its maximum effect at precisely the point where it would do the Allies the greatest good. Even before the editorial repercussions had time to roll in, the House, on that same Thursday afternoon, passed the armed ship bill with a vote of 403 to 13.

In the Senate Mr. Lodge had seen at once that the telegram would be 'of almost unlimited use in forcing the situation.... One would think that note would make the whole country demand war.' Senator La Follette, however, had not been made to demand war by the Zimmermann telegram; and on Friday, March 2, he was again able to block the armed ship resolution. The Senate paused to vote the enormous naval appropriation bill, and then went on with the debate. Only a few more hours of the session remained, and that night they sat late under crowded galleries and in an intense excitement. In London that day Mr. Page had been in conference with Mr. Balfour and Mr. Bonar Law. There was, it seemed, a growing difficulty about 'exchange' and consequently about paying for American food and munitions. 'Could a great popular loan be got in the United States (like the great Victory Loan here)?' Mr. Page thought it likely, if the right men took hold of it. At about the same hour, Senator Vardaman, holding the crumbling pacifist front at the Capitol, was denouncing the munition-makers for stampeding opinion, was assailing militarism and declaring that there was a gigantic move on foot to frighten, deceive and plunder the American people. Senator Kirby, one of the two Bryanites who had voted against endorsing the break with Germany, was crying in an unparliamentary confusion: 'Fellow citizens — gentlemen of the convention — the public mind has been inflamed by a hireling sensational press... to a point where... we can hardly deliberate here....'

The pressures were tremendous. Spring Rice reported the 'strong peace movement' in the Senate but thought it plain that 'feeling in the country' was growing hourly more powerful. With the morning of Saturday, March 3, but one day remained; the session would end at midday on Sunday. Mr. William Randolph Hearst, in his winter retreat at Palm Beach, was writing out telegrams for his editors: 'Mr. McCay should make strong eight-column cartoon... showing Uncle Sam and Germany shaking their fists at each other on left side page and on right side big head and shoulders of Japan with knife in hand leaning over into picture evidently watching chance to strike U.S. in back.' President Wilson had received Austria-Hungary's reply to his telegram of February 22, and was making a last attempt on Count Czernin; but even the President could have put little hope in the Austrian negotiation then. His one chance was to get discretionary powers as to the ships and send Congress home. He had gambled with the Zimmermann telegram on forcing the ship bill through at the risk of inflaming the public beyond all possibility of control. As the long Saturday wore away the worst result of all — no bill and a passionate public insisting upon immediate action — stared the President in the face. As Senator La Follette grimly rallied the pacifist forces, Senator Lodge and his 'militant party' (as he called them) could not have been better satisfied.

Emotions were passing beyond all bounds. Mr. Alton B. Parker, who had once been the Democratic party's nominee for the Presidency, fired a blazing telegram at Mr. Bryan, who had three times held the same honor:

If you and your friend Senator La Follette and all your joint followers and sympathizers had gone to Heaven three years ago, Germany would not have attempted to drive the United States from the seas or to conspire to make war upon her.... Nor would you have had occasion to sneak out of Washington upon the discovery of the German plot. While you can never undo the mischief you have planned, yet if you act quickly you may be able to persuade those now ambitious to become the Benedict Arnolds of Congress to end the shameful scene now being enacted.

But the shameful scene dragged on. Senators Norris, Cummins and Gronna were now fighting with Mr. La Follette, blocking every effort to bring the bill to a vote. Early on Sunday morning, March 4, seventy-five of the ninety-six members of the Senate signed a statement protesting against the filibuster and putting it on record that they would have voted for the bill had the rules offered them any way of doing so. But the pacifists stood their ground. Senator Stone, toward the end, supported them with a four-hour speech against the bill. Senator La Follette's own speech was never given; the patriots, since he would not permit them to pass the bill, retaliated by denying him the opportunity to state his case. 'I have a great speech undelivered,' he said, 'which I propose to deliver throughout the country.' But in the meanwhile the armed ship bill was dead. Sunday morning was 'dark and gloomy, with high winds and floods of rain.' The Senate finished up what business it could; the President drove down to the Capitol to sign any last-minute legislation, and at noon the gavel fell. The battle was won. But the ship bill had carried down with it not only the independent offices and general deficiency bills but the Army appropriation bill as well. There was no longer any question about an extra session.

When Senator La Follette thus assured the Republicans their 'say' he may have believed that an extra session of Congress — directly representative, as it was supposed to be, of the people — was necessary to prevent the President from taking the nation into war. What he had actually done, of course, was merely to deliver the President over to Senator Lodge and the militant party. Perhaps it was a realization of this, as well as personal intolerance of opposition, which lent bitterness to Mr. Wilson's celebrated outburst. It came that Sunday evening in a long public statement from the White House:

Although as a matter of fact the nation and the representatives of the nation stand back of the Executive with unprecedented unanimity of spirit, the impression made abroad will of course be that it is not so and that other Governments may act as they please without

"HERE IS YOUR AMBASSADOR!"
From *L'Illustrazione* (Milan)

HAULED DOWN FOR THE FIRST TIME
From the *News* (Dayton, Ohio)

"Hauling down the flag" is what it seemed like to many citizens when the President's bill giving him authority to arm our merchant ships failed to pass the Senate. Our readers will find this Congressional episode discussed in the editorial pages of this issue.

"DAMN THE TORPEDOES! GO AHEAD!"
From the *Times* (New York)

PUTTING THE JACK IN THE BOX
From the *Oregonian* (Portland)

THE AMERICAN AND THE GERMAN EAGLES ABOUT
TO CLASH
From *O Malho* (Rio de Janeiro)

fear that this Government can do anything at all. We cannot explain. The explanation is incredible. The Senate of the United States is the only legislative body in the world which cannot act when its majority is ready for action. A little group of willful men, representing no opinion but their own, have rendered the great Government of the United States helpless and contemptible.

In addition to Senator La Follette, those who participated in the filibuster or refused to support the bill were five Democrats: Stone of Missouri, O'Gorman of New York, Kirby of Arkansas, Lane of Oregon and Vardaman of Mississippi; and five Progressive-Republicans: Norris of Nebraska, Cummins of Iowa, Gronna of North Dakota, Clapp of Minnesota and Works of California. Some of them, perhaps, were not oblivious to powerful German or Irish minorities in their constituencies; but on the whole their impulse seems a noble and honorable one. Yet the President was right. The only opinion which they represented was the opinion of a distant future. They were standing in a breach already carried; the most they could do was to confuse or destroy whatever control the President might still exert for peace, while they had nothing to put in its place. Nothing, that is, except Congress; and Congress was to prove a far weaker reed than Mr. Wilson.

iv

In the second inaugural of Woodrow Wilson there was little to suggest the splendors of that great day, four years before, when Democracy had returned to the White House and the bright sun of the New Freedom had dawned over a happy land in a world at peace. It was across chasms more profound than those of time that one had now to look back into that far-off age. Its innocent sunshine could now be seen — when it could be seen at all — only as a traveller, pressing onward through a storm, sometimes sees a shaft of light against some serene mountain peak that he has left far behind him. Could one have really believed in those days that the sunshine would last forever, that Privilege was dead and war a grotesque anachronism? Had Theodore Roosevelt actually been a battler for the Lord; and was it really Woodrow Wilson who had once said: 'I tell you, ladies and gentlemen, I take off my cap to Bob La Follette.... Taunted, laughed at, called back, going steadfastly on.... I love these lonely figures'?

Even the day was wintry, though a pale sun broke through after the speechmaking began. As the parade came down Pennsylvania Avenue the customary plumes and gold lace, the absurdly brilliant uniforms of the militia and the marching clubs, were noticeably absent. For the first time since the Civil War the troops were there with the thought that they might be needed. National Guard regiments in field service equipment lined the Avenue — a duty which had always been left to the police in the past — and near the Capitol a machine gun was mounted and ready on the pavement. The President's four-horse carriage (it was the last time that a horse-drawn vehicle was to be used for an inaugural parade) was surrounded as it advanced by a hollow square of thirty-two secret service men, and the troop of regular cavalry which acted as escort rode in olive drab. No one was allowed within the Capitol grounds unless he carried a pass. The inaugural address was brief, and largely a repetition of what had gone before.

But in New York City that evening a wildly enthusiastic mob was pouring into Carnegie Hall to denounce the recalcitrant Senators for the crime of having tried to save them from the most terrible war in history. 'The Rev. Dr. Lyman Abbott was greeted with roars of approval when he called the filibustering Senators "Germany's allies."' 'Traitors! Hang them!' came the answering shouts from the audience. The Hon. James Beck devoted his legal talents to the proof that the President had a right to arm merchant ships anyway, and the cheers resounded. They cheered the proposal that Mr. Root should be made Secretary of State and Mr. Roosevelt Secretary of the Navy; and at every declaration that Germany was at war with the United States already they yelled and waved their little American flags in an orgy of patriotism.

Spring Rice reported that the action of the eleven 'Iscariots, as they are called' was 'an evident proof of the direct authority exercised by Germany in Congress.... Rumors of plots and discoveries of plots by German-Americans are rife, and some of them authenticated.' The second great 'conspiracy scare' was in fact now fully under way, as the precautions of the inaugural bore witness. Again there were everywhere visions of great armies of trained German reservists arising suddenly, as from the dragon's teeth, out of the heart of the nation. Bombs were discerned under every country bridge, and every tennis court was already a German gun-emplacement. In the War Department and the Council of National Defence they were furiously at work upon the vast mobilization plans; while Mr. Roosevelt, who hoped to get a division, was 'as yet holding in; but if [Wilson] does not go to war with Germany I shall skin him alive. To think of the folly of having cursed this country with the really hideous misfortune of four years more of Wilson in this great and terrible world crisis.'

On March 9, the Friday after the inauguration, Mr. Wilson issued the call for the extra session which was now unavoidable. But he set the date for April 16 — over a month away. In the meanwhile, however, could he continue simply to do nothing about the merchant ships? It was also on March 9 that an anxious, and perhaps slightly disingenuous, cable arrived from Mr. Page: 'I find that continued delay in sending out American ships, especially American liners, [!] is producing an increasingly unfavorable impression.... There is a tendency even in high government circles to regard the reasons for delay which are published here as technicalities which a national crisis should sweep aside.' That Sunday, March 11, was 'War Sunday' in the New York churches. The New York Federation of Churches had decided to 'mobilize its Christian strength behind President Wilson.' The ministers proclaimed the holy war from many pulpits. In Brooklyn Dr. Newell Dwight Hillis brought his congregation to its feet in un-ecclesiastical cheers with his sermon: 'Why We Should Go to War With Germany.' A resolution in favor of conscription and pledging support for war was adopted by 158 congregations in the city. 'Our churches,' said the Rev. Charles A. Eaton in the Madison Avenue Baptist Church, 'have been preaching what amounts to a moral asphyxiation. Pacifists afflict the country.... They make me want to swear, pray, laugh and weep.' It was a performance echoed in countless other cities. On the Monday it appeared that organized labor would not be behind organized religion, when Mr. Gompers summoned the American Federation of Labor chieftains to Washington to decide upon labor's attitude in 'the impending crisis.' It was to take them but a day to pledge labor's services to the cause without reservation. Before they had done so, however, President Wilson, on Monday evening, March 12, formally announced that naval guns and gun crews would be supplied to American merchant ships even without Congressional authorization.

On the same day the American steamer Algonquin was sunk without warning off Plymouth. No lives were lost; but it constituted the second in a series of 'overt acts' that were now to come in an ever more rapid succession.

From the preceding November down to that moment, President Wilson had clung consistently to his policy of preserving the United States from war by buying a peace in Europe with an American guaranty of a world peace system. Now, he was without the means to develop it farther. Should he attempt to continue in that course, his authority would be at an end — at a moment when his four-year term of office was just beginning. Mr. Wilson was not a man easily to accept a loss of personal power. But if he now felt that the re-establishment of his command over the situation was a matter of absolutely vital importance to the nation which he represented, one can hardly ascribe the feeling wholly to personal egotism.

He had endeavored to retain command by making peace; and the peace solution lay shattered before him. There remained the alternative — the easy, the profoundly tempting alternative — of making war. The more vigorously he intervened the more complete a hold would he regain over Allied policy; while as for his own public, no ruler ever wields so absolute a power as that of the head of a modern democratic state leading his people into war. Yet President Wilson — and it is the fact which has earned him his great place in human history — was not willing to sentence perhaps hundreds of thousands of his countrymen to death or mutilation on the battlefield for the utterly barren satisfaction of taking revenge upon the Germans. The lives lost at sea could not be restored by the sacrifice of countless others. The military defeat of Germany could not return the submarine into the brains of its inventors, nor solve the baffling intricacies of sea war and neutral right for which the Entente was quite as much responsible as were the Germans. Simple victory over the Central Powers would not in itself serve any American national interest remotely commensurate with the human costs of a large-scale intervention in Europe. If President Wilson was to take this one tempting exit from the *impasse* at which he had arrived, he must find some reason that would make it worth while for the common men and women who would pay the price. But it was just here, as chance would have it, that the war solution assumed its most tempting aspect.

The great vision of a world remade, of peace, justice and equal opportunity enthroned among the nations, of the armies disbanded and the old curse of war lifted at last from the scarred backs of men, arose to beckon him forward. He would have been more than human had so vast a role not appealed to his personal ambition. Yet if his egotism was at work, it was an egotism which all sides had been earnestly striving to arouse through the past two years. It was Mr. Lloyd George who, speaking as Prime Minister of Great Britain, had just told him that he must save the Allies from themselves, that 'he must help make peace if the peace made at that conference is to be worth keeping.' Is it strange that such promptings should have had an effect? Jane Addams saw the President in those days and remembered the conversation:

[He said that] as head of a nation participating in the war, the President of the United States would have a seat at the peace table, but that if he remained the representative of a neutral country he could at best only 'call through a crack in the door.'... The foreign policies which we so extravagantly admired could have a chance if he were to push and defend them, but not otherwise.

On March 15, the Czar of Russia abdicated and the news of the Russian revolution reached the United States. Germany had won the greatest, the most nearly decisive, victory in her whole four years of effort. Yet, so strong were the Entente propagandas and so imperfect was the American understanding of the war that it was received by our public as only another augury of the early success of the Allies. Was not 'autocracy' the great enemy, and had not the unusually extreme form of autocracy in Russia always constituted one of the most obvious and embarrassing weaknesses of the Allied cause? It was so no longer. The Czarist court, it was now everywhere discovered, had throughout been pro-German at heart; its overthrow would only release the full energies of the Russian people and nerve their armies to fight with redoubled vigor for freedom, justice and humanity. The fact that a chief reason for the overthrow was the weariness of the Russian people with fighting of any sort escaped our editors. It also escaped our statesmen; and the Russian revolution supplied only a fresh impulsion toward our own entry into the conflict.

The ten days from March 11 to March 21 would seem to have been the decisive period. They had opened with 'War Sunday,' with the orders to arm the merchantmen, with the sinking of the Algonquin and Mr. Gompers's rallying of labor to the cause of militant patriotism. The Russian revolution was an accomplished fact by Thursday, the 15th. On Friday there came the startling discovery of something that looked, in the heated atmosphere of the moment, almost like revolution in the United States. The powerful railway brotherhoods — key trades unions which did not belong to Mr. Gompers's A. F. of L. — had been waiting for the Supreme Court to determine the constitutionality of the Adamson eight-hour law, a Federal enactment which they had won some time before under threat of a strike. It was known that the Court was about to hand down its decision. On Friday evening the railway unions abruptly called their strike throughout the nation, with the demand that the provisions of the Adamson act be granted them by the owners regardless of the constitutionality of the law. On the verge of a war in which transportation would be all-important, it was an unnerving crisis.

Some, at any rate, of the railway executives felt that it would be grossly unpatriotic of them to enter the European struggle burdened with an eight-hour day; and as they mobilized the war passion to defeat the union demand they were convinced that they were 'standing out for a principle' which was 'the very foundation of practical patriotism.' The brotherhoods, on the other hand, had no intention of seeing their own interests sacrificed upon those altars of patriotism which were to bring so rich a yield to most of its high priests. The week-end passed in a high tension. Secretary Lane, active in the negotiations, thought that 'we came near to having something akin to a civil war.' It was a close thing; but in the end the patriotism of the brotherhoods was to prove more practical than that of their employers, and they got their eight-hour day. On Monday the Supreme Court (which may also have been mixing practicality with its patriotism) upheld the act with a five-to-four decision.

On the Saturday that the railway executives and the government were struggling with the brotherhoods, the Council of National Defence was taking another great step toward industrial mobilization. The Munitions Standards Board was set up that day under Mr. Frank A. Scott of the Warner & Swazey Company. It was to develop into the chief agency of munitions procurement upon our entry into the war. It was also on this Saturday, the 17th, that the War College tore up all its tables of munitions requirements to rewrite them upon a larger scale. The new schedules were based upon an army of 1,000,000 men fighting under European trench war conditions.

During this same week-end there came the definite news of the famous German retreat upon the Hindenburg Line. On their war maps, our public saw the black lines, so long and so tragically immobile, suddenly leap forward at the rate of whole miles a day. The cities of Bapaume and Péronne, upon which every mind had been fastened all through the terrible last half of 1916, but which had continued to stand inaccessible behind the heaps of dead, now fell within a week. The public had heard about 'strategic retreats' too often to believe that this was in fact one of the true strategic retreats of the war. Hopes leapt high again, bringing new fuel to the war fever. Only later was the grim irony to sink in and the truth to appear that the Entente had again suffered what was in reality a severe reverse.

Finally, it was together with all these events that three more American steamers — the Vigilancia, City of Memphis and Illinois — were sunk in quick succession on Friday, Saturday and Sunday. In two of the sinkings there was no loss of life, but fifteen men, six of them American citizens, were drowned with the Vigilancia. 'Prepare! prepare! prepare!' the Reverend S. Parkes Cadman was shouting at a Y.M.C.A. meeting in Brooklyn that Sunday. In the remoter wilds of Kansas and Missouri a newspaperman, Mr. Edward G. Lowry, was finding the hinterlands still opposed to war but ready 'to follow the President.' In Washington the bureaucracy had worked itself into an almost unbearable state of tension, and was exerting all its influence to hurry the President forward. 'Armed neutrality' was becoming a byword and a joke. On Monday, March 19, with the news of the latest sinkings, the War Department suspended further demobilization of the National Guard troops returning from the border, while Secretary Daniels was reported to have convened the Navy General Board 'for discussion of plans of co-operation with the Entente.'

Colonel House, content to await the inevitable in his New York apartment, heard from one visitor in the early days of that week that 'something akin to a panic' was developing at the capital and that there was a 'feeling in Government circles that if the President did not act promptly, a strike would come about in

Cabinet and official circles.' On Monday another friend called
the Colonel twice by telephone from Washington. 'He is disturbed at the President's inertia, and he and Lansing want me to
come to Washington to see if I cannot stir him into action.' On
Tuesday still another visitor was 'disturbed' at the lack of activity.
'He believes there will be an unfavorable reaction against the
President unless he formulates a plan... and follows it vigorously.'
That evening House summoned Captain Guy Gaunt to give him
a private explanation of the delay. The President, House said, was
'rather hesitating about the attitude the new Congress may adopt,'
and House himself was 'loath' to advise his chief, for the interesting
reason that 'if he goes wrong he will lose influence with him.' On
the other hand, the Colonel explained that the Cabinet 'is for war
and is trying to force the issue'; and Downing Street was secretly
reassured with the extraordinary hint that the Administration,
while 'uncertain of Congress,' was 'anxious about *danger of cooling
down of public feeling.*' Was it partly for this reason, perhaps, that
at the regular Tuesday Cabinet that day the 'disturbance' had
already reached the point of open rebellion?

According to Mr. Houston, it was the President himself who
opened the discussion by asking flatly whether he should advance
the summons to Congress and what he should say to it. There
was silence, until Mr. Houston sprang into the breach:

> Germany is now making war on us.... We ought to recognize that
> a state of war exists. What can we do? We can get a big army and
> navy started. We can further prepare financially.... First of all,
> find out from the Allies just what aid we can most quickly and effec-
> tively give.... We were drifting.... Call Congress and ask it to declare
> that a state of war existed.... War could not be waged mildly.

Secretary Baker thought 'that immediate steps should be taken
... to raise a great army and that universal training should be
inaugurated.' Secretary McAdoo supported Houston. 'Lansing
said little or nothing, as usual.' William B. Wilson, Secretary of
Labor and one of the pacific faction, 'said that he had reluctantly

made up his mind that action had to be taken. We were at war.'
Secretaries Gregory and Redfield, also of the milder wing, 'expressed the same opinion.' Two remained; both had been hesitant in the past.

> The President said: 'Burleson, you and Daniels have said nothing.'
> Burleson replied quietly: 'We are at war. I am in favor of calling Congress at the earliest moment.'
> Daniels gave us the views of the naval experts.

The Cabinet, as Secretary Lane put it, was 'at last a unit. We can stand Germany's insolence and murderous policy no longer. Burleson, Gregory, Daniels and [William B.] Wilson were the last to come over.' Confronted with this unanimity among his advisers, the President appears to have said little. He did let drop one idea: 'If our entering the war would hasten and fix the [revolutionary] movements in Russia and Germany, it would be a marked gain to the world and would tend to give additional justification for the whole struggle.' When they broke up they did not know what his decision would be. But next morning small doubt remained. On Wednesday, March 21, a new Presidential proclamation advanced by two weeks the date for convening the extra session. It was now summoned for April 2 — a week from the following Monday.

V

'It is either war or it is submission to oppression,' Mr. Elihu Root told the Union League Club of New York. 'There is no question about "going to war." Germany is already at war with us.' That convincing slogan, so nicely calculated to relieve those who uttered it of any necessity for thought and any responsibility for the consequences, now re-echoed everywhere through the press. It was proclaimed by editorial 'pages in New England and in Southern California, in the cotton South and the industrial Middle West. So unanswerable did it seem that the chief debate turned not upon the question of war but upon the magnitude of the war effort that we should put forth.

The Governor of Connecticut, a pillar of the Baptist Church, was already mobilizing the clergy of his state to take a census of its human war material. The Governor had not forgotten, he explained, that 'our God is the God of Love,' but he felt that 'this country has a mission to perform in the world.' So, no doubt, did the American Peace Society, the oldest of the American pacifist organizations, with a history stemming directly from the horror and exhaustion which the Napoleonic Wars had left behind them. It, too, was now 'standing behind the President,' while the Springfield *Republican* congratulated it for being such a 'good loser.' On Thursday, the 22d, there was still another huge rally in Madison Square Garden in New York. Again Mr. Root was a chief speaker:

> All history teaches us that the rich and defenceless peoples, the peoples who are too luxurious, too fond of their comfort, their prosperity, their wealth, their ease, to make sacrifice for their liberty, surely fall a prey to the aggressor. So Rome fell.... So Persia fell.... So poor, peaceful China fell, three hundred years ago....

Mr. Root, like Mr. Lloyd George and Mr. Wilson, wanted the United States to enter the war in order to attain a place at the peace table, but for a different purpose.

> I hate war, but I welcome the coming of the inevitable at the beginning.... I say that upon the issue of the war in Europe hangs the question whether America shall, at the close of that war, be turned into one armed camp, or whether America shall be a subject nation. There is no nation on earth — not England nor France, nor Belgium nor Italy nor Russia, with a greater stake in the success of the Allies in this war against German militarism than the United States. We are able to hold this peaceful meeting — with a few weak explosions — and why? Because we are protected by the navies and armies of the Allies!
> *A Voice:* That's a lie! [Followed by the ejection of the interrupter.]

One thing more.... Every true American heart should respond with joy, amid its sorrow, to the feeling that if we enter this war ... we shall be fighting over again the battle of American democracy, along with the democracy of England, the democracy of France, the democracy of Italy, and now, God be praised, the great democracy of Russia; fighting for the principle of free self-government against the principle of old-time autocracy and military power.

'Enough has been said and hinted,' Spring Rice was advising his Government next day, 'to justify the assertion that the die has been cast and that this country has drifted into war.' Already Colonel House had sent off a glowing message, through an English visitor: 'Tell them we are with you to the finish of our resources in supplies, money and men. We are prepared to go the whole hog.... Give my warmest regards to my friends over there, Lloyd George, Balfour, Asquith and Grey. Tell them all I am thinking of them all every hour.' It was a melting sentimentalism not shared by the more hard-headed agents of Great Britain; and together with Spring Rice's report of Friday, the 23d, there went another from one of the British 'representatives' in the United States who was 'in close touch with events at Washington':

It looks as if W[ilson] would in fact help us *pretty* well: almost all he can: but I think he will try not to be *technically* an ally. He's the most agile pussy-footer ever made, and when any serious decision is taken always tries to unload the responsibility on to someone else.... But it does seem as if the Huns had fairly driven him into a corner out of which he can't possibly wriggle!

The private communications of the British, however, were safe from interception. It was on this same Friday that Mr. Lansing finally ordered Mr. Whitlock to withdraw with all his staff from Brussels, leaving the Belgian Relief in the hands of the Dutch. In the Friday Cabinet, during the same hours, the time was consumed with 'routine matters of preparation.' The reporters were told afterward that the President and his Cabinet had now decided upon an 'aggressive warfare' in addition to the mere protection of American shipping. Next day the great industrialists of our Council of National Defence were formally demanding a conscript army of 1,000,000 men; while Secretary Baker was engaging to urge 'strongly' upon the President their decision in favor of a draft as opposed to volunteer enlistment.

One bellicose mind was conceiving even stranger plans. On the day after the submarine declaration Mr. Roosevelt had filed his request with Mr. Baker to be notified 'at once' if there was any chance that there would be a war. The notification had never arrived. With all the fierce excitement of preparation now going forward on every side, Mr. Baker, it seemed, was taking no interest in the great, the long-cherished project of a personal Roosevelt army. Desperately, the former Colonel of the Rough Riders appealed to his old friend, Senator Lodge, to circumvent a hostile Administration by getting direct authorization for the plan from Congress. Nor was that all:

> Meanwhile, I have notified Jusserand of the facts, and told him that if either Congress or the Administration declares that a state of war exists, I shall take an expeditionary infantry division to France (under the American flag) on my own account if his Government thinks it worth while to pay for us. If his Government does not, I shall try whether Canada would like to pay for an American division (under our flag) — I understand that they need more men.

There could be no more eloquent testimony to the extraordinary psychology of the moment than the fact that a former President of the United States could advance this remarkable and distinctly treasonable proposal. But perhaps it is a question whether Mr. Roosevelt — a prey to a raging furnace of emotion within his own breast, fed by war madness, by ambition, jealousy and disappointment — was by this time altogether rational. And Secretary Baker knew, as Marshal Joffre was soon to tell him, that in the real war upon which the American people were now about to embark, 'it cost from ten to fifteen thousand lives to train a major-general.'

Nor was Mr. Roosevelt the only independent and ambitious soldier. On March 24 the axe, poised for so long above the insubordinate neck of General Wood, fell with a cruel abruptness. In his
stronghold at Governor's Island the general was suddenly notified that his command was to be divided up, and he was politely
offered his choice between the task of defending Charleston,
South Carolina, from invasion or exile to the even more 'important' and remote commands at Hawaii or Manila. Incredulous,
the general telephoned to the Adjutant-General for confirmation
of this order, and was told that it was final. He hung up. 'Wood's
comment was, "I guess he thinks he's got me now." ' And he had.
Preparedness, after all, is not war.

There was to be a storm of protest from the general's adherents,
and the Republicans sought patriotically to exploit it as another
means of hamstringing Mr. Wilson. 'We can conceive of no service to the Government more worth while at the moment,' the
Boston *Transcript* severely observed, 'than that its head shall be
made to understand, with all the speed and solemnity possible,
that his attack upon a citizen soldier of the character, courage and
capacity of Leonard Wood is looked upon at home and abroad
as a national disgrace.' But in war one does not make heads of
governments understand things — it is the other way around.

In his Brooklyn church on Sunday, March 25, the fire-eating
Rev. Newell Dwight Hillis was suggesting that the eagle upon the
Great Seal of the United States should be replaced by a tortoise,
with the motto: 'God made every creeping thing.' It is true that
when Senator Wadsworth, at another meeting in Brooklyn, cried
for war to the hilt and the immediate despatch of a regular division
to France, the utterance 'curiously' drew 'quite a number of hisses.'
But they were drowned at once in roars of applause. The quiet
seclusion of East Fifty-Third Street was being broken that Sunday
morning as the pacifists — Amos Pinchot, Paul Kellogg, Lillian
Wald — led a last forlorn hope against Colonel House himself.
But the Colonel easily put them off. At his Embassy in London
Mr. Page was already at war, setting his whole staff to 'asking

everybody what the Americans can best do to help the cause along,' and cataloguing the results for the guidance of Washington. Most of the British leaders talked ships, naval patrols and credits, but the military men, significantly enough, wanted 'an expeditionary force, no matter how small.'

The Sunday passed. A bare week now remained before the Congress would convene. President Wilson turned to call the National Guard back into service as a defence against that long-anticipated uprising of the pro-Germans (which never happened), but what his Message would be no one knew — not even the President, for it was as yet unwritten. Colonel House at last began to feel some anxiety. Through all the critical period since the break with Germany the President had rather noticeably failed to call his adviser into consultation. The Colonel, convinced of the inevitability of the outcome, had been satisfied to wait; but the strain seems to have been growing more severe, for he now wrote suggesting that it might be well for the President to see him. There was no reply. On Monday, however, the Colonel had a long conference with Mr. Howard Coffin, one of the industrialists of the Council of National Defence, which disturbed him so much that he resolved to go at once to Washington. He thought the war preparations required attention; he was also 'anxious to talk with [Mr. Wilson] concerning his message to Congress.' Thus self-invited, the Colonel reached the White House on Tuesday afternoon. His doubts, he found, had been unnecessary. What the President asked him was whether the Message should call for a declaration of war or should announce that war already existed and merely request the means to wage it.

Colonel House immediately advised the latter course, for 'I was afraid of an acrimonious debate if he puts it up to Congress to declare war' — as the Constitution would seem to have required. At any rate, the main point had evidently been decided. Yet the President, strangely enough, seemed not to share his adviser's mood of cheerful relief. 'He was not well, and complained of a headache.' The Colonel sought to restore him to a proper frame of mind and nerve him for the slaughter with the old, old argument that he should act 'in a creditable way so that his influence would not be lessened when he came to do the great work which would necessarily follow the war.' But perhaps the President, standing upon that somber verge, had a clearer realization of how distant, how unattainable, those splendid visions really were. He said that 'he did not believe he was fitted for the Presidency under such conditions.' House answered with ready encouragements — fighting a world war would be easier, even, than such peacetime achievements as the passage of the Federal Reserve Act or the Panama Canal tolls repealer. 'He listened with a kindly and sympathetic attention, and, while he argued with me on many points, he did it dispassionately.' It is possible that for the time being the Colonel, like Mr. Page, no longer counted.

Next morning, Wednesday, the President played golf. While he was on the links Mr. McAdoo arrived to see House — breathing fire and desolation. 'McAdoo wants war — war to the hilt. He said his appetite for it was so strong that he would like to quit the Cabinet, raise a regiment and go to the front. All three of his sons have enlisted.' So perhaps Mr. McAdoo, too, had remembered the splendors of San Juan Hill. When Mr. Wilson returned he called in Colonel House to show him, at last, the first rough notes of the Message which had to be delivered five days later. House 'approved' them and returned to New York.

In the War Department, in the Council of National Defence and among the passionate patriots of preparedness, the pressures which were to take an A.E.F. of 2,000,000 men to Europe were rapidly being worked up. The most that Allied opinion was suggesting at the time was a relatively small American contingent for the Western Front; indeed, it is possible that some, even, of their military men were still a little cautious about inviting an American intervention on too great a scale. Yet 'this did not change the War Department's policy, which had been formed before we entered the war. We went on with our plan for a great army.' In the

Cabinet on Friday, March 30, the President was still raising that obstinate question about the 'sentiment of the country,' but they assured him that although there would presumably be 'a great many disaffected individuals,' no 'situation would develop which could not be readily handled.' So far had we already come in our war against militarism and autocracy. When the Cabinet rose, the members felt confident that the President was going to ask, not for a declaration of war, but for the more compelling 'declaration of a state of war,' and that the nation would 'pledge all its resources to the prosecution of the struggle to a speedy end.' Next day, Saturday, the Council of National Defence was adopting a resolution by Secretary Lane providing that all the military contracts should be written on the basis of a three years' program. 'We may win in two years,' Mr. Lane thought. 'If we had the nerve to raise five million men at once we could end it in six months.' Could they?

That Saturday evening fell. Within less than forty-eight hours, the Congress would be in its place and waiting. According to Winkler:

On the night of March 31, the President stirred restlessly in his bed. Finally he rose, donned bathrobe and slippers and took his small typewriter out on the south portico of the White House. Mrs. Wilson, hearing him, slipped into the kitchen and prepared a bowl of milk and crackers which she silently placed at his side. There, in the stillness of the night, Wilson wrote his War Message.

Sunday morning came — the last Sunday of that peace which the President had striven courageously, if perhaps mistakenly and too tardily, to maintain. In Vienna, Count Czernin was devoting it, by a rather tragic irony, to a public call for a conference and a negotiated settlement among the war-weary peoples. In London Mr. Page was pouring out another of his endless letters:

The Administration can save itself from becoming a black blot on American history only by vigorous action — acts such as these:

... We must go in with the Allies.... We must sign the pact of London — not make a separate peace.... (1) The Navy — full strength, no 'grapejuice' action. (2) An immediate expeditionary force. (3) A larger expeditionary force very soon. (4) A large loan, at low interest. (5) Ships, ships, ships. (6) A clear cut expression of the moral issue.

The day wore on. The bellicose Lane was writing happily to his brother. The die was cast. Even in the Far West they were standing behind the President, for Mr. Lane had collected telegraphic reports on the local feeling there and the replies had all been in that sense. 'Yet none came back,' Mr. Lane added, 'that spoke as if they felt that we had been outraged or that it was necessary for humanity that Germany be brought to a Democracy. There is little pride or sense of national dignity in most of our politicians.' Mr. Lane had a better spirit and a clearer understanding of the needs of humanity.

At about the same hour the freighter Aztec, the first armed American merchantman to sail from the United States, was foundering in the dusk and a stormy sea off the island of Ushant. She had been torpedoed, efficiently and without warning; one of her boats was smashed in launching and there was a heavy loss of life. Her two five-inch naval guns — our first answer to the U-boat — had not fired a shot; their crews had not seen even the track of the torpedo, much less the submarine which discharged it. As the Aztec's people were drowning in the cold, black seas off Finisterre, the pacifist forces in New York that Sunday afternoon were organizing for one last, desperate effort — a mass descent upon the capital in the morning. But at Columbia University a group of patriotic professors were hastily preparing a counter-demonstration. Professor Walter B. Pitkin was rushed off to Washington as an advance guard; several ministers — Dr. William T. Manning, Dr. George R. Van de Water and Dr. Karl Reiland — were enlisted as aids; reinforcements were summoned from Yale under Professor Henry W. Farnum, and a statement was issued by the committee through Professor Charles A. Beard: 'The hour has struck to put an end to the Prussian oligarchy.... Every advocate of peace at any price... is now playing into the hands of Prussian militarism.'

There was one minister of the Gospel who refused to be swept away by the tides of war emotion. At the Church of the Messiah at Park Avenue and Thirty-Fourth Street, the Rev. John Haynes Holmes's morning sermon had been a passionate declaration of faith: 'If war is right, then Christianity is wrong, false, a lie.... No order of a President or a Governor will persuade me or force me to this business of killing.... Other clergymen may pray to God for victory for our arms. I will not. In this church, if nowhere else, the Germans will still be included in the family of God's children.' It gave his trustees a bad afternoon. 'Dr. Holmes is an idealist,' one of them explained to the reporters, but this was not 'the time to put his idealism into practice. We are not going to lie down and let Germany or anybody else wipe up the floor with us.... The Church of the Messiah is going to fight first... to protect American right and American lives, and after we have protected them we will go on with our ideals.' Elsewhere that Sunday the churches overwhelmingly agreed, not with Dr. Holmes, but with his trustees. Throughout the nation the pulpits were mobilized for the Christian conflict; and even in the remote fastness of the Rocky Mountain states (where the politicians might be backward) the clergy were holding flag-raising services and proclaiming the holy war. The nation as a whole, whatever it may actually have wanted, was now standing behind the President; the War Message was written and ready; only a few hours remained before the irrevocable step would be taken. But in all the moral fervor and war hysteria of the moment there was one statesman who retained a clearer and a sadder understanding of what the great crusade was in reality to imply. That man was Woodrow Wilson, President of the United States.

As the day dragged on, Mr. Wilson despatched a sudden summons, not to Colonel House, but to Mr. Frank I. Cobb, who presided so ably and so loyally over the editorial page of the New

York *World.* Mr. Cobb could not get to Washington until after midnight, and it was about one o'clock on Monday morning when he finally reached the White House:

> The 'old man' was... sitting in his study with the typewriter on his table.... He looked as if he hadn't slept.... For nights, he said, he'd been lying awake going over the whole situation.... He said he couldn't see any alternative, that he had tried every way he knew to avoid war.... I told him his hand had been forced by Germany, that so far as I could see we couldn't keep out.... 'Yes,' he said, 'but do you know what that means?... It would mean that we should lose our heads along with the rest, and stop weighing right and wrong.'... The President said a declaration of war would mean that Germany would be beaten and so badly beaten that there would be a dictated peace, a victorious peace.
>
> 'It means,' he said, 'an attempt to reconstruct a peacetime civilization with war standards, and at the end of the war there will be no bystanders with sufficient power to influence the terms. There won't be any peace standards left to work with. There will be only war standards.'...
>
> He went on to say that so far as he knew he had considered every loophole of escape, and as fast as they were discovered Germany deliberately blocked them with some new outrage.... He had no illusions about the fashion in which we were likely to fight the war. He said when a war got going it was just war, and there weren't two kinds of it.... We couldn't fight Germany and maintain the ideals of government that all thinking men shared. He said we would try it, but it would be too much for us.
>
> 'Once lead this people into war,' he said, 'and they'll forget there ever was such a thing as tolerance. To fight you must be brutal and ruthless, and the spirit of ruthless brutality will enter into the very fibre of our national life, infecting Congress, the courts, the policeman on the beat, the man in the street.'... He foresaw too clearly the probable influence of a declaration of war on his own fortunes; the adulation certain to follow the certain victory, the derision and attack which would come with the deflation of excessive hopes, and in the presence of world responsibility. But... it was just a choice of evils.

The President foresaw it all, down even to the bitter end. Yet Mr. Wilson, no less than his countrymen, was the prisoner of his own policies, of fate, of human limitations. He was powerless to check the course of history now. What he could do was to strive to turn this moral disaster to the highest possible ends. He could still dedicate himself to the task of salvaging, if it was possible, that settlement of justice, humanity and reason for which all sides had convinced themselves that the Great War was being waged. President Wilson knew how enormous now would be the difficulty of an attempt 'to reconstruct a peacetime civilization with war standards.' But he would try.

The sky paled. The morning of April 2, 1917, was dawning.

XII. WAR TO END WAR

i

AS President Wilson and Mr. Cobb were talking in the White House, 'one thousand militant pacifists, each armed with a white tulip' were crowding the railway station in New York, ready to take the night train for Washington. 'They are going,' according to one hostile account, 'to keep the nation out of war, and 14,000 other flower bearers from the rest of the United States are going to help them do it.' Colonel House, hurrying likewise for the night train, must have passed through the curious spectacle. The lights glared over the crowd; the white tulips waved their pathetic way through the gates, and the trains trundled off in the darkness toward Washington. In their mail-cars there went the morning editions, whose headlines already assumed that it was all over:

CONGRESS READY TO DECLARE
STATE OF WAR NOW EXISTS;
COUNTRY IN MILITANT MOOD

The day came in raw and stormy. President Wilson had sat late with his visitor, but he was up much earlier than usual. Before breakfast the White House reporters saw a messenger emerge with a sealed envelope — it was the War Message, in the President's own typescript, on its way to the public printer. Mr. Tumulty was at the White House an hour before his usual time; Colonel House arrived for breakfast, but the President was already leaving for the golf links with Mrs. Wilson, and House saw him 'for a moment only.' Until Congress should be convened and organized there was nothing to do but to kill time. Mr. Wilson spent the whole morning playing golf. Colonel House motored with Mr. Polk of the State Department, or answered anxious telephone inquiries from Mr. McAdoo as to whether the War Message would prove adequate. The Colonel, who had himself seen only the rough notes for it as yet, felt certain that it would 'meet every expectation.' Outside the whole city was clothed with flags — a sufficient indication of what Washington expected — while on Capitol Hill the Senators and Representatives were collecting in their offices, waiting for the opening of the session, which was fixed for noon.

The pacifist host, led by Dr. David Starr Jordan, was milling about the Capitol in the damp weather, considerably at a loss. They had tried to organize a parade and had been sternly refused a police permit. They had tried to see the President and had been denied; they had tried to storm the State, War and Navy Building and had been repelled by the heavy guards posted there. Most of them drifted back to the other end of Pennsylvania Avenue, to invade the Senate and House office buildings or sit about on the Capitol steps, watching one of their number who bore a solemn banner: 'Is this the United States of Great Britain?' Senator La Follette tried to get authorization for them to hold a formal demonstration, but failed; and no one else paid very much attention until, shortly before noon, there arose a sudden fracas in one of the corridors of the Senate Office Building.

Six or seven Massachusetts pacifists, among them Mrs. Anna May Peabody, the Rev. Paul Harris Drake and Mr. Alexander Bannwart, a youngish man of German-Swiss parentage, had penetrated to the door of Senator Henry Cabot Lodge himself to make their protest, as his constituents, against a declaration of war. The Senator was busy. They insisted. The Senator, stepping to the door, consented at least to hear them. 'There followed the usual pacifist harangue' ending with the argument that Massachusetts sentiment was strongly against war. With dignity Mr. Lodge replied 'that he alone could be judge of sentiment in Massachusetts'; the pacifists, unsuppressed, told him that war was cowardly. 'National degeneracy and cowardice,' Mr. Lodge answered, 'are worse than war,' and backed toward the office door. The heroic episode which followed has been recorded in Mr. Lodge's own words:

> They were very violent and very abusive, and I was engaged in backing away from them and saying that we must agree to differ when the German member of their party said, 'You are a damned coward.' I walked up to hit him and said, 'You are a damned liar,' and he hit me and I hit him. Then all the pacifists rushed at me and I thought I was in for a bad time, but my secretaries sallied forth to my rescue and there was a mixup.

Mr. Bannwart was thirty-six and athletic; the Senator was spare and sixty-seven, but according to some witnesses he floored the traitor with his first blow. The secretarial reinforcements came pouring out of the office; a gallant Western Union messenger, passing through the corridor, sprang into the fray. 'I saw an old man in a fight,' he modestly told the reporters afterward, 'and I thought it my duty to help him.' The help, at all events, was efficacious. 'The pacifist who attacked me got badly beaten up and it all ended very comfortably and without hurt to me'; the mauled and bleeding Bannwart was finally borne off to custody by the Capitol police, and the thrilling news ran through the Senate Office Building that Senator Henry Cabot Lodge, striking our first blow for freedom, had personally punched a pacifist in the nose. 'I am glad that I hit him,' Mr. Lodge concluded. 'The Senators all appeared to be perfectly delighted,' and Mr. Lodge himself was momentarily a national hero.

The forces of peace had been routed at the beginning. Other Senatorial doors were hastily closed upon them; the police presently broke up an incipient demonstration on the Capitol steps, and ultimately they adjourned to a public hall for a conventional and impotent mass meeting. The hall, as it happened, was next door to a National Guard armory, and the young citizen soldiers — whose lives, after all, they were trying to preserve — booed and jeered them as they went by. Later there were some other meetings and speechmakings, but it was not of the slightest use, and before the day was over the peace army was dissolving.

At noon Congress convened; it was to require the whole afternoon, however, to complete the organization of the House of Representatives, and the serious business could not begin until evening. Among the members taking their seats for the first time there was one who attracted particular attention — Miss Jeannette Rankin, Representative from Montana and the first woman to sit in the Congress of the United States. As to the attitude of the statesmen there was little doubt, although it was, perhaps, rather less than unanimous. One newspaper survey discovered that the Congressmen 'are beginning to look upon defence of our trade routes as merely incidental. The members of the House of Representatives, all fresh from home, now interpret the sentiment of their communities to mean that when the United States enters the war it will be as a great democracy aiding in the overthrow of an autocracy of the worst sort'; while a poll revealed seventy-six of the Representatives for war as against only fifteen definitely opposed. Yet there were twenty-five others who were doubtful or noncommittal, while one lingers over the curious detail that this survey showed a two-to-one sentiment against sending any troops to Europe, or even formally joining the Entente alliance.

In the House the routine business droned on; the Senate was temporarily in recess. In New York that afternoon a crowd stopped to mob a pacifist speaking from a cart-tail, but there was little excitement. Far away in Brussels Mr. Whitlock was paying his farewell visit to General von Bissing, whom our newspaper readers had known so long as the ogre of the Belgian occupation:

'*Vous partez donc?*' '*Oui, Excellence!*' And then in a kind of rage he almost roared: '*Et pourquoi?*'... He said that he was sorry to see me go.

The Germans gave them every courtesy; while the Belgians gathered in silent crowds at every street corner and before the railway station to wave farewell. The train finally rolled away toward Switzerland with Mr. Whitlock and his staff, and another famous mission was at an end. In the White House they whiled away the time. Mr. Wilson finally read his message to the Colonel, and the adviser noted happily that none of the Wilson papers had pleased him more. Superficially the President seemed calm, but House's trained eye could detect 'signs of nervousness.' The afternoon lengthened; until word came at last that Congress would be ready at eight-thirty, and they sat down to an early dinner in order to be in time. Only House and the members of the family were there, and they talked 'of everything excepting the matter in hand.' Beyond the windows the evening fell, in mist and a soft rain; the crowds were already lining the avenue to cheer the President on his way to the Capitol, while a troop of United States cavalry was drawing up as an escort to safeguard his passage — from the embattled pacifists!

By nightfall two more troops had been thrown around the Capitol; the whole building was swarming with secret service men, Post-office inspectors and police, and it was impossible for any pacific disturber to 'get within pistol shot' of the place. The House galleries were filling again with a brilliant assemblage of the authorized; the Representatives were taking their places; the Supreme Court was seated, this time, directly before the Speaker's desk; the Cabinet was on one side, while behind them the Diplomatic Corps, in full evening dress, occupied a place upon the floor of the House for the first time in anyone's memory. In an atmosphere of intense excitement the House was called to order; two minutes later the doors were flung open, and the Vice-President entered, followed once more by the Senate, marching two by two, with every man — or almost every man — 'wearing or carrying a small American flag.' Solemnly that impressive and patriotic spectacle moved down the aisle to the seats reserved. Senator La Follette was flagless; so was Senator Vardaman, but there was no time to check up on the others, for a moment later the Speaker was announcing: 'The President of the United States.'

The chamber had never witnessed an ovation such as that which followed. The Supreme Court rose *en masse* to lead the applause; the Senate, the Representatives, the packed galleries, stood up to clap and then to cheer. Mr. Houston glanced back at the Diplomatic Corps and 'bowed to Spring Rice and Jusserand, who were expectant and happy.' Not for two minutes could the demonstration be quelled. 'At eight-thirty-five o'clock tonight,' the New York *Times* correspondent was writing as the cheers resounded, 'the United States virtually made its entrance into the war. At that hour President Wilson appeared before a joint session...' The noise died at last; and as the President opened the sheets of note paper before him an intent and absolute silence fell. Without looking up the President began:

> Gentlemen of the Congress: I have called the Congress into extraordinary session because there are serious, very serious, choices of policy to be made, and made immediately....

The opening paragraphs were a brief recital of the submarine controversy and the failure to check the progress of that 'cruel and unmanly business.' The 'German submarine warfare against commerce,' the President said, 'is a warfare against mankind.' Chief Justice White, prominent in the foreground, was seen to give a vigorous nod of approval. The voice went on: 'The challenge is to all mankind. Each nation must decide for itself how it will meet it. The choice we make for ourselves must be made with a moderation of counsel and a temperateness of judgment befitting our character and our motives.... But armed neutrality, it now appears, is impracticable.' At once the close attention 'deepened into a breathless silence.' On the Chief Justice's face there appeared an expression of profound satisfaction. The President continued, pointing out the weaknesses of that solution, the practical certainty that it could only lead to the war it had been designed to prevent. And then — did he draw a breath? — 'There is one choice we cannot make, we are incapable of making: we will not choose the path of submission —'

At the word, the Chief Justice, 'with an expression of joy and thankfulness, dropped the big soft hat he had been holding, raised his hands high in the air and brought them together with a heartfelt bang; and House, Senate and galleries followed him with a roar.' The President finished the sentence: '— and suffer the most sacred rights of our nation and our people to be ignored or vio· lated,' and then swept on:

> With a profound sense of the solemn and even tragical character of the step I am taking and of the grave responsibilities which it involves, but in unhesitating obedience to what I deem my constitutional duty, I advise that the Congress declare the recent course of the Imperial German Government to be in fact nothing less than war against the Government and people of the United States; that it formally accept the status of belligerent which has thus been thrust upon it; and that it take immediate steps not only to put the country in a more thorough state of defence but also to exert all its power and employ all its resources to bring the Government of the German Empire to terms and end the war.

The Chief Justice rose to his feet, 'leading the Supreme Court and the entire assembly. His face was a study. It worked almost convulsively and great tears began to roll down his cheeks.' Behind him 'the Senators and Representatives were cheering.... Heflin of Alabama sprang to his feet. In a second the whole Democratic side of the House was up after him, and then Ollie James of Kentucky rose in his turn, followed immediately by the Democratic side of the Senate... cheering at the top of their lungs.' The tension was broken in a fierce tide of emotion. From that moment until the end the Chief Justice 'was vigorously applauding everything'; the others were not behind him. The President went on to catalogue the measures which such a declaration as he asked would call for — the 'mobilization of all the material resources of the country,' further great naval expansion, an immediate addition of 500,000 men to the Army, to be raised by conscription, with subsequent increases as rapidly as the men could be trained. It made no difference. Whatever some of them may have thought in saner moments, they cheered it all now; they even cheered as the President turned to the attempt to fix the great effort which he was invoking upon the highest of ends:

> Our object... is to vindicate the principles of peace and justice in the life of the world as against selfish and autocratic power, and to set up amongst the really free and self-governed peoples of the world such a concert of purpose and of action as will henceforth ensure the observance of those principles. Neutrality is no longer feasible or desirable where the peace of the world is involved and the freedom of its peoples.... We have seen the last of neutrality in such circumstances. We are at the beginning of an age in which it will be insisted that the same standards of conduct and of responsibility for wrong done shall be observed among nations and their governments that are observed among the individual citizens of civilized states.

Could they have failed to realize that the duties and responsibilities of that new age must apply to the United States equally with other peoples? There was, at any rate, no sign of dissent; and the President changed his theme. 'We have no quarrel,' he went on, 'with the German people' — just as he had long before announced, upon the verge of a lesser war, that we had no quarrel with the people of Mexico. 'We have no feeling towards them but one of sympathy and friendship.' He launched into a long denunciation of the crimes their government, however, had committed — crimes of spying, intrigue and propaganda of which 'self-governed nations' could never, of course, have been guilty. 'We are glad, now that we see the facts with no veil of false pretense about them, to fight thus for the ultimate peace of the world and for the liberation of its peoples, the German peoples included; for the rights of nations great and small and the privilege of men everywhere to choose their way of life and of obedience. The world must be made safe for democracy.' In the tide of the President's rolling prose the phrase might have passed without accent had not Senator John Sharp Williams of Mississippi, who had been listening intently and in silence, 'instantly seized the full and immense meaning of it. Alone he began to applaud, and he did it gravely and emphatically' until one after another took it up and the whole Chamber burst into another uproar. It died again, and President Wilson passed on at last to his peroration:

It is a distressing and oppressive duty, Gentlemen of the Congress, which I have performed in thus addressing you. There are, it may be, many months of fiery trial and sacrifice ahead of us. It is a fearful thing to lead this great peaceful people... into the most terrible and disastrous of all wars.... But the right is more precious than peace, and we shall fight for the things which we have always carried nearest our hearts — for democracy, for the right of those who submit to authority to have a voice in their own governments, for the rights and liberties of small nations, for a universal dominion of right by such a concert of free peoples as shall bring peace and safety to all nations and make the world itself at last free. To such a task we can dedicate our lives and our fortunes... with the pride of those who know that the day has come when America is privileged to spend her blood... for the principles that gave her birth and happiness and the peace which she has treasured. God helping her, she can do no other.

It had taken him just thirty-six minutes. As the last words fell, another hurricane of cheering swept the Chamber. Secretary Redfield was near Jusserand; his hand met that of the Ambassador and 'grasped it firmly. I shall not forget the expression of his eyes.' Everyone was on their feet again, shouting, clapping, waving the American flags they had brought or tearing the miniature emblems from their lapels to wave them too. All but one:

Senator Robert Marion La Follette, however, stood motionless with his arms folded tight and high on his chest, so that nobody could have an excuse for mistaking his attitude; and there he stood, chewing gum with a sardonic smile.

The President walked quickly from the desk. People crowded around him as he went with their congratulations. Senator Henry Cabot Lodge, fresh from that magnificent appeal for a new world order of peace and international responsibility, 'shook his hand warmly and said: "Mr. President, you have expressed in the loft-iest manner possible the sentiments of the American people."' Mr. Houston, an almost equally determined war hawk, poured out his congratulations. The President 'smiled, thanked me and passed on.' Behind him, within five minutes after he had left the desk, the House was being called to order to adopt a rule making possible the swift passage of the great war appropriations bills. In the Senate, Mr. Stone was summoning the Foreign Relations Committee for 10 o'clock next day to draft the declaration of war. 'I am against a declaration of war,' said the Senator, who had fought against it so long, 'but when it is declared I will be a war eagle screaming as loud as the rest. Blood is thicker than water.' By that time the President was out of the crowd and glare, on the way back to the White House through the darkness and the rain.

Beyond the radius of that fierce, mass hysteria at the Capitol it did not seem, for some reason, so exciting. Perhaps the nation had discounted it all too long; perhaps the statesmen had been more deeply moved by mere dramatic suggestion than they quite realized themselves. In New York the city editors found it hard to work up anything worthy of the day. The streets were calm, except at Carnegie Hall, where there had been a pacifist meeting. Someone remembered that next day would be the eightieth birth-day of Mr. John Burroughs, the celebrated naturalist; and a re-porter routed out the old man by long distance telephone. He was found to be 'awaiting patiently the entrance of the United States into war.... He particularly wished to live to see the day when militarism was crushed.' Before the bulletin boards in Herald Square only some hundred loungers could be counted; and they appeared to receive the news without enthusiasm. In the more elegant atmospheres of the Metropolitan Opera House, however, there was a response more fitting to the occasion, though even there it required a little stimulation. Ambassador Gerard, who was in the audience — the piece was De Koven's 'The Canterbury Pilgrims' — heard the extras being shouted between the acts. He was in the act of telephoning Mr. Swope of the *Worla* for confirmation of the news, when one of the directors of the opera company passed. Mr. Gerard told him what had happened and demanded that he do something — 'order the news read from the stage, for example, and the Star Spangled Banner played.' The reply was disappointing. 'No,' the director said, 'the opera company is neutral.' Shocked, the former Ambassador hurried back to his box, 'and stepping to the front, called on the house to cheer President Wilson. There was, for a moment, surprise at such unconventional action, but the whole house soon broke into cheers,' and as the orchestra responded then with the Star Spangled Banner on its own account, 'conventionalism was dead.' It ended in a queer climax. When the last act curtain rose upon the dying cheers, they could see that Margarete Ober, the German singer playing the Wife of Bath, was nervous; and the action had progressed for only a moment or two when she collapsed in a dead faint and had to be carried from the stage. The opera went on without her.

But in the White House, as on the streets, the feeling was subdued. For a time they talked it all over again in the Oval Room, 'as families are prone to do after some eventful occasion' — the President, Mrs. Wilson, Margaret Wilson and Colonel House. The Colonel told him how great was the position he had taken; Mazzini, the Colonel thought, was the one modern statesman who could approach the grandeur of these policies. Mr. Wilson protested, citing Webster, Lincoln, Gladstone; but the Colonel begged to differ. Apparently, Mr. Wilson let it go, and they broke up. 'I could see the President was relieved that the tension was over and the die was cast. I knew this would happen.' But if one dares to trust Mr. Tumulty's memory, there was another scene in the White House that night, when the secretary talked alone with his chief in the Cabinet room. The applause from the sidewalk crowds as he had driven to the Capitol returned to the President's ears. 'My message today,' Tumulty remembers his saying, 'was a message of death for our young men. How strange it seems to applaud that.' And afterward, in the secretary's account, the President broke down and wept, with his head on the Cabinet table.

ii

Four swift, strange days were to follow. They were exciting; yet there was a curious sense of the automatic — almost of the synthetic — about the excitement. Each day the newspapers splashed bigger and blacker headlines across their front pages, just as they had done in July and August, 1914, yet it was not the same. On the one hand, there had been too much talk. People could not believe, even now, that it was the real thing at last; they still could not imagine that young Americans were actually to be raised and shipped by the million into the bloody trenches of Northern France. On the other hand, the outcome had been taken too much for granted. We were at war already. Germany had made war on us. What could we do about it? Competent observers, looking back upon it all afterward, were to feel that Congress had been 'dragooned' into declaring war by the President and the newspapers. The statesmen at heart did not want to declare war. Perhaps. Yet few of them had attempted, even, to check the steady flow of history to that end; almost none had possessed the strength to accept and commit themselves to an alternative, and now, in these last minutes of the eleventh hour, there was but one man among them with the resolute courage not only to stand against the tide but stake his reputation and his career upon an uncompromising battle for his convictions. Congress and the vocal elements in the country rejected his proffered leadership; and the United States fell with a queer helplessness into the war, on the comforting assumption that it was an inevitable and foregone conclusion.

When the Senate met at noon on Tuesday the legislative machinery was oiled for the instant passage of the war resolution. The Senators spent a few moments reading into the record the floods of letters, telegrams, petitions and memorials they had received from all over the country. They fill no less than twenty-four of the big pages of *The Congressional Record* with a fine minion type; they came from every kind of source — state legislatures, farmhouse meetings, churches, 'committees of public safety,' fraternal lodges, expensive clubs and popular mass meetings. Pacifist sentiment was strongly represented, especially from the West and Far West; but much the larger number were calling for war and 'universal service,' and wherever the memorial represented an official vote of a legislature it was on the belligerent side. It did not take long to present them, and the Senate moved on to the great business of the day. In the morning the Foreign Relations Committee had adopted the war resolution; but Senator Stone, as chairman, had cast a lone vote in opposition, and it was therefore reported out by Senator Gilbert M. Hitchcock of Nebraska:

> *Resolved by the Senate and House of Representatives of the United States of America in Congress assembled,* That the state of war between the United States and the Imperial German Government which has thus been thrust upon the United States is hereby formally declared; and that the President be, and he is hereby, authorized and directed to take immediate steps not only to put the country in a thorough state of defence but also to exert all of its power and employ all of its resources to carry on war against the Imperial German Government and to bring the conflict to a successful termination.[1]

The resolution was read; Senator Hitchcock asked unanimous consent for its immediate consideration. But at once the grim figure of Senator La Follette arose in its place in the front row of the Senate Chamber. 'Mr. President, I ask,' he said, 'that the joint resolution go over for the day under the rule. I object to the request for unanimous consent.' There was dismayed expostulation from Mr. Hitchcock, from Mr. Martin, the majority leader, and from others. Senator La Follette was unmoved; 'I ask,' he said, with 'his peculiarly exasperating smile,' 'for the regular order.'

---

[1] This is the resolution as adopted, which differed slightly from that reported to the Senate.

Martin tried again: 'The joint resolution goes over, of course, but I have a right to make some comments on this situation ——' The sentence was cut in two. 'I have asked for the regular order,' interrupted La Follette with sarcastic emphasis, 'and I ask for a ruling upon that request.'

Under the rules they were helpless; no comment was allowable and the resolution could not be considered until next day. In an effort to save something out of the anti-climax the Senate adjourned upon the spot, to meet at ten on the following morning; while the leaders went at once into conference to arrange, as an answer to the threatened filibuster, for a continuous session from that hour until war had been declared. It was a disconcerting check; but the New York *Times* correspondent did his best to make out of it what he could:

And while [the leaders] were conferring on the street floor of the Capitol on the way to save the nation from the undeserved imputation of being laggardly to meet the President's call to arms, Senator La Follette far underground below their feet, in a little cubbyhole of a room in the sub-basement reached by a labyrinth, was busily whispering cheek by jowl with a dozen pacifists.

The House adjourned to wait upon the Senate, and again there was nothing to do save to kill time or watch the reaction now rolling in from the President's message of the night before. Mr. Roosevelt actually left his card and his congratulations at the White House: 'The President's Message is a great state paper,' he told the reporters, and then went on to see Senator Lodge. The New York *Tribune* devoted the day to the exposure of a vast new German conspiracy to raise 'a black rebellion through the South.' The facts, according to the *Tribune*, were 'difficult of access' and 'no one knows how serious the situation is'; but the plot provided that the American Negroes 'should rise, free themselves of the white man's bondage, seize Texas and turn it into a black republic' in which 'Mexicans and Japanese were to have equal rights with the Negro.' Patriots were still pouring into Washington on Tuesday to combat the pacifist army, but the latter was already broken, and the sidewalk crowds amused themselves hooting and harrying its remnants wherever they were recognized. The Navy posted a destroyer in the North River with her guns trained upon the interned German liners, and many cities hastened to place themselves in readiness against the anticipated German uprising. In New York the Police Commissioner mobilized 12,000 men as a 'fighting force,' threw guards about all the bridges and organized a flying squadron of 180 motor trucks, prepared with machine guns and 'sharpshooters' to suppress Teutonic rebellion wherever it might raise its head. But there was one rather disconcerting development. The patriots might flock to Washington; they were not, unfortunately, flocking into the naval recruiting stations in anything like the numbers which had been expected, and in New York 'a determined effort' was undertaken to speed up recruiting. 'The members of the Women's Auxiliary of the Naval Reserve, which has just opened headquarters in the north corridor of the Hotel Biltmore,... made automobile tours throughout the city urging young men to enter the service.'

Such things, however, were mere details compared with the great response which came pouring over the cables from abroad. The news of the President's Message was in the European capitals on Tuesday morning. In Berlin there was a rather feeble effort to deprecate the whole affair: 'Even if Congress adopts the President's views, Germany will not declare war nor take any steps to wage war against the United States.' But in Paris the American flags began to blossom within fifteen minutes after the first despatches had arrived; soon the whole length of the Grands Boulevards was alive with them and the offices of *Le Matin* 'looked like one huge American flag when the decorators were through with the building.' In London, Lord Bryce was concluding that there had been 'nothing finer in our time' than the President's Message and 'few things so fine.' When Mr. Wilson's name was mentioned in the House of Commons that afternoon the members actually applauded, and when Spring Rice's report was read they cheered.

Mr. Herbert Hoover, speaking as head of the Belgian Relief, cabled the President his joy and admiration. Mr. Page spent a long afternoon with Balfour and Lord Robert Cecil. Mr. Balfour 'shook my hand warmly and said: "It's a great day for the world"'; he then plunged into a long list of matters in which the British wanted immediate American help, yet again and again he would break off in the midst of the enumeration to tell the Ambassador 'how the action of the United States had moved him.' Throughout Great Britain the Message was to be read at meetings, in schools and from the pulpit; printed editions of it were quickly sold out. One man, in retirement now and resting in a village of the far northwest Highlands, must have read it with a peculiar satisfaction. Sir Edward Grey, now Viscount Grey of Fallodon, perceived that the long and patient course of his diplomacy had yielded its fruit at last.

On Wednesday morning the newspapers were crying the Wisconsin pacifist's stroke of the day before in eight-column streamer heads:

LA FOLLETTE BLOCKS FOR A DAY ACTION ON WAR RESOLUTION

ALLIES LAUD WILSON; CABINET HURRIES ARMY AND NAVY PLANS

PEACE, DEMOCRACY AND NO WAR ON US THE TALK IN BERLIN

On the front page of the New York *Tribune* there was a powerful cartoon by J. N. Darling; it showed the Earth hanging in space with a huge, bloody sword — 'Imperialistic Rule of Might' — thrust through it, and the caption read: 'There Can Be No Healing of the Wound Till the Thorn is Removed.' In Washington at ten o'clock the Senate met under galleries already filling. There were a few minutes of routine business — more memorials, presentation of bills, and so on — and then the statesmen turned to the War Resolution. Senator Hitchcock introduced it with a statement of his own conversion: 'I have opposed war; I have been bitterly opposed to it' but 'I cannot at this moment cast my vote against war without doing a vain and foolish thing.' Senator Swanson of Virginia (who had so readily 'fallen into line' with Mr. Lodge on the great naval building program) continued the debate with a long exposition of the history; and Senator Lodge himself followed with a ringing call to action and a repetition of the sterling sentiment with which he had demolished Mr. Bannwart:

> No one feels the horrors of war more than I.... But there are, in my opinion, some things worse for a nation than war. National degeneracy is worse; national cowardice is worse. The division of our people into race groups, striving to direct the course of the United States in the interest of some other country... is far worse.... Whatever suffering and misery war may bring it will at least sweep these foul things away.

Nor did the Senator fail to dedicate himself to a higher end:

> This war is a war, as I see it, against barbarism,... organized barbarism panoplied in all the devices for the destruction of human life which science, beneficent science, can bring forth.... We are fighting against a nation which, in the fashion of centuries ago, drags the inhabitants of conquered lands into slavery; which carries off women and girls for even worse purposes; which in its mad desire to conquer mankind and trample them under foot has stopped at no wrong, has regarded no treaty.... What we want most of all by this victory which we shall help to win is to secure the world's peace, broad-based on freedom and democracy.... We shall achieve this result, and when we achieve it we shall be able to say that... we have not fought in vain. [Manifestations of applause in the galleries.]

The galleries were packed now to the doors; and as Senator Vardaman of Mississippi arose with the first speech in opposition, the white faces of the listeners reached up in an unbroken sweep to the eaves of the Chamber. On the floor, the rail was lined with members of the House, who came in to stand there by the hour. Senator Vardaman made his appeal — 'But, Mr. President, I do not feel like sacrificing a million men..., in order to liberate Germany from the cruel domination of kings, without first consulting the people who are to be sacrificed for the deliverance.' If it was wrong for the European autocrats to have plunged their peoples into war without their consent, how could the President and the Congress of the United States do the same? But there were no manifestations of applause from the galleries at that. Senator Stone was brief. He opposed war. He would vote against it. But argument was useless, and when the vote had been taken he would stand ready with the rest.

The afternoon was wearing on. Senator McCumber of North Dakota made a feeble attempt to soften and neutralize the resolution, and failed ignominiously. No one voted for his amendment except himself. Senator George W. Norris of Nebraska, Mr. Hitchcock's colleague, took up the fight with the bitter accusation that the war was being forced by a servile press and a vast propaganda to increase 'the enormous profits of munition manufacturers, stockbrokers and bond dealers.' With passion he swept on:

> We are going into war upon the command of gold.... I know that I am powerless to stop it. I know that this war madness has taken possession of the financial and political powers of our country.... I feel that we are committing a sin against humanity and against our countrymen. I would like to say to this war god, You shall not coin into gold the lifeblood of my brethren.... I feel that we are about to put the dollar sign upon the American flag.

At that for the first time the debate quickened to anger as the celebrated 'Jim' Reed of Missouri leapt to his feet to repel the traitorous thought: 'If that be not giving aid and comfort to the enemy on the very eve of the opening of hostilities then I do not know what would bring comfort to the heart of a Hapsburg or a Hohenzollern.' So opposition was already treason; and as Norris went down under a barrage from John Sharp Williams, Ollie James and others, the great war machine which was so soon to crush every free expression of criticism or objection had begun to roll. The excitement died away again in a steady drone of speech-making beneath galleries crowded, hushed and intent. They heard noble sentiments from the war faction and weak explanations from one or two of the pacifists who were now yielding to the inevitable, until at last, well on in the afternoon, Robert La Follette arose to take the floor:

> Mr. President, I had supposed until recently that it was the duty of Senators and Representatives in Congress to vote and act according to their convictions.... Quite another doctrine has recently been promulgated ... and that is the doctrine of 'standing back of the President' without inquiring whether the President is right or wrong. For myself, I have never subscribed to that doctrine and never shall. I shall support the President in the measures he proposes when I believe them to be right. I shall oppose measures proposed by the President when I believe them to be wrong....

He began in a long and reasoned defence of his filibuster against the armed ship bill, appealing from the passion of the moment to the verdicts of the future. In using all his constitutional powers to obstruct that precipitate decision, he had been acting from conviction. If he had been wrong, there still remained 'the sovereign power of the people' to 'correct our errors and mistakes and our wrongdoing.' Once more he repeated his unwavering faith in that power:

> There is always lodged, and always will be, thank the God above us, power in the people supreme. Sometimes it sleeps, sometimes it seems the sleep of death; but, sir, the sovereign power of the people never dies. It may be suppressed for a time, it may be misled, be fooled, silenced. I think, Mr. President, that it is being denied expression now. I think there will come a day when it will have expression.
>
> The poor, sir, who are the ones called upon to rot in the trenches, have no organized power, have no press to voice their will on this question of peace or war; but oh, Mr. President, at some time they will be heard.... I think, sir, if we take this step, when the people to-day who are staggering under the burden of supporting families ... find ... prices multiplied, ... when ... those who pay taxes come to have their taxes doubled ... there will come an awakening; they will have their day and they will be heard. It will be as certain and as inevitable as the return of the tides, and as resistless, too.

And with that confession of faith he turned to a deliberate, a coldly logical dissection of the President's War Message. Almost sentence by sentence he exposed and attacked the assumptions which underlay it. In resuming her submarine war, Germany had violated no 'pledge' for the reason that none had been given. Her undertaking had rested expressly upon the condition that the Allies should be brought to modify their blockade measures, and that condition had never been fulfilled. The idea that the sub-marine campaign was 'a warfare against mankind' was fantastic; there were many still neutral nations who did not so regard it. The idea that we had no 'quarrel with the German people' was absurd; 'it is idle to talk of war upon a government only' when it was the enemy people who must sustain the costs and sufferings that our warfare would inflict. The idea that this could be made a war for democracy was inconsistent with the nature of the situa-tion. Of all the nations with which we were about to ally ourselves only France and the new Russia were actual democracies, and no one could pretend that we would not have been entering the war in precisely the same way had Russia remained a Czarist des-potism. And what would the war do for American democracy? It was being entered with no popular mandate; 'the espionage bills, the conscription bills and other forcible military measures which we understand are being ground out of the war machine in this country is [sic] the complete proof that those responsible for this war fear that it has no popular support.'

Topic by topic the speech flowed on. Outside the darkness was falling; the lights presently came on, but they let him continue without interruption and without response. He turned to the broader assumptions upon which the whole crusade was based. For the origin of the war the German Government could not be held solely responsible — all the rival powers were in part at fault. The Allies equally with Germany had violated international law and denied American rights. The British, in first declaring the North Sea a war zone, had authorized the German submarine reply. The United States had failed in her neutral duty by holding

Germany to a 'strict accountability' not demanded of the Entente. The great distinction between human rights and property rights was inadmissible at law and irrelevant. There was no rhetoric in the speech; after that moving introduction there was no emotion in it. It was dry, awkwardly worded argument, but it was earnest. The time dragged by; the character of the gallery crowd was changing. 'Brilliantly dressed women, with escorts in evening clothes, came from dinner parties or theaters' to witness the end of this final effort by the hard-minded champion of the people. Sir Cecil Spring Rice appeared; Mr. and Mrs. McAdoo were there; Secretary Lansing and Mr. Polk and others from the State Department looked on. The Senator spoke for four hours altogether, to end at last without even a peroration. If we had actually remained neutral, he said abruptly, we would not be facing war. There remained two possible alternatives — to enforce our commercial rights impartially against both sides or simply to cut off our commerce from both. Suddenly, almost lamely, he sat down.

It was John Sharp Williams who sprang up to sweep the whole effort aside as a 'verbal eternity' that 'would better have become Herr Bethmann-Hollweg of the German Parliament than an American Senator'; and as the Mississippian arose upon that note into 'a flight of patriotic oratory' on the old model, it 'gave the galleries the throb and thrill that they had been waiting for.' The junior Senator from Wisconsin, Mr. Husting, rebutted Mr. La Follette with a long and learned effort. Senator Hardwick of Georgia pledged 'the sons of Dixie' to the firing line in a burst of eloquence. The conservative Republicans were for the most part silent, wanting only to get it over with; but the leonine Borah endorsed the war in a speech as lofty, as patriotic and as perplexing as usual, while Senator Warren Gamaliel Harding of Ohio, ignorant that he was so soon to sit in President Wilson's chair, paused to make it entirely clear that he was 'not voting for war in the name of democracy.' It was 'the maintenance of just American rights' that he was interested in. Senator Smoot offered up a three-line prayer for Divine blessing upon their action; more batches of

WEATHER
To-day overcast. To-morrow, probably fair and continued cold. Strong west winds
Full Report on Page 11

New York Tribune

First to Last — the Truth: News · Editorials · Advertisements

CIRCULATION
Over 100,000 Daily
Net Paid, Non-Returnable

Vol. LXXVI No. 25,710

SATURDAY, APRIL 7, 1917

ONE CENT In New York City

Round Up Germans As Plotters

U. S. Arrests Eight Leaders Here, Twelve in Illinois

Sixty in the First List of Suspects

Men Held Incommunicado; Secret Agents Watching Reservist Army

Year of War May Cost 5 Billions; Heavier Taxes for Rich and Poor

Incomes as Low as $1,000 Probably To Be Assessed—Excess Profits to Pay Higher Percentages—Big Bond Issue to Aid Allies

90 German Ships Seized In U.S. Ports

McAdoo Issues Order Immediately After Passage of War Resolution

Value of Vessels Taken $148,674,000

Customs Officers Board 27 Liners in New York—2,014 Seamen Held

America in Armageddon; Country Is Called to War; All Its Forces Mobilizing

The War Proclamation

WASHINGTON, April 6.—At 1:11 o'clock this afternoon President Wilson signed the joint war resolution adopted by Congress and immediately issued the following proclamation:

Joint War Resolution Signed by President Without Ceremony

News Flashed to Army and Navy

Wilson Approves Compulsory Service Bill, Hoping War Will End War

Domestic

telegrams were quickly read into the record, and at eleven minutes past eleven the vote was reached.

The names were called in an intense silence. 'On the floor the Senators themselves were unusually grave and quiet.... The great crowd was awed by the solemnity of the occasion and sobered by the speeches they had heard'; and when the result was announced there was no demonstration. The Senate had adopted the War Resolution by a vote of 82 to 6. There were eight absentees; each sent word that he would have voted for the resolution save one — Gore of Oklahoma, who had led the peace fight of the year before. The six Senators who had the courage to stand until the end against what they believed to be a folly and a crime were Asle J. Gronna of North Dakota, Robert M. La Follette of Wisconsin, Harry Lane of Oregon, George W. Norris of Nebraska, William J. Stone of Missouri and James K. Vardaman of Mississippi. All were to suffer for it, but none more bitterly than La Follette, over whose head there was to break a storm of passionate hatred and villification almost without parallel in our history. The Senate, stopping only to receive a resolution congratulating the people of Russia upon their adoption of 'a democratic form of government,' adjourned.

iii

Only the House remained; and at ten o'clock next day, Thursday, April 5, the Representatives began their debate. All morning, all afternoon, all evening, the speechmaking flowed on while the nation waited for the foregone conclusion. Again the floor and galleries were crowded as the whole ground was rehearsed once more. The arguments were the same; the emotional appeals, the oratory and the bathos were a repetition of what the Senate had heard. The war party was overwhelming in its strength; yet again there was a small and earnest opposition, and early in the day one of these — Representative Fred A. Britten, a conservative Republican from Illinois — sounded a curious note. He was speaking of a Chicago crowd which had watched a war demonstration in silence. 'They stood in silence, gentlemen,' he said, 'because their heartstrings and their sympathies were not with the movement that is slowly but surely dragging us into this terrible European mire'; and on the word there came applause, not only from the gallery but from the floor. Mr. Britten went on: 'Ask your friends around you on the floor of the House, "Are you going to vote for this bill?" "Yes; I hate like the devil to vote for it, but I am going to." Why do they hate to vote for it?' Instantly there came horrified interruptions and demands for names. Mr. Britten stuck to his declaration that he could name 'probably seventy-five per cent of the Members' secretly opposed to the War Resolution:

The truth of the matter is that ninety per cent of your people and mine do not want this declaration of war and are distinctly opposed to our going into that bloody mire on the other side. There is something in the air, gentlemen, and I do not know what it is, whether it be the hand of destiny or some superhuman movement, something stronger than you and I can realize or resist, that seems to be picking us up bodily and literally forcing us to vote for this declaration of war when way down deep in our hearts we are just as opposed to it as are our people back home.

Was it true? Mr. Carter Glass, later destined to become, in the Senate, a pillar of conservative Democracy, interjected an angry rebuttal; there was applause for that, too, and Mr. Britten passed on to another subject. The note did not recur. But was it true? As the steady procession of speakers ground on, the House applauded the peace advocates almost as readily as the war hawks. There was a moment of surprise when Representative Claude Kitchin of North Carolina, the majority leader, announced that he would vote against the War Resolution:

I know that for my vote I shall be not only criticized but denounced from one end of the country to the other. The whole yelping pack of defamers and revilers in the Nation will at once be set upon my heels.

My friends, I cannot leave my children lands and riches — I cannot leave them fame — but I can leave them the name of an ancestor who, mattering not the consequences to himself, never dared to hesitate to do his duty as God gave him to see it.

Again the applause followed. Perhaps it may be, as some believe, that on a secret ballot the House would have defeated the resolution; if so, however, there were too few of Mr. Kitchin's colleagues who dared to face the 'defamers and revilers' which all of them knew to stand in wait. Speech followed speech for the record, most of them belligerent, some poetical, nearly all leaving behind them today a queer flavor of the unreal, as if the statesmen knew themselves only to be going through the motions of a debate no longer relevant. Outside a heavy northeast storm was blowing its sheets of rain against the building; while in other offices in the city and in other cities throughout the nation the soldiers and sailors, the politicians, the industrialists, the editors and preachers and educators, the patriots and the publicity-seekers, were bending every effort to the starting of the great war machine on the course now assumed to be inevitable. For a time the Representatives even amused themselves by baiting two colleagues from the same state into a floor quarrel; it brought a touch of levity into the proceedings but that presently died away and the talk ground on.

The evening wore through; midnight came, and the representatives of the people were still committing their views, one after another, to history and *The Congressional Record*. By twenty minutes past one on Friday morning the reporters keeping tally had counted eighty speeches; by half-past two the number had passed one hundred, and the long flood was drying up. The rollcall came at last, after nearly seventeen hours of oratory, at a quarter to three in the morning. While the names were being droned out, Representative Rankin of Montana entered and took her seat. Her name was reached; she made no answer, and the clerk passed on. The first woman Member had failed to vote. 'Uncle Joe' Cannon, the veteran of so many years, of so many moments, great and little, in that Chamber, heard what had happened and went up to speak

to her. 'He is understood to have said: "Little woman, you cannot afford not to vote. You represent the womanhood of the country in the American Congress. I shall not advise you how to vote, but you should, one way or the other, as your conscience dictates." '
On the second call the clerk reached her name: 'Miss Rankin.' For a moment there was again no answer; she was clutching nervously at her throat, in evident distress, with every person in the chamber watching her. At last she rose to her feet, looking straight ahead. 'I want,' she said, with her voice breaking, 'to stand by my country, but I cannot vote for war.' The voice trailed away in a kind of sob. 'I vote No,' she finished, barely audibly, and fell back into her seat, 'pressed her forehead and began to cry.' The rollcall went on remorselessly; and at a few minutes past three the result was announced. The House had followed the Senate by the overwhelming vote of 373 to 50. It was the morning of Friday, April 6, 1917. The nation, save for the formalities, was at war.

Of the fifty negative votes, sixteen were Democratic, thirty-two came from Republicans — mostly of the western progressive wing — one was that of an independent and the remaining one that of Meyer London, the Socialist member.[1] There were, altogether, 528 Senators and Representatives; only 56, or just over one in ten, had dared to cast their votes against the tide. That day was not out before most of them were answering for it. At once Miss Rankin was being accused of having gravely injured the cause of woman suffrage by her failure 'to recognize the big

[1] The Northeastern states contributed but one negative vote — that of London, the Socialist from New York. There were nine scattering votes from the South, four of them from Mississippi. Six from Illinois and one each from Ohio and Michigan made eight for the east-central states. Wisconsin and the states west of the Mississippi contributed twenty-seven, with five more from the Pacific Coast. If Illinois can be included with the West, that section, in other words, cast thirty-eight of the fifty negative votes. Nevada's delegation, consisting of only one man, was the only one unanimous against. Nine of Wisconsin's eleven representatives voted in the negative, and two of the three from South Dakota; in no other state did more than half the representatives vote negative. The negative votes came from only twenty states; a few members, of course, were absent, but every Representative present from the remaining twenty-eight states voted for the declaration of war.

issue.' Mrs. Carrie Chapman Catt forgave her; Mrs. Norman Whitehouse, on the other hand, the chairman of the New York State suffrage party who had already pledged her support to the war, refused to comment. In the Senate cloakrooms a movement was under way to destroy Senator Stone, and it was doubted that he could long retain his post of Chairman of the Foreign Relations Committee. Mr. Kitchin's prediction was borne out as the hot wires poured in from his North Carolina district; his vote, they said, did not represent five per cent of his constituents and the local newspapers were already beginning the campaign of defamation and reviling: 'Remember the first blood of the Confederacy, Henry W. Wyatt, of Edgecombe! His sons are not degenerates.'

Seventeen years later it was to occur to the Associated Press, upon the anniversary, to seek out the men who had voted against the declaration of war upon Germany. It could discover only seven of them; but of the seven it found not one who, in the gray aftermath of experience, either believed that his vote had been wrong or regretted that he had cast it.

Within a few hours after the session's end the morning headlines were streaming once more:

HOUSE, AT 3:15 A.M., VOTES FOR WAR, 373 TO 50;
$3,000,000,000 ASKED FOR ARMY OF 1,000,000;
NATION'S GIGANTIC RESOURCES MOBILIZED

At Governor's Island, as the oratory had been flowing, the Twenty-Second United States Infantry had 'slept on its arms,' awaiting the first call to battle — against the interned German liners in the North River. At their piers Mr. Dudley Field Malone, the Collector of the Port, had massed 600 Customs agents ready for the seizure, and at five in the morning Mr. Malone himself was routed out by a telephone call from Washington announcing that the hour had come. 'The word was flashed to Governor's Island, and Army tugs steamed alongside the ordnance dock to embark the veterans of the Twenty-Second.' Rapidly the troops were distributed to the various piers, the police and the reporters were

ready, and presently Mr. Malone came hurrying upon the scene
in the early light. At the gangway of the Vaterland he found
Commodore Hans Ruser, the master of the great ship. The two
men, who were acquainted, smiled at each other. 'We are ready,'
the German observed, a little sadly, and the vessel was handed
over and her crew marched off to internment. It was not exactly
heroic, perhaps, but it was the first act of war.

In Boston, Philadelphia and most other ports similar scenes were
being enacted. The ships were quickly swept up — and all of
them found to have been disabled long before. Attorney General
Gregory at the same time was launching a great drive to round up
'the ringleaders of the German plots,' and before nightfall some
sixty unhappy suspects had been gathered in. It was announced
during the day that the university authorities were everywhere
cancelling their athletic schedules, and organized intercollegiate
athletics came to an abrupt end for the duration of the war. The
pacifist organizations were silent at last. It was noticed that recruiting, on the other hand, failed to show any marked improve-
ment that day; but the eastern cities were at least 'aglow with
flags,' and in New York the great mansions of the captains of
industry and finance in upper Fifth Avenue were observed to be
patriotically displaying the Stars and Stripes. Otherwise, the
day seemed strangely quiet; here and there crowds would collect
before National Guard armories as if vaguely expecting something,
but the police who had everywhere been mobilized against un-
known peril found nothing in particular to do. There were few if
any disturbances; there was no rising of those famous half a
million trained German reservists. It was a little difficult to make
the moment appear as exciting as it should have been, but in
Washington, when the Senate met at noon with the House's
action before it, a New York *Times* correspondent once more did
his best:

> The Senate had its first taste of real war activity today. When
> Vice-President Marshall was signing the resolution which proclaimed
> the existence of a state of war between the Imperial German Govern-

ment and the Government of the United States, some observers
noticed two young ladies busily engaged in knitting military socks
in the gallery.... Investigation proved them to be Miss Elsie Calder,
daughter of the Senator from New York, and Miss Sarah Murphy of
Brooklyn, her guest.

Solemnly, but without ceremony, Mr. Marshall signed the resolution and laid the historic pen away; and as the document was
sent on its way to the White House, the Senate turned to vote the
first $100,000,000 war credit — a teacup from the oceans of
expenditure which were to follow. Even at the White House the
queer air of anti-climax persisted. The President was at luncheon
with Mrs. Wilson and his cousin, Miss Helen Woodrow Bones,
when the official parchment draft arrived at about half past
twelve. The party went at once to the usher's room in the lobby,
where Rudolph Foster, the President's executive clerk, was waiting
with the resolution. Ike Hoover, the Chief Usher, who had watched
so many Presidents come and go, was there as well, but no one
else — not even Colonel House or the faithful Tumulty. Mrs.
Wilson handed her husband a pen as he sat down, and the signature was affixed. Mr. Foster hurried in to the reporters waiting in
the executive offices, and a moment later they saw a young naval
officer run out onto the sidewalk and begin to signal in naval
semaphore to another in a window of the Navy Department across
the street. The face vanished from the window; and they knew
that the wireless operators at the communications office within
were already pouring out the messages to all ships and shore
stations announcing that the United States was at war with
Germany.

That was all. At the Metropolitan Opera House that night,
Geraldine Farrar stepped before the curtain bearing a great
American flag and sang the Star Spangled Banner; while in the
offices of the New York *Tribune* they were preparing a single,
three-word head. 'America in Armageddon' it would say next
morning. On the Western Front that day, in Italy and the Balkans,
along the crumbling battle lines in Russia, in the far north and in

the tropics and on the grey seas, the war had mangled its usual number of human bodies, inflicted its usual hurts and tortures, closed another day in its long, routine tale of agony. But all that, for the moment, was very far away. America, men simply thought, was in the war; and among them all, none quite knew how it had happened, nor why, nor what precisely it might mean.

America was in the war.

THE END

INDEX